HOW DATA NEED PEOPLE

From genome sequencing to large sky surveys, digital technologies produce massive datasets that promise unprecedented scientific insights. But data, for being good to use and reuse, need people – scientists, technicians, and administrators – as embodied, evaluative, social humans. In this book, anthropologist Götz Hoeppe draws on an ethnography of astronomical research to examine the media and practices that scientists and technicians use to instruct graduate students, make diagrams for data calibration and discovery, organize collaborative work, negotiate the ethics of open access, encode their knowledge in datasets – and undertake social inquiries along the way. This book offers a reflection on the sociality of data-rich research that will benefit attempts to integrate human and machine learning. It will be of interest for students and scholars in data science and science and technology studies, as well as in anthropology, sociology, history, and the philosophy of science. This book is also available Open Access on Cambridge Core.

GÖTZ HOEPPE is Associate Professor of Sociology at the University of Waterloo, Canada. He is the author of *Conversations on the Beach: Fishermen's Knowledge, Metaphor and Environmental Change in South India* (2007) and *Why the Sky is Blue: Discovering the Color of Life* (2007), which received the American Meteorological Society's Louis J. Battan Author's Award.

HOW DATA NEED PEOPLE

*The Social and Epistemic Practice of
a Data-Rich Science*

GÖTZ HOEPPE

University of Waterloo

CAMBRIDGE
UNIVERSITY PRESS

Shaftesbury Road, Cambridge CB2 8EA, United Kingdom

One Liberty Plaza, 20th Floor, New York, NY 10006, USA

477 Williamstown Road, Port Melbourne, VIC 3207, Australia

314–321, 3rd Floor, Plot 3, Splendor Forum, Jasola District Centre,
New Delhi – 110025, India

Cambridge University Press is part of Cambridge University Press & Assessment,
a department of the University of Cambridge.

We share the University's mission to contribute to society through the pursuit of
education, learning and research at the highest international levels of excellence.

www.cambridge.org
Information on this title: www.cambridge.org/9781009686730
DOI: 10.1017/9781009686754

First published 2026

A catalogue record for this publication is available from the British Library

A Cataloging-in-Publication data record for this book is available from the Library of Congress

ISBN 978-1-009-68672-3 Hardback
ISBN 978-1-009-68673-0 Paperback

Cambridge University Press & Assessment has no responsibility for the persistence
or accuracy of URLs for external or third-party internet websites referred to in this
publication and does not guarantee that any content on such websites is, or will remain,
accurate or appropriate.

For EU product safety concerns, contact us at Calle de José Abascal, 56, 1°, 28003 Madrid,
Spain, or email eugpsr@cambridge.org.

To Steffi

Contents

Figures

List of Figures

Preface

For being good to be used and reused, scientific data need people – scientists, technicians, and administrators – as embodied, cognizant, social, and cultural human beings. This book examines how scientific data not only represent information, but are also deeply implicated in social actions and accountabilities. Scientific data are the remarkable epistemic and social "stuff" that scientists use to learn about nature, instruct students, build connections, transmit knowledge, grow trust, and evaluate the work of other researchers. These uses often go together. What data are like shapes how these interactions and relations unfold, and vice versa. Drawing on an ethnographic study of research in astronomy, I focus on instruction, practical reasoning, and decision-making as lenses into scientific work with large datasets (but also with smaller ones).

I set out from the tenet that humans are fundamentally evaluative. We are concerned that others understand our intentions adequately, knowing that our actions are being evaluated, and we examine others' actions and intentions likewise. We pursue our goals while seeking to avoid blame and embarrassment. How ordinary members of various societies do this has long been of interest to anthropologists and sociologists. I adopt this perspective to examine the work of researchers, students, and technicians in contemporary scientific work. A second theme, resulting from the first, is my focus on what I call data-centric socialities: forms of social coordination unfolding in the making, use, and publication of data. My notion of data-centrism – that making, using, and publishing data causes people to interact and engage in specifiable ways – is inspired by sociologist Georg Simmel.

I begin with identifying digital data as media that afford certain uses and interactions and then examine successively how researchers learn from technicians about data production, instruct new data users, use diagrams to cultivate data, engage mundane reasoning to resolve disjunctive findings, organize collaborative work, manage normative issues in the open access to data, and seek to encode their collective knowledge in a data-set. If scientific data are epistemic and social stuff, then natural scientists are, by necessity, also social inquirers. As I approached research work as an ethnographer, I realized that scientists and technicians were, at times, doing a sort of ethnography themselves, using practices that are bound to become more important in the future.

These matters become visible only at the fine granularity of social inter-action and the technical detail of a specific science. But their lessons are more general, because uses of social accounting practices are so widespread and common. Sciences other than astronomy may, of course, use other media, engage other disciplinary objects, and use other epistemic orders to organize their work. But they will need to train new members, use diagrams to interpret data, use forms of mundane reasoning, organize joint work, act normatively, transmit knowledge – and engage accounting practices along the way.

How Data Need People is published as high-volume data flows, cloud-based databases, machine learning, and generative artificial intelligence are transforming much scientific work. This is a time of rapid technological and conceptual change, but I am confident that attending to interactions and accounting practices will help when making sense of the future social fabric of science, data-rich or otherwise, whatever the participant or medi-atory statuses of machines may be. I hope that this approach will also contribute to a rapprochement of the history and philosophy of science with the sociology of science, which some critics have reduced to Actor-Network Theory and the Sociology of Scientific Knowledge at the expense of alternatives, including the naturalistic and interactionist approach that I pursue here. Some philosophers' recent interest in epistemic agents (Chang 2022) and their application of social science methods (Veigl and Currie 2025) offer an opening. After all, epistemic agents are unavoidably also social agents, and, as such, users and subjects of accounting practices.

This book marks the end of what became, for me, a long journey. It began with an ethnographic study – inspired by Ludwik Fleck's (1979 [1935]) *Genesis and Development of a Scientific Fact* as well as Bruno Latour and Steve Woolgar's (1986 [1979]) *Laboratory Life: The Construction of Scientific Facts* – of how astronomers make, process, and use digital data in the construction of a scientific fact. But in doing so I was drawn to attend to scientists as people. I was also inspired by historical and epistemologi-cal studies, like Hans-Jörg Rheinberger's (1997) fascinating account of the discovery of protein synthesis, but missed more attention to human actors and their social commitments in them.

At first unsure where to start, I began with detailed examinations of extended sequences of work that I had witnessed, from the training of PhD students over two years (Chapter 3) to the collaborative fixation of a dataset over several months (Chapter 8). Doing so made me revisit my anthropological toolbox and learn about, and from, interactionist approaches like ethnomethodology. Along the way I continued my field-work with revisits, additional ethnography, interviews, and attendance at workshops and conferences. Thus equipped, I examined a series of topics that seemed to be of enduring importance for scientific research with large datasets (and smaller ones). Even though this book presents an account of research in astronomy, its conceptual work owes much to my ongoing study of research in paleoceanography as well.

Acknowledgments

I thank my astronomical interlocutors for their help, patience, and understanding during my fieldwork. I am very grateful to the director of "the Institute," where I did most of my fieldwork, and the directors and staff of Calar Alto Observatory and the European Southern Observatory at La Silla for making my stays there possible and immensely enjoyable. Anthropologists commonly introduce pseudonyms when writing about their ethnographic subjects and conversationalists. I am especially grateful to the scientists and technicians whom I call Anna, Antonio, Ben, Carlos, Catalina, Christina, Chuang, Curt, Eddie, Elias, Francesca, Henry, Joe, Jorge, Ken, Mallory, Mary, Mike, Nadine, Nora, Norman, Olli, Oscar, Otfried, Otto, Owen, Pablo, Patrick, Peter, Susheela, and Tim. I hope that you recognize yourselves and feel adequately represented. Anton M. Koekemoer kindly shared the audio recording on which Transcript 4.8 is based. I am very grateful to Karin Knorr Cetina for affiliating my initial project to her former Unit of Knowledge, Finance, and Society at the University of Konstanz. Conversations with Klaus Meisenheimer, Christian Wolf, and David W. Hogg have profoundly influenced my view of data-rich science.

A number of colleagues and friends have read and commented on manuscripts that became part of this book: Jesus Aceituno, Debbora Battaglia, Ulrich Buczilowski, David DeVorkin, Abou Farman, Christian Greiffenhagen, Martin Harwit, Christian Heath, Webb Keane, Ann H. Kelly, Karin Knorr Cetina, Yaël Kreplak, Stefan Laube, Kenneth Liberman, Michael Lynch, David Martin, Klaus Meisenheimer, Curtis Moyer, Marie-Hélène Nicol, Hans-Jörg Rheinberger, Tanya Richardson, Hilmar Schäfer, Sergio Sismondo, Arjen van der Wel, Niklas Woehrmann, and Christian Wolf. I am particularly indebted to Grey Gundaker for her guidance when I made my first steps into ethnomethodology, her encouragement, and a close reading of the manuscript. I thank Christian Greiffenhagen for nudging me toward the title. I am grateful to the anonymous reviewers of the articles of which parts are included in this book. Anonymous reviewers of the book proposal and the manuscript kindly provided essential advice. Of course, the responsibility for remaining mistakes is mine alone.

I have presented some of the results and materials from this study at seminars and workshops at the Universities of Konstanz, Southern Denmark, Waterloo, Wilfrid Laurier, Exeter, and the College of William & Mary, at the National Air and Space Museum in Washington, DC, meetings of the International Institute for Ethnomethodology and Conversation Analysis, the Society for Social Studies of Science, the American Anthropological Association, the Society for Cultural Anthropology, at the Alfred Wegener Institute for Polar and Marine Research, and onboard the research vessel *Polarstern*. For their comments I am particularly grateful to Nancy Barrickman, Debbora Battaglia, Catelijne Coopmans, David DeVorkin, Vanessa Dirksen, Clemens Eisenmann, Mariana Fereira, Paul Forman, Barbara Grimpe, Barbara J. King, Karin Knorr Cetina, Stefan Laube, Sabina Leonelli, Kenneth Liberman, Douglas Macbeth, Werner Reichmann, Arpita Roy, Hilmar Schäfer, David Teira, Johannes Wagner, Leon Wansleben, and Kath Weston.

Several research assistants did excellent work for this project: Mike Bernhardt, Ulrich Buczilowski, Sonja Froitzheim, Sarah Heupel, Eva-Maria Kaufmann, Jaclyn Kuizon, Sabrina Lehner, Karoline Lukaschek, Frederik Schönebeck, Friederike Sontag, Ayala Stein, Brooke Sutcliffe, and Victoria Zinyuk. Regina Vera-Quinn kindly translated Spanish recordings for me. I thank Sara LeBlanc and Michael Reyers for their work on the illustrations. Sean Speers and Herbert Balagtas rescued me from various computer troubles. Franka Heise saved me at two critical moments. I am grateful to Nadine Albert and the team of the Havenhostel Bremerhaven, where I wrote parts of this book.

At Cambridge University Press I am very grateful to David Repetto for his guidance, and to Anna Hubbard and Aleksandra Serocka for their meticulous work, help, and patience. I thank Polly Chester for her painstaking copy-editing and Ramya Selvaraj for the project management.

I am deeply grateful to my family and friends for enduring support and encouragement.

My greatest thanks are to Stefanie Hoeppe, my partner, for being with me on this journey. Without her love, understanding, and support I would not have been able to finish this book.

I am very grateful to the Deutsche Forschungsgemeinschaft (grant HO 3986/2-1), the Daniel and Florence Guggenheim Foundation, the College of William & Mary, and the Social Sciences and Humanities

Research Council of Canada (Insight Grant #435-2018-1397) for essential financial support.

This book draws in part on material published in the following journal articles: "Working Data Together: The Accountability and Reflexivity of Digital Astronomical Practice," *Social Studies of Science*, 44(2) (2014), 243–270; "Tensions of Accountability: Scientists, Technicians and the Ethical Life of Data Production in Astronomy," *Science* as *Culture*, 27(4) (2018), 488–512; "Mediating Environments and Objects as Knowledge Infrastructure," *Computer Supported Cooperative Work*, 28(1–2) (2019), 25–59; "Medium, Calculation, Play: On Digital Images in Scientific Practice," *Social Studies of Science*, 49(5) (2019), 758–784; "Members Doing Ethnography? On Some Uses of Irony and Failed Translation, Witnessed in an Episode of Data Sharing in Open Science," *Ethnographic Studies*, 17 (2020), 1–21; and "Encoding Collective Knowledge, Instructing Data Reusers: The Collaborative Fixation of a Digital Scientific Data Set," *Computer Supported Cooperative Work*, 30(4) (2021), 463–505. I am grateful to the publishers Sage, Springer Nature, and Taylor & Francis for their permission to reproduce this material. Figures 3.8, 3.9, 4.5, 4.6, 8.1, and 8.2 are reproduced by permission of the American Astronomical Society.

Introduction
Making Sense of Data-Centric Socialities

Scientists need data. Data are scientists' records of observation, collection, and experimentation. Data are the materials that scientists use to construct empirical knowledge. But data also need scientists. Whether in the laboratory or the field, scientific equipment and detectors do not work by themselves. Someone builds, maintains, and operates these recording devices. Someone calibrates, analyzes, and interprets their output, and someone archives these records. Yet there is another, deeper sense in which data, if good to use and good to reuse, need people – scientists, technicians, and administrators – as social beings: embodied humans who communicate; share cultural, normative, and ethical notions; monitor other's actions; build trust; hold others to account; and navigate potential challenges to their reputation. Science may be exceptional because of its systematic ways of learning about the world,[1] but scientists and technicians are in many ways not different from ordinary people. Some studies of science with large datasets broadly acknowledge cultural and social influences, but there is much more to learn when we engage a refined view of what people are like and how they act. We can do this by witnessing scientific work ethnographically, paying close attention to interactions between scientists, students, and technicians.

But as ethnographic fieldworkers we cannot study science in general. We can only witness *this* work in *this* discipline, done *here* and *now*. To study data-rich science ethnographically, we need a science and an example of its workings. *How Data Need People* focuses on astronomy, which is arguably not only the oldest science, but has also been at the forefront of new developments in working with large datasets, the open access to data and software, and uses of machine learning.[2] Allow me to declare right away that

---

[1] That science is characterized by its systematicity is a view articulated by philosopher Paul Hoyningen-Huene (2013).
[2] Astronomical data are almost entirely digital and largely homogenous – recorded from basically the same viewpoint (planet Earth and nearby spacecraft) with a limited set of detector technologies – are

many of the practices and resources that we find in data-rich astronomy are similar to those in other sciences, making many of this study's findings transferable to them. So let us begin by considering one astronomical data-set and two scenes of its production and publication in some detail. In the rest of this introduction, I will keep returning to this case as I specify my anthropological approach, review my argument, and introduce my study.

I.1   Scientific Data Are Epistemic and Social Stuff

Figure I.1 shows a photograph of a small patch of the night sky, made using an infrared camera attached to the 3.5-meter telescope of Calar Alto Observatory in the mountains of Andalusia, Spain. Taken in what astronomers call the H band, this is a recording of near-infrared light invisible to human eyes.[3] It is a composite image, a so-called mosaic, the result of adding 580 exposures totaling 10 hours of "integration time." Collected in several observing campaigns over 3½ years, these exposures were recorded using a detector with 2048 × 2048 pixels, cooled with liquid nitrogen to –120 degrees Celsius. The image is a photographic negative. Small black and grey dots, about 32.000 altogether, are traces of light attributed to distant galaxies, some estimated to be 9 billion light years away, two thirds of the way to the end of the visible universe.

Making this mosaic was a distributed and collaborative effort. The observatory's staff astronomers recorded the exposures (at times in the company of a visiting graduate student) and sent them to researchers in Heidelberg, Germany, largely on mobile hard drives.[4] There, members of a research team processed, calibrated, and added them. This mosaic was prepared mostly by Nadine,[5] a PhD student. Senior scientists instructed her to assemble a consistent set of exposures from various observing campaigns, to detect objects and to combine these data with those from an earlier project to measure the distances and physical properties of galaxies in this field. Because of the high data rate of many short exposures taken with a large detector array, Nadine processed these exposures semi-automatically using a so-called pipeline. The target of these observations was A2713, a

---

rarely monetized, lack economic uses, and come with few privacy concerns. This makes the social study of their use in certain ways less complex and may help to foreground elementary issues and practices.

[3] The H band is the near-infrared wavelength range of 1.5 to 1.8 micrometers.

[4] At times, it seems, data need people for transportation and delivery.

[5] When appearing by themselves, all first names in this book are pseudonyms. Combined first and last names are actual names.

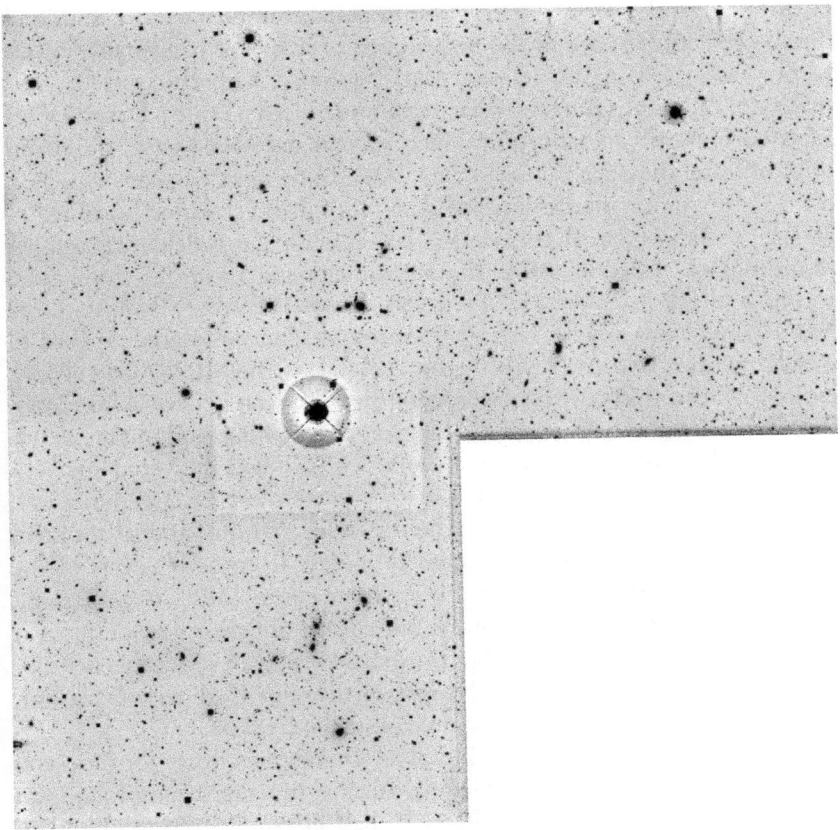

Figure I.1   Mosaic of photographic exposures of the A2713 field.
(Reproduced with permission).
Note: The online version shows the colors of the original figure.

supercluster (a "cluster of clusters") of galaxies, as well as galaxies in the universe behind it.[6]

Nadine belongs to MAMBO (pseudo-acronym), a research group that investigates deep fields: small parts of the sky selected for offering views of the distant universe which are little obstructed by the stars, dust, and gas of our Milky Way galaxy.[7] Taking particularly long ("deep") exposures of these fields, these astronomers aim to detect and characterize faint and distant objects. Because of the finite speed of light, we see distant objects as they appeared in the remote past. Equipped with this sort of time machine, the group pursues what astronomers call "lookback studies" of galaxy evolution.[8] In astronomy, such surveys have been at the forefront of promoting the open access to data, assembling large datasets, as well as using computational techniques of data mining and machine learning.[9]

The mosaic of Figure I.1 is part of a dataset of the A2713 field that includes recordings of radiation across the electromagnetic spectrum from radio waves to ultraviolet radiation and x-rays. It was made by MUWAGS, the Multi-Wavelength Galaxy Survey (pseudonym), an international team to which members of the MAMBO group belonged. The MUWAGS collaboration included thirty astronomers from the European Union, Switzerland, the United Kingdom, Canada, the United States, China, and India, including tenured senior scientists, postdoctoral scholars, and PhD students.

The brightest feature in the mosaic is a large dot left (east) of the center. Situated in an apparent square brighter than its environs, and surrounded by a circle of light, four spikes seem to radiate from it. It is one of the nearest objects seen here: an old and cool star in our Milky Way, perhaps only a few hundred light years away, but comparatively bright in the near infrared. In the optical (visible light) exposures used to select this field for study it did not seem particularly noteworthy. For Nadine and her colleagues, it is now a concern as a source of image artifacts.

The mosaic's peculiar outline hints at an even greater worry for the team: the bottom right (southwest) quadrant is missing. Initially, the team's aim was to photograph a square of half a degree by half a degree, covering a bit more than the size of the full moon on the sky. Yet, due to persistent bad weather and limited access to the telescope, team leaders decided to drop a quarter of this field from their observing program. They preferred to "go deeper"

---

[6] The acronym A2713 stands for the pseudonumeral entry (#2713) in the Abell catalog of galaxy clusters (Abell 1958).

[7] I use the term "deep fields" to include all fields on the sky observed for extragalactic studies with long exposures at multiple wavelengths.

[8] See Blumenberg (1987), Jay (2000), and Cimatti et al. (2019).

[9] See Ivezić et al. (2020) and Ting (2025).

(making, processing, and adding more exposures to obtain a more sensitive mosaic) in the other parts, instead of arriving at a "shallow" sum exposure. Three quadrants remain, each corresponding to a set of telescope pointings.

Bad luck with weather at the observatory and its impact on the dataset was an enduring concern for the team. It surfaced again one day at a group meeting, at which Otfried, a senior researcher and Nadine's thesis supervisor, was to report on the status of new observations of A2713 and A2714, another galaxy cluster the team studied. Besides Otfried and Nadine, Otto, and Owen (two other senior astronomers), two PhD students and two postdoctoral scholars were present, as well as myself, an ethnographer. The following exchange occurred at the beginning of this meeting. To capture consequential pragmatic aspects of talk in this transcript, underlining marks emphasis, an ellipsis (…) marks a brief audible pause, hhhh marks an outbreath characteristic of chuckling or giggling, HA-HA-HA marks loud laughter, and double parentheses include verbal descriptions of the talk's delivery.[10] Having received a message from the observatory with the latest update on the observations earlier in the morning, Otfried reports:

Transcript I.1

1	Otfried:	Okay … so ehm … maybe it would be good to give a brief … eh … account where we … where we stand at the moment with MAMBO … I want to mention before that … from my side we have … new observations in A2714 … ehh … we had new observations in A2714 already a week ago … or a bit more than a week ago … and tonight hhhh the first observations of A2713 for more than a year hhhhh have happened hhhhh
2	Owen:	It is still … it is still there?
3	Otfried:	hhh ((chuckles))
4	(Group):	hhhh HA-HA-HA-HA-HA-HA-HA-HA ((collective laughter))
5	Otfried:	So … it seems that we make some progress … I am pretty sure …
6	(Group):	HA-HA-HA-HA-HA-HA-HA-HA-HA-HA-HA ((collective laughter continues))
7	Otto:	((whispers)) It has drifted away
8	(Group):	HA-HA-HA-HA-HA-ha-ha-ha ((collective laughter recedes and ends abruptly as Otfried continues to talk))
9	Otfried:	I … I think we have a good chance to get … a very good … to decent data base for A2714 in this year … we have already collected quite a bit

---

[10] In this book I use elementary conventions of conversation analysis for my transcriptions, simplified from Jefferson's (2004) scheme. See the Appendix for details.

These scientists' shared concern for their dataset animates this discussion. Arguably, Owen's question (in line 2) of whether the galaxy cluster A2713 was "still there" is rhetorical. Astronomers do not expect a galaxy cluster to disappear or to "drift away" in the sky, as Otto intimates with his commentary (in line 7), certainly not after a year or so of bad weather. However, despite this being implausible to everyone present, Owen's question elicits collective laughter (lines 4, 6, and 8). Unable to ascribe this laughter to individual participants I have labeled its authors as "(Group)." Otfried can be heard as having invited their laughter. Not only could his choice of words, that the new observations "have <u>happened</u>" (instead of being made), signal irony – his passive voice suggesting that their making was out of the team's control. His chuckling (toward the end of line 1) also opens a slot for Owen to position his question, to which Otfried reacts with a brief, sharp outbreath that continues his chuckling (in line 3).[11] Yet the laughter that follows is contained. It ends abruptly (line 8) and Otfried goes on to give his account on the current state of observations for the project (line 9). One may hear him calling for the group to go on with business as usual, astronomically speaking.

Members of the group probably heard Owen's interjection as a quip on their notoriously bad luck with weather at the observatory. But they may have also heard it as suspending the backgrounded assumption of the night sky's stability, a commonplace for astronomers since antiquity and all too familiar to leisurely stargazers who recognize constellations like Orion and the Big Dipper in the night sky year after year. If galaxies and galaxy clusters were to "drift away," the sky – and astronomical work practices – would literally be "out of order." Anthropologist Mary Douglas writes that a joke "affords the opportunity for realizing that an accepted pattern has no necessity" (1975, 96). The laughter that a joke elicits illuminates a social world held in common with others. Joining the laughter affirms one's membership in it.

That people hold worlds in common with others through sharing classifications and methods of sensemaking is basic to human social life. This is essential for our communications to succeed. Owen's quip points at once to the natural order that astronomers unravel and to the social order of research through which they do so.[12] These two orders go together.[13] Owen's quip suggests that there ought to be shared practices of achieving reference – of

[11] On invited laughter, see Jefferson (1984) and Sacks (1992, vol. 2, 570–575).
[12] As Barnes (1995, 66) notes, we can conceive of social order as the absence of conflict, as the stability of a pattern over time, and as a pattern. Implicated in the other conceptions, the latter is of greatest sociological interest. Following Garfinkel (1956, 1967), I shall consider social order not as a given, but examine how participants (members) constitute, recognize, and maintain it.
[13] Garfinkel (1967, vii) remarks that "in doing sociology, lay and professional, every reference to the 'real world,' even where the reference is to physical or biological events, is a reference to the organized activities of everyday life."

finding the galaxy cluster again – which themselves are unproblematic to these researchers. The sudden end of laughter (in line 8) may well mark that these researchers cannot afford to be skeptics. Their work, and much research with large datasets, inhabits a space of nonskepticism.[14]

If this scene thus leads us to ponder the metaphysical and communicational foundations of these researchers' data production, another demonstrates how they seek to enable absent others to learn from their processed data. When Nadine and her colleagues pondered the weather at Calar Alto the team was also busy assembling its first public release of their A2713 dataset. It was not to contain Nadine's near-infrared observations, but the team's core data comprising of visible-light photographs taken with a telescope in Chile, high-resolution exposures taken with the Hubble Space Telescope, and a mid-infrared map produced with the Spitzer spacecraft, along with a large object catalog – a table of measured and estimated properties of galaxies in this field –, based on these data. An early catalog version included the output of diverse algorithms applied to images like Figure I.1 – positions, measured radiation fluxes, photometric redshifts, error estimates and so on –, merged into a single large table with ca. 88.000 lines (one per detected object) and about 700 columns (one for each measured or estimated parameter). At a collaboration meeting it was cut down to 200 columns, a more manageable size for users beyond the team.

In the team's work, this table became a remarkable thing. To be published along with it, a journal article was to describe the catalog entries and how they were made. MUWAGS team members worried that, as with so many manuals we encounter in all walks of life, users may ignore these instructions or not read them properly, only to blame the MUWAGS team for mistaken uses thereafter. But there was yet another concern about the table: that with any reasonable amount of work its description would be incomplete. Peter, a postdoctoral scholar and MUWAGS member, explained to me:

> Transcript I.2
> How should data users <u>know</u> this all? You as a team <u>cannot</u> put all your complex shared knowledge into the documentation. You <u>forget</u> things. You take <u>stuff</u> that you know and work with for five years as a given. You <u>forget</u> to include it in the documentation. That happens <u>all</u> the time. (...) Perhaps you could write a massive <u>project</u> blog or a website to explain all that could go <u>wrong</u> with using the data ... but we are probably not even aware <u>ourselves</u> of what we would have to describe since this is a years-long trained ... but perhaps already intuitive ... process.

---

[14] I thank Douglas Macbeth for this formulation. Like other scientists and everyone else, astronomers cannot meaningfully question presumptions foundational to their work from within their practices. Much of Wittgenstein's (1969) *On Certainty* explores this point. See also Pollner (1987) and Gebauer (2009).

Given how hard it is to convey the team's knowledge of their data by describing it, Peter and his colleagues would prefer the catalog itself to encode it. And indeed, catalog entries contain and conserve, somehow, parts of the team's collective knowledge of their data, "frozen in" for future uses and users. Notably, several of the table entries are likelihoods – such as those resulting from the probabilistic classification algorithms used to estimate whether any specific dot or blob in Figure I.1 is a star, a galaxy, or a quasar (a luminous and apparently compact extragalactic object). It is through such likelihoods that the team communicates its beliefs about its data to users, who can employ catalog entries to address new questions, generate further likelihoods, and change their beliefs about the galaxy cluster, its member galaxies, other objects of this kind, the distribution of cosmic dark matter, and so on.[15] To change one's beliefs means to learn. Computation and human learning thus are entangled and the team's challenge is: "How can we share our data so that others can use it to update their beliefs?"

The photographic mosaic and these scenes of its making and publication illustrate how data have become peculiar stuff that scientists use to learn about nature, instruct students, build connections, transmit knowledge, grow trust, and evaluate the work of others.[16] The mosaic of Figure I.1 is one image of the night sky made for scientific analyses, a recording of radiation from deep space. But it is also a deposit of social relations, metaphysical assumptions, and economic considerations.[17] First, the recording medium is central to these astronomers' work. They can add digital exposures to form a single image in which faint signals rise over the noise, becoming detectable and measurable.[18] Second, that these exposures, taken at different times, can be added to form an image is contingent on the night sky's stability – a key aspect of astronomy's natural order. (Other sciences engage other natural orders.) Third, data-rich research and the training of junior scientists go together. Indeed, much scientific work is done in instructional settings, but students learn also by participating in

[15] Here astronomers use "belief" not as something hidden in a private mind (cf. Ryle 1949), but as in Bayesian inference, where it stands for the prior distribution as an estimate of the probability of a hypothesis. Bayesian inference is about updating prior beliefs with likelihoods (Jaynes 2003; MacKay 2003; Sivia 2006). I describe these catalog entries as likelihoods for simplicity. Many are in fact posterior probabilities that cannot be simply converted to likelihoods.
[16] By writing of "stuff" I emphasize the probing and open-ended nature of my inquiry in which I do not know in advance all that matters to the scientists and technicians whose work I witnessed.
[17] For the notion of an image as a "deposit of social relations" see Baxandall (1972).
[18] This additivity is one of the "affordances" (Gibson 1977) of digital imaging in astronomy (cf. Chapter 1).

group meetings and other gatherings, such as when they make sense of a quip like Owen's. And they learn on their own and with other students by encountering data, computer code, diagrams, models, and phenomena.

By implication, fourth, a lack of data threatens the group's social organization as a unit of research and training. As with many collaborations in astronomy, MUWAGS did not plan an instrument, build it, and use it to produce data. Instead, its members wrote a series of proposals and were lucky, being granted observing time at major observatories. For a certain period of exclusive proprietary use, the data they obtained were their epistemic and social "stuff," with which they established connections and collaborations.[19] Fifth, for Nadine the lack of data due to bad weather turned into professional and personal trouble. "Her" deep field's depth – variously expressed as integration time or the magnitude of the faintest detectable signal – was her enduring concern. One night at the observatory, when yet another of her observing runs was "clouded out," Nadine worried that "a deep field that does not go deep is not a deep field." With this truism she arguably signaled to me that her aspiration to membership in the community of deep field astronomers was at stake. Contributing to the production of a dataset was a key to her participation and belonging in this community.

The MAMBO team's exposures contributed to the MUWAGS dataset. Its members' give and take of data – as well as the mosaic's missing corner (Figure I.1) – suggests that, sixth, the "economic" is intertwined with the "epistemic" and the "social." These three cannot be properly separated. (And there is always politics as well.) Seventh, issues of knowledge and proper use reach beyond the Heidelberg team and the MUWAGS collaboration toward users of their data, who may hold the MUWAGS team accountable for their work.

There is also a lesson for methodology here. The pervasiveness of instruction in science is a boon for ethnographers who can witness researchers explicating what they usually take for granted. With students being common onlookers to laboratory and data analysis work, there is a place at their side for ethnographers to gain insights into its material and social orders, standards of judgment, background assumptions, and accounting practices of such work. Much of this is lost in studies based on interviews and documents.

---

[19] The competitive use of shared facilities is not unique to astronomy, as studies of particle accelerators, research ships, and spacecraft demonstrate (Traweek 1988; Law and Akrich 1994; Doing 2009; Vertesi 2015, 2020; Goodwin 2018).

We have a lot to learn even from brief moments of interaction. Take Owen's question, for example. The problem of how to interpret it was "thrown back" to participants, whose laughter made it recognizable as a pun.[20] With their response the analyst's position shifts from social scientists to participants in the field. The first to analyze Owen's utterance and recognize it as humor is not the ethnographer – everyone at the meeting arguably did so. As Douglas Macbeth (2007, 200) puts it, "ordinary cultural members are the first analysts on the scene." And so it is not only with laughter but with talk in general. Attending to what is witnessable rather than conjecturing about what goes on in people's minds, not seeking to pass judgments on people's utterances and actions using external standards, as well as not grafting concepts onto observations quickly, means to adopt a naturalistic attitude. This is the approach I take in this book.

I.2   Data-centrism Is a Social Process

The work of the Heidelberg group is but one example of how data are central to social relations and social interactions of scientists and technicians, students and their mentors, teams that collaborate and compete. In their professional lives, scientific data are epistemic and social things. Data are also entangled in economic and political relations, but *How Data Need People* considers the social as foundational, not least because economic and political action also is, at its core, accomplished socially. There is a data-centrism here in the sense that making, using, and publishing data causes humans to interact and engage with each other in specifiable ways. Making and using scientific data necessarily involves people's evaluative tendencies, and, as such, their concerns with their actions being adequately understood by others, with being held accountable for the products of their work, with referring to the same world together, and with becoming – and remaining – adequate members of professional communities.

Adopting this viewpoint helps us to formulate an ethnographic, interactional, practice-focused complement to a rich literature on the production, use, and management of scientific data. When sociologists first began to study scientific work ethnographically, they challenged portraits of science that philosophers had sketched and produced accounts of the (social) construction of facts. Data were a topic of their descriptions, but not a central concern. Thus, in one of the first ethnographies of laboratory work in

---

[20] See Sacks et al. (1974, 728). The formulation "thrown back" is due to Lindwall et al. (2015, 144).

science, sociologist Karin Knorr Cetina (1981) noticed that scientists and technicians used an array of machines to generate and fixate a variety of records and traces on paper, photographic film, and other media. But as these marks were subsequently processed to "manufacture" scientific facts, few of these records seemed to leave the laboratory – unlike the arguments they supported. Bruno Latour and Steve Woolgar (1986, 45–53) called the marks that laboratory machines produced "inscriptions." In their sketch of a biochemistry lab as a site of production, Latour and Woolgar (1986, 46) depict how energy, chemicals, animals, as well as mail and telephone connections enter the laboratory. What leaves it are "ARTICLES" (capitals in original) – presumably containing arguments and newly constructed facts –, but not "inscriptions" or "data."[21]

When these studies appeared in the 1980s, online databases began to transform research in many disciplines, first perhaps in molecular biology, mobilizing data beyond individual laboratories like never before. Stephen Hilgartner (1995) argues that such databases constitute a novel regime of science communication, impact research practices as well as institutional arrangements, and reshape the boundaries of what counts as public and private and possibly even the contents of knowledge. Nowadays, online databases are common and widely used, from genetics to the environmental and climate sciences, astronomy, and linguistics.[22]

With data thus mobilized, social scientists have used notions like communities of practice, moral economies, and gift exchange to capture the social and moral dimension of using, sharing, and publishing data. By doing so they hint at the potential of anthropological and sociological analyses. Thus, Jeremy Birnholtz and Matthew Bietz (2003) argue that data are implicated in scientists' social worlds and communities of practice through ownership and access. Bruno Strasser (2019) emphasizes the diversity of scientists' moral economies in the sharing and withholding of genetic-sequencing data. Christine Borgman and her coauthors recognize data as a collaboration's "glue" (Borgman et al. 2012, 485). Echoing Marcel

---

[21] Bogen and Woodward (1988) define data as local evidence for nonlocal phenomena. Leonelli (2016, 77) defines scientific data inclusively as "any product of research activities (…) that is collected, stored, and disseminated *in order to be used as evidence for knowledge claims*" (emphasis in original). Bokulich and Parker (2021) restrict their definition to records that are separate from the system or phenomenon under study. By following Hacking (1992a, 48) and considering only the products of data generators (typically forms of writing or inscription, broadly conceived) as data, my view is yet narrower and more specific.

[22] See Hine (2008), Leonelli (2016), Hilgartner (2017), and Strasser (2019) on genetics; Edwards (2010) and Borgman (2015) on environmental sciences; McCray (2014, 2017) on astronomy; and MacWhinney (2025) on linguistics.

Mauss (2016 [1923–1924]), they identify a gift culture in which datasets are assets that can be traded with other researchers, used as leverage in collaborations, and brought as dowry (Wallis et al. 2013). If data are released, Borgman (2015, 217) argues, they can lose their value as "assets" to "barter."

But owning, accessing, and publishing them as resources is only a part of how data are implicated in the social, economic, and political lives of scientists and technicians. Philosopher Sabina Leonelli connects an understanding of data as "tools for communication" (2016, 69) with an examination of their epistemic function and economic value. Drawing on interviews with database curators, Leonelli argues that data-centrism marks a shift away from considering data as single-use products of the research process toward recognizing "efforts to mobilize, integrate, and visualize data (…) as contributions to discovery in their own right" (Leonelli 2016, 2). In her view, it "consists of a normative vision of how scientific knowledge should be produced in order for the research process to be efficient and trustworthy" (Leonelli 2016, 197). Good data, it seems, need curators who, literally, care for them.[23]

Studies of information infrastructures also highlight how important human action and skill are for enabling the reuse of data. Christine Borgman (2015, 4) argues that data "exist within knowledge infrastructure – an ecology of people, practices, technologies, institutions, material objects, and relationships." Paul Edwards' (2010) historical study of research about climate change argues that this phenomenon becomes recognizable to scientists only through the stable background that the knowledge infrastructures of climate science provide. These include networks for standardizing and calibrating instruments as well as practices of measuring, distributing, and repairing meteorological data. Edwards and his coauthors (2011) note that where proper infrastructures are not established, users often understand others' data only through elaborate communications with data makers that they call "data friction." They recognize the parallel of this process to everyday social interaction, in which "common ground" – shared understandings fundamental to mutual sensemaking – is typically provisional and contingent. For data to be usable, people need to do this work, but here, as well, these people's commitments and accountabilities remain largely unspecified.[24]

---

[23] See also Pinel et al. (2020) and Pinel and Svendsen (2024).

[24] On "common ground," see Lewis (1969), Clark (1996), and Enfield (2013). Scientists widely recognize the importance of infrastructures for data-rich research (cf. Wynholds et al. 2011; Blanton et al. 2023). Nevertheless, as I focus on practices of making, using, and preparing data for publication,

We can probe yet further into the socialness of data-rich science and find it also in how scientists draw inferences from data by computational means. Linguistic anthropologist Paul Kockelman (2017, 2025) proposes a Bayesian anthropology that treats reasoning as probabilistic and computational. He seeks to align this approach with the semiotics of Charles Sanders Peirce, who argued that meaning is generated in chain-like processes of semiosis in which signs instigate the production of new interpretants (objects of interpretation). However, Kockelman does not address how embodied, evaluative, social humans participate in this process and strive to be accountable to other researchers. This is what a naturalistic anthropological approach to data-rich science can examine.

I.3 An Anthropological Perspective

An anthropological approach, as I understand it here, puts people – embodied, cognizant, social, and cultural human beings – and their practices at the center of attention. It begins neither with ready-made concepts nor with individuals and "private ratiocination" (Douglas 1992, 240), but with public understandings and shared practices. That we are social before we are individual is a viewpoint owed to Émile Durkheim, a founder of sociology and anthropology.[25] It is a sense of anthropology endorsed by philosopher Ludwig Wittgenstein, who in his late work observed shared social practices and wondered how knowing something is a witnessable ability.[26] Wittgenstein insists that learning to do what others do by attending to what they make explicit and what they take for granted does not require access to their private thoughts but can be achieved through participating in a shared form of life. Thus understood, what novices in science (and elsewhere) do bears some resemblance with an ethnographer's practice of participant observation.

Such an anthropological approach ought to focus on communication and do so in a fine-grained way that is alert to social action and interaction. Language is arguably our principal means to coordinate social actions, to build and maintain social relations, to commit ourselves to social projects, and to hold each other accountable. There is a tyranny of accountability in

---

but not archiving or retrieving them, infrastructures play a relatively small role in my account. See Genova (2018) and Borgman and Wofford (2021) on astronomy's data infrastructures.

[25] Durkheim makes this point in *Elementary Forms of the Religious Life* (1915 [1912]). Interaction-minded scholars like Mead (1934) and Blumer (1969) share this viewpoint.

[26] Consider, as an example, paragraphs 143 to 184, on understanding and ability, in Wittgenstein's (2009 [1953]) *Philosophical Investigations*.

social life, "an ever-present possibility of being noticed, praised, blamed, questioned, called out, and judged" (Enfield and Sidnell 2022, 21). This accountability is exercised largely through uses of language.[27] If an ethnographic study can sketch a "model of the human" in data-rich science, social accounting practices are bound to be one of its foundations.[28] But such an anthropological approach, and such a model, must also acknowledge the biographical nature of participants' lives.[29] Membership in a community and culture, credibility, and reputation are biographical matters, and so are assessments of genealogy ("Who was her supervisor?") and expertise, such as when someone's "track record" is examined (Collins and Evans 2007). Biographies are repositories of trustworthiness.

When anthropologists explore an unknown domain, they are often wary that diverse actors, agencies, and objects, not all human, may matter to a social setting. They cannot know in advance which forms social life may take, nor if these actors and agencies are members of a culture or community. Compared with terms like community, moral economy, or culture, the notion of "sociality" is more inclusive and open-ended, less laden with presumptions about the workings of social relations, interactions, and practices. Some anthropologists use sociality as a term that is not in need of a definition (Graeber 2011; Wilf 2013; Miller 2015). Others have defined it as the "art of living together" (Lee 1927), as "the capacity to be social" (Schick 1984), as "referring to the creating and maintaining of relationships" (Strathern 1988, 13), as a "condition of social co-presence" (Chau 2006, 147), as "the character of social interaction that underpins social life" (Enfield and Levinson 2006, 2), and as the "range of possibilities for social coordination with others" (Ochs and Solomon 2010, 69).[30]

---

[27] See Evans-Pritchard (1937), Douglas (1980), Levinson (1983), and Enfield and Sidnell (2017).

[28] Such a model may be a caricature, but it could turn out to be a useful heuristic for the social study of future developments in science. The study of accounting practices can also complement and develop pragmatic philosophical views of what "epistemic agents" (Chang 2011, 2022) are like. After all, epistemic agents are unavoidably also social agents, and as such users and subjects of accounting practices. It could also contribute to a rapprochement of the history and philosophy of science with the sociology of science, which some critics (like Daston 2009) have regrettably reduced to approaches like Actor-Network Theory and the Sociology of Scientific Knowledge, to the neglect of alternatives (Kinzel 2012), including the naturalistic and interactional viewpoint that I adopt. This would also benefit approaches like cognitive ethnography (Nersessian and MacLeod 2022) and discipline-specific studies (e.g., Boyd et al. 2023), which, so far, lack interactional views of human reasoners and actors. See Veigl and Currie (2025) for the use of social science methods in the philosophy of science.

[29] Note that, for Gell (1998, 10), anthropology "tends to focus on the 'act' in the context of the 'life' – or more precisely, the 'stage of life' – of the agent. The fundamental periodicity of anthropology is the life cycle."

[30] Notions of sociality are also popular with philosophers (Tuomela 2007; Nguyen 2020) and behavioral scientists (Ward and Webster 2016).

In this book I examine data-centric socialities as forms of social coordination unfolding in the making, use, publication, and reuse of digital scientific data. My notion of data-centrism – that making, using, and publishing data causes people to interact and engage in specifiable ways – is inspired by Georg Simmel, who early in the twentieth century proposed the study of sociations (*Vergesellschaftungen*) as the proper object of sociology. Simmel noticed that "neither hunger nor love, neither work nor religiosity, neither technology nor the functions and results of intelligence (…) are themselves sociation. The latter is manifested only when individuals' isolation is transformed into forms of togetherness and for-each-otherness that count as interaction" (Simmel 1992 [1908], 18–19, my translation). He continues that the "specific subject matter and the form of sociation are always a unit, since a social form cannot have an existence when dissolved from any content, as much as a spatial form cannot exist without the matter whose shape it is" (19). Simmel sensed that "minor forms of sociation" (34), which ought to be studied "microscopically" (34), shape society at large. He distinguished forms of sociation at different scales, from fleeting encounters to lifelong and generational forms of belonging to families, medieval guilds, and nation-states.[31]

Elsewhere, Simmel (2004 [1900]) pondered the effects of money, a quantitative medium like many forms of data, on forms of sociation.[32] Simmel argued that, unlike barter, uses of money always introduce the community as a "third party" to an exchange. Money, he writes, therefore is a "claim upon society" (Simmel 2004 [1900], 176–177). Thus inspired, I consider a variety of data-centric socialities that involve scientists and technicians, students and their mentors, teams that collaborate and compete, participants of hack weeks, as well as the technologies and media that they use together.

Inspired by Simmel, we benefit from a change in perspective. For good reasons a growing body of studies has probed into pressing ethical issues of contemporary data uses in science and society.[33] But when we attend to interactions of data makers and data users ethnographically, a subtle ethical landscape comes into view that is consequential for those affected, yet unrecognized by existing studies. Scientists and technicians emerge as social inquirers themselves (Chapters 2, 3, 7, 8, and Outlook). Combining

[31] On Simmel as an inspiration, but not a model, for empirical investigations of social interaction, see Bergmann (2011).
[32] See also Dodd (2014).
[33] See, for example, Floridi and Taddeo (2016), Mayernik (2017), White et al. (2022), Poole (2023), and Padmapriya and Parthasarathy (2024).

data from different sources for analysis – a common, often challenging problem of data-rich science – becomes a window into a discipline's community and culture (Chapter 3). We discover how diagrams are sites for "cultivating data" (Chapter 4) and domains for practicing mundane reason (Chapter 5), and we learn how scientists use collaborations as organizational experiments to manage their work with large datasets (Chapter 6). Probing into the "inner conversations" among members of a research team gives us novel insights into the normative expectations of "open science" (Chapter 7). And we learn that scientists commonly presume a "reciprocity of perspectives" (Schütz 1962, 1964), assuming that data users act like themselves, as they seek to encode their knowledge in a dataset and design it for others to use it properly (Chapter 8).

As suggested, my approach is naturalistic. I attend to what I can witness as an ethnographer. I accept Edwin Hutchins and Brian Hazlehurst's (1995, 54) "no telepathy assumption": "No mind can influence another except via mediating structure." I refrain from conjecturing about what goes on in people's minds and do not seek to pass judgments on their utterances and actions using external standards. Instead, I aim to make sense of data-centric socialities from the viewpoints of their participants: scientists and technicians, novices and old hands.

My perspective is aligned in many ways with ethnomethodology, a sociological approach to the study of practical actions and practical reasoning. Ethnomethodology is not a method and it is not ethnography. Ethnography is the empirical study of people living and acting in their life worlds, undertaken by observing and participating in these settings.[34] Ethnomethodology is the study of the methodical ways in which people make sense of ordinary and professional activities and do so in ways that others can recognize. Following Harold Garfinkel (1967), who modified advice that Durkheim (1982 [1895]) gave in *Rules of Sociological Method*, ethnomethodological investigations are guided by the heuristic to treat social facts as accomplishments: "Where others might see 'things,' 'givens' or 'facts of life', the ethnomethodologist sees (or attempts to see) process: the process through which the perceivedly stable features of socially organized environments are continually created and sustained" (Pollner 1974a, 27). As Michael Lynch puts it, "[w]hat is at stake is not the

---

[34] In my view, ethnography is not simply a method either, but an approach that is imbued with a particular epistemology and ontology, such as by situating "language deeply and inextricably in social life" (Blommaert and Jie 2020, 7), by attending to the viewpoints of participating humans (Agar 1995; Fabian 1995; Hymes 1996), and by examining their sensemaking practices. Uses of numbers, measurements, and diagrams are, likewise, situated in the social life of data-rich science.

theoretical problem of order, but the substantive *production* of order on singular occasions" (2001, 140; emphasis in original). This order is typically brought about sequentially and it can often be analyzed as such. Consider again the conversation of Otfried, Owen, and their colleagues that I witnessed, recorded, and transcribed (Transcript I.1). Following Otfried's complaint about weather at the observatory, Owen posed his question and participants analyzed it "on the fly" to act thereupon: they laughed. Thus, ethnography can yield materials for an ethnomethodological inquiry.

Ethnomethodologists and conversation analysts argue that we analyze each other's actions all the time and that we can gain insights into participants' understandings by attending closely to how they respond to each other, as it reveals the order that they create, recognize, sustain, and take for granted.[35] In fact, we can conceive of any social actor as a lay sociologist or anthropologist, who is "an inquirer into the practical circumstances that confront the member going about the business of everyday life, an ethnographer of its culture, a methodologist separating truth from falsity, fact from fancy, valid from invalid inferences, reality from fantasy" (Hester and Eglin 2017, 200).

If anthropologists have emphasized the importance of social accountability for social order and mutual sensemaking, a notion of accountability is, likewise, central to ethnomethodology. There it refers to the self-organization of social settings by its members who "make its properties as an organized environment of practical activities detectable, countable, recordable, reportable, tell-a-story-aboutable, analyzable – in short, *accountable*" (Garfinkel 1967, 33; emphasis in original) to each other. There are two aspects of this accountability: producing the order as well as making it witnessably available so that it can be reproduced. Achieved through "situated practices of looking-and-telling" (Garfinkel 1967, 1), this communicative work establishes the participants' trust and the moral order of their interaction.[36]

Note the important distinction between accountability as a concern with being held to account (a reflective stance) and ethnomethodological

---

[35] Thus understood, human sociality is characterized by processes of mutual, methodical sensemaking. Talk-in-interaction in copresence may be its foundational site. Schegloff (2006, 70–71) summarizes an enormous body of scholarship when he writes that "[p]eople talk in turns, which compose orderly sequences through which courses of action are developed; they deal with transient problems of speaking, hearing or understanding the talk and reset the interaction on its course; they organize themselves so as to allow stories to be told; they fill out occasions of interaction from approaches and greetings through to closure, and part in an orderly way." See also Sacks (1992) and Sidnell (2010).

[36] See Garfinkel (1963); Lempert (2013).

accountability as situated within lived practice (and thus often nonreflec-
tive), shaping how actions are organized. The former requires language
for becoming socially relevant, whereas the latter may include uses of
language but is commonly prelinguistic or even nonlinguistic. I consider accountability-as-responsibility as a second-order phenomenon that
commonly presumes ethnomethodological accountability. I shall refer to
"accounting practices" inclusively as the actions oriented to the achievement of either kind of accountability.

As ethnomethodologists understand it, reflexivity is a characteristic feature of social interaction, during which participants continually reassess
earlier observations, utterances, and interpretations. Always understood
as temporal and sequential, ethnomethodological reflexivity is different,
for example, from the postmodern concern of ethnographers about their
role in fieldwork. For ethnomethodologists, reflexivity is implicated in the
phenomenon of accountability.[37]

I.4   The Social, the Numerical, and the Computational

As a "social communication technology" (Dor 2015) language may be our
principal means to coordinate social actions, to commit to social projects,
to hold each other accountable, and to build and maintain social relations.[38] But numbers, computations, diagrams, and pieces of computer
code are other means to do so. Wittgenstein (1978) noticed that confusion would result if we were not to agree routinely on the result of simple
calculations, such as that 25×25 is 625. Making such calculations and
routinely agreeing on their outcome is, for him, an anthropological fact.
This numerical accountability is a social accountability.[39] Given that most

---

[37] See Heritage (1984) and Lynch (1993). Barnes et al. (1996, 205fn4) describe ethnomethodology as "a
means of studying realisms," and this suggestion, I believe, makes it rewarding to bring it into conversation with recent work in the philosophy of science that strives for "realistic" views of (scientific)
realism (Chang 2022). If anthropologist Tim Ingold (2018, 2) is right to claim that "anthropology
is philosophy with the people in" then one might as well wonder what a "(scientific) realism with
the people in" would look like. Sharrock and Anderson (1991, 74) argued long ago that the question
of "whether scientists are right in their 'realistic' construal of their achievements gives way to the
question of whether the scientists' sense of the reality of the phenomena they deal with has in fact
been identified at all." Ethnomethodological studies are valuable for this purpose, but see Hoeppe
(2023) for some reservations about ethnomethodological studies of scientific practice.
[38] However, see Leroi-Gourhan (1993 [1964]), Gundaker (1998), and Rutherford (2025) on uses of
touch, gestures, inscriptions, and graphisms.
[39] Rawls (2002), Pollner (2012), vom Lehn (2016), and Koschmann (2019) speculate that Harold
Garfinkel's notion of accountability may have been inspired by the bookkeeping he witnessed at his
parents' furniture company.

scientific measurements are numbers, and digital data are intrinsically numerical, this medial microstructure must be consequential for data-centric socialities (Chapter 5).

Digital images like Figure I.1 are two-dimensional arrays of numbers. They are used for diverse analyses and measurements in astronomy and other sciences. Their numerical accountability reaches beyond dimensionless single numerical values and extends to one, two, or even higher dimensions (cf. Chapters 1 and 5). How digital photographic exposures are formatted is essential to what astronomers can do with them, such as adding, subtracting, or dividing exposures. It is also essential to this work's social organization – such as when several smaller teams combine data taken at different telescopes into a joint dataset, as was the case with the MUWAGS collaboration. The call is, therefore, to include the material properties and medial formats of data in an anthropological analysis.[40]

In pondering how data, as media, shape social forms, we can take inspiration from anthropological views of money use throughout human history. Keith Hart (2001, 2016) observes that, as a symbolic medium, money not only reduces the value of diverse entities to a single scale and conveys information more easily. It is also a "store of memory linking individuals to their various communities, a kind of memory bank (…) and thus a source of identity" (Hart 2016, 7).[41] Nadine's quest for membership in the community of astronomical deep field researchers by contributing to the production of a dataset resonates with this observation, as it does with Simmel's view of money as a "claim upon society" (Simmel 2004 [1900], 176–177).

Many anthropologists take a negative view of money, highlighting its coercive function in exploitative and unequal economic relations, but Hart recognizes in money a medium that humans can shape to their needs, a medium that also has redemptive features: "Money is how we learn to be truly human" (2016, 11). Hart's argument for a "human economy" from which no one is excluded resonates with demands for the open access to data and other resources in the sciences. This aspiration arguably guides many hackathons and hack weeks – meetings at which participants work together with public datasets on shared problems, teaching each other methods and hacks along the way (Chapter 6).

---

[40] Diverse material artifacts can mediate human action and knowledge (Goody 1977; Vygotsky 1978; Marx 1990 [1867]; Hutchins 1995; Klein 2003; Latour 2005; Goodwin 2013, 2018; Madianou and Miller 2013). See Munro (2001) for a view on how numbers mediate social life, an important topic for accounting studies and the sociology of science (Heintz 2007; Mennicken and Vollmer 2007).

[41] See also Dodd (2014) and Maurer (2021).

I.5   Data Economies

Christine Borgman argues that datasets are assets that can be traded with other researchers, used as leverage in collaborations, and brought in as dowry. Released data, Borgman (2015, 217) reports, lose their value as "assets" to "barter." She adds that data may also be regarded as "liabilities" (2015, 217) due to the costs and efforts of storing and managing them or because of legal implications, such as when guarding rights to anonymity and privacy. These descriptions focus on concerns over ownership and access, but do not address how data would be used.

As Hart (2001) points out, we are increasingly imagining living together as an economy. Many astronomers are acutely aware of their work's economic dimension and their references to it go along with a shift toward data-centrism. I was intrigued by how pervasively my interlocutors used a vocabulary borrowed from capitalist economy to describe the organization of contemporary observing. Astronomers commonly refer to data as commodities, talk about where best (on the sky) to invest a block of telescope time, and describe observing projects as enterprises oriented to making profits. Although some astronomers had referred to data as commodities before,[42] this metaphor arguably gained traction in the early 2000s. By then several major research institutes had cut long-term contracts with observatories and instead joined collaborative projects where they would share the financial costs of building and operating instruments for access to their data products.[43]

As a notion to describe the access to and use rights of data, "economy" is both a member's term and an analyst's term. But analysts like Borgman and participants use it only to highlight specific aspects and not to describe the workings of an entire discipline. Considering a domain of practice as an economy might suggest that an exchange principle is basic to all its activities, or that all these operate according to a capitalist logic. This can be misleading.[44]

I.6   Scales of Organizing: Collaboration, Friendship, Hack Weeks

Doing science with large datasets involves diverse actors and relations. It is differentiated. To get at this differentiation, we need to develop

---

[42] For example, Léna (1988, 1).

[43] Hoeppe (2018a). The ALLSKY survey described in Chapter 7 was such a project.

[44] See Chapter 7 on the notion of "moral economy."

both a more fine-grained vocabulary and an understanding of diverse scales of sociality in terms of the number of participants and the complexity of technology involved, as well as the temporality that unfolds. Contemporary astronomers are not liberal subjects who own data privately and permanently. Large amounts of observing time at public observatories are made by, and given to, collectives only. Structured and often hierarchical, collaborations are dominant in data-rich science and central to much of what I observed. Collaborations have lifetimes from a few years to decades. Many of the long-lasting collaborations described in the literature are formal organizations marked by their privileged or even exclusive access to data-generating facilities.[45] When focusing on facility users, I find that many collaborations are "organizational experiments" (Sharrock 2011, 29) that draw on diverse resources to order their affairs, often in improvisational ways (Chapters 6, 7, and 8).

Several large data-centric collaborations in astronomy have developed from the friendship of actors in influential organizational roles. Thus, "old boys'" networks (McDonald 2011) certainly matter. But friendship, as a form of social relation characteristic of settings in which other rights and obligations are suspended, is important more generally in a field in which shorter-lived and often fluid social forms emerge. In astronomy's diverse ecology of data production, where access to many, but not all, facilities is nominally open to all researchers, networks of friends and ties of academic genealogy provide diverse ways of "mutual aid" in organizing access to data, assembling the expertise to analyze it, and establishing coauthorship (Chapter 6). Human work lives are these ties' characteristic timescales.

Compared to long-lasting formal collaborations and the affective ties of friendship, hackathons are fleetingly short. Rarely lasting more than the five days of a "hack week" (a common format), hackathons in astronomy are typically marked by a diverse group of participants who work ostensibly free from hierarchies on newly released datasets, with open software, and on shared problems. Hackathons are thus a social form contingent on openness. Instruction, learning, and building new relations are their goals.[46] While hackathons may be brief, participants' relations are often more enduring.

An interactional approach to these scales of sociality could be reductionist and trace all social structures to patterns of interaction. But, in adopting it, analysts would ignore the diverse contexts of accountability and

---

[45] Knorr Cetina (1999), Shrum et al. (2007), Vertesi (2015, 2020), and Roy (2024).
[46] Huppenkothen et al. (2018) and Falk et al. (2024).

accounting practices in which members engage. As Egon Bittner (1965) noted long ago, people use "organizational constructs" – understandings of how to act as a member of an organization – as resources for achieving, and mutually making sense of, intelligible actions.[47] Inspired by Bittner I examine how this inherent reflexivity shapes courses of practical action. I find that scientists use diverse resources, including medial and epistemic orders as well as a dataset's projected coherence, for organizing collaborative work (Chapter 6).

I.7   Learning from Instruction

As mentioned, the pervasiveness of instruction in science is fortunate for ethnographers, as there is already a place for them available at the side of students, inviting insights into backgrounded assumptions and into how practices unfold in real time. Thus, we can identify problems of data-rich science, consider how they are "staffed" with people in a specific case, and witness ethnographically how they are managed.[48] In this way, scientists' social, epistemic, political, and economic accountabilities become unavoidably part of our analysis. Yet more intriguing is a convergence of learners' practices that includes junior scientists and ethnographers, a theme that I shall examine in several contexts (Chapters 2, 3, 7, 8, and Outlook).

Data-centric socialities are inevitably media-centric socialities, and thus my exploration of instruction begins in Chapter 1 with an inquiry into what scientists can do with digital media that they could not do before. Setting out from a lecture on image processing to undergraduate students, it traces astronomers' understandings of digital data's affordances. It argues that the introduction of charge-coupled devices in the 1980s provided solutions to a set of practical problems that astronomers had formulated with increasing clarity since the 1950s. Subsequently, new organizational possibilities for astronomical research emerged. These include mobilizing data beyond local contexts, rendering abstract time as an object of management, sharing data as nonrivalrous goods, assessing others' work remotely, and building new forms of collaboration – elements of a novel medial middle ground for data-rich science.

---

[47] Weick (1979, 1995), Anderson et al. (1989), and Anderson and Sharrock (2018).

[48] My approach to consider how problems are "staffed" is inspired by Garfinkel's examination of variously populated waiting lines as examples of "immortal ordinary society" (2002, 65), but sociological studies of situationalism (e.g., Marres and Stark 2020) are relevant as well.

Chapter 2 returns to human sociality and supplements my introduction to elements of ethnomethodology (earlier in this introduction) with a review of how humans are fundamentally evaluative and what the ethical implications of this entail. I examine this by joining graduate students, junior scientists, and technicians as they record data at an astronomical observatory. The "legitimate peripheral participation" in "communities of practice" (Lave and Wenger 1991) has become a catchphrase for the situatedness of apprenticeship. Considering situated interactional engagements of instructors and students can shed light on how this "peripheral participation" succeeds, I show how learning and instruction are situated locally while being subject to accountabilities that extend far beyond any single site. I argue that the visitors' ordinary interactional competence enables much of their learning. The telescope control room's progressive redesign and relocation has modified this experience and facilitated its transfer. But it turns out that technicians' ethical evaluations of researchers do not travel as easily. This is part of an ethical landscape that was invisible to prior studies.

Chapter 3 identifies PhD student training as a curious process in which instruction and the advancement of science go together. It examines how Nadine, the PhD student encountered earlier, was instructed to tackle a common, though often challenging, problem of data-rich science: calibrating a new dataset and combining it with data from a different source for analysis. By following Nadine around over two years as she achieved this goal, we learn how she became a competent member in the community and culture of extragalactic astronomy. Conversely, we gain insights into what makes combining scientific datasets often so challenging. I introduce and adopt Trevor Pinch's (1985) notions of "externality" and "evidential context" as aids for comparing epistemic practices; examine how models are used to calibrate a dataset; study the use of shared, but backgrounded notions about the world; and probe into uses of diagrams and visualizations.

Instruction in data-rich science unfolds not only in face-to-face situations and through user manuals. Ideally, data themselves would instruct their users. How can scientists pass on to potential users what they have learned about their data? Chapter 8 proposes answers to this question by focusing on the medium of data and its social uses. It argues that scientific data do not merely represent information but can be structured and presented to have a pragmatic function oriented to enable users' understanding. It demonstrates this by describing how the MUWAGS collaboration designed its catalog to guide users to self-correct wrong uses and delimit being held accountable for misuses. Some astronomers argue that catalogs encode their makers' collective knowledge of their data. Chapter 8 examines this claim ethnographically, identifies elements of a pragmatics of data reuse, and ends with a reflection on socio-computational orders – entanglements of the social and the computational in data-rich science.

The MUWAGS team succeeded in making its catalog "more-than-representational" or "more-than-evidential" by projecting its members' own conduct onto imagined catalog users. As such, they assumed a "reciprocity of perspectives" reminiscent of what social theorists following Alfred Schütz (1962) have recognized as a foundational feature of human intersubjectivity. This is not the only instance in which elementary aspects of social interaction and intersubjectivity help us to make sense of data-centric socialities even where scientists do not meet face to face. Other examples are the sequentiality of actions, participants' mutual monitoring, and the reflexive maintenance of inhabiting a shared world, as well as the omnipresence of accounting practices. *How Data Need People* thus examines the uses and limits of interactional understandings when scientists use media in orienting toward others who are commonly absent.

I.8 Learning from Practical Reasoning

Successful instruction often engages learners in experts' practical reasoning. It is instructive to distill elements of this reasoning, not least for making ethnographic insights into one scientific discipline relevant for studies of others. Garfinkel (2022) called for specifying the "discovering sciences of practical action," arguing that scientists "are *investigating* as well as *using* practical actions, reflexively discovering a local organization of practical actions as well as *what* those practical actions disclose, stumble upon, negate, or prove" (Lynch 2022, 10; emphasis in original). Whether novices or old hands, scientists invariably reason "in the midst of things," as Garfinkel (2002, 101, 249, 250) put it. For practical reasoning there is "no time out" (Garfinkel 2002, 118). It is always situated in the here and now, responds to actions, and calls for responses. It is necessarily prospective (looking forward to what is meant to be achieved) and retrospective (informed by what has happened before), open to correction and oriented to various accountabilities – epistemic, social, and otherwise. What scientists do invariably relates to work done by others elsewhere, and is oriented toward writing a report – the long-lasting record of their research.

The things in whose midst scientists reason are typically defined by their discipline's subject matter. Geologists study rocks and sediments, botanists study plants, and astronomers study objects "on" the sky. Consequently, research work in astronomy differs from that done in botany or geology. Scientists' reasoning is tied to the materials and tools at hand, including computer code, databases, and data of specific formats.[49] But how does this matter to screenwork's virtuality in data-rich science, which, at first glance, erases the material differences of disciplinary work?

How Data Need People examines how discipline-specific objects and structures become actionable through their mediation. Chapter 5 takes uses of the sky in astronomy as an example. Astronomer David W. Hogg once wrote in a blog post that "[a]ll of astronomy and astrophysics is built on the observation and reobservation of sources on the sky."[50] This apparently self-evident statement came to intrigue me as I witnessed data analyses and listened to conversations such as the one of Otfried, Owen, and their colleagues (Transcript I.1). I noticed that the sky's phenomenal properties – its apparent immutability and the richness of its visible features – pervaded astronomical research and provided infrastructural resources for actions that researchers rarely acknowledge in their publications. The sky (and objects on it) is both a topic of research and a resource for its conduct, as it provides saliences that scientists use alongside existing records for ordering work, diagnosing trouble, and repairing data. It is a resource for relieving data users from trusting data makers. Other sciences, I argue, can dwell on other resources to do so.

Note that this work engages what sociologist Melvin Pollner called "mundane reasoning": recognizing and resolving disjunctive experiences using shared sensemaking practices that draw on the presumption that "reality is coherent, determinate and intersubjectively accessible" (Pollner 1987, 47). Mundane reasoning pervades scientific work with data. Diagrams are one of its resources. Diagrams exhibit data in various stages of processing, from "raw" detector outputs to "science plots" that present measured and derived physical values, such as, say, the masses or

---

[49] Thomas Kuhn hints at this with his notion of "disciplinary matrix" (1970, 182), a discipline-specific ensemble of equipment, practices, and discourse.

[50] hoggresearch.blogspot.ca/2008/03/budavari-and-szalay.html (accessed July 7, 2025). The formulation "on the sky" is prevalent in astronomers' talk. It acknowledges the "celestial sphere" as a perceived two-dimensional surface and arguably also the mediated nature of astronomical research, where the "sky" is sometimes defined as "a two-dimensional distribution of intensity of electromagnetic radiation" (Léna 1989, 245; cf. Chapter 5).

luminosities of stars and galaxies. Scientists rarely talk with each other about their work without also looking at plots or sketches on paper, blackboards, or computer screens.[51] Previous studies have pointed out how diagrams make data, models, and phenomena accessible intersubjectively and available for experimenting, exploring, and operating. I examine how diagrams thus become not only "places of thinking" and discovery,[52] but also spaces in which scientists prune and cultivate datasets in light of epistemic and social accountabilities (Chapters 3, 4, and 5).

Scientists are practical reasoners also when organizing collaboration – inevitable for making, processing, and analyzing large datasets. Chapter 6 examines data-centric collaborations as "organizational experiments" (Sharrock 2011, 29) that draw on diverse resources to order their affairs, often in improvisational ways. These resources include medial formats, epistemic orders, and a team's joint orientation to produce a consistent dataset. Diverse in origin and structure, such data-centric collaborations typically lack features of formal organization, such as organizational charts and legally binding contracts. They often emerge from ties of academic genealogy and friendship. For a certain period of exclusive proprietary use, the data that such teams obtain and make is their epistemic and social "stuff," which members use to establish connections and collaborations.

As practical reasoners, natural scientists are also social inquirers. For many scientists the emergence of "open science" has been a practical problem. Chapter 7 considers how researchers examine the social and moral accountabilities of the open access to data and the tensions that result from them. I noticed that as two collaborations prepared datasets for public release, their members became both inquirers into and actors in what many astronomers refer to as their discipline's culture of open data access. Both teams can be described as groups of practical methodologists who used "inner dialogues" to explore the normative expectations and tensions of this domain, seeking to inhabit proper statuses in it. The chapter argues that examining scientists' understanding of statuses and their achievement offers resources for a refined critique of "open science" that is considerate of the context sensitivity of data production and use. Along the way, it examines some methods of how scientists, as members, are doing ethnography.

---

[51] See Ochs et al. (1994, 1996) and Alač (2011).
[52] Compare Wittgenstein's (1960, 7) remarks in the *Blue Book* on paper as a place of thinking.

I.9 Varieties of Data-Centric Socialities

The episodes examined in this book lead us to discover a data-centrism in contemporary science in the sense that making and using data invites humans to interact and engage in specifiable ways – from moments of instruction to striving for membership in a community and organizing collaborative work. We can find data-centric socialities at many scales. They involve scientists and technicians (Chapter 2), students and their supervisors (Chapters 3, 4, and 5), teams that collaborate and compete (Chapters 4, 6, 7, and 8), makers and users of data (Chapter 8) – and always also the technologies and media that they use together. Never is "the social" simply grafted upon something that is otherwise not social. It is always a constitutive and essential aspect of scientific work with data. Its explorers are not just visiting anthropologists and sociologists, but students, scientists, and technicians themselves (Chapters 2, 3, 7, 8, and Outlook).

As I described earlier, my notion of data-centrism is inspired by Georg Simmel's explorations of the diversity of social forms in the early twentieth century. Probing into a wide array of social forms in his *Sociology* (1992 [1908]), Simmel realized that many forms of sociation await discovery – not least by means of more detailed, "microscopic" studies, but also because new forms keep emerging while others fade away. This, certainly, is to be expected, as well, of data-rich science in the twenty-first century. The chapters that follow offer microscopic examinations of some of its dominant forms of sociality and their resources. While these become visible only at the fine granularity of social interaction and the technical detail of a specific science, the lessons we learn are more general, because uses of social accounting practices are. Sciences other than astronomy may, of course, use other media, engage other disciplinary objects, and use other epistemic orders to organize their work. But they will need to train new members, use diagrams to interpret data, use forms of mundane reasoning, organize collaborations by engaging certain orders, act normatively, transmit knowledge – and engage accounting practices along the way.

I.10 This Study

This study began with eighteen months of ethnographic fieldwork by the MAMBO team – the MUWAGS collaboration – as well as associated and competing researchers in 2007–2010, followed by annual revisits in 2010–2019, additional fieldwork in 2023, and ongoing conversations and exchanges with former team members and other scientists. I witnessed data analysis work, instructional meetings, team meetings, and teleconferences; conducted interviews; accessed emails; read publications relevant to the team's work; and assisted in a small part of their research. I recorded oral histories and biographical interviews and studied documents archived by participants. I also attended collaboration meetings, seminar talks, workshops, and conferences. I pursued my fieldwork in Germany, at observatories in Spain and Chile, at a research institute in the United States and at a university in Canada, as well as at conferences, meetings, and at a hack week in Italy, the United Kingdom, the United States, Canada, Germany, France, and Malaysia.

My aim was to witness how astronomers make and use large datasets. They typically do their research in projects, that is, in sequences of work in pursuit of a specific research goal, typically involving several people, extending over months and years, entailing many moments of retrospection and prospection, ideally resulting in publications jointly authored by participating scientists (but, usually, not data-producing technicians). One focus of my ethnography was to follow three PhD students through their thesis projects. Partly overlapping, the other was to witness various stages of the "data life cycle" in action, from the planning and making of observations to their calibration, analysis, and publication. I took detailed fieldnotes and many photographs, and made 434 audio recordings, including 151 interviews, 85 naturally occurring work scenes, 56 work sessions of collaborations, 10 teleconferences, and 52 recordings of academic presentations and discussions.

Even though most of what I witnessed occurred at a small number of sites, *How Data Need People* is not a laboratory ethnography. Much of what I witnessed happened "in-between" places: data were made for users elsewhere; scientists, distributed globally, met in teleconferences, videoconferences, and meetings, and engaged in work done at many places; and papers were written (in part) for unknown readers. Thereby, "the distant" was always present in work that was ostensibly local and the distinction between locality and distance became both problematic and a lens into the workings of data-rich research (cf. Chapter 4).

As I focus on the sequential unfolding of projects over days, months, and years, I have ordered and analyzed my ethnographic material as "streams" that map the temporal, prospective, and retrospective organization of work. In doing so my study differs from those that are based on historical material (Edwards 2010), on surveys (Tenopir et al. 2015), or on interviews (Kriesberg et al. 2013; Leonelli 2016). These are commonly analyzed with approaches like Grounded Theory (Corbin and Strauss 2014), which cannot attend in detail to the always lived and sequential work of scientists and technicians that interests me. Events like Owen's pun (Transcript I.1) and their interpretation would likely be missing from an interview-based account.

I was attracted to the MAMBO team because of its influential technical innovations. The team analyzed images with semi-automatic software pipelines, made and combined large datasets from telescopes on the ground and in space, developed probabilistic data models, and automated object classification techniques. A few years earlier, team members had drastically improved a technique for estimating photometric redshifts (a measure of cosmic distance) from multicolor photographs (Chapter 3). It enabled them to assemble samples of distant galaxies ten times larger than any other team had produced, and thus to do novel statistical studies of galaxy evolution. When I began my fieldwork, a report on the status of observational cosmology had recently considered it the best-performing survey of its kind worldwide. MAMBO was the foundation for a series of international collaborations, including MUWAGS. Even though the team continued to extend its observing program, it could not compete with a team from the United States that had implemented its technique, had access to an observatory with better weather conditions, and then arguably scooped its key science results. Revisiting the team after 2010, I witnessed its decline. It dissolved in 2016.

One of MAMBO's successes is its afterlife in contemporary science. Its improved photometric redshift technique proved to be an important step for ongoing and planned projects, including analyses of data from the James Webb Space Telescope (as of 2022), the European Space Agency's Euclid spacecraft (launched in 2023), and the Legacy Survey of Space and Time at Vera Rubin Observatory (operating since 2025). The years of my study also mark the widespread use of machine-learning techniques in astronomy. Here again, the MAMBO team's work was prescient as it incorporated methods of probabilistic inference from the start.

My access to the team was facilitated by earlier contacts with some of its members when I was an editor and staff writer of *Spektrum der Wissenschaft*, the German-language edition of *Scientific American*, before I returned to academia. I benefitted from my own training and research experience in extragalactic astronomy, as a MSc student in the 1990s (Hoeppe et al. 1994), before I began to study social anthropology. By doing so I arguably acquired "unique adequacy" to do the present study, the "vulgar competence" that Garfinkel and Wieder (1992) deem necessary for ethnomethodological analysts of work.

While my presence as an ethnographer was marked by some astronomers initially ("Now we all have to wear a tie!"), I was quickly taken for granted as a temporary presence and not deemed as someone in need of particular care. My competence and sense of membership became audible to myself, for example, when listening to the recording of the conversation represented in Transcript I.1, in which I heard myself participating in the laughter following Owen's pun. I shared much of the cultural background of the MAMBO and MUWAGS team members and was of a similar age as its postdoctoral scholars and junior faculty members. At times I was a proper participant-observer, such as when I participated in classifying galaxy images for the MUWAGS collaboration, but in many situations of instruction and technical deliberation I tried to be more like a "fly on the wall."

Anthropologists and sociologists debate how the presence of an ethnographer affects a social setting and whether one could then still talk of "naturally occurring situations." I share this concern but note that people need to get their work done – work that other members must eventually recognize as adequate. Witnessing both this work and settings in which others scrutinized it assured me that what I had understood was meaningful to members. Despite the ethnographer onlooking, there is only so much that people can do differently if they want to produce work that their peers will accept.

A further point is how ethnographers can claim any deeper significance for apparently singular events like Owen's pun in Transcript I.1. To generalize from it or claim its representativeness, would one not need to witness, say, five, or ten, or fifteen similar scenes first? This demand for statistics and quantification as sole measures of evidentiality frustrates interaction-minded ethnographers (Crabtree et al. 2013). As Wes Sharrock and Bob Anderson (1986, 93) point out, "from ethnomethodology's point of view, the location of regularity has much more to do with demeanour than with statistical representativeness," and they elaborate: "We do not determine that something is commonplace because we have witnessed thousands of occurrences of it. Seeing it once might be enough to establish for us just how commonplace it is" (Sharrock and Anderson 1986, 93). As with Transcript I.1, and as elaborated earlier, what matters is the "inside view" of how participants in a situation react to certain actions and utterances, signaling unwittingly, for example, that a certain action or its absence is commonplace in a given setting. The regularity and generalizability of social actions is not reducible to extraneous criteria like sample size or the duration of fieldwork.

CHAPTER 1

Medium
Digital Affordances

1.1 This Chapter's Plan

Data-centric socialities are media-centric socialities. Ostensibly, media are "means of transmitting some matter or content from a source to a site of reception" (Davies 2005, 181). This is what the air does when carrying sound waves or a letter that contains a lover's words. But media do not only transmit. As philosopher Sybille Krämer (2019, 833) insists, media are fundamentally generative: they "always shape and constitute what they represent." Throughout history, new media have generated new possibilities, enabling people to do new things. Astronomers have worked with diverse media, from tabulating observations in cuneiform writing on clay tablets and various graphical explorations on paper to photographs on glass plates and printed materials that allow researchers anywhere to compare identical records made at different times and places.[1] So, what do digital media add to, or change about, these practices? What can scientists do with them that they could not do before?

This chapter attempts to answer these questions for digital imaging in astronomy. I begin with a scientist's assessment of its novelty and then describe how a detector technology and a data standard became dominant. I focus on the work of ground-based optical astronomers, but it turns out that their interactions with radio astronomers and space astronomers (who use observatories on spacecraft) – members of different "instrumental communities" (Mody 2011) – have shaped the social organization and sociality of data-rich astronomy. I describe a technological convergence in astronomical practice that affords mobilizing data beyond local contexts, rendering abstract time as an object of management, sharing data as nonrivalrous goods, monitoring and assessing others' work remotely,

---

[1] See Rochberg (2016) on cuneiform records, Nasim (2013) on paper sketches, Pang (2002) on photography, as well as Eisenstein (1979) and Latour (1986) on print media.

and building new forms of collaboration. As identical copies of observing records, digital data do not only "spread the word" about research, but also the "work" itself (cf. Kohler 1999, 252). These uses unfold in a novel medial middle ground. Elementary operations with digital exposures are its foundation.

1.2   "The Big Trick of Optical Astronomy": Quantitative Imaging with Digital Outputs

Let us begin with an introductory class in observational astronomy taught for undergraduate students at a North American university. Following a review of various imaging detectors, the Professor turns to charge-coupled devices (CCDs). These sensitive solid-state detectors use the photoelectric effect to produce grid-shaped pixel images which can be read out and then stored, retrieved, and transmitted as digital files. CCDs are found in digital cameras from smartphones to large telescopes.[2] Once cooled with liquid nitrogen to reduce quantum noise, CCDs can be exposed for several hours. Figure 1.1 illustrates how digital images are both visual and numerical. It shows a small fraction of a calibrated astronomical CCD image as a formatted, bounded, two-dimensional surface of nonoverlapping square picture elements (pixels). A progression of shades of gray represents the radiation flux registered in individual pixels. The grayscale from white to black encodes the number of detected photons and corresponds to increasing exposure, with black indicating the CCD's maximum exposure and saturation.

The Professor cares about making images of sources on the sky and measuring their brightness, size, and shape. But artifacts in data – imprints of the observing situation, including noise –, are this work's ever-present burden. By enabling "quantitative imaging with digital outputs,"[3] CCDs promise a remedy. As the Professor explains, CCDs in use are not only "very efficient" (sensitive) and "very linear" (recording incoming light in proportion to the exposure time). What is more, their output is "born-digital" (McCray 2014), that is, numerical and, as such, symbolic. It is directly amenable to arithmetic calculations, including the pixel-by-pixel

---

[2] In recent years CMOS (Complementary Metal Oxide Semiconductor) detectors have increasingly replaced CCDs. Their output is processed very much like that of CCDs.

[3] The formulation "quantitative imaging with digital outputs" is due to James E. Gunn. See Galison (1997), Beaulieu (2002), Joyce (2006), Alač (2011), and Hoeppe (2019b) for accounts of scientific representations that use numbers and visuals in conjunction. On digital imaging in astronomy, see also Kessler (2012) and Brooker et al. (2019).

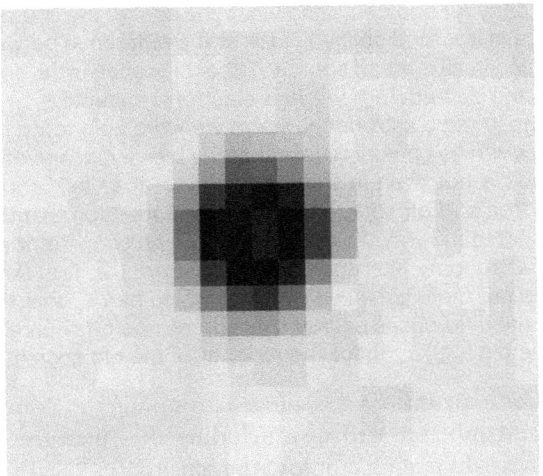

Figure 1.1   Detail of the negative of a calibrated photographic exposure of a source on
the sky, a grid of 21 × 19 pixels (picture elements).
Note: The online version shows the colors of the original figure.

addition, subtraction, and division of exposures. In concert, these properties offer unprecedented possibilities to remove artifacts from data. The
Professor explains:[4]

Transcript 1.1
Now that we have gone over some of the basics ... ehm ... I think it's time
to get into ... to some of the tricks. The <u>big</u> <u>trick</u> of optical astronomy is
that everything is a <u>differential</u> observation. This is not true of absolutely
all observational astronomy. And I am gonna talk a little bit about what
I mean by this. In <u>older</u> astronomy this was almost <u>never</u> the case. <u>Old</u>
astronomy was photographic plates ... where somebody took a picture
of the sky ... and they just collected photons for 20 or 30 minutes ... or
two hours ... or they did spectra for hours and hours (...) And so why is
((*differential observation*)) an improvement? The thing is ... there are all
these effects that ... we can <u>remove</u> by differential imaging. So ... for
example ... the instrument response shouldn't care where you look in
the sky ... it shouldn't matter ... the instrument is the instrument ... we
can look here ((*the Professor points with his hand toward the ceiling in
various directions*)) ... and here ... and here ... The instrument response
should be the <u>same</u>. So .... you can look <u>on</u> your source ... and then you

[4] In this transcript, <u>underlining</u> marks emphasis, ellipses (...) mark brief audible pauses, and double
parentheses contain descriptions, in italics, of context and witnessed actions. See the Appendix for
the transcription conventions I adopt.

can look off your source ... and what you see off the source should have no source in it ... and so if you look at the difference between on source observation versus an off source ... the difference is the source. And this was not the case before we had electronic detectors ... There were a few things in radio astronomy where we were able to do this ... but this on source versus off source is one of the big ... it is one of the unspoken things ... it's not even in the textbooks ... they talk about techniques of on source and off source but they don't mention that this is a funda-mental shift in the way we do astronomy ... it is one of the reasons why modern astronomy is so much more powerful ... it is not just that the detectors are more sensitive ... it's that you can ... that they are digital and that the differences between on source and off source are vital ... So that is the big trick in optical astronomy ... the big secret.

As the Professor explains, CCDs allow astronomers to count photons of cosmic light and subtract artifacts, including the "instrument response," from it. Differential imaging employs the sensitivity, linearity, and "born-digitality" of CCD's output. But why is this move from analog photogra-phy – an element of what the Professor calls "old astronomy" – to digital imaging so spectacular and productive? In analog photography an emul-sion of silver halogenide grains is exposed by incoming light and fixed chemically. This process is much less sensitive than photography with CCDs: of 100 incoming photons a CCD registers up to 80, whereas pho-tographic film records only 1 or 2 (McLean 2008). Thus, film loses most incoming photons. Photographic film is also highly nonlinear: it does not record incident light in proportion to its intensity. An emulsion's charac-teristic curve plots the density of dark grains as a function of light expo-sure. It is approximately linear for a certain part only, but nonlinear for shorter as well as longer exposures, where film saturates.[5]

Analog photography is not "born-digital." To analyze analog photo-graphs with a computer, one must digitize them first, that is, scan devel-oped film with a densitometer to measure its transmission and transform this information into numerical values. Doing so requires sampling and quantization.[6] It loses information. Measuring the characteristic curve for each plate and applying the linearization correction to the measured trans-missions of scanned pixels involves decisions that are difficult to reproduce. Nowhere is there a simple subtraction of "off-source" from "on-source" exposures. Differential imaging with CCDs bypasses these challenges. No

---

[5] More precisely, the characteristic curve plots the logarithm of optical density versus the logarithm of exposure time.
[6] See Manovich (2001, 28).

wonder that it amazes the Professor. But the success of differential imaging depends on the stability of detector ("the instrument response should be the same") and sky over the period of observation. Subtracting "off-source" from "on-source" would not make sense otherwise.

Differential observation may be called an affordance of CCDs in use. Psychologist J. J. Gibson (1977, 67–68) argues that "the affordance of anything is a specific combination of the properties of its substance and its surface" for use in any perceiving animal's project. Widely adopted, the notion of affordance seeks to capture potential, often unplanned and unanticipated uses of objects in specific courses of practical action.[7] Differential observation of astronomical sources was not a design feature of CCDs. Astronomers at work recognized its do-ability with this new detector. I will review more affordances of digital imaging in astronomy later in this chapter, including those that matter to its social organization of observing and data use. But let us briefly consider its history first to understand the options and decisions that led to its widespread use.

1.3 How to Count Light? Defining an "Ideal Detector" and Trying to Build It

In retrospect, work done in the 1970s and 1980s laid a foundation for data-rich astronomy, thanks largely to the invention of CCDs and the rising computing power available to scientists. Many astronomers realized quickly that CCDs offered solutions to a set of problems that researchers had formulated since the 1950s, and to which a variety of detector designs were attempts at a solution. In putting it this way I follow George Kubler, who writes in *The Shape of Time* that "[e]very important work of art can be regarded both as a historical event and as a hard-won solution to some problem" (Kubler 1962, 30). This art historian's way of pondering the historical and social meaning of artifacts is worth adopting for making sense of technical inventions and their social uses.[8]

---

[7] "Affordances are invitations, not demands" (Grey Gundaker, personal communication). Gibson's notion of affordance is used in studies of design (Norman 2002), computer-supported work (Sellen and Harper 2002), and ethics (Keane 2016), among many others. I adopt it in this chapter to sketch the diverse uses that detectors like CCDs enable in astronomical practice without claiming that technical features determine them. Sharrock and Coulter (1998) have formulated an important critique of Gibson's understanding. A related notion, from phenomenology, is saliency (Gurwitsch 1964), which, however, is commonly used to address acts of perception only.

[8] By considering technologies as solutions to problems I sidestep social constructionist and technological determinist accounts, which posit relatively direct relations between communities and technologies (cf. Pinch and Bijker 1984; Wyatt 2008). Astronomers were marginal to the invention of both analog photography and CCDs.

So, which problems did CCDs solve for astronomers? We know parts of the answer from Section 1.2. But let us develop a more comprehensive understanding by contrasting the two detector technologies that dominated optical astronomy in the 1950s, well before CCDs were invented. One was analog photography. It was praised for its capability to record wide-field images, for its high resolution, as well as for its easy processing and archiving (Hearnshaw 1996, 327). But as we have seen, these affordances came along with serious downsides: low sensitivity, nonlinearity, as well as the need to scan developed film to generate digital output. Photomultipliers were the other technology. Used for photometric measurements of starlight since the 1910s, these devices used the photoelectric effect to let incoming photons trigger electron cascades that were registered with voltmeters. Their advantages were their relatively high sensitivity (ten to twenty times that of photographic plates), linear response, and ease of calibration. Their output could be digital or analog. Photomultipliers are essentially 1-pixel detectors, suited for measuring the radiation flux of point sources such as bright stars.

Attempts to design the best possible detector in optical astronomy were efforts to combine the advantages of analog photography with those of photomultipliers while avoiding the downsides of either. As researchers and technicians at various observatories sought to come up with new designs, they pondered what an ideal detector would be like.[9] This development was guided by metrics of performance. Light sensitivity became the most discussed metric. Quantum physics posits the countability of photons of light, and thus the detective quantum efficiency (DQE) – the efficiency of an actual system compared to an idealized, perfect photon-counting system – seemed to be a useful measure of sensitivity.[10]

Because of their high quantum efficiency and linearity, photomultipliers were the starting point for developing electronic detectors that could produce images. An early design that the French astronomer Albert Lallemand proposed already in the 1930s was called electronography. It used photocathodes to make images by recording the output electrons on photographic film. But electronographic cameras were difficult to use, and extracting information from the recorded films was challenging.[11] Thus, high sensitivity alone would not define a desirable imaging detector.

---

[9] See Baum (1955, 1964).

[10] Rose (1946) and Fellgett (1955). Schröter et al. (2022) review the role of quantum physics in the distinction between analog and digital media.

[11] See Worswick (1976), McMullin (1980), and Hearnshaw (1996, 465).

Image intensifiers also used photocathode tubes but focused the electron beam onto a photo-emitting screen that was scanned by a television camera. As such, their output was electronic and could be digitized easily. The most successful image intensifiers were both sensitive and linear but worked only for observing faint light sources (Boksenberg 1976). Bright sources were quickly saturated. Consequently, a wide dynamic range – a large span between the brightest and the faintest recordable signal – was desirable as well, along with the demand for detectors to produce stable images whose neighboring parts would not influence each other's response, as some image intensifiers tended to do.

Unlike electronographic cameras, image intensifiers became popular in the late 1960s and 1970s. Several designs were developed, but none was built in large numbers. Alexander Boksenberg and his team at the University College London built four copies of the Image Photon Counting System (IPCS) that were used as traveling instruments, for example, at the 5-meter telescope on Mount Palomar in California and the European Southern Observatory's 3.6-meter telescope at La Silla in Chile (McCray 2014). Its main competitor was Joseph Wampler and Lloyd Robinson's Image Dissection Scanner (IDS) at Lick Observatory in California, of which five copies were built. This was the only instrument that visiting astronomers could use. As with the IPCS, the IDS's internal noise could be controlled when used only as one-dimensional detectors to record spectra, but not images (Robinson and Wampler 1972).

In 1977, after more than two decades of experimentation with electronic detectors, Peter Boyce, the program director for astronomical instrumentation and development at the National Science Foundation (USA), observed that there was "an almost bewildering variety of detectors being used for ground-based astronomical observations" (1977, 148). A handful of researchers developed these designs, and their knowledge and skill could not be transferred easily. Boyce noted that "enthusiastic instrument developers" tended to overlook the requirement of "simplicity of use and reliability over extended periods at the telescope" (1977, 148). He concluded:

> The ultimate test of a new detector is not the pictorial quality of its first images but the new knowledge ultimately derived from its use by a wide range of working astronomers. In one or two cases where sufficient resources have been available, it has been possible to use a very complicated detector in a relatively routine manner. But the most useful scientific tool continues to be that one which can be used by a large number of scientists without the need for a long or complicated introduction or training period. (Boyce 1977, 145)

Boyce echoed a sentiment that many astronomers shared when he noticed that years of developing alternatives to analog photography only demonstrated the latter's enduring qualities in terms of its high resolution, wide field of view, and storage capacity (cf. also Ford 1979). With the emergence of digitization techniques and digital detectors, the storage capacity of photographic plates was measured in terms of pixel number. Digitized in standard ways, a 30 cm × 30 cm photographic plate (a typical format) yielded one billion pixels. This was several orders of magnitude above the largest digital detectors available in the 1990s (Bland-Hawthorn et al. 1993). This, of course, did not remedy analog photography's low sensitivity, nonlinearity, and not-born-digitality.

When Boyce formulated his critical assessment in 1977, a consensus developed that CCDs – invented in 1969, but still at an early stage of development – would soon become dominant. A main driver for their use in astronomy was the plan of NASA, the US National Aeronautics and Space Administration, to build a large Space Telescope. As this Space Telescope was to be operated remotely in a low Earth orbit, using analog photography seemed impractical. Not only would the radiation deflected by the Earth's magnetic field saturate the film. It would also be difficult to develop and scan exposed film and transmit these data to Earth. Image intensifiers seemed more promising, but their capriciousness remained worrisome. In the 1970s, CCDs were small and sensitive only at short visible wavelengths. But despite their early stage of development, they seemed more promising than any other detector design. The hundred-fold sensitivity of CCDs over classical photography transforms the light collecting power of a 2-meter telescope into that of an imaginary 20-meter telescope. Their "born-digital" output and linear response promised that data could be worked with easily. And what is more, CCD detectors were stable, light, and rugged enough to be flown on spacecraft (Smith and Tatarewicz 1985).

Robert Smith and Joseph Tatarewicz (1985, 1994) argue that what I call the affordances of CCDs defined a "pull" for their development. But Smith and Tatarewicz note that there was also a "push": the effort by Bell and other companies to develop CCDs for a broader market, including for military uses. NASA and the US government supported this effort. The development and production of CCDs as commodities resonates with Boyce's observation that the success of a detector depends not alone on its optical performance, but also on its widespread availability and ease of use. Mass production entails standardization and an increased scale of operations (Hart 2001). Produced as commodities, CCDs promised to be suited for the use by a global community of researchers. Initially, some astronomers worried that, in a field of larger economic forces that promoted CCDs as a new commodity, their specialist requirements would be ignored (Illingworth and Butcher 1980). But this did not hinder astronomers from adopting this technology. Carnegie Institution astronomer Vera Rubin put it succinctly: "I took my first CCD spectra in [19]84, and virtually never went back" (Thompson 2019, 181).

1.4 Data Format: FITS, the Flexible Image Transport System

One hallmark definition of "the digital" is that it enables the loss-less encoding and decoding of information (cf. Stetter 1997, 67). But this alone is insufficient to make digital records an effective communication medium. Data makers and users need to define shared standard data formats. First formulated in 1979, the FITS (Flexible Image Transport System) standard became a milestone for the interoperability of astronomical data. By the 2000s, the success of FITS had spread widely. It inspired data standards beyond astronomy, being used, for example, by the Vatican Library as the format to store and process digitized scans of its manuscript and document collection.[12] How the FITS standard was defined and developed is instructive for an understanding of data-centric socialities. Let us take the viewpoint of optical ground-based astronomers to make sense of how the FITS standard enabled communications between previously autonomous "instrumental communities."[13]

Throughout the 1970s, formatting data, that is, encoding the recorded information of gridded pixel images as well as the metadata that named and described them, was an individual scientist's decision. Constrained by their computer's architecture, they could not pick any format they wanted. Formats differed in how numbers were represented in the binary system, resulting in problems of interoperability. For example, a magnetic tape written on a Digital VAX computer, could not be read easily on an IBM 360, then the other popular mainframe computer (MacKenzie 1993).

Otto, one of the Heidelberg team's senior astronomers, remembers his troubles with deciphering other researchers' data tapes:

---

[12] See vaticanlibrary.va/en/in-digitalizzation/the-current-digital-project.html (accessed July 7, 2025).
[13] I use Mody's (2011) notion of "instrumental community" loosely, to indicate that the research practices of radio, x-ray, and optical astronomers are contingent on the distinct technologies they use.

Transcript 1.2

1 Otto: Back then everyone wrote their own format and when you got
          a tape from someone at times you had to spend a week or so
          until you could read it.

2 Götz: Which formats were these?

3 Otto: Well ... you first had to find out! ((*Our systems manager*)) once
          wrote some code ... and gave it to me ... that made a dump
          of a tape so you could see how long a record was. What was
          there ... after all? Some folks gave us tapes that were poorly
          documented. A file that is well organized tells you right away
          ... this the record length ... byte number so-and-so means <u>this</u>
          ... byte number so-and-so means <u>that</u> ... and so on. And then
          you had to sit down and write code to read the tape record
          by record ... and fiddle with these records so that you could
          make anything with it. Whether it was an image or a table or
          whatever. Often it was quite a hassle to make it usable.

4 Götz: With tapes from observatories?

5 Otto: Yes ... or from colleagues who had worked with the data and
          told us ... "Good ... here ... take my <u>data</u>!" And then we had to
          fiddle with the tapes.

An informal discussion of Ronald Harten and Donald Wells in 1976 eventually led to a shared astronomical data standard. Harten, a radio astronomer, worked at the Westerbork Synthesis Radio Telescope (WSRT) in the Netherlands, while Wells, an optical astronomer, was at the National Optical Astronomy Observatory at Kitt Peak (Arizona, USA). In the mid-1970s new developments in telescope design made radio astronomers and optical astronomers eager to define a format for sharing digital data. Most older radio telescopes had been single dish antennas capable of making low-resolution maps of the sky only, but now a new generation of radio interferometers became available. With this design, the signals of antennas kilometers apart could be correlated to reveal details comparable with those of optical images. Opened in 1968, the WSRT was the first large radio interferometer, followed by the Very Large Array (VLA) in New Mexico (USA), which became operational in 1976.[14] Now capable of seeing "the same" sky at different wavelengths, radio and optical astronomers were eager to compare and combine their data. No single organization could produce both radio and optical data, and thus the members of distinct organizations and instrumental communities had to cooperate. The

---

[14] For a brief history of the WSRT, see astron.nl/telescopes/history-of-wsrt/ (accessed July 7, 2025). For a history of the VLA, see Kellermann et al. (2020).

FITS standard was designed to enable this cooperation. Harten and Wells were soon joined by Eric Greisen of the US National Radio Astronomy Observatory that operates the VLA.

FITS was meant to "facilitate the unambiguous transmission of n-dimensional, regularly spaced data arrays" (Wells and Greisen 1979, 446), that is, images, tables, and data cubes. It is not a compression format like JPEG or MP3, but a standard to store and transport scientific data at arbitrarily chosen precision along with textual descriptions and numerical information. FITS files are composed of one or more "header-data units."[15] The header is encoded in the ASCII format and thus – unlike files in a binary format – can be read by machines and humans alike. It begins with an identifier of the file type, lists keywords whose values describe the telescope and instrument details, observing date and coordinates, the specific binary format adopted, as well as the dimension of the header-data units' data portion. Users can define their own keywords and include text of arbitrary length to maximize a file's "self-documentation" (Wells and Greisen 1979, 446). All records have a length of 23.040 bits (2880 8-bit bytes). The lengths of the header and of each subsequent data unit can be multiples of this record size. Data units are typically stored in a binary format to speed up their processing. Users can specify the binary format in which floating point numbers are represented at a precision of their choice (MacKenzie 1993).

Apart from developing this technical description, Wells, Greisen, and Harten suggested principles for how astronomers should use and manage the FITS standard. Greisen (2003, 78) argues that, in hindsight, "the decision that no addition to the format should make existing data sets obsolete" was most important. This demand for backward compatibility became known as the Once FITS, always FITS rule. It is what makes the format valuable for archives like the Vatican Library. Despite the commitment to the long-term usability of existing FITS files, frequent changes to the standard were made over years and decades (Scroggins and Boscoe 2020). These were mandated through communal governance, in which regional FITS user groups collected and debated proposed changes to the standard, to be then endorsed by the International Astronomical Union's FITS Working Group. Over time, email discussions replaced the regional working groups (Scroggins and Boscoe 2020, 43). The FITS Working Group includes representatives of main observatories and space

---

[15] fits.gsfc.nasa.gov/fits_primer.html (accessed July 7, 2025).

agencies. In 1990, NASA endorsed the FITS format for its astronomical data (Hanisch et al. 2001).[16]

1.5   Affordances for the Social Organization of Data Production and Use

Distinguishing an "old astronomy" from a "new" one, as the Professor did, is not about a "material analog" versus an "immaterial digital." In both "made-digital" analog and "born-digital" photography, data are inherently material. Information is bound to substrates – glass plates, punched cards, magnetic tapes, DVDs, or hard disks.[17] But digital information is non-rivalrous: "We can share it without dividing it and consume it without diminishing it" (Suber 2012, 46). The substrates and formatting of data afford diverse uses.

First, there are the benefits of commensuration, additivity, and experimentation that digital records enable (see also Chapter 4).

Second, different substrates afford distinct practices of data ownership and access. For most North American, European, and Australian researchers in the 1960s to 1990s, doing "old astronomy" meant writing proposals and applying for observing time at national or international observatories (McCray 2000). Time allocation committees adjudicated these proposals. If granted some nights of observing time, researchers would travel to an observatory as visiting astronomers. The observatory offered capabilities and services to record data.[18] Working in the dome at night, using the equipment allocated to them with the help (and often guidance) of night assistants, researchers recorded images and spectra on glass plates, photographic film, or, later, on magnetic tapes. Observing techniques could be idiosyncratic, adjusted to the science case at hand, but were also shaped by visiting astronomers' limited skills and understanding

---

[16] This was part of NASA adopting the recommendations of the Squibb and Cheung (1988) report. The emergence of multi-messenger astrophysics and a new generation of instruments producing large higher dimensional datasets has instigated a debate on whether a new standard besides FITS is desirable (Mink 2015). The Advanced Science Data Format (Greenfield et al. 2015) is a candidate that has been used for archiving and processing James Webb Space Telescope data (Graham et al. 2023).

[17] See Blanchette (2011) and Dourish (2017).

[18] When representatives of major observatories debated possible new observing modes at a 1995 conference in Hilo (Hawaii), they debated whether observatories should deliver "a product, a service, or a capability" and whether researchers would, accordingly, now be "customers, clients, or users" (Boroson 1996, 245). The existing visitor mode was meant to offer a capacity for users. Depending on the ranking of approved observing programs, service-mode observing offered products, services, or capabilities to users.

of the observatory's technology. Visitors took photographic plates to their home institutions to analyze and digitize them, but did not typically return them to the observatory. Even when some observatories claimed plates as their property, the plates' return was not usually enforced and neither were breaches sanctioned.[19] These "makers" seemed to adopt a Lockean notion of private property, which ascribes legitimate ownership to human labor (Locke 1988 [1690]), understanding the plates to be the products of visiting astronomers' labor. Photographic plates and magnetic tapes were at times exchanged and passed on to students – but also stored away without leaving much of a trace, being forgotten or even discarded. If they traveled at all, then it was usually within personal networks.

Third, the additivity and linearity of CCD exposures afford new observing modes. Only around 2000, when CCDs were already dominant, did service-mode observing become an alternative to the visiting mode (see Chapter 2). In service mode, technicians record data for absent researchers. This was meant to improve the data quality and the efficiency of telescope use by scheduling observations for approved projects according to weather conditions at the observatory. It largely removed researchers from the observatory and allowed projects to be split into several components that could be observed over some time. This was possible thanks to the additivity of digital exposures, which enabled their combination; the linearity of CCDs, which allowed calculating necessary exposure times; and the sky's stability at the timescales of this work.

Fourth, data's digitality affords holding its producers accountable remotely. Moving from visitor-mode to service-mode observing shifted the responsibility for data quality from visiting astronomers to observatory technicians (Giacconi 2008, 233), an issue that I examine further in Chapter 2. Note how the born-digitality of data matters here. Faults in born-digital, numerical data can presumably be blamed on the performance of observatory technicians. As data's digitality offers novel possibilities to hold others to account, this blame can travel far. By contrast, in "old astronomy" photographic plates were often chemically developed and fixated during the observing night itself and approved as "good enough" by visiting astronomers at the place of production. But when scientists work with open data, they, too, can be held to account more easily (see Section 1.6).

---

[19] I draw on conversations with scientists who used the European Southern Observatory at La Silla, Calar Alto Observatory, Kitt Peak National Observatory, and the Cerro Tololo Inter-American Observatory.

Fifth, service-mode observations following standard procedures yield data that can be archived and reused more easily. Into the 1990s, many ground-based optical observatories deemed the costs of setting up archives excessive. Dennis Crabtree and his colleagues (1996, 207) argue that, in contrast to the expensive operation of space telescopes, at ground-based observatories "the cost of the technology to archive data safely, develop the software for searching and accessing the archives, etc. was too high given the relative cost of redoing an observation." This argument about costs implies these astronomers' sense that the sky will be sufficiently "the same" at the time of reobservation. Only when telescope construction and operating costs rose swiftly in the 1990s, did the "cost-per-byte of the data" (Benacchio 1997, 391) mandate systematic archiving. But initially the value of archives was questionable because many visitors recorded and documented their data idiosyncratically. Piero Benvenuti (1994, 3) lamented that an archive of such data would be a "graveyard of zombies" of little benefit for future uses. To make a difference one had to follow standardized observing and archiving protocols – an import from the operation of radio and space observatories.[20]

Sixth, and harking back to my second point, digital data that are thus accessible and usable afford new modes of research collaboration. Data made using different technologies (sensitive to radio, x-ray, optical, and ultraviolet radiation), stored in a single format, are commensurable and combinable. They allow researchers with expertise in different technologies and wavelength ranges to collaborate more effectively than before. Calibrations and analyses of one constituent dataset can retroact on others. The shared access to data archives and repositories facilitates the work of globally distributed research teams. The public availability of data at the end of proprietary periods enables specific temporalities of teamwork, as I will examine later in this book (Chapters 6 to 8).

---

[20] Giacconi (2008). Radio and space astronomers had adopted standard observing protocols and maintained public data archives since the 1970s. For example, the VLA, mentioned earlier in this chapter, is a public, national facility whose data are broadly accessible. With the beginning of its operations in 1976, data were archived and became publicly available after a one-year propriety period. Likewise, satellite data were generally recorded in standard ways suited for archiving. Beginning in 1978, data of NASA's and the European Space Agency's (ESA's) spacecraft became available to the public after certain proprietary periods. In 1976, a conference in Williamsburg, Virginia, formulated recommendations for archiving and the public access to NASA's astronomical satellite data (Goody and Massey 1976). In 1978, the International Ultraviolet Explorer, a project of NASA, ESA, and the British Space Agency, was the first space observatory to institute a proprietary period (of six months; Willis 2013). In the 1990s, several initiatives promoted interdisciplinary forms of collaboration for computing-intense science (Hine 2008, 23–24). At the same time there was an increased demand for the accountability of tax-funded science, enforced in the United States, for example, through the 1993 Government Performance and Results Act.

Seventh, these capacities are expanded with novel architectures for large databases, which "move the analysis to the data" (Szalay 2018, 202). Pioneered by the Sloan Digital Sky Survey (see Chapter 6), these are now widely used beyond astronomy.

These affordances of digital data "conspire" with astronomy's phenomenal setting, where all scientists observe the "same" stable sky. These affordances structure and define the disciplinary character of astronomical research. Not only are its "born-digital" data amenable to symbol processing. Given that almost all information is due to the sense of vision (versus touch or smell) – or rather, the detection and processing of quantized ("digital") radiation –, multimodality appears to offer astronomers no insights into their research objects beyond what is visual and measurable. The numerical, computable nature of astronomical data makes such data available to probabilistic inference and suited for machine-learning applications.[21]

1.6   A Digital Middle Ground

In the 1970s and 1980s, when they were early career researchers, the Professor and Otto used a variety of media and apparatuses, including printed catalogs (tables of the measured properties of celestial objects) and atlases, and photographic plates they recorded themselves at the telescope, as well as optical and mechanical machines for analyzing photographic plates exposed at various observatories. They used blink comparators for spotting differences between photographs, x-y measuring machines for determining celestial coordinates, and digitized plates with microdensitometers. Since the 1990s, this machinery of optical, mechanical, and electronic instrumentation has been largely collapsed into computers. Technologies for data production and analysis have converged. Technological convergence is, of course, not exclusive to astronomy.[22] But compared to other sciences it is particularly pronounced there because astronomers work almost exclusively with recordings of light, whose nature as discrete, countable quanta is commensurate with that of digital detectors and computers, and with being processed as symbols.

[21]   As such, astronomical practices seem exemplary for what Alač (2020, 493) calls the "dominant orientation toward the visual modality" in scientific work. However, embodied practices clearly matter in astronomical data production and analysis (see Chapters 2 and 4). See Nasim (2021) for a historical study of embodiment in astronomical observation. Helmreich (2016) illustrates uses of hearing in interpreting one kind of astronomical data.

[22]   See Hart (2001) and Arthur (2009).

We can regard technological convergence in astronomy as a key element of a novel medial middle ground and examine its implications for data-rich science and data-centric socialities. The notion of a medial middle ground is due to historian of science Hans-Jörg Rheinberger (2011), for whom it pertains to mediations characteristic of laboratories, where it is "the *apparatus* in all its complexity and intricacy that comes to stand *between* the knowing subjects and the objects of knowledge" (2011, 340; emphasis in original). For him, "the medial world of knowledge-making" (340) includes diverse recording media which enlarge and reduce, speed things up, and slow them down for examination. Rheinberger (2011; 2023) suggests that attending closely to how scientists use laboratory equipment is the best way to identify the medial middle grounds of science.

Like Rheinberger I want to understand the workings of specific media and apparatuses, but I extend the notion of middle ground, which I use loosely, beyond individual laboratories to include what they share and what connects them: data, computers, code, networks, and standards (like the FITS format). This makes it a sort of infrastructure, but I also include social practices and resources like diagrams to represent data.[23] The affordances listed in Section 1.5 mark its scope. For me as an anthropologist, Rheinberger's "knowing subjects" are unavoidably a differentiated bunch: researchers at various places, at various stages in their education and career, in diverse institutions and collaborations, situated in a variety of networks and communities. What makes astronomy's digital middle ground unprecedented is not only the technological convergence and the diversity of its human participants, but also the practical aspects of its "flatness," to borrow journalist Thomas Friedman's (2005) term for describing how the internet changed networked global trade. For astronomer Matt Mountain (2014), it is the public availability of astronomical data that has "flattened the astronomy world," contributing to a sense of placelessness that some contemporary astronomers notice in their work. As one researcher told me, "to do research in astronomy all you need is a laptop computer and a connection to the Internet."

Describing the work of early twentieth-century drosophila geneticists, who developed extensive networks for sharing domesticated fruit flies

---

[23] See Star and Bowker (2006) and the discussion in Chapter 5 on infrastructuring. The notion of an "accounting regime" (Jones and Dugdale 2001) locates calculative practices in such a domain. Besides them, practices like mundane reasoning (Chapter 5) and conventional diagrams (Chapter 4) are means to extend social accountability, which is essential for a medial middle ground to have any social use. It would be worthwhile exploring the connection of this medial middle ground alongside the pragmatist notion of common ground (Lewis 1969; Clark 1996; Enfield 2013).

for experimentation, Robert Kohler noticed that "[f]ormal publications spread the *word* of mapping and the standard fly, but exchange of stocks and know-how spread the *work*" (Kohler 1999, 252; emphasis in original). Sharing and exchanging digital data, formatted in FITS, is one means for astronomers' work to meet closer to the "shop floor," for making data and actions available for inspection, and for holding not only observatory technicians, but also researchers, to account.[24] In moving from publishing results and arguments to also circulating digital data and software, a medial middle ground enables scientists to build and contest trust, gain interdependence, and grow coordination, learning, and skills in novel and often unnoticed ways. Marshall McLuhan (1964) famously argued that media are "extensions of man," but it seems that, in astronomy, digital data have become social extensions that connect multiple instrumental and epistemic communities, transforming the workings of each. When astronomers contribute to data archives, they care for the needs of future researchers while also creating possibilities that data users will blame them. Thus, a medial middle ground is not merely a technological matter. It is also a space for ethical evaluations, as I will examine in Chapter 2.

---

[24] In Hoeppe (2020b), I describe how the authors of a discovery claim were held to account by critics who reanalyzed their public data.

Evaluations
The Ethical Life of Data Production

2.1 This Chapter's Plan

This chapter focuses on evaluations of persons as a lens into data production in science and its ethics. That humans are fundamentally evaluative is a basic tenet of social interaction and social life. We are concerned that others understand our intentions adequately, knowing that our actions are being evaluated, and we examine others' actions and intentions likewise. In many sciences, data production has become a service, with technicians generating data in researchers' absence. This chapter traces scientists' and technicians' evaluations through several contexts. As such, it takes a common problem of data-rich science – the production of data as a service –, considers how it is "staffed" in a specific case, and follows its management ethnographically.

I begin with describing the separation of data-producing technicians from data-using scientists and examine how researchers in astronomy interpret recorded data not only as representing information about the sky, but also as second-order information about the conduct of technicians and the functioning of apparatus. Then I turn to how technicians experience observing in the absence of data users – ever mindful that these can later inspect their work. Eventually, I examine an instructional setting in which junior scientists as apprentices learn from technicians to record data. While I joined these students and technicians as an ethnographer, I realized that both were doing a sort of ethnography themselves. Students are inquirers into locally situated practices who learn from various cues, make sense of how locals react to their actions, and discover how technicians are subject to accountabilities that extend far beyond the local setting. Technicians, in turn, are ethnographers of visiting researchers' evaluative practices. Thus understood, ethnographic practices support and enable scientific data production while also revealing its ethical tensions.

2.2 Producing Data as a Service

Outsourcing data production and analysis has swiftly gained importance in much scientific work. Genome sequencing is a prominent example. David R. Smith, a microbiologist at the University of Western Ontario (Canada) who studies the genomes of algae, reports that he can now

> select an algal strain of interest from the NCMA [National Center for Marine Algae and Microbiota] culture collection, have the NCMA grow the organism, extract DNA, and then send the DNA to a commercial facility of my choosing for high-throughput sequencing, followed by professional bioinformatics consulting and analysis, catered to my project needs. (Smith 2015, 16)

Much of the sequencing information is generated in factory-like establishments (Cyranoski 2016). In this arrangement, data are commodities that companies produce as a service and sell on a market. Smith notes that "[n]ew technologies and the burgeoning biotech industry have made it quick, cheap, and easy for researchers to generate massive amounts of molecular sequence information" (2015, 15). Yet he is also concerned that using such services removes scientists from the objects of their research, possibly impeding their creativity (Smith 2015). Biologists Franz Pichler and Susan Turner (2007) have expressed concerns regarding the trustworthiness and the quality of data produced in outsourcing, pointing to issues of confidentiality and worry about scientists losing the expertise to use novel laboratory techniques. Nevertheless, they describe these issues as technical problems that proper management can fix.

These commentaries acknowledge, albeit implicitly, the work of technical experts who have previously worked in copresence with researchers but are now separated from them in space and time. This is curious for ethnographers who found that technicians have manual skills that scientists lack (Doing 2009), are guardians of technology as well as gatekeepers to the phenomena of science (Barley and Bechky 1994), and are central to reconciling the temporalities of laboratory work (Law and Akrich 1994; Doing 2009). In these accounts, technicians' work typically becomes visible only when problems arise.[1] Thus, Steven Shapin demonstrates that Robert Boyle's trust in his technicians was a key element of his laboratory's "moral texture" and essential to its success. Yet he also notes that Boyle commonly erased references to technicians from accounts of successful work and blamed them for experimental failure (Shapin 1994, 383).

---

[1] See Barley and Bechky (1994), Suchman (1995), Star and Strauss (1999), and Doing (2009).

What happens to scientist–technician relations when data production is outsourced, widely separating scientists and technicians? Has trust in institutions replaced personal trust? How would either case manifest itself and how would this matter to scientific practice? In pursuing these questions, this chapter takes Shapin's concern with the "moral texture" of knowledge-making relations into the twenty-first century and considers how data are produced in service work.[2]

Changes in astronomical observation offer a compelling case for examining such questions. Prior to the early 2000s, most astronomers submitted observing proposals to time allocation committees staffed by peers who ranked the proposals and allocated telescope observing time. Successful astronomers then traveled to observatories for a certain number of nights to work with the support of staff technicians. Around the year 2000, several major observatories adopted service-mode observing, in which technicians observe in the absence of researchers. Approved projects are ranked in categories and scheduled flexibly according to the requirements specified in approved proposals.[3] Thus, the ESO delivers data as a product to the authors of the highest-ranked programs, while it offers applicants of lower-ranked programs a capability that they can use at their own risk (of an observing run being "rained out," for example). Ranked classes thus mark a new distinction of what kind of place the observatory is for staff and scientists, and what it is meant to deliver. In the absence of scientists, observatory staff are now responsible for the quality of data.[4] Researchers of differently ranked observing programs are "customers, clients, or users" (Boroson 1996, 245).

Service-mode observing is widely regarded as having improved the quality of astronomical data and the efficiency of telescope use (Giacconi 2008), but it is not without critics. Senior astronomers worry that practicing service-mode observing exclusively will result in young researchers' insufficient sense of what is a doable observing program and a lack of

---

[2] Stating that "all jobs involve work on materials, information or people," Korczynski and Macdonald (2009, 3) define "service work" as "work that involves working on people." It includes settings in which service workers are not in direct contact with service recipients.

[3] In service mode, projects are ranked in categories. The European Southern Observatory (ESO) uses the following classes for its Very Large Telescopes (VLTs): "The top-ranked proposals are assigned an A rank, followed by B rank, and the filler programmes, with more relaxed observing constraints, receive rank class C" (Sterzik et al. 2015, 2). ESO guarantees the completion of A-ranked programs at the specified requirements. A-ranked programs that are not completed in one semester are continued in the next one, while B- and C-ranked programs are not carried over. See also Comerón (2004) and Rejkuba et al. (2018, 2024).

[4] See Giacconi (2008) and Sterzik et al. (2015).

responsibility for the costly and sensitive equipment on which their work depends. Novices could lack essential insights into how data are produced. Otfried, a senior researcher who regularly supervises PhD students, explains:[5]

> *Transcript 2.1*
> Operating telescopes in pure service mode is troublesome in that astronomers do not know anymore how their data are coming <u>about</u> and therefore they ... they do not know the details of their data. (...) I <u>must</u> <u>know</u> how one observes ... which restrictions there are ... how <u>this</u> works ... what ... yes ... what happens ... how does the <u>weather</u> affect it ... and all those things. Otherwise you lose touch with what can be achieved and what is a <u>good</u> observing program. You don't get a good observing program just by having a brilliant idea. It has to be <u>doable</u>. You need to know how things are actually done ... and you don't know this if you've never seen a telescope in action.

Otfried acknowledges the functioning of instrumentation and the specific temporalities of observing, but he alludes at most implicitly to the technicians who mediate "all those things" that one must know. While there appears to be a consensus among senior astronomers that data-using researchers need to be familiar with the work done at observatories, the degree of familiarity required is controversial (Lockman 2005). Scientists like Otfried argue that experiencing observing at one observatory is sufficient for developing proposals more generally, given that many observatories are "one of a kind" – standardized places whose operation historians of science have linked to factories and industrial work.[6]

2.3 Evaluations and Accountabilities

Steven Shapin (1994, 367) argues that scientists' and technicians' "knowledge-making relations" have a "moral texture." He uses historical sources to locate the foundations of this moral texture in trust and moments of praise, blame, and justification. But how could such relationships unfold when data makers and data users do not work in copresence?

[5] See the Appendix for a full description of the transcription scheme I use.
[6] See Schaffer (1994) and Pang (2002). Another critique is that the low completion rate of lower-ranked programs endangers their utility. In 2014, a review of the first fifteen years of service-mode operations at the VLT demonstrated that more than 90 per cent of A-ranked proposals had been completed, but only 45 per cent of B-ranked programs. This was particularly troubling since half of the service-observing time had been scheduled for B-ranked programs (Primas et al. 2014; Sterzik et al. 2015).

Whatever distance does to scientific work, one can assume that it does not undo the fact that humans are fundamentally evaluative (Laidlaw 2014). Praise, blame, and justification pervade social life, whether people meet face to face, talk about others in their absence, or use various communication media. The prospect of being evaluated informs much of what we do and don't do. Ethnomethodologist Kenneth Liberman argues that the first "rule" of participating in social life is to avoid embarrassment.[7] Linguist Stephen Levinson (1983, 321fn16) points out that participants in conversation "are constrained to utilize the expected procedures [of talk in interaction] not (or not only) because failure to do so would yield 'incoherent discourses,' but because if they don't, they find themselves accountable for specific inferences that their behaviour will have generated." After all, participants in conversation mutually monitor each other (Goffman 1964).

Is such mutual monitoring also practiced in service encounters and in service work done at a distance? Unlike many other encounters, exchanges between clients and service providers are asymmetrical, and this is bound to affect how its participants evaluate each other (Goffman 1983). Paul Manning's (2008) interpretation of the imagined conversations that baristas of the coffee chain Starbucks post at an online site about their face-to-face encounters with "Stupid Customers of the Week" provides an example. Manning argues that these imagined conversations illustrate how these service providers are dissatisfied with customers not recognizing their skills. Manning finds two ideal models of talk in tension with each other:

> One of these is a technical script based on craft knowledge possessed by the baristas which contradicts the notion that "the customer is always right" (…). The other is a normative egalitarian model of talk between peers in which the barista deserves the same treatment as is normatively expected by customers. (Manning 2008, 115–116)

Service encounters are thus fraught with ethical tension. But, of course, ethical evaluations matter not only there. Ethics pervades everyday interactions from turn-taking in conversation to expressions and gestures of politeness, and may well be fundamental to social interaction itself.[8] Thus conceived,

---

[7] Remark made at a lecture at the workshop on ethnomethodology and conversation analysis at Syddansk Universitet, Sønderborg, Denmark (December 2013).

[8] See Garfinkel (1963), Goffman (1983), and Lempert (2013). Various understandings of ethics and morality conflict. Following Williams (1985), Keane (2016, 16–20) points out that these terms tend to portray social relations differently: "morality" typically alludes to universal rules that can be contemplated on one's own, whereas "ethics" is invariably socially situated.

ethics is everywhere. But why should one attend to its situated visibility and focus on face-to-face encounters in the service work of data production if the latter appears to be marked by the *absence* of such interactions between producers and users?

First, even when labor is divided and distributed, people and their work are commonly assessed in their absence. As Karl Marx writes in volume 1 of *Capital*, "it is by their imperfections that the means of production in any process bring to our attention their character of being the products of past labour. A knife which fails to cut, a piece of thread which keeps on snapping, forcibly remind us of Mr A, the cutler, or Mr B, the spinner" (1990 [1867], 289). Although Marx does not explicitly formulate this as an instance of (personified) blame, such evaluations, and appertaining typifications, could easily be invoked here. Second, attending ethnographically to ethical evaluations in interactions and ordinary encounters is a means for avoiding privileging rational reflection and alleged choice-making. It calls for looking beneath normative and institutionalized discourses. Third, if ethics pervades social interactions and knowledge production, it is pointless to seek to define its borders. However, it remains the case that for ethics to matter beyond face-to-face encounters, evaluations must be communicated. Ethnographers can witness the "communicative methods and labor" of making ethics "recognizable and effective in discursive interaction" (Lempert 2013, 387).

Thus conceived, ethics must be fundamental to data production – distributed or not –, as it is to all collaborative scientific work. But merely positing its existence fails to address how it unfolds and what it can tell us about the conditions of service work in data-rich science. Aiming to develop a more fine-grained analysis, I draw on studies that have adopted an interactional approach in the study of what anthropologist Webb Keane (2016, 100) calls "ethical life": the "saturation of social existence with evaluations of persons, their relations, and their actions."[9] Philosopher Bernard Williams (1985; 1986) is intrigued by the possibility of making sense of ethical variety by taking an "ethnographic stance": "the situation of an observer who has an imaginative understanding of a society's ethical concepts and can understand its life from the inside, but does not share those concepts" (Williams 1986, 203–204). This perspective aims at attaining the experiencing subject's first-person perspective, while maintaining the reflective distance of a third-person view.

---

[9] See also Keane (2014), Laidlaw (2014), and Lambek (2015).

By contrast, it is from the second-person perspective that people "are compelled to account for themselves to another – for example, with excuses, accusations, justifications, praise, or blame." It is the "natural home for ethical reasoning, explanations, justifications, and all the other dynamics that prompt reflexivity" (Keane 2016, 243, 244). This perspective always requires an interlocutor for its realization.[10] At times, this may be an ethnographer. Erving Goffman (1963) illustrates the third-person perspective when he observes that stigmatized persons are highly skilled in seeing themselves from another's perspective, often as a type of person.

Keane emphasizes that ethics is eventful, with ethical evaluations being instigated by what, inspired by J. J. Gibson (1977), he calls ethical affordances – "any aspects of people's experiences of themselves, of other people, or of their surround, that they may draw on as they make ethical evaluations and decisions, whether consciously or not" (Keane 2014, 7). Ethical affordances can matter in contexts of production – remember Marx's observation of "Mr A, the cutler, or Mr B, the spinner."

Now consider, again, the work of David R. Smith, the biologist introduced in Section 2.2. He describes how he can complete a "shopping list" for the collection of microbiotic algae cultures and end up receiving sequence information from a commercial company. Of course, shopping involves many intricate decisions that a shopping list cannot specify: "how to find things, which aisles to go down in what order, how to decide between competing brands, etc." (Suchman 2007, 119). The list only states how the activity is to turn out. Imagine that this work is done as a service. It is likely to occur under constraints of time and available resources, and then accusations of blame may be just around the corner. What if the requested organic apples are not in stock today? What if a certain cheese is currently available only at another branch at the other side of town? Always tied to the here and now, the temporality of shopping is bound to be distinct from how, for example, Pierre Bourdieu has portrayed scholarly work as being characterized by *skholé*, the free time of philosophical reflection.[11]

As Manning (2008) and Keane (2016) illustrate, we can study ethical evaluations by attending to narratives and imagined conversations. Here, accountability-as-responsibility is a second-order phenomenon that

---

[10] Judith Butler (2005) follows Nietzsche in noticing that an account of oneself is commonly given as a response to being questioned.

[11] Bourdieu (2000, 13) uses the Greek word *skholé* for alluding to the distinction that Plato makes when comparing philosophers' "talk at their leisure in peace" with the hurried talk in the courts.

presumes ethnomethodological accountability. But we can also witness ethical evaluations in social interaction, including conversation. How joking together and formulating utterances collaboratively may be heard as levelling hierarchies,[12] and how pauses may instigate justifications or explanations demonstrates the constitutive role of conversation in ethical life.[13] I shall attend to such uses in considering my ethnographic material. Focusing on the actors' perspectives and attending to situated actions, including talk, I do so by considering service-mode observing from three viewpoints: scientists using data, technicians producing data in their absence, and a case where scientists joined technicians in a run of service-mode observing.

2.4   Scientists Using Data in the Absence of Technicians

Let us now turn to the use of data produced in service mode, and there to the evaluation of persons and their actions in a situation where the smooth flow of work with digital photographic exposures was suspended.

All optical astronomical exposures contain artifacts of the observing situation, including image distortions of the telescope and camera and the blurring of images due to atmospheric turbulence. Digital pixel images are "arrays of numbers" (Lynch 1991a) that researchers use arithmetically, for example, by adding, subtracting, or dividing entire images pixel by pixel (see Chapter 1).[14] One of the first steps in processing them is to divide the science exposures (recorded at night) by so-called flatfield frames, which are recorded before or after stars appear in the sky. As images of the twilight sky, flatfield exposures record the camera's pixel-to-pixel sensitivity variations only. Dividing the science exposures (which contain the same variations but also traces of stars, etc.) by the flatfields is meant to "cancel out" these artifactual variations and yield science images with desired "flat" backgrounds, that is, uniform noise levels.[15]

However, this was not what Nadine, the PhD student whom we met in the Introduction, found with exposures made in service mode by technicians operating Omega2000, a near-infrared camera attached to the 3.5-meter telescope at Calar Alto Observatory (Spain). A ring-like feature

---

[12] See Heritage and Watson (1979), Sacks (1992), and Sidnell (2010a).
[13] See Pomerantz (1980) and Goodwin (1987).
[14] Pössel (2020) provides a useful introduction to astronomical data and their analysis.
[15] In flatfield division, science exposures are the dividend and flatfields the divisor, a divisor that is a unitless number (the relative sensitivity of pixels).

in her exposures that seemed to be due to excess light in the telescope troubled Nadine. She worried about its detrimental effect on her data analysis, particularly when combining these data with another dataset: optical (visible light) exposures taken with the Wide-Field Imager (WFI), a camera installed at the 2.2-meter telescope at La Silla Observatory (Chile; see Figure 2.1). As it was not resolved easily in dialogue with Otfried, her supervisor, Nadine's problem became a topic at the next group meeting.

There, the team's conversation focused on the computational uses of their exposures, such as subtracting an artifactual "detector distribution" (instrumental response) and dividing images by flatfield exposures. It includes evaluations of data, telescope, camera, and the observatory staff member ("night assistant") who recorded them. Half an hour into the meeting, the following exchange ensued between Otfried, Otto, and Owen, all senior group members and experienced observers:

Transcript 2.2

1	Otfried:	...but if you take out the overall detector distribution first. You know it from all the runs you have with Omega2000 over the last years ... and take it <u>out</u>. Then you would see at least more easily whether the flatfield [is
2	Otto:	[This would be one possibility ... if the flatfield is ... you do this ... take a master-flat in all the main filters and <u>divide</u> your incoming flatfield ... you can do this in Omega with this ... and then you can better judge what has
3	Otfried:	<u>Sure</u>!
4	Otto:	This would be one possibility ... but this is not specific to Omega. If I want to compare ... for instance WFI flatfields ... they are completely different on the 10 ... 15 percent level also.
5	Owen:	Mm hm
6	Otfried:	The <u>flatfields</u> ... yeah ... <u>sure</u>!
7	Otto:	But <u>that</u> is not the flatfield. It is bad illumination. But this is ... in the case of WFI it is an error made by the night assistant ... because the scattered light is strange ... they pointed at the Schmidt telescope ((*located at the observatory in the neighboring dome*)) or whatever they did wrong ... I don't know. But for <u>Omega</u> it's the sky.
8	Otfried:	It happened to me as well ... I would not blame the night assistant.
9	Otto:	For Omega it is the sky illumination which changes wildly ... in some cases. It's also because ... I had to point

              this out to Calar Alto ... because in our service run ...
              what they did was ... they took one series of flatfields
              ... four or five images in the first night and <u>that</u> <u>was</u> <u>it</u>!
              And you should <u>never</u> do this with Omega. You should
              try to get a flatfield every night in order just to pick the
              best ones.

10   ((*9 seconds*))
11   Otfried: Anyway ... it looks as if we had [( )
12   Otto: [and I am puzzled by this
              circular thing.

In this exchange, data are inspected as a window into the functioning of the telescopic apparatus and the work of those who operate it. As these scientists debate a compromised flatfield exposure, two sets of choices are in focus: observers decide when and how to take flatfields and data analysts decide which flatfields to work with. Otfried and Otto draw on their experiences at two observatories. Otto refers to the artifact that troubles Nadine with the indexical "that" (line 7) and describes it as "this circular thing" (line 12). He acknowledges that picking a "good" flatfield calibration exposure is difficult, as their shape differs from case to case in a way that he specifies quantitatively (line 4). Otto and Otfried agree that the artifact was not due to a bad flatfield exposure (lines 6 and 7), but they are unable to reconstruct the observing situation with the data they have. Otfried hears Otto as "blaming the night assistant" at La Silla for having, perhaps, pointed the telescope in the wrong direction in the twilight sky (line 8), and informing "Calar Alto" (line 9). Otto then proceeds to admonish the observatory for not taking proper flatfield exposures every night, thus moving from criticizing a type of person to criticizing an organization. Conceivably, someone higher up in its hierarchy could sanction technicians.

That these researchers noticed an artifact instigated this discussion. It prompted Otto to evaluate the actions of observatory technicians who are absent physically and who are otherwise not mentioned when discussing data analyses. Both Otto and Otfried acknowledge that observers have the power to act and to do things differently. However, the staff observer's possible judgment and resulting choice to point the telescope "wrongly" remains unattended in this brief exchange. A complex situation at the observatory, which may have been largely out of the observer's control (perhaps due to technical malfunctions or poor weather conditions), is collapsed into "troublesome" digital recordings for which an unspecified individual, a member of the category of "night assistants," is held accountable.[16] But those who could give an account are not present.

Accusing an observatory staff member of a technical error, as Otto does, may not suffice to identify the artifact as an ethical affordance, even when Otfried hears it as an instance of blame. Perhaps more telling is a comment that Curt, a postdoctoral scholar, made. In a conversation with fellow group members he mused that "perhaps the night assistant does not like me" when a smaller-than-expected fraction of his B-ranked service-mode program had been executed.[17] This is another instance of where the smooth progress of work seemed suspended, now due not to the troubling quality of data, but because of the limited amount of data delivered. Of course, personal sympathy should not affect the operations of a formal organization like an observatory, but here a researcher (who has been a visiting astronomer before) imagines himself as being evaluated ("not liked") by "the night assistant." This is a third-person view of himself by an imagined other, a view in which "the night assistant" is recognized as a person imbued with the capacity to evaluate and make decisions.

Curt's remark may well have been ironical or even a joke that highlights the otherwise backgrounded expectation that observatory staff ought not to make decisions based on evaluating persons. Curt added that he presumed that staff observers try to play it safe and "prefer imaging over spectroscopy." Recording spectra (which involves positioning a slit on the sky and deciding on its width) is generally considered as more challenging, and prone to mistakes, than taking images. Thus, imaging poses smaller risks of retrospective blame. Much as in the conversation of Transcript 2.2, Curt typifies the "night assistant" as an "ethical figure" (Keane 2016, 153).

2.5   Technicians Producing Data in the Absence of Researchers

As researchers like Otto interpret some artifacts as ethical affordances in evaluating the work of observatory staff, these technicians are aware, and wary, that they become thus visible to data users. Oscar, a telescope and instrument operator (TIO) at Calar Alto, explains: "If the observation is good ... of course ... that's our job. If the observation is bad ... is not okay ... well ... everybody can say ... well ... you are not working okay."

---

[16] Blaming the "night assistant" is a slippage, since night assistants support astronomers in visiting mode, whereas Otto here refers to service-mode observing.

[17] At the ESO (to which Curt refers), B-ranked projects are terminated at the end of an observing semester whether completed or not, whereas uncompleted parts of A-ranked projects are carried over to the next semester for completion.

Separated from data users, Oscar is wary of having no chance to respond to this criticism.[18]

One night, as I was attending service-mode observations at Calar Alto Observatory with Jorge, a night astronomer, he noticed sudden variations in the "seeing" – the undesired blurring of images due to atmospheric turbulence (measured in arc seconds, a unit of angular scale). Observing programs specify a maximal allowable seeing limit, but sudden variations in seeing can make adhering to such limits challenging. Staff observers are faced with the decision to continue or stop an ongoing observing block (OB). In the following, I transcribe in quotations marks what I heard as reported direct speech. Jorge told me:

> Transcript 2.3
> In a night like this ... the seeing can change very <u>fast</u> ... so probably during a focus series you are below a certain value ... but five minutes later it is probably very different ... and then it is very <u>difficult</u> to decide what to do ... because the observer wants <u>exactly</u> 1.4 ((arc seconds)) but what happens if it is 1.5 ... and if it is dancing between 1.2 and 1.5 or 1.6 ... so this is ... ehhh ... a <u>difficult</u> part ... because (...) so ... some observers ... you have a situation like this ... for example ... if the seeing is 1.5 then you decide ... well ... if I don't do this then ... hmmm ... the other thing that I can do is just close the telescope ... so ... I will <u>do</u> it anyway ... <u>just in case</u> that the observer ... finally wants this observation ... they can send it to the trash or whatever ... but then ... the main observer ... that one using the data ... as well... goes ... well ... ((*mimicking an angry voice*)) "<u>Come on! I told you specifically that the seeing limit was 1.4</u> ... <u>so why did you take the data?</u>"

Speaking in the ethnographer's presence, Jorge gives an account of himself as making a reasoned decision aimed at benefitting an imagined researcher, whom he typifies as a third person. Conditions of fluctuating seeing, for which existing rules do not apply, call for observers to decide and reflect on being held accountable for their actions. Jorge describes his decision to go on with observing as a virtuous act, done for the potential benefit of a researcher.

Bypassing the rigid scheduling of OBs, Jorge describes himself as offering "free data" to a researcher who can discard them without foregoing the observatory's promised delivery of data meeting the specifications. Not shutting the telescope down when data of potentially usable quality can be taken attests to a sense of workmanship that is valued at the observatory. Performed while conducting service-mode observations, it is "an act that does not call attention to itself" (Lambek 2015, 292), an act that

---

[18] Note that telescope and instrument operators are accountable not only to academic users, but also to the observatory's hierarchy, operations, and data quality monitoring.

may remain unrecognized and that users may not value. Note that Jorge typifies the researcher's imagined reaction, and with it the researcher, suggesting that this is not a singular incident. Jorge portrays this researcher as excessively demanding in terms that are not neutral but evaluative.

2.6   A Ship, Not a Factory: Conflicting Senses of Place

Conflicting senses of place inform evaluations of researchers and technicians in service-mode observing. We have so far explored the ethical figure of observatory staff members being blamed for taking poor data. Let us now meet its counter-figure: researchers as excessively demanding data users.

Although service-mode observing is prevalent today, few observatories have abandoned the visitor mode altogether. Some researchers still visit observatories for training and for conducting programs requiring on-the-spot decisions. Staff members generally appreciate that researchers visit the observatory to witness their work, to accept responsibility themselves, and to learn to write OBs that are considerate of the overheads that are unavoidably part of observing. Thus, Catalina, a colleague of Jorge at Calar Alto Observatory, insists that astronomers would do well to "remember that there is a moon in the sky that can disturb your observations and that you need time for the calibrations." She also notes that "astronomers always want to observe" and, when pushing too hard, must be stopped from putting instrumentation at risk. Catalina recalls a situation prior to the introduction of the service mode at Calar Alto:

Transcript 2.4
We were having dinner ... and it was <u>raining</u>. And then the astronomer tells me "I am going to the ..." That was when we were observing in the dome. Was quite six years ago. He tells me "I'm going to the ... telescope." And I say "Okay ... but please don't open the dome ... because it's raining." And he says "<u>Ah</u>... okay." And then I was relaxed ... having my dinner. And then I come here to the office. It was <u>raining</u>. I was coming with the car. I see the 2.2 ((*meter telescope*)) with the dome <u>open</u>. And I just go to him and I say "What are you doing? It's <u>raining</u>!" And he says to me "Yes ... but it's the time for the sky flat ... and I can't lose them." And I say "You can <u>lose</u> ((*them*)) because it's <u>raining</u>!" And he says "<u>No no no</u> ... I have to take my sky flats." And it was <u>raining</u>! And then I go quite fast to the dome and I close the dome.

Addressing the ethnographer, Catalina uses reported direct speech, conserving the dialogue (in second-person address) which documents this astronomer's lack of attention to her instructions and his lack of acknowledging her as a person who merits proper attention. This visiting astronomer not only demonstrated poor judgment and made a technical mistake, but also committed an ethical breach. That he put the observatory's equipment at risk of damage is apparent. Catalina does not emphasize this further as she recalls acting as the equipment's guardian. But she adds that she went to call the technical director to the scene who spoke with the visitor and reminded him of the observatory's social order and the need to abide by Catalina's command.

At times it may be the observatory's weather officer who intervenes. The term "officer" here alludes to the hierarchical organization of observatory work and echoes a notion that many staff members share: that the observatory resembles a ship, and not a factory that delivers ready-made commodities. The resemblance between observatory and ship, which is also perceived among staff at La Silla Observatory, is furthered by its isolation, its rigid scheduling of work tasks, its code of conduct, the typical duration of work stints on the mountain (ten to fourteen days), as well as the uncertainty of navigating in a changing environment of which one is not entirely in control.[19]

Visitors' eagerness not to lose any observing time may take a turn for the odd, as Pablo, an administrator at La Silla Observatory, illustrates:

> Transcript 2.5
> Astronomers are not better than other people. I have been here for many years and I have seen <u>everything</u>. (…) There was a professor who observed at the 3.6-meter telescope … and we found him <u>peeing</u> in a corner of the <u>building</u>! The 3.6 dome is fairly <u>big</u> and there are lots of rooms that are not used. It is over-constructed in a way. But the <u>toilet</u> is on the third floor. In the old times the control room was on the <u>fifth</u> floor. And this professor was too lazy to go down … he had no <u>time</u> for that … he did not want to lose <u>one</u> <u>minute</u> of his observing.

The stories that Catalina and Jorge retell illustrate how critical data are to these scientists' professional lives. Numerous similar narratives, usually featuring astronomers' excessive concern over maximizing their exposure time, circulate among staff members at observatories, but they do not seem to travel far beyond. Along with a distant data user's imagined blame (see Jorge in Transcript 2.3), they illustrate the ethical figure of the excessively demanding user. For observatory staff members, such narratives affirm

---

[19] This simile may remind one of how Plato, in the *Republic*, compares ruling a state with navigating a ship, emphasizing that a ship cannot be run democratically. Instead, he argues that it ought to be steered under the guidance of a knowledgeable expert, a "stargazer" (*meteorologicon*), who must "pay attention to the seasons of the year, the sky, the stars, the winds, and all that pertains to his craft" (*Republic* 488d; Plato 1997, 1111).

what it means to do the right thing at the right time in the right way, that is, to act in ways that are valued locally.[20]

2.7 Scientists and Technicians Observing Together

Many of the Heidelberg Institute's graduate students are sent to observatories to experience a week or two of the work and life there. They experience observatories' spatial and temporal organization (mealtimes, places forbidden to visit at certain times, closing window shutters at twilight) and are taken on informal tours of the telescopes (Figure 2.1). They interact

Figure 2.1   Staff scientists and visiting astronomers at the 2.2-meter telescope at La Silla Observatory. The WFI camera is visible as the metallic cylinder under the primary mirror encasement. Visiting astronomers commonly take tours of the observatory, where they witness and experience the observatory as a rigorously and accountably organized space-time. (Photograph: Götz Hoeppe)
Note: The online version shows the colors of the original figure.

[20] In her ethnography of pilots who navigate container ships on the Hooghly, a river connecting Kolkata with the Indian Ocean, Laura Bear finds that these pilots consider ethical action as fundamental to their work as they mediate "temporal rhythms, representations, and technologies in an orchestration of human action towards their temporary reconciliation" (Bear 2014, 72). Bear argues that it is the pilots' workmanship that fixes the spatiotemporal flow of capital.

with the observatory's technical staff, mostly at night in the telescope control room. It is there that, in Keane's (2016) terms, visitors interact with staff technicians in the second-person perspective.

In December 2009, I joined Nora and Mary on their observing run with the WFI camera at the 2.2-meter telescope at La Silla Observatory.[21] Nora, a PhD student, visited the observatory for ten nights of observing as part of her training. She did not have an observing program of her own. Mary was a postdoctoral member of the MAMBO research group whose observations were scheduled for this period. Mary had applied for thirty one-hour-long exposures that were required to reach the sensitivity she needed for her project of supplementing an existing dataset of the Chandra Deep Field South. The time allocation committee ranked her program relatively low, making its completion unlikely.[22] Although she was not required to be present for her relatively undemanding observations, she decided to join the observing run in which her project was scheduled. Mary explains:

> *Transcript 2.6*
> I had this project for <u>three</u> years now ... <u>every</u> year it was ranked low ... although I was never told why. I don't know. In the <u>first</u> year I got nothing ... because it was just bad weather for a week ... basically. In the <u>second</u> year it was also hampered by bad weather ... which meant I got two hours. And so when I now got the <u>third</u> year approved ... but low ranking ... I thought I have better chances of getting data if I actually go there. (...) Of course ... it's a little bit <u>devious</u> of me ... I guess ... is the word ((*laughs cautiously*)) ... to try to come here just to make sure that <u>my</u> program gets observed. But I mean ... I hope that I do not push <u>too</u> much for my program ... because I realize that ((*other*)) people have higher priority.

Mindful of her project's low ranking, Mary hopes to influence nightly decision-making. In doing so, she orients to an "ethic of fair treatment" (Goffman 1983, 14–15) that encompasses not only the proposal review process and the act of observing, but also her previous, largely failed attempts to obtain data for her project.

Mary is accompanied by Olli, her husband, who, too, is an astronomer. Also visiting is Anna, a PhD student in charge of operating the GROND (Gamma Ray Burst Optical/Near-Infrared Detector) instrument, a camera designed to record the afterglows of distant cosmic explosions.

---

[21] This is the instrument mentioned in Transcript 2.2 and shown in Figure 2.1.
[22] The time allocation committee for the 2.2-meter telescope assigns programs as rank A, B, C, but, unlike in scheduling VLT observations, A-ranked programs are not guaranteed completion.

Apart from WFI and GROND, the Fiber-Fed Extended Range Optical Spectrograph (FEROS) is attached to the telescope. Only one instrument can be used at a given time; switching between them takes about one minute.

Late in one afternoon, before Nora's fifth and Mary's third observing night at the telescope, Nora meets with Tim, the night astronomer responsible for the telescope. They develop a draft schedule for the upcoming night that includes OBs pertaining to three different programs. This schedule is bound to be modified throughout the night.

With twilight approaching, visitors and TIOs meet in the control room, situated in a building 500 meters away from the telescope. The observatory's three largest telescopes are operated from there.[23] Each is controlled from a niche equipped with a workstation for the telescope controls as well as with a so-called BOB (Broker for Observing Blocks) terminal, at which the schedule – a sequence of OBs pertaining to the individual programs – is displayed and rearranged. Additional screens display measurements of the weather conditions, an all-sky camera, and camera view into the telescope dome (Figure 2.2). In the control room, a complex set of technical operations is collapsed into screen work.[24]

Observing begins during twilight with a series of flatfield exposures. Sitting at the telescope controls, Carlos, the TIO, completes these exposures with input from Tim. Taking flatfields demands staying in tune with the fading daylight. The two work with visibly intense concentration and talk in Spanish, precluding interventions from the visitors (who are unable to speak Spanish with any fluency). In auditory copresence, Nora sits a few meters away at the BOB terminal (Figure 2.3). She waits for Tim and Carlos to tell her the details of finished exposures that she records by hand in the observing log.

[23] Since the 2.2-meter telescope was first used in 1984, its controls have been progressively removed from it. Initially, the control desk was in the dome near the telescope. In 1990, it was moved to a separate room in the dome building, then to another building among the domes on the summit (2004), and then to the current building furthest away on the mountaintop (2009), where it still is in 2025. This was done to shield sensitive detectors better from traces of human activity and reduce the operation costs. With operators and visitors progressively removed, less stringent demands are placed on their discipline and comportment.

[24] Together in the control room with visiting astronomers, working on computer terminals like them, some TIOs feel their expertise in the telescope's functioning and repair to be denigrated, as they can act only through computer terminals and structures of talk-in-interaction. On the other hand, visitors' experience of screenwork in the control room is transferable to other sites of digital work. Control rooms are sites for the standardization of experience. This may contribute to the sense of placelessness that some contemporary astronomers notice about their work (cf. Hoeppe 2012) – a feature of astronomy's digital middle ground (Chapter 1).

Figure 2.2 At twilight in the control room of the 2.2-meter telescope at La Silla Observatory. A visiting astronomer (standing) looks on as the TIO (seated, right) and the night astronomer (seated, left) record a series of calibration exposures. (Photograph: Götz Hoeppe)
Note: The online version shows the colors of the original figure.

At 20:34 CST (Chilean Standard Time), while calibration exposures are recorded, Mary joins Nora at the BOB terminal. Nora has just returned to the control room from a brief walk outside:

Transcript 2.7 (20:34 Chilean Standard Time)
1 Nora: The wind was very strong when I went
2 Mary: ((*looks at current weather data on the La Silla MeteoMonitor*)) It says <u>stable</u> at eleven ((*meters per second*)) ... on <u>this</u> one
3 Nora: Ahh: ahh: ehm ... I just don't know when we close (the) dome heh
4 Mary: Fifteen ... I think ... ((*examines the telescope manual*)) <u>close</u> is <u>twenty</u> ((*meters per second*))
5 Nora: Yeah ... but the pointing limit ... was ... what does it mean?
6 Mary: Well I guess it means you can't point so that the wind comes right into the wing ... the <u>hole</u> ((*the dome slit*)) ... because that would destroy everything ... but I ... I ... I wouldn't actually know ... exactly ... which targets that meant we would have to skip

Figure 2.3   At the BOB terminal. This visiting astronomer examines an air mass plot; the handwritten observing log is visible in front of the keyboard. (Photograph: Götz Hoeppe) Note: The online version shows the colors of the original figure.

7 Nora: You have to check the <u>direc</u>tion ... of the wind
8 Mary: Yea:h: ... but (if) we are like picking my objects hhhh ... I don't know where that is (hhhh)

Nora's experience of the wind outside instigates a joint attempt with Mary to understand how it will affect their scheduling (line 6), since the dome has to be shut above a certain wind speed and wind direction. Mary appears to be concerned about whether her targets may be affected (line 8).

Thirty minutes later, about halfway through the calibrations, the wind remains worrisome. Tim and Olli have now joined Nora and Mary at the BOB terminal:

Transcript 2.8 (21:03 Chilean Standard Time)
1 Olli: How's the wind doing?
2 Mary: It's the same
3 Tim: The wind will be an <u>issue</u>
4 Mary: Do you <u>think</u> so? I thought it will go down
5 Tim: I mean we are very close to not being able to go south ... and I don't know where the things are (   )

6	Mary:	( )
7	Tim:	What's south?
8	Nora:	What is the declination?
9	Olli:	<u>Latitude</u>
10	Tim:	We are minus 27 or something
11	Nora:	Minus 29 … so (say) minus 30 … so everything above minus 30 is north and everything below minus thirty is south (('*Tim inspects the air-mass diagrams, which list the target objects' coordinates*))
12	Tim:	This is minus 33 … this target is minus 33

Olli's question (line 1), whose significance Tim affirms and specifies (in lines 3 and 5), triggers participants' assessments of the wind's possible impact on the observing program. Above a certain wind speed, the dome slit must not face the wind. Thus, certain observing targets may need to be excluded from the schedule. Tim's questioning of the visitors in line 7 can be read as posing them an "exam question" (Mehan 1979), for as a night astronomer at this observatory he should know the answer, but he may have also asked about the targets' coordinates. To identify which targets may be affected, the celestial coordinates ("declination" in line 8) must be compared with the observatory's geographical latitude. This is what Tim, Nora, and Olli do (in lines 7 to 11). At least one target seems to be affected (line 12).

Unlike the many exchanges between the visiting astronomers and Tim that punctuate the observing night, the visitors rarely talk with Carlos, the TIO. Mary does so just as her program's first hour-long WFI exposure was to begin. For doing so, the telescope is pointed to the celestial coordinates of Mary's target:

Transcript 2.9 (22:07 Chilean Standard Time)

1	Carlos:	So what now?
2	Mary:	<u>WFI</u>
3	Carlos:	<u>WFI</u>? … okay … change
4		((26 seconds)) ((*Carlos types into the keyboard of the telescope controls*))
5	Carlos:	<u>Same</u> settings?
6	Mary:	We do the <u>pointing</u>
7	Carlos:	<u>Focus</u>
8	Mary:	<u>Focus</u> … but <u>no</u> standards
9	Carlos:	<u>No</u> standards?
10	Mary:	Not … just yet … maybe later
11	Carlos:	Okay
12	Mary:	Maybe next time

Carlos' question (in line 1) may be rhetorical since he should have seen WFI indicated on his terminal as the next instrument to be used. After preparing the observations at the telescope control, he corrects how Mary references the upcoming activity (lines 7 and 8). Her decision not to observe standard stars for her program apparently surprises him, but he accepts Mary's decision and executes her instructions. Willing to forego one set of standard star observations, Mary can be heard as aspiring to save time for another of her long exposures.

Once this exposure is completed, Carlos examines it for the shape of stellar images (expressing his satisfaction when these look round as required) and measures the seeing (the blurring of starlight by the atmosphere) using the images of stars visible in it. Carlos seems focused on producing data with accountably round, well-focused stellar images. Mary and Carlos thus seem wary of making the exposures suit their respective computational uses and accountabilities, epistemic (Mary) and institutional (Carlos). Nora records Carlos' seeing measurement in the observing log.

As Mary's long exposure is in progress, the schedule is reassessed:

Transcript 2.10 (22:13 Chilean Standard Time)

1	Olli:	So what's the plan?
2	Nora:	Ehm ... so now we do one of Mary's fields
3	Olli:	Yeah
4	Nora:	and then just one of John's ... maybe ... and then going back to hers or to the FEROS thing which will ... we should go back to
5	Mary:	Then UTC ((Coordinated Universal Time)) would be three ... that is two hours away
6	Nora:	Yeah ... we could also do maybe two of John's ... if that is possible ... and then do the FEROS and then go back to your field
7	Mary:	Eh:: ... but we have (said) first ... we have said to do FEROS as late as possible [if that could be
8	Nora:	[mm hm yes we could also do two fields of yours ... yeah ... I just would want to do this one ... [( )
9	Mary:	[Yes so
10	Nora:	and I think ( ) these I want ( )
11	Mary:	so ( ) specifically ... the east is done
12	Nora:	and there is only one left and there is no VR left and ... I mean ... we could do the 40 fields, but I would rather ( )

Figure 2.4   Visiting astronomers (sitting) and a staff night astronomer (standing) inspecting air mass plots pertaining to three observing projects. (Photograph: Götz Hoeppe)
Note: The online version shows the colors of the original figure.

Prompted by Olli's question, Nora formulates an account of the ongoing observation and of possible ways to continue (lines 2, 4, and 6). Mary intercepts Nora (line 7) by reminding her of her promise to schedule FEROS observations late (this would make Mary's and John's observations with WFI possible beforehand, thus gaining her program another OB). Nora acknowledges this (line 8), but alludes to her responsibility of scheduling a target from the A-ranked proposal ("<u>this</u> one") of John, an absent astronomer. She continues in lines 10 and 12 with recounting her bookkeeping of OBs for John's program, which involve several filters and positions on the sky. In line 12, "VR" is a shorthand for the V and R band filters used for John's project, while "40 fields" is a shortcut reference to the celestial coordinates of target fields in John's program (at a declination of 40 degrees south). Throughout the night, Nora and Mary cannot agree among themselves on a sequence of OBs for implementation.

Later in the night, Tim joins Nora, Mary, and Olli at the BOB terminal (Figure 2.4). He looks at the monitor and comments:

Transcript 2.11 (23:14 Chilean Standard Time)
1   Tim: Well ... so here again ... we are doing WFI ... So it's WFI WFI WFI and then the ( )
2   ((3 seconds))
3   Mary: FEROS GROND WFI
4   ((2.5 seconds))
5   Tim: Good

Tim begins reciting the upcoming plan. He thus makes it audibly available to everybody in at the telescope controls. A long pause (line 2) suggests that he does not finish reciting the sequence. This pause opens a slot that Mary fills, continuing Tim's list of instrument names that index the respective upcoming OBs. By doing so she acknowledges Tim's first part of the formulation. Tim's response (in line 5) may signal his approval of the plan or his confidence in Mary's ability to continue formulating the sequence he had begun. Tim may have tested Mary's competence or "fished for information" about upcoming observations.[25]

Minor as this scene may appear, it is throughout the night that Tim initiates formulations and reformulations of the upcoming schedule. Mary and Nora contribute their more specialized knowledge of the observing programs and thus participate in the formulation-building. As he guides the formulating, Tim consistently assesses calibration exposures and monitors the instrument performances for which the observatory and its staff are held accountable. Tim's lack of knowledge may have been prompted the paired structure of talk in Transcript 2.11, but it encapsulates a pattern of talk that emerges throughout the night: Tim initiating collective formulations and modifications of the observing plan.

Let us now jump three days ahead, to the end of Mary's and Olli's last night on the mountain. At this point, fifteen of the thirty-hour-long exposures that she needed had been taken. Mary leaves the documents pertaining to her program behind at the BOB terminal, appending them with a handwritten note that said, "Basically no seeing constraint (I'll take what I get)," adding a smiley face to her message (Figure 2.5). As such, she authorizes overriding the specifications that her proposal defined. Not only does this suggest Mary's recognition of staff technicians' decision-making powers. Her personalized style and the humbleness of phrasing the request also contrast markedly with what might have been expected of an excessively demanding user, as characterized earlier in this chapter.

[25] See Pomerantz (1980) and Goodwin (1987).

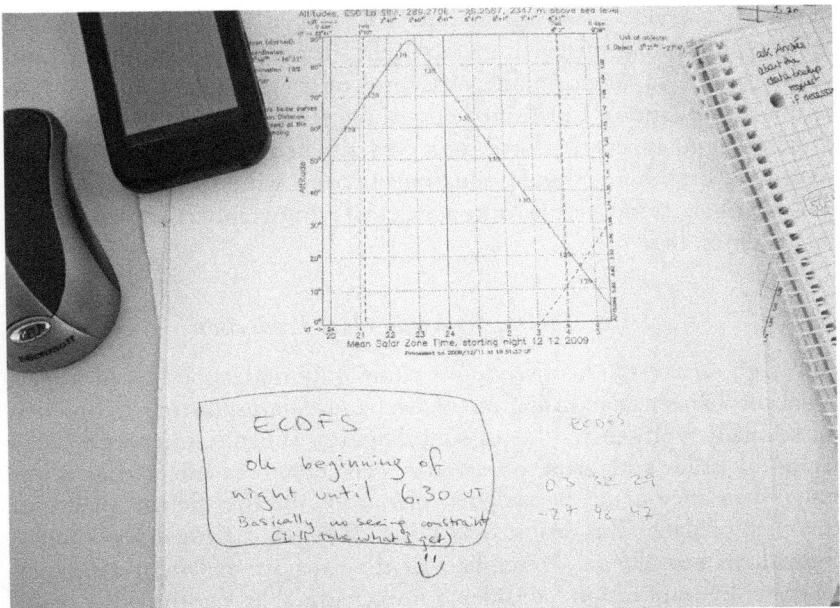

Figure 2.5   Air mass plot pertaining to Mary's observing program. The curve (above) shows her target objects' altitude above the horizon (in degrees) throughout the night (continuous line). The diagram also shows the end of twilight and the beginning of dawn (vertical dashed lines) as well as the rising moon (rising dashed line in the bottom right corner). Mary's handwritten note (below), added shortly before she left the observatory, specifies the conditions needed for observing her program and advertises its relative lack of meteorological constraints to the observer in charge of nightly scheduling. (Photograph: Götz Hoeppe)
Note: The online version shows the colors of the original figure.

2.8   Discussion

In science and technology studies it is commonly analysts who examine ethical issues, such as when they point out that aspirations to openness lead to "unethical" scientific knowledge, or when the trustworthiness of data, dealing responsibly with the privacy of human subjects, uses of algorithms, and regulating data access are at stake.[26] By attending to "ethical life," the "saturation of social existence with evaluations of persons, their relations, and their actions" (Keane 2016, 100), I consider ethics differently. I took a common problem of data-rich science – the production

---

[26] See Floridi and Taddeo (2016), Mayernik (2017), White et al. (2022), Leonelli (2023), Poole (2023), and Padmapriya and Parthasarathy (2024). These concerns about ethics are in addition to philosophical understandings of ethics as integral to epistemology (cf. Harding 1995).

of data as a service –, considered how it is "staffed" in a specific case, and followed its management ethnographically. The move in astronomy from visiting-mode to service-mode observing offers exemplary insights into ordinary evaluations. I identified ethical figures that ascribe certain forms of conduct to types of people, observed situated actions in the control room as a site where ethical evaluations become witnessable, and noticed how visiting astronomers became accidental ethnographers of the observatory's ethical life.

2.8.1 Ethical Figures in Data Production

Although service-mode observing is commonly understood as an impersonal mechanism, data-using researchers and data-producing technicians occasionally typify each other as ethical figures. When researchers debated technical issues with data, observatory staff members emerged as actors only when they could be assigned blame for the insufficient quality or quantity of data. This blame was never directed at named (or known) individuals but always at members of the category of "night assistant," who are, by implication, considered interchangeable. On the other hand, staff observers regard some scientists as members of another category: excessively demanding users who disregard what kind of organization the observatory is – more a ship than a factory. Usually shared with fellow staff members only, their audience is local.

The accountability of interaction that visiting astronomers experience in the observatory's control room is confined to its situated enactment. The disjuncture between researchers' and technicians' accountabilities, and the resulting disappointment and blame, is a tension in service-mode observing. As scientist–technician interactions have become discontinuous and fraught, ethical figures and ethical accounts travel unevenly in the landscape of data production, and the importance of social interactions often remains unrecognized.

2.8.2 Situated Actions and Ethical Practice

Taking interlocutors seriously, and acknowledging them as meriting attention, is an ethical practice.[27] For visiting scientists, it is only at night in the control room that the category of "night assistant," or rather, "telescope and instrument operator," becomes filled with life. Mary experienced

---

[27] See Liberman (1999), Sidnell (2010b), Darwall (2006), and De Stefani and Mondada (2025).

this on her visit to La Silla. Seeking to complete more of her low-ranked observing program, she engaged in the mutual accountability of social interaction. Whereas ethical figures emerged in third-person perspective (Transcripts 2.2 to 2.5), it is in the control room that visitors interact with staff technicians in the second-person perspective. Visitors draw on their interactional competence and become thereby available to staff members' mutual monitoring.

In recording science exposures of documented absolute time (duration), temporality is a dominant concern for all participants in the control room. Their shared task is to accommodate preliminary schedules with a dynamic environment. There is "no time out" (Garfinkel 2002, 118, 259) from the joint work of getting through the observing night together. This night's irreversible temporality is critically different from the visitors' scholarly work back home. Only at night in the control room can data users witness the accountabilities and dilemmas that staff members face as they seek to move from a "shopping list" to obtaining useful data. As visiting astronomers come to learn from those who work for them, the hierarchy characteristic of service encounters is, for the time being, flattened or even reversed.

Observatory staff members and visiting astronomers collaborate in formulating and reformulating plans for the night, but they do not contribute to this work equally. Staff astronomers have institutional rights to initiate and guide the formulation and reformulation of the schedule, thus instructing visitors about the social and temporal order of observing. In the conversation of Transcript 2.10, Tim is not present when Nora, Mary, and Olli contemplate the schedule. On their own, they hesitate to formulate a revision for adoption. Perhaps they are wary of being held accountable for it. Later in the night, Tim set out to formulate a "best-case scenario" for the rest of the observing night. He drew Anna, Mary, and Nora – who knew specific programs and their ranking in greater detail – into making this knowledge consequential for subsequent actions. In contributing to such formulations, visitors learn without being visibly taught (cf. Schwartz 1976, 64).

2.8.3 Members Doing Ethnography

It seems far-fetched that novice researchers could learn how to control telescope and detectors during their brief stays on the mountain. They could not possibly deal with a malfunction of equipment. And they would quickly forget many details if they did not practice their observing skills. If so, what of lasting value could they possibly learn during their brief stays at the observatory? What kind of expertise do they acquire? What, after all, is the point of their visit to the mountain?

When junior scientists visit an observatory, they experience its organizational hierarchy, rigorously disciplined space-time, and the unfolding of the observing night in its control room. There, they can dwell on their ordinary interactional competence in negotiating the nightly observing program and witnessing how staff astronomers deal with their work's accountabilities and dilemmas. There, they experience which "overheads" are involved and what it means for observations that there is a moon in the sky, as Catalina remarked dryly (in Section 2.6). There, they are "*investigating* as well as *using* practical actions, reflexively discovering a local organization of practical actions" (Lynch 2022, 10; emphasis in original). Much of this local organization is a social organization. Are these visiting astronomers, then, doing a sort of ethnography? Conversely, when we ponder the accounts that Jorge, Catalina, and Pablo give in Transcripts 2.3 to 2.5, are observatory staff members like them also doing a sort of ethnography, but of the visiting astronomers' culture? After all, Jorge, Catalina, and Pablo appeared to have acquired a sort of what Bernard Williams (1986, 203–204) called an "ethnographic stance" – an understanding of visitors' ethical concepts, without sharing them.

Early in his *Studies in Ethnomethodology*, Harold Garfinkel remarks that it is in "doing, recognizing, and using ethnographies" that members accomplish the "analyzability of actions-in-context" (1967, 10). Garfinkel does not specify what exactly he means with "ethnography," but, following Alex Dennis (2024, 101), we can suspect that his use of the term is "deflationary": "[b]eing able to see what is being done in a setting is field-work, and being able to describe that to others is ethnography." This inclusive understanding is shared by ethnomethodologists like Stephen Hester and Peter Eglin (2017, 200). Rawls and Lynch (2024) call it "endogenous ethnography." However, one may feel like responding that if everyone is an ethnographer, nobody is. Is calling what these scientists and technicians do "ethnography" not a stretch of what is already a "catchall phrase" whose "meaning is extremely general and vague" (Harper 2000, 241)?

Sociological and anthropological ways of doing ethnography are informed by an epistemology and ontology and are oriented toward the production of written accounts for nonmembers (Blommaert and Jie 2020). As such, they differ from these scientists' and technicians' apparently quotidian practices. There is an important sense in which what these scientists do goes beyond a deflationary sense of doing ethnography, if the latter regards them as inquirers into the "practical circumstances that confront the member going about the business of everyday life" (Hester and Eglin 2017, 200). After all, being at the observatory is *not* part of visiting astronomers' everyday life. As we have seen, some of them may, in fact, disturb the observatory's regular and ordinary life. Scientists and technicians thus inquire into what are, to them, an unfamiliar sociotechnical environment and visitors of uncertain power, respectively. Some of them make their experiences accountable as narratives (cf. Transcripts 2.3, 2.4, and 2.5) and written notes (Figure 2.5).[28] These inquiries are part of their professional work, but seem less conspicuous than, for example, statisticians' routine ethnographic forays in search of categories that they can subsequently probe quantitatively, such as by censuses (Mair et al. 2016). In his ethnographic study of a halfway house for narcotics offenders, Lawrence Wieder (1974) noticed that the house's new residents were in much the same situation as the ethnographer, having to make sense of a "convict code," an unspecified set of maxims that seemed binding for residents and staff. This suggests a convergence of learners' practices, including those of the ethnographer. In Chapter 3, I use Wieder's (1974) study as a resource for understanding graduate student learning in the making and use of large datasets.[29] Thus understood, the quality of data produced at the observatory, and the maintenance of communal skills, are accomplished thanks to a twofold ethnographic move.

2.8.4 Experience beyond Interaction

Let me end this chapter with a note on astronomers' experience of nightly observing beyond social interaction, probing further into their reasons for visiting observatories. One night, at the end of an hour-long exposure, Mary seemed captivated when watching the CCD readout slowly emerging on screen over half a minute. I perceived this to be somber moments of raised attention and pause. When I asked her about this a few weeks later, she replied in an email:

> It brought tears to my eyes to think that these photons have traveled for billions of years, crossing endless distances, and then I caught them here. They

---

[28] In Chapters 7 and 8, I will add to these observations by examining uses of translation and irony as members' methods of doing ethnography. See also the Outlook on scientists as social inquirers.

[29] See also Sormani (2014, ch. 2) on student learning in a physics laboratory. Hahn et al. (2018) note a similarity of the ways in which information systems are used and designed and how social scientists study them. They call this an "actor/analyst symmetry."

will not travel any further. And it happened just nearby where I am, just then. I am serious, and it is very silly, but I certainly do get a strong feeling of awe when the CCD reads out. It is not at all the same when you go home and see it on the computer. Then it is just pixels with varying intensity, it is just numbers and digits and data to crunch. But on the mountain, I know that those photons that have been traveling on their own for that long are falling on my head. And I can catch some of them. It is poetic. And silly. :)

In this response, Mary gives importance to the observing situation's "here and now." Invoking contemporary physics and cosmology, which describe light as photons traversing a vast universe for billions of years, she links vision to touch: photons can be caught or fall on your head. Conceived as such, the distant universe is, at the observatory, a part of the tangible world to which astronomers can expose their detectors and their bodies, the observational machinery functioning as a tool that extends human senses. What the readout CCD image shows are traces. But what makes it possible "to leave traces and to read them is the material continuity, physicality, and sensuousness of the world," as Sybille Krämer (2007, 15; my translation) argues. A figure–ground reversal is invoked, the observatory being the figure that makes the ground, the universe-filled-with-radiation, conceivable. Arguably, temporal sequences of activity contribute to this astronomer's experience of immediacy, which includes waiting for the exposure to end. During the exposure, the social, the technical, and messengers of a nature distant in space and time ("photons") are copresent or coeval, and Mary is aware of this.[30] That she remembers this experience so vividly weeks later suggests that this memory endures, giving meaning to her work at other times and other places.

---

[30] I use the notion of "coevalness" with hesitation, as it is linked with the arguments Fabian (1983) put forth in *Time and the Other*, aiming at exposing critically the use of time in older anthropological writing. See also Merleau-Ponty (1968), on experiencing connections between vision and touch, and Hoeppe (2012), for a fuller account of the place of the observatory and astronomers' experience of observing.

CHAPTER 3

Membership

Learning to Become a Competent Data User

3.1 This Chapter's Plan

I argued in Chapter 2 that experiencing work in an observatory control room develops students' abilities to use observational data competently. But nobody expects that, by visiting an observatory for a few days and nights, they would become members of its staff's community and culture. By contrast, educating PhD students aims at making them competent members in the community and culture of a science. This process takes much longer than a few nights in the control room. In this chapter I examine how Nadine, the PhD student we encountered in the Introduction, was instructed to tackle a common, often challenging problem: calibrating a new dataset and combining it with data from a different source for analysis. By following her around over two years as she achieved this goal, we learn how she became a competent member in the community and culture of extragalactic astronomy, not the least by being an explorer of social norms. Conversely, we gain insights into what makes combining scientific datasets often so challenging. As such, this chapter applies the tactics of Chapter 2 – take a problem of data-rich science, consider how it is "staffed" in a specific case, and follow its management ethnographically – to another setting.

I begin with reviewing graduate student training as a curious process in which instruction and the advancement of science go together, introduce the setting of Nadine's PhD project, and then follow it through four critical moments. This account of Nadine's work will also serve as a starting point for Chapters 4 and 5, on uses of diagrams (Chapter 4) and mundane reason (Chapter 5) in scientific research with large datasets.

3.2 Instruction and Membership

Even a casual visitor of a research setting notices that science is replete with situations of training and instruction. PhD students did almost all the data processing that I witnessed during my study. Of course, there is a lot more instruction in science than educating students. Scientists and technicians of all ages and career stages are taught how to use new instruments, new data, new computer code, and yet unfamiliar diagrams. Not all instruction is face to face. Far from it. Written descriptions and manuals instruct, too. But except for a few independently working postdoctoral scholars, every scientist at the Institute found themselves at one end or the other of one or more instructional relationships.[1]

In PhD projects, training students and advancing science go together.[2] At the Institute, supervising bachelor and master thesis projects was often delegated to junior scientists, including PhD students and postdoctoral scholars. By contrast, PhD students were typically supervised by senior scientists, including the Institute's directors. Senior scientists told me informally that good PhD students offered a better return on investment into their training than master students, who, they declared, need more guidance. Typically, three years long and with defined objectives, PhD thesis projects are important units in the organization of many collaborative projects.[3]

Finishing a PhD is often understood to be more than acquiring certain skills, completing data analyses, and writing up a thesis, followed by the award of formal credentials. Ideally, it also signals the achievement of membership in a community and culture.[4] Doing so entails being able to accommodate to this social world's normative expectations, epistemic and social orders, and social accountabilities. David Kaiser (2005, 1) argued that "scientists are not born, they are made." I would add that they are made by doing science.

Witnessing unfolding PhD projects provides ethnographers both with an opportunity and a difficult challenge. It is an opportunity because not only is the position of an onlooking learner already defined (for students), it may be filled also by ethnographers, who can thereby witness acts of instruction. In the process, ethnographers can learn about researchers' implicit, backgrounded assumptions. But doing so is challenging, since

---

[1] This does not mean that all instruction was personalized in pairs of masters and apprentices. Much instruction happens through students' participation in research groups.

[2] Delamont and Atkinson (2001), Larivière (2012), and Sverdlik et al. (2018).

[3] Many senior scientists are wary that relying on the outcomes of student work poses a risk for the success of complex projects. Some argue critically that PhD students are, at times, denigrated to a cheap source of skilled labor for coding and data-reduction work.

[4] The formulation "culture and community" is meant to indicate that these notions are not identical, and neither is, in general, the membership of these categories.

one does not achieve membership in a community and culture overnight, but over years. Scientists' PhD projects take as long social scientists' PhD projects and research grants. This makes it difficult for ethnographers to document and analyze this process. To make sense of it, ethnographers may also need substantial expertise in the work they witness.

Given these difficulties, social studies of PhD student education in science have relied mostly on interviews. Thus informed, Sara Delamont and Paul Atkinson (2001, 88) argue that the "replication of science in undergraduate years (…) constructs a domain of relative stability," whereas "doctoral students discover that 'real' science is more complex, and that failure is a normal outcome of routine work." Once mastering their work, however, successful PhD students "remove all mention of the context, of the messy realities and of the tacit" from their publications (Delamont and Atkinson 2001, 89). Other interview-based studies refine, qualify, and supplement this picture.[5]

Wolff-Michael Roth and G. Michael Bowen (2001) note in response to Delamont and Atkinson (2001) that interviews give us insights into how interviewees account for their experiences retrospectively, but they do not tell us reliably how interviewees have mastered their skills in the real time of practice. As a counterpoint, Roth and Bowen present an ethnographic account of how an advanced undergraduate student in field ecology learned to generate and analyze data in an independent research project. In her insightful ethnography of dendrochronologists, Meritxell Ramirez-i-Olle (2020) follows a PhD student through his project, but she does not make his learning experience her topic. Ethnographic studies of PhD student learning remain rare, and they typically focus on brief moments of interaction. Thus, Morana Alač (2011) uses video recordings to study multimodal interactions in graduate student instruction in neuroscience, whereas Philippe Sormani (2014) combines a self-study, as an ethnographer, of using laboratory equipment without in-person instruction with an account of a PhD student's discovery work in experimental physics. This chapter aims to complement these studies by witnessing a PhD student's training over two years. It follows Nadine around as she mastered a common, often challenging problem: combining data from different sources for analysis. I shall argue that her achievement of membership hinged on this success.

That the successful instruction of science students goes along with their achievement of membership is a point that Ludwik Fleck and Thomas

---

[5] Campbell (2003), Bhattacharya and Bodner (2014), Sverdlik et al. (2018), Shibayama (2019), Wylie (2019), and Maher et al. (2020).

Kuhn made long ago. Fleck (1979 [1935], 141) observed that junior scientists' "thought style" appears to them as "natural and, like breathing, almost unconscious, as a result of education and training as well as through [their] participation in the communication of thoughts within [their] collective." Kuhn insisted that students generate meaning not solely by comprehending statements (propositions) but through extensive practice, particularly when dealing with exemplars – "concrete problem-solutions that students encounter from the start of their scientific education (…) that (…) show them by example how their job is to be done" (Kuhn 1970, 187). Communal practices are founded on exemplars. Training to be a scientist is not altogether different from learning a craft as an apprentice. It is a form of socialization – and thereby of the "reproduction of social worlds" (Macbeth 1994, 312) – that may be necessarily dogmatic. Seeking to unite Garfinkel's and Kuhn's insights on education, Mary Douglas (1992, 244) adds that exemplars must be "used in regular procedures of accountability" to be effective in founding collective beliefs. She notices that "puzzle-solving techniques are prime in the process of community creation" (Douglas 1992, 244).

However, these studies do not tell us how "procedures of accountability" are engaged sequentially in creating new members. Thus interested, I am inspired by an unusual source for the social study of science: Lawrence Wieder's (1974) ethnography of the "convict code" in a halfway house for released ex-convicts. The halfway house that Wieder studied was meant to prevent convicted narcotics offenders from relapsing into new offenses upon their release from prison. Wieder discovered that its convict residents kept referring to a loose set of maxims by which residents ought to abide, for example, not to "snitch" – that is, not to display cooperation with the halfway house's staff. What Wieder came to call the convict code also included references to types of people – such as "kiss asses" and "snitches."

Wieder recognized that this code, although never specified in detail (and never in writing), was familiar and binding to both the halfway house's residents and staff. New residents and Wieder, as their ethnographer, had to familiarize themselves with it by using what Garfinkel (1967, 78) called a documentary method.[6] As if provided only with fragments of a document, new residents and staff members (as well as the ethnographer) had to draw

---

[6] The notion of "documentary method" is Karl Mannheim's (1952, ch. 2). It is closely related to the hermeneutical circle that Gadamer (1960) and others discussed. Garfinkel (2002, 112–113) later became wary of the circularity involved in its use (cf. also Baccus 1986; Koschmann and Zemel 2014; and Button et al. 2015).

on what they experienced to make informed guesses for how to act in yet unfamiliar circumstances. They did so by witnessing long-term residents' reactions and learned about the "convict code" by entering into its domain of accountability. The code became a collection of "embedded instructions for perception" (Wieder 1974, 203) that was used reflexively: it was "a constitutive feature of the setting [it made] observable" (Garfinkel 1967, 8). The code and its enactment are instructive for linking learning and discovery to the achievement of membership in science. Wieder's study points to a convergence of ethnographic practice and doing science that I have pointed out already in Chapter 2.

3.3 A Domain of Practice: Photometric Redshift Surveys of Galaxy Evolution

Nadine's PhD project brought her into a research group known for innovative studies of cosmological deep fields: small parts of the sky selected for offering views of the distant universe to study galaxy evolution. Since early in the twentieth century astronomers have been using the finite speed of light as a "tool" for studying galaxies' distant past by observing faraway objects (Peebles 2020). Assembling a chronology of their evolution requires knowing the distances to many galaxies. What astronomers call redshift (abbreviated as z) is a measure of distance. It indicates how much the wavelengths of the light emitted by cosmic objects are stretched due to cosmic expansion, shifting specific spectral features to longer wavelengths. Introductory textbooks describe how redshifts are measured with spectrograph equipped with a glass prism or grating to disperse incident light into its constituent wavelengths (Chromey 2010). For the study of large samples of distant galaxies this technique is limited due to the prohibitively large amount of telescope time needed to record the spectra of faint galaxies one after another. This hindered statistical studies of galaxy populations.

In the late 1950s, William Baum proposed a way to circumvent this problem. By taking photographs through a variety of color filters, he was able to construct low-resolution spectra of several galaxies per field of view and estimate the redshift of prominent spectral features by comparing these with the template spectrum of a nearby galaxy (Baum 1962). At the price of a decreased spectral resolution Baum could measure many "photometric redshifts" in a certain amount of telescope observing time. When sensitive large digital detectors became available in the 1980s and 1990s, this technique was taken up and developed by several researchers who improved the template-fitting technique. While promising, red-shifts inferred from such "multicolor" observations remained controversial for several years, largely because of occasional "catastrophic outliers" (Koo 1999).

In 1999, the MAMBO (pseudo-acronym) team (see the Introduction) set out to improve photometric redshifts by modifying earlier work in three ways. First, they decided to use seventeen filters instead of the five to seven that researchers had typically used. In the new project, five filters were "broad-band" filters covering the visible spectrum from blue to red evenly. The other twelve were "medium-band" filters covering the same spectral range in a more fine-grained way. Thus, instead of one orange filter there were now three filters transmitting different hues of orange light. For measuring photometric redshifts, medium-band filters had not been used before in a systematic way. Second, the team built the Wide-Field Imager (WFI), a new charge-coupled device camera for the 2.2-meter telescope at La Silla Observatory in Chile, to which they had privileged access through their home institute. This camera's wide field of view allowed recording the light of many objects in every single exposure. Third, they improved the fitting technique by developing a digital template library of a large set of galaxy types, as well as of stars and "active galactic nuclei" at various redshifts.[7] Observing five fields in the sky, the MAMBO team produced by 2003 a catalog of 25,000 galaxies up to red-shift one, corresponding to a lookback time of half the universe's age. This sample of distant galaxies was ten times larger than any other available at this time (Lin et al. 1999).

When I began my ethnographic study of the MAMBO project in mid-2007, work on the survey proceeded in two directions. First, to detect more distant galaxies whose spectral light is stretched to longer wavelengths, the team added near-infrared observations of three of the five fields, using a new camera attached to the 3.5-meter telescope of Calar Alto Observatory in Spain. Second, they constructed an improved template library of simulated galaxy spectra for the purpose of extending the spectral range from optical (visual) wavelengths to the near infrared. This was meant to make template fitting feasible for more distant (higher red-shift) objects in the new observations and to obtain more precise clues about their physical properties.

---

[7] Active galactic nuclei are central regions of galaxies whose excessive luminosity is linked to the radiative effects of massive black holes.

3.4 Four Reflexive Moments in Nadine's PhD Project

In 2005, MAMBO team members had begun supplementing an existing (optical) dataset from La Silla Observatory in Chile with new (near-infrared) observations at longer wavelengths taken at Calar Alto Observatory in Spain. They wanted to extend the survey's outer limit from redshift $z = 1$ to $z = 2$, covering the last 9 billion years. Obtaining a sizeable sample of several thousand distant galaxies and using it to trace statistically how the colors, luminosities, and masses of galaxies have evolved over this period was to be Nadine's PhD thesis project.[8]

Recording and calibrating data to assemble a catalog – a table of measurements and estimated information – was at the heart of Nadine's project. Patrick, a postdoctoral researcher who was already familiar with template fitting, summarized the data-reduction and analysis tasks that lay ahead of her in the form of a recipe:[9]

Transcript 3.1
The <u>first</u> thing is to <u>upload</u> the exposures ... check the FITS headers and do all that. (...) The <u>next</u> steps are bias subtraction ... <u>correcting</u> for nonlinear effects and some other small tidbits ... <u>making</u> the flat field ... <u>divide</u> all science images by it (...) and <u>correct</u> for cosmics. (...) Then comes the <u>photometry</u>. If you have made a catalog <u>already</u> with SExtractor[10] and know where the galaxies are on your exposures ... you do the photometry in each filter (...) meaning that you have to determine the instrumental <u>magnitudes</u> at these positions ... and then <u>calibrate</u> all of that (...). At the end you have magnitudes ... <u>normal</u> magnitudes ... and those are plugged into the multi-color classification. For that you first have to calculate <u>colors</u> (...) and they all go into the classification where you use the colors to decide not only what kind of <u>object</u> it is ... but also at which <u>redshift</u> it is ... and when you have the redshift and the object type and spectral type you can derive <u>other</u> parameters ... like mass ... total luminosity and the like (...). The data are stored in <u>tables</u> ... and they tell me ... star number 1828 has got 18 counts per second in this image taken with this filter ... and this information is saved in a large table ... which is created when instrumental <u>magnitudes</u> are computed ... and you keep working with these tables (...).

---

[8] Following Alač (2011), pseudonyms in this chapter distinguish between newcomers (Nadine, Norman, etc.) and old-timers (Otfried, Otto, Oliver, etc.). I add postdoctoral fellows (Peter, Patrick, etc.) as an intermediate category.

[9] See the Appendix for a complete list of the transcription conventions adopted.

[10] Source Extractor, or SExtractor, is an open-source software code for detecting objects in digital images (Bertin and Arnouts 1996).

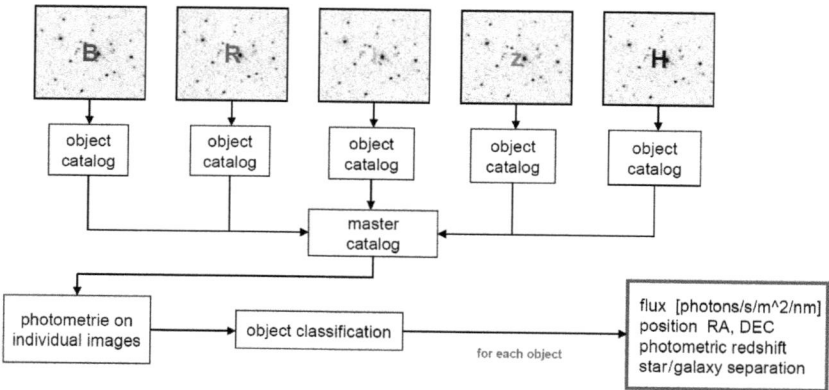

Figure 3.1   Flowchart of the MAMBO research group's data reductions as taken from a conference presentation of one of its members. It depicts the work as a sequence of operations. First, a set of exposures is taken of specific selected fields in the sky through a series of color filters (B, R, I, z, H). These are then used to algorithmically detect objects, take photometric measurements at the object positions, and classify objects by identifying the best-fitting match from a library of template spectra. The results are object positions, radiation flux densities, classifications of the object type (star, galaxy), and estimates of the photometric redshift, a measure of cosmic distance. (Reproduced with permission by the author)
Note: The online version shows the colors of the original figure.

Patrick describes this progression from "raw data" to calibrated data as a single sequence of tasks,[11] much as it is commonly described in the methods sections of research publications.[12] One of the last steps in this sequence is to use a cosmological model to convert redshifts to distances and convert measurements to absolute, distance-independent values.

Team members used a flowchart to depict how their work proceeded from locally specific records to claims about physical objects and phenomena (Figure 3.1). Drawing on Patrick's account and using material from Nadine's work, I add specific detail in Figure 3.2.

[11] "Raw data" is a member's term, used by the astronomers whose work I witnessed. It has been argued that due to the unavoidably context-dependent nature of data production, there are no "raw" data (Bowker 2005; Gitelman 2013). However, a meaningful distinction can still be made between "primary" data – unprocessed and uninterpreted outputs of data generators or instrumental recordings that have been variously called "inscriptions" (Latour and Woolgar 1986), "data" (Hacking 1992a), and "traces" (Rheinberger 2011) – and the outcome of calibrations and processed materials deemed useful for the production of a scientific result – for which Rheinberger (2011), for example, reserves the term "data," which are arguably more profoundly "theory-laden" (Hanson 1958) than unprocessed instrumental recordings.
[12] Examples are Lin et al. (1999, 535), Capak et al. (2007, 103f.), and Nicol et al. (2011).

(a)   (b)

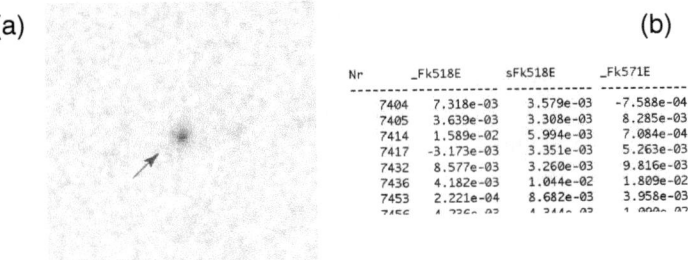

Nr	_Fk518E	sFk518E	_Fk571E
7404	7.318e-03	3.579e-03	-7.588e-04
7405	3.639e-03	3.308e-03	8.285e-03
7414	1.589e-02	5.994e-03	7.084e-04
7417	-3.173e-02	3.351e-03	5.263e-03
7432	8.577e-03	3.260e-03	9.816e-03
7436	4.182e-03	1.044e-02	1.809e-02
7453	2.221e-04	8.682e-03	3.958e-03
7456	4.776e-03	4.344e-03	1.000e-02

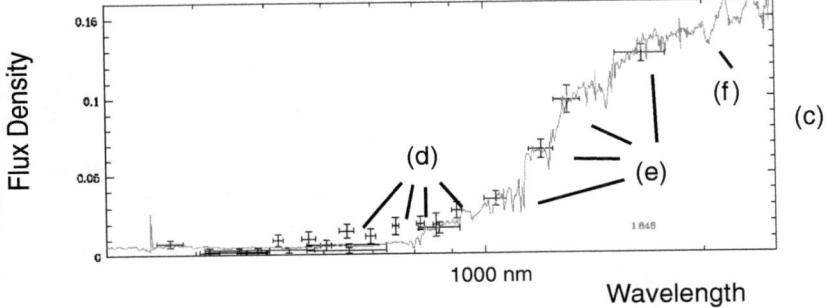

(c)

(f)

(d)   (e)

1.848

Flux Density

1000 nm

Wavelength

Nr	prob_star	prob_gal	MC_z	MC_sz
7404	*	*	1.570	0.348
7405	0.0	97.8	1.630	0.239
7414	*	*	1.555	0.368
7417	0.0	99.5	1.878	0.296
7432	0.0	100.0	1.845	0.069
7436	0.0	98.5	2.053	0.113
7453	0.1	99.7	1.611	0.327
7456	0.0	97.7	1.747	0.225

(g)

Figure 3.2   Scheme depicting basic steps of the MAMBO team's spectral energy distribution template-fitting technique. First, exposures taken through each color filter are processed and calibrated with standard data-reduction procedures (a). In the resulting images, objects are detected algorithmically and assigned catalog numbers, their fluxes are measured, converted into magnitudes, and saved in a table (b). These can then be plotted as a spectral energy distribution (c), wherein measurements taken with the telescope in Chile (d) join those taken with the telescope in Spain (e). Crosses indicate measurement errors. Next, the best-fitting spectral energy distribution template, shown here as a continuous line, is selected algorithmically from the template library (f). Using the best-fitting template, the object is classified as a "star" or "galaxy," and, in case of the latter, its redshift and physical parameters, such as mass and luminosity, are inferred from this fit and entered in the catalog (g).
Note: The online version shows the colors of the original figure.

In the following, I shall give an account of how Nadine's work unfolded over two years, focusing on four episodes in which the sequential following of protocols became problematic. For this description it will be useful to employ Trevor Pinch's (1985) notions of "externality" and "evidential context." They allow us to compare practices of data production and use across disciplines.

Box 3.1 Externality and evidential context

Trevor Pinch (1985) notes that observational reports in physics are contingent on chains of inference, and this affects how they are assessed. He examines how a claim about the number of neutrinos emitted from the solar interior was made. As neutrinos hardly interact with matter, it is very difficult to detect and count them. The team running the experiment that Pinch describes placed a large tank in a deep underground mine to shield it from terrestrial and cosmic radiation and filled it with tetrachloroethylene (dry-cleaning fluid). When neutrinos hit chlorine atoms in the tank, these turned into atoms of radioactive argon. Once a week the tank was flushed to detect radioactive decays and record them with a chart recorder. The team then used the recorded wiggles to estimate the amount of radioactivity produced. After subtracting a background signal (ascribed to radioactivity from the subterranean environment), they converted the measured amount of radioactivity into the number of chlorine atoms hit, and this in turn to the number of neutrinos that had entered the tank. Researchers subsequently attributed the detected neutrinos to have come from the solar interior and not from other cosmic sources.

   Pinch notices that the chart recorder's wiggles were uncontroversial, but uninteresting for anyone except the research team's members. As an observational report, these wiggles were of what Pinch called "low externality" – tied to their specific, local context – and "low evidential significance" – themselves not supporting interesting or risky knowledge claims. It was only by adding a series of assumptions that team members were able to claim that they had detected neutrinos from the sun. Freed from specific local details, their report was now of "high externality" (Pinch 1985, 13). As such it was suited to address evidential contexts of "high evidential significance," of interest to researchers studying the solar interior, theories of gravitation, and climate change on Earth (Collins 1992).[13]

   Two aspects make Pinch's notions particularly salient for examining research with diverse datasets. First, as Steven Shapin (1995, 265) observes, moving up along the "axes" of externality and evidential significance can be seen as taking a "credibility risk": "critics can pick away at the gap between

---

[13] These descriptive terms speak to philosophical accounts of the theory-ladenness of observations (Duhem 1954 [1914]; Hanson 1958; Quine 1970), but Pinch (1985, 14, 33fn21) insists that the externality of observation reports does not correspond to theory-ladenness in a simple way.

elements in the metonymic relationship," but data makers can also "bid for rich credibility-rewards." Shapin argues that this offers "a framework for describing the moral economy of risk and reward in the relevant community" (Shapin 1995, 265). Second, as I show in this chapter, members engage evidential contexts and their diagrammatic representation as contexts of accountability. Diagrams are cultural resources that become meeting places of epistemic and social action. What is negotiated in their use commonly retroacts on data calibrations and interpretations (see also Chapter 4).

3.4.1 Galaxies That Are "Too Bright for Their Distance"

In September 2007, eighteen months into Nadine's thesis project, the new dataset consisted of about 1,300 near-infrared exposures taken through three medium-band filters and one broad-band filter (the so-called H band). Using pipelines, semi-automated computer code that senior team members had developed to process telescopic exposures, Nadine removed biases and dark currents, divided science exposures by flatfields, confirmed the detector's linear response, and applied algorithms for removing cosmic ray hits. She then brought all images to a common point spread function,[14] a requirement for making the photometric measurements in different exposures comparable and combinable. Nadine considered this task accomplished when Otfried told her that the output images were "looking fine." He encouraged her to proceed to measure the near-infrared fluxes at the positions in the field where objects had been detected in the previous optical imaging.[15]

After Nadine ran the photometry algorithm and generated a first catalog (a table of the flux measurements of objects previously detected in the optical exposures), Otfried explained how to apply the template-fitting technique to the combined optical and near-infrared dataset. Using it so resulted in a table that listed for each object the best-matching template, object class (star, galaxy, quasar), photometric redshift, and – in case of galaxies – luminosity and mass (see Figure 3.2g). Thus equipped, Nadine's study had gained in externality.

Most entries in the new catalog seemed inconspicuous, but a few dozen objects that had been previously classified as relatively nearby galaxies were

[14] Point spread functions quantify the blurring of telescopic images due to atmospheric conditions and the telescope's aperture (Chromey 2010, 310f.).
[15] Photometric calibrations in astronomy have been propagated by beginning with a single standard star, the primary calibrator (most often Vega, α Lyrae), to calibrate the brightness of secondary standard stars around the sky by comparison with Vega, and tertiary standard stars (calibrated in respect to the secondary standards, usually with declining precision; Hearnshaw 1996).

now identified as bright and massive, distant galaxies at redshift 1.8 or so. Nadine was intrigued to find such objects. But while accepting that Nadine had done everything as instructed, Otfried remained noticeably reserved. He was puzzled by how bright the objects appeared given their distance and suggested they discuss her work at the next team meeting. In preparation for this, Otfried asked Nadine to make a set of plots, including a graph showing the old versus the new redshift for each object (i.e., the ones based on optical-only data versus those based on optical plus near-infrared data), as well as the spectral energy distributions of objects now reclassified as high-redshift galaxies.

Otfried opened the meeting by presenting and describing Nadine's plots, focusing on how the new template fits differed from those derived from the optical-only data (Figure 3.3). He noticed an offset between the near-infrared and optical magnitudes and suspected that it had caused the template-fitting code to pick wrong templates. He thus regarded the combined dataset as erroneous.

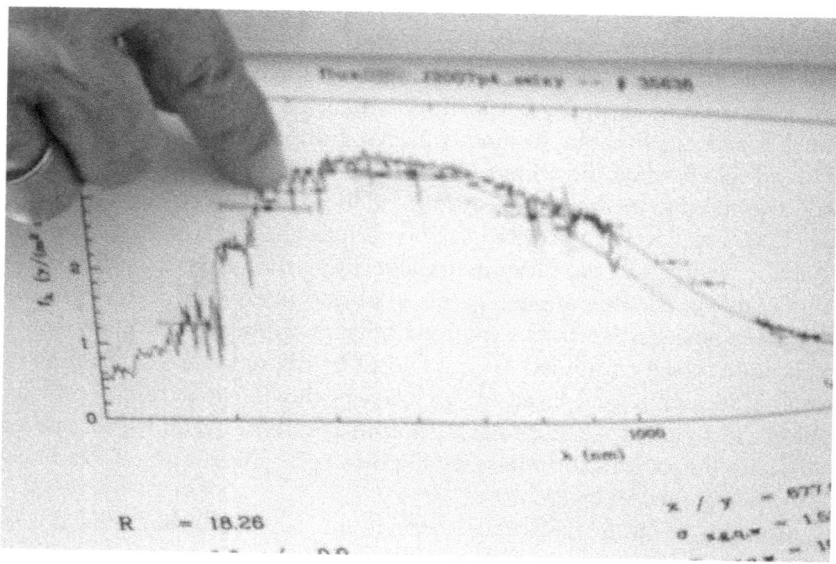

Figure 3.3   At a team meeting, Otfried is concerned about an offset visible in some galaxy spectral energy distribution fits that Nadine had prepared. This diagram depicts measurements of flux density over wavelength for one of these galaxies. As in Figure 3.2, dots with error bars represent the measurements and the continuous line represents the template model. (Photograph: Götz Hoeppe)
Note: The online version shows the colors of the original figure.

Within a few turns the conversation largely became an exchange between Otfried and Otto, who had overseen the construction and calibration of the near-infrared camera used for the new observations. Both were concerned about Nadine's plots and debated them in light of their previous observing experience. Long before Nadine had joined the team, Otfried and Otto had struggled with what turned out to be straylight in the WFI at the 2.2-meter telescope. This had resulted in a troublesome flatfield that corrupted all flux measurements. Otfried surmised that Nadine's result implied that this old problem had not been fully resolved.[16]

At this point several options seemed possible. Nadine's dataset comprised observations in twenty-one filters, recorded with two cameras attached to telescopes on different continents over seven years. Otfried and Otto knew that neither the cameras nor the telescopes would remain entirely stable over such a long period. But how could this be checked? Aware that the deep field Nadine studied is in a part of the sky that the Two Micron All Sky Survey (2MASS; Skrutskie et al. 2006) had observed previously, Otto suggested comparing the new observations with this survey's photometric catalog, which was freely available on the internet. Many astronomers regard 2MASS as a reliable source of object positions and near-infrared photometry.

Prior to this discussion, Otto had written a computer program to compare the new photometry with entries in the 2MASS catalog. Within two days of the team meeting, Nadine managed to download the 2MASS data and used Otto's program for preparing a diagram visualizing the differences in the fluxes of stars measured at various positions on the images. While the fluxes appeared to agree in the image's center, there was a marked offset in a ring-like shape around it (Figure 3.4). To Otto and Otfried this suggested that they were dealing with an artifact in the new data, possibly due to stray light in the camera. Otfried concluded:

Transcript 3.2
I think ... what we have to do is to remove the ring ... and see whether what comes out then is good enough. The problem is that we have something which is now ... we had something which is clearly not good enough. We had objects which do not exist. I mean ... the redshift two galaxies of twenty-first or twenty-second magnitude which clearly indicate that we have a problem ... which is too bad ... which is worse than what we can accept.

---

[16] Otfried's belief that there may have been a problem with the WFI camera (which he had codesigned) rather than with the Omega2000 camera (in whose construction he was not directly involved) can be interpreted as a case of "distance lending enchantment" as noted in studies of expertise (Collins 1992) or of the "certainty trough" that MacKenzie (2001, 333–334) has described.

Figure 3.4   Following the group meeting, Nadine and Otfried assess the flatfield frames visually. (Photograph: Götz Hoeppe)
Note: The online version shows the colors of the original figure.

Here "magnitudes" is a measure of how bright objects appear on the sky and "redshift" is a measure of the distance to cosmic objects. Otfried implies that, at a certain distance, galaxies can only be *that* bright to be proper members of their class. Linking the brightness of galaxies to their distance is a statement about the universe's geometric structure and light propagation in it.

Using Otto's code and the 2MASS catalog, Nadine, Otfried, Otto, and Patrick went on to quantify the excess light in the flatfield image (Figure 3.5). Following a series of discussions at blackboards, and while regarding paper printouts, they developed a recipe for subtracting the ring from the flatfield image (Figure 3.6). Nadine then used the corrected flatfield image for reducing all 1,300 raw exposures. After she had rerun the photometry and template-fitting codes, the presumed excess of massive galaxies at redshift 1.8 had disappeared.

By progressing from calibrating "raw data" to revealing astronomical phenomena, Nadine had gone from a context of low evidential specificity (Pinch 1985) – detecting faint light sources and measuring their brightness – to a highly specific, and perhaps risky, epistemic claim: identifying these sources

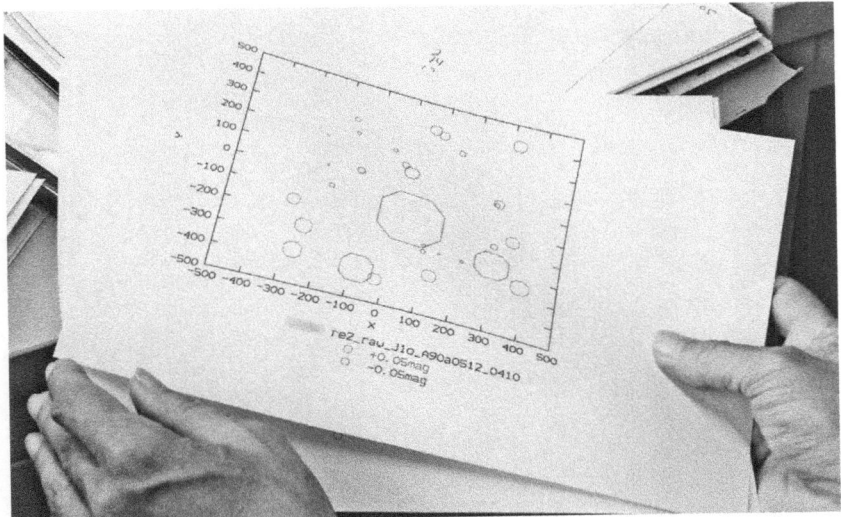

Figure 3.5   Guided by Otto, Nadine assesses the flatfield frame quantitatively by plotting differences of her brightness measurements of stars in the field with those of the public 2MASS catalog. (Photograph: Götz Hoeppe)
Note: The online version shows the colors of the original figure.

as distant, massive galaxies. She had to go to a higher externality to be able to "lose the phenomenon" (Garfinkel 2002, 264). At lower externality there were no phenomena to be lost. Individual traces of light in the exposures that Nadine worked with were never "just these traces," but were – if epistemically productive – accountable to a galaxy's spectral energy distribution, whose further constituent traces were revealed in the dataset's other images.[17]

Otfried and Otto made educated guesses about how reflections on lenses and glass filters in the camera might cause straylight in its images, but neither they themselves nor the observatory's engineers attempted to find a quantitative physical explanation for it. These astronomers seemed interested only in being able to correct for the excess light recorded in

---

[17] In this episode one may consider the flatfield ring as a phenomenon that these astronomers do not simply lose, but control for. However, given that their joint work is to find astronomical objects, I follow their usage of considering phenomena as regularities that can be abstracted from pertaining to individual objects and are characteristically linked to disciplinary representational spaces (see Chapter 4). Similarly, Bogen and Woodward (1988) distinguish phenomena from data by considering the former, unlike the latter, as detached from the observing situation. In doing so, (spectral template) models were used to correct data (cf. Edwards (2010) and Bokulich (2021)). One may add that this episode was not so much about losing an astronomical phenomenon as it was about how not to find objects that do not exist.

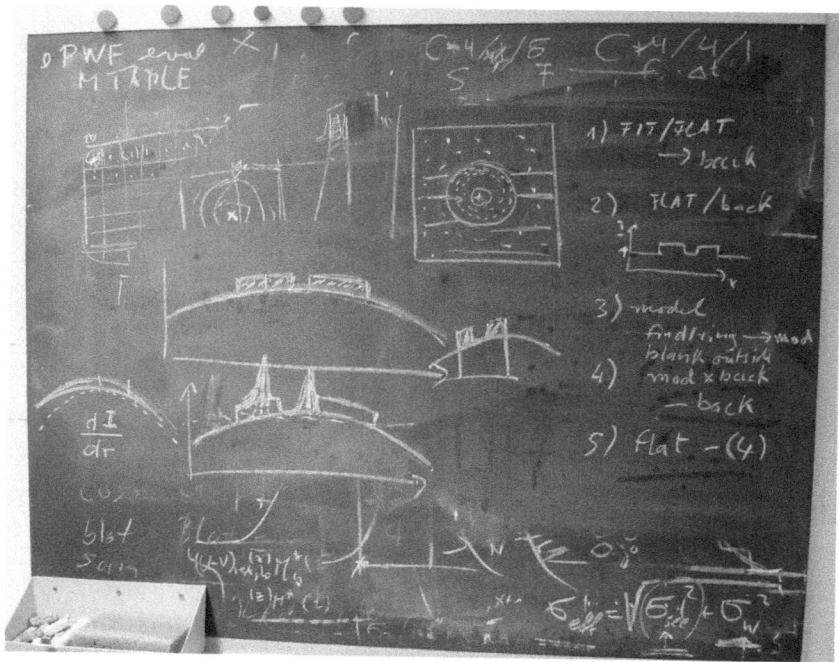

Figure 3.6   Summarized on Otto's office blackboard, a group discussion yields a recipe to correct for the flatfield ring that is now considered an artifact due to scattered light in the infrared camera. A sequence of arithmetic operations to the flatfield frames specifies its remedy (steps 1 to 5, as seen on the right). (Photograph: Götz Hoeppe)
Note: The online version shows the colors of the original figure.

the flatfield exposures computationally, a task for which access to the 2MASS proved valuable. The ring-like feature in the flatfield images thus became accountable not to a physical description of telescope and camera, but to the documented record of astronomical observations available to all researchers through the internet. For Otfried and Otto, making the artifactual ring (and, by implication, the camera's performance) accountable to a "globally" stabilized catalog such as 2MASS appeared to be more secure and convincing than making it accountable to a local calibration. Indexical cues in the local setting thus triggered team members to recruit a wider set of accounting practices into their project. Until discovering the ring-like feature in the near-infrared exposures, both constituent digital datasets were regarded as equally malleable, being subject to possible correction.

3.4.2 An Overdensity of Galaxies That "Cannot Exist"

In the previous episode, Nadine had worked with the team's "old" catalog of objects detected in optical wavebands. It lacks objects detected exclusively in the four newly observed near-infrared bands and thus misses the more distant objects that her project was searching. Rather than resolving the straylight issue to its possible conclusion, Otfried considered the flat-field images as "good enough for now." He was now eager for Nadine to prepare a near-infrared selected galaxy catalog. In making this catalog, Nadine did everything as instructed. But again, a surprise ensued. In late 2008, when I was traveling abroad, she wrote to me, in an email message,

> I would like you to be here to share our amazing discovery. I still have to convince myself to believe it. I have discovered a very high number (around 100) of red massive galaxies at [redshift] z around 1.6! We did check if it was a problem with the library but the SEDs [Spectral Energy Densities] look very good! I think that the library is good. We still have to calculate the mass for these objects, but they look massive. I don't see obvious clustering, those galaxies are sparse across the field.

When I returned to the Institute, I learned that old-timers had done all "diagnostic work." Nadine had not been involved. Otfried explained to me:

Transcript 3.3
At first I thought that there really is something there ... an overdensity at a redshift of 1.6 in our field. But then ... discussing this with Oliver ((*another old-timer*)) convinced me that this has to be nonsense. First ... you cannot expect such an overdensity to exist ... and secondly ... how these objects are distributed in the field ... they are all over ... and a ((*galaxy*)) cluster ... even a supercluster (...) would cover only a fraction of our field if it were at a redshift of 1.6. Then you would see it as an overdensity ((*in celestial coordinates*)). (...) So I had to admit that it would be mistaken to assume that there is an overdensity ... as it now seemed to be obviously wrong ... if you like. And after a while I realized that the overdensity may be due to the asinh magnitude producing wrong colors.

As in the first episode, the plausibility of Nadine's analysis was assessed with respect to the phenomena that template fitting revealed, such as "overdensities of objects" or "superclusters" of galaxies. The apparent over-density – a clustering of objects in a part of the field – emerged after combining the two datasets. The optical-only dataset alone had not revealed it. Otfried realized that template fitting is sensitive to how one computes so-called color indices, which, in turn, depends on how one defines and measures magnitudes.

Astronomers commonly define magnitudes as a logarithm of the incoming radiation flux and color indices as the difference of two magnitudes pertaining to two wavebands (Chromey 2010, 27). In the MAMBO system, templates are fitted (and redshifts measured) in color space, that is, by comparing sets of observed color indices with those derived from the template library. However, for faint objects at the noise limit of an exposure, magnitudes and color indices become ill-defined due to the asymptotic behavior of the logarithm of near-zero arguments. Other astronomers had tried to remedy this problem by introducing a modified magnitude definition that uses the inverse hyperbolic sine (asinh) instead of the logarithm. This function resembles the logarithm for small fluxes, but is "better behaved" for small positive arguments.[18] Various astronomical survey projects, including MAMBO, adopted these "asinh magnitudes."

Alerted by Oliver's concern with the overdensity at redshift 1.6 being implausible cosmologically, Otfried suspected that this modified magnitude definition might produce artifacts when applied to the MAMBO filter set because of its combination of broad-band and medium-band filters. For an object that has been detected in a broad band, but is too faint to be detected in a medium band, spurious color indices can result, making the algorithm pick the wrong template. Specific combinations of wrongly assigned color indices can make the algorithm preferentially select templates with a specific redshift for a range of spectral energy diagram shapes, resulting in what some practitioners call "redshift focusing."

After some experimenting, Otfried arrived at a new definition for computing magnitudes at low signal-to-noise ratios that seemed to "behave well" for color indices derived from combinations of broad- and medium-band photometry. For brighter objects, this definition converges with the traditional logarithmic magnitude definition. After Otfried had included the new magnitude definition into the MAMBO photometry algorithm, it became Nadine's task to recalculate the photometry for all objects in all filters. Using these to run the template-fitting algorithm again made the overdensity of galaxies at redshift 1.6 disappear. It was now considered an artifact.

As in the first episode, it was the perceived implausibility of a finding at presumably high externality – a statement about a large-scale structure in the distant universe – that prompted a return to lower externality and a less specific evidential context. However, in this instance, accounting

---

[18] Lupton et al. (1999). Whereas the logarithm function is asymptotic, tending toward negative infinity for decreasing positive arguments, the inverse hyperbolic sine function is linear near the origin.

practices were not cast wider than before, but local procedures were refined to enable an intertwining of astronomical phenomena, observing procedures, and reduced digital data.[19]

3.4.3 *A Luminosity Function That "Nicely Agrees"*

Nadine's next task was to assess whether her new measurements could reproduce published statistical findings about distant galaxies that other teams had made. Otfried now asked her to prepare a galaxy luminosity function, a graph depicting the number of galaxies in a specific volume as a function of galaxy luminosity. Such graphs are commonly used for inferring evolutionary changes in the galaxy population statistically.

Equipped with widely used recipes and aided by Oliver, Nadine wrote computer code for preparing luminosity function diagrams from the combined catalog. After considering her work, Otfried complimented Nadine by saying that her diagrams "look okay." He then pulled out a paper copy of an article that a team of US astronomers had recently published. This team of renowned scientists had assembled luminosity functions derived from several deep fields at different parts in the sky in one plot, including one they had made using earlier data released by the MAMBO team. Working with pencil and ruler, Otfried copied measurements from Nadine's plot to the published graph and then held printouts on top of each other against the light to assess these diagrams' "sameness" or "difference." Thus, he noticed a systematic offset between the graphs that puzzled him and asked Nadine to check carefully what she had done, concluding that "if it is not too far away from what everyone has found I would be happy." Within a day Nadine noticed that she had introduced an erroneous factor of two in adopting the software code. Remedying it made both plots "agree quite nicely," as Otfried declared upon further visual inspection.

By preparing the luminosity function, Nadine again moved to work at higher externality where a concern for individual objects gave way to considering the statistical properties of the galaxy population and its evolution. Unlike in the previous cases, accounting practices involved manual craftwork in addition to the visual assessment of "reasonable agreement"

---

[19] This is reminiscent of Duhem's (1954 [1914]) account of introducing auxiliary hypotheses to "save the phenomena" in scientific observation. Note that in the sequential work that I describe, potential discoveries are discarded as being unlikely, whereas in Duhem's account an astronomical phenomenon is saved in the light of anomalous data.

(Kuhn 1977, 185) with existing data or representations of previously established phenomena. Comparing Nadine's work with that of well-known and respected astronomers who drew on the same data, and finding them to be in reasonable agreement, raised Otfried's trust in Nadine's computations and made both datasets accountable to the work of these other scientists.[20]

3.4.4   A Troubling "Hole in the Universe"

A few months later, after Nadine had defended her PhD thesis, she had finished a draft journal manuscript describing her work. When Peter, a former PhD student of Otto's who had been instrumental in developing and conducting the MAMBO survey, visited the Institute they met with Otfried to discuss the manuscript. Nadine's draft included several graphs that the described the galaxy sample. The first of these was a histogram showing the number of objects (n) as a function of redshift (z), a so-called $n(z)$ plot (Figure 3.7).[21]

This histogram's shape troubled Peter. He doubted it was cosmologically plausible and suspected that it hinted at a bias in their sample's faint end, where it would be more complete for bright galaxies of a certain color or shape. Otfried agreed with Peter that the graph is accountable to what the distribution of galaxies in the universe is like, but he disagreed about what this implied for its shape. He argued that the dip seen in the diagram between redshifts 0.3 and 0.9 documents a dearth of galaxies in the appertaining distance interval, a "hole" in the universe.[22]

In the discussion that followed, Peter used his laptop computer to generate additional plots from the data. These showed how a change in the faint magnitude limit affects the histogram's shape. Otfried conceded that the sample's degree of completeness did indeed vary with galaxy color and magnitude, that this was likely to cause the dip seen in the histogram, and that they had to redefine their galaxy sample. Otfried agreed that, after all, there seemed to be no hole at this part of the universe.

---

[20] On "agreement" in scientific practice, see also Lynch (1985a, ch. 6).
[21] I examine this episode in greater detail in Chapter 4, focusing on their use of diagrams.
[22] Suspecting a "hole in the universe" in form of a galaxy underdensity is not as outlandish as it may seem. One of the most observed fields in the sky, the Chandra Deep Field South, is known to be underdense at intermediate redshifts (Hartlap et al. 2009).

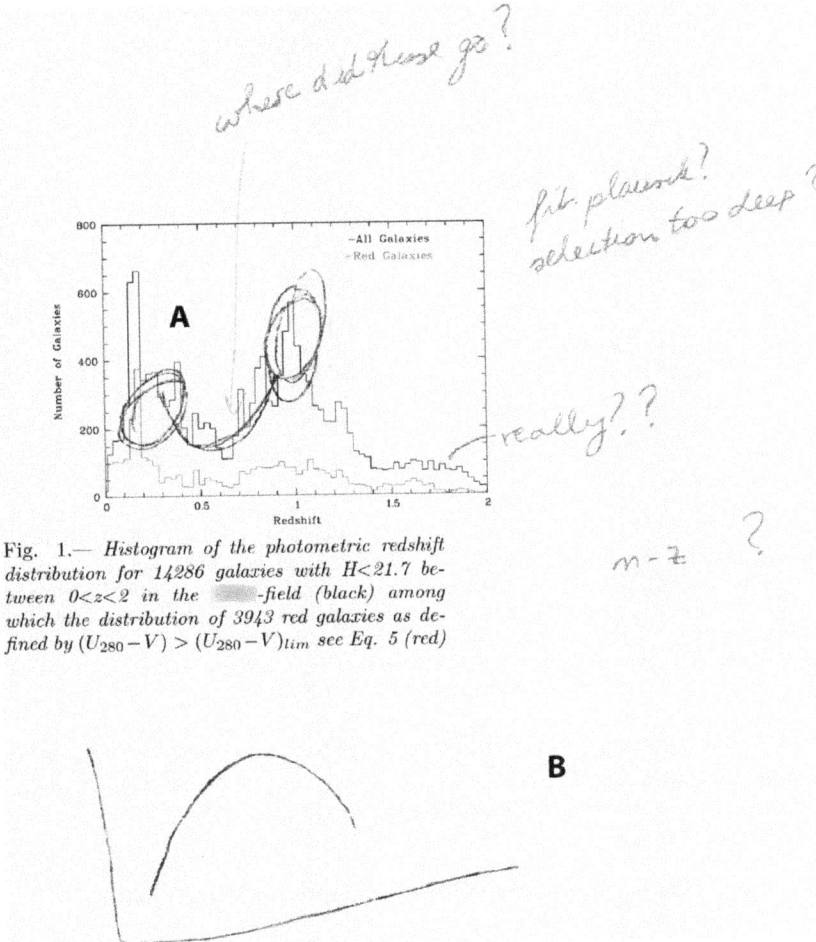

Fig. 1.— *Histogram of the photometric redshift distribution for 14286 galaxies with H<21.7 between 0<z<2 in the* ▮▮▮▮*-field (black) among which the distribution of 3943 red galaxies as defined by* $(U_{280} - V) > (U_{280} - V)_{lim}$ *see Eq. 5 (red)*

Figure 3.7   Histogram in Nadine's draft manuscript, showing the number of galaxies as a function of redshift for all objects detected in the A2713 field. This printout includes Peter's handwritten notes as made prior to the group meeting (unlabeled) as well as the marks he added during the discussion with Nadine and Otfried as described in the text (labeled A and B).
Note: The online version shows the colors of the original figure.

In this instance, in which two old-timers initially disagreed about "what the universe is like," Nadine was not forced to return to work at lower externality. Instead, her task was to remove objects from her sample, starting with the faintest galaxies and progressing to brighter ones until obtaining a sample that was "reasonably complete." Eventually, Otfried,

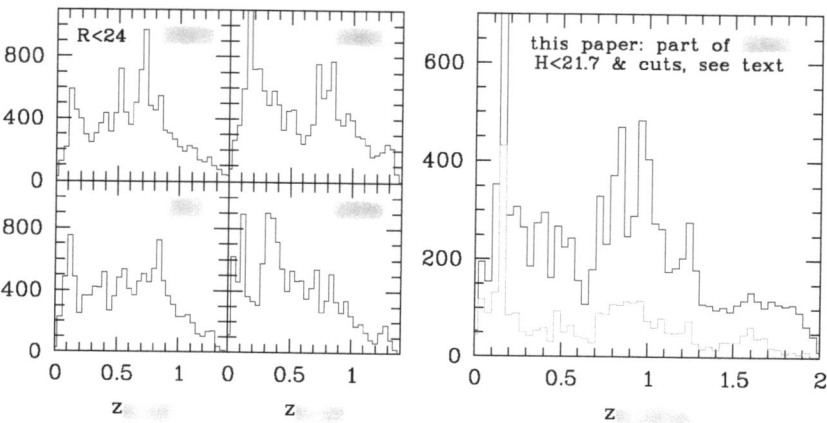

Figure 3.8   Revised histogram as it appeared in the published paper, showing on the right the number of galaxies as a function of redshift for all objects in the same field as in Figure 3.7, selected according to refined criteria from Nadine's optical plus near-infrared galaxy catalog. The dip seen around $z = 0.5$ in the earlier version is less prominent due to the adoption of different selection criteria for the galaxy sample. On the left, four similar histograms are now included, each depicting one of four fields that the MAMBO team observed. These histograms use the "old" (optical-only) dataset. They illustrate "cosmic variance," that is, how much the numbers and volume densities of galaxies vary when observed with the same technique in different parts of the sky. (© American Astronomical Society. Reproduced with permission)

Nadine, and Peter agreed to remove galaxies that were fainter than a limit magnitude that depended on the redshift, arriving at the sample that was subsequently used for the published analysis (Figure 3.8).

3.5   Discussion: Instruction, Reflexivity, Membership

By following Nadine's work over two years we get a sense of how she became a competent member in the community and culture of extra-galactic astronomy. Conversely, we gain insights into what can often make combining new data with an existing dataset so challenging. As we have seen, astronomers describe this work as a single linear sequence of operations (Transcript 3.1 and Figure 3.1), but I witnessed that their practices were reflexive in an ethnomethodological sense, in that earlier steps of work were reassessed and modified, subject to the outcome of later steps in the sequence.[23] This prospective and retrospective reasoning

---

[23] I do not mean to suggest that the flowchart in Figure 3.1 is wrong, but that its proper use is embedded in members' practices.

engaged discipline-specific representational formats and contexts of accountability.

In the midst of her project, exasperated yet again from trying to run computer code for basic data reductions, Nadine once exclaimed: "My job is to get error messages!" At that time, her challenge was to run this code so that it would not crash but generate meaningful output. Two years later, after Nadine had defended her PhD thesis, I asked her how many times she had done the reductions of her dataset. She replied:

> *Transcript 3.4*
> I don't <u>know</u> ... <u>many</u> times! From the <u>raw</u> frames to the fully <u>reduced</u> frames ... and then many times the <u>photometry</u> ... <u>again</u> and <u>again</u> and <u>again</u>! (...) I think that in astrophysics it <u>never</u> fits. You always need to use your knowledge to verify what you are doing. <u>Every</u> calculation. You have an idea how it <u>can</u> be ... but you have to be very careful with all the <u>details</u>. And you have to <u>verify</u> each step to go on and continue with the recipe. And with <u>each</u> part of a recipe you have to see if there is any <u>problem</u> there ... because the recipes are never perfect.

In this retrospective account, Nadine alludes to her experience of the unavoidable incompleteness of written instructions that always require researchers' "ad hocing" (Garfinkel 1967, 22), that is, their on-the-spot use of contextual knowledge for making decisions that are "good enough for now." She also hints at the necessary "willingness to wait" (Garfinkel 2002, 202) in learning a practice. From despairing over troubleshooting computer code to engaging multiple contexts of accountability, Nadine acquired not only a sense of the limitations of rule-following, and of the reflexivity necessarily involved in working data together: considering their outcome, she learned to review and repair past actions. She mastered the task of proceeding from knowing about a cosmology to using it. And she discovered how critical well-calibrated data are to a scientific analysis.

What, then, about Nadine's achievement of membership? In this discussion I approach this question by first specifying how images and diagram were constitutive of her team's work. Then I characterize the domain-specific body of assumptions that team members used as a resource for achieving accountability. Eventually, I ask what its use implies for data calibration and the training of junior scientists.

3.5.1 *Scaffoldings of Graphs, Contexts of Accountability*

The documentary practices that constituted Nadine's work involved a range of marks and inscriptions: telescopic exposures, spectral energy distributions, color–color plots of stars and galaxies, as well as galaxy color-magnitude diagrams, luminosity functions, and the $n(z)$ plot (see Figures 3.3 and 3.7).

These diagram formats are conventionally used in astronomy for interpreting data in evidential contexts of increasing externality: a spectral energy distribution is made for individual objects, color-magnitude diagrams display measurements of many objects in a scatterplot (where individual objects are recognizable), whereas all individual object information is erased in luminosity functions, which describe populations of galaxies. In the work that I witnessed, these diagrams were not only constitutive of the phenomena observed, but were also engaged to provide contexts of accountability. Each trace that Nadine's work revealed, that is, each flux measured in an exposure at a position where a signal had been detected algorithmically, was never "just this trace," but was regarded as one of several constituents of an object's spectral energy distribution that the dataset's exposures revealed, all of which were made accountable to a library spectral energy distribution template.

A spectral energy distribution is often represented as a graph of radiation flux density ("intensity") as a function of wavelength (cf. Figures 3.2 and 3.3). The team's old template library consisted of a set of spectral energy distributions observed with a spectrograph. The new library's templates were derived from computer simulations of the spectral light emitted from a model of stellar populations. They were made to match the old templates where these were available and extended the template library to longer wavelengths and higher redshifts. In this work, template fitting never is a comparison of "nature" with "models" but a comparison of the momentary endpoints of two different trajectories of documentary practices in the representational space of observational astronomy (cf. Rheinberger 1997, ch. 7). The templates – a kind of model – were a means to constitute phenomena from data and were thus used as tools to move from lower externality toward higher externality for addressing more general evidential contexts.

Note that, in this team's work, contexts of accountability do not dwell in some abstract space but are defined by diagrams. Many of these are conventional and used by astronomers worldwide (Figures 3.3, 3.7, 3.8, and 3.9), but others are used only within the team (such as Figure 3.5). Diagrams essentially define contexts of accountability.[24] They are meeting places of epistemic and social action, as I will examine further in Chapter 4.

---

[24] This contrasts with language use in social life, where the definition and recognition of "context" is an enduring challenge for members and analysts (Durranti and Goodwin 1992; Fabian 1995).

3.5.2 Cosmology as a Convict Code

When Otfried, Otto, Oliver, and Peter instructed Nadine, they used assumptions about the universe that they agreed upon or negotiated on using. They regarded galaxies at redshift 2 as "unlikely" to appear as bright as 20 mag, did not "expect" overdensities at redshift 1.6 to extend across the field of view under consideration, agreed that galaxy luminosity functions made from observations of different parts of the sky should look "more or less the same," and argued about whether there is a "hole" in the "universe as we have known it before." Otfried, Otto, Oliver, and Peter thus oriented to the observed world as having a single "underlying pattern" (Garfinkel 1967, 40, 78). This assumption informed their assessments when jointly regarding the diagrams that Nadine had prepared. Like the other PhD students they instructed, she was guided to apply a "documentary method" (see footnote 6) to elicit it.

Authors of research articles on galaxy evolution routinely make the cosmological assumptions they use explicit. In their "Introduction" sections, articles typically include a sentence which specifies the "cosmology," such as

> We use the standard Lambda cold dark matter (ΛCDM) cosmology with $H_o = 70$ km Mpc^{-1} s^{-1}, $\Omega_\Lambda = 0.70$, and $\Omega_M = 0.30$. (Ronayne et al. 2023)

or

> Throughout this paper, we assume a Planck Collaboration et al. (2020) cosmology of $H_o = 67.4$ km s^{-1} Mpc^{-1}, $\Omega_m = 0.315$ and $\Omega_\Lambda = 0.685$. (Leung et al. 2023)

Here H_o (the Hubble constant), Ω_M or Ω_m, and Ω_Λ (the fractions of matter and dark energy of what astronomers call the critical density) are three of six numerical parameters characterizing the world model that is currently dominant.[25] Both Patrick's account of this team's work (Transcript 3.1) and research publications on galaxy evolution suggest that astronomers use this cosmology and the parameters specifying it only to convert observed redshifts into physical distances and magnitudes into luminosities. Apart from contexts of instruction, these astronomers did not make the phenomenal properties of the sky and of stabilized astronomical phenomena

---

[25] An often-cited article summarizes this model succinctly: "In this model the universe is spatially flat, homogeneous, and isotropic on large scales, composed of radiation, ordinary matter (electrons, protons, neutrons, and neutrinos), nonbaryonic cold dark matter, and dark energy" (Spergel et al. 2003, 175).

explicit as resources for combining new and existing data. However, as seen earlier, references to these phenomena permeated the work that I witnessed. It is in this practical way that an "implicit cosmology" is used both constructively and descriptively as a shared view of "what the universe looks like" as seen through the representational (diagrammatical) formats of observational astronomy, a view that novices must learn to adopt. Thus understood, an "implicit cosmology" is a collection of "embedded instructions for perception" (Wieder 1974, 203), much like the "convict code" in the halfway house that Wieder described.

Wieder's account resonates with Melvin Pollner's study of mundane reasoning. Pollner argues that because of their mutual orientation to the assumption of an "incorrigibly objective and commonly shared world" (Pollner 1974b, 53) members of a practice can recognize and resolve disjunctive experiences (as they typically occur in the combination of datasets). In doing so, members commonly rely on *ceteris paribus* clauses.[26] Embedded in members' reasoning, "incorrigible propositions" (Gasking 1955) are resources for reflexively preserving their own validity. As Pollner (1987, 18) argues, "mundane reason is not an empirical version of reality but an *a priori* specification of its features in terms of which empirical claims are reviewed for their adequacy." I explore this further in Chapter 5.

Nadine and her supervisors inferred the distant galaxy population's properties through a sequential intertwining of data, phenomena, and equipment. In achieving this, the elements of their "implicit cosmology" remained stable. But is an "implicit cosmology" as stable as the convict code appeared to Wieder during his fieldwork in the halfway house? The fourth episode, where Peter and Otfried debated the existence of a "hole in the universe," demonstrates that "sameness" is negotiable in light of what astronomers call "cosmic variance." Theorists claim that the homogeneity and isotropy of the universe that the standard model postulates are realized on the largest scales only (Spergel et al. 2003, 175). Whenever astronomers observe a small part of the sky (as they do when studying deep fields), the "sameness" of these fields with other small parts of the sky is not guaranteed outright but needs to be established empirically in the course of work. This is what Otfried, Peter, and Nadine did by including the left panel shown in Figure 3.8. It depicts the number of galaxies as a function of redshift in four distinct fields on the sky,

---

[26] *Ceteris paribus* clauses posit that a law only holds if "other things are equal." It provides members with a resource to account for disjunctive experiences by attributing them to "things not having been equal" (cf. Cartwright 1983; Earman et al. 2002).

illustrating the range of possible cosmic variation. In this way the reflexive use of an "implicit cosmology" is delimited in this inductive work.

As observational astronomy develops, the elements of a cosmology are incorrigible until further notice only.[27] Would revisions or refinements of the "implicit cosmology" affect astronomy's social order, or have they done so in the recent past? For their practices to be mutually recognizable, astronomers need to work with a cosmology. Throughout the late twentieth century there was a notorious uncertainty among astronomers about basic cosmological parameters, dividing researchers, by and large, into two factions.[28] In 2003, the widely publicized release of observations taken with the NASA spacecraft Wilkinson Microwave Anisotropy Probe (WMAP) resulted in a set of precisely determined cosmological parameters that most researchers came to agree upon (Spergel et al. 2003), ushering in what has been called an era of "precision cosmology" (Primack 2005). Years after this release I heard researchers referring to it as "The Gospel according to WMAP." By doing so they seemed to allude not only to its authority and hegemony, but also to the moral implications of mutually sharing an order of (and for) practice.

As it is through a cosmology that people consider the world as organized, this is where the astronomers' cosmology meets the ones that anthropologists are more familiar with. It is through cosmology, anthropologist Michael Herzfeld (2001, 194) writes, that "people treat the universe as organized: rather than a collection of random physical components, it is a highly ordered disposition of matter and energy structured in different levels of size and complexity." A cosmology is not merely a set of beliefs, but also a resource for action. It defines a normativity that has epistemic and social uses. Or, as Mary Douglas (1975, xix) put it, "[t]he known cosmos is constructed for helping arguments of a practical kind."[29]

3.5.3 Calibration

Patrick's description of the team's workflow (Transcript 3.1) and Otto's diagram thereof (Figure 3.1) suggest that data calibration and analysis are two distinct parts of a project. But it turns out that they are closely

---

[27] A completely incorrigible proposition would be devoid of any information about the world (Gasking 1955, 208), which is clearly not how astronomers understand a world model.
[28] See Freedman and Madore (2010) and Matarese and McCoy (2024) on controversies about the Hubble constant.
[29] See Hoeppe (2018b) on practical uses of cosmologies beyond astronomy.

enmeshed. As in physics, calibration in astronomy is often understood as the "use of a surrogate signal to standardize an instrument" (Franklin 1997, 31). In astronomical photometry, optical flux and color standards are derived from the star Vega (α Lyrae) as the primary calibrator, which is used to calibrate secondary and then tertiary standard stars all over the sky, whose fluxes are subsequently used as reference signals.[30]

Up to her first run of template fitting, Nadine's calibrations had proceeded in this way, but her calibration did not end there. Her work oscillated between making representations which could be interpreted as revealing phenomena at high externality and probing into the observing situation and data analysis where artifacts in the (malleable) data can be removed or analysis procedures corrected. Along this way these researchers replicated phenomena deemed already stabilized.[31]

Astronomers argue that they subject reduced and calibrated data to specific evidential contexts solely to obtain a "sanity check" of the calibrations. They insist they do not "tune" them to make the data replicate known phenomena through enforcing their "sameness."[32] As in the MAMBO team's work, publications describing new observations of deep fields typically contain flux measurements of objects much fainter than those included in published (and stabilized) all-sky catalogs such as the 2MASS mentioned earlier. One means to assert and to demonstrate their reliability and trustworthiness is to represent them in a standard format along with observations of other fields that are deemed comparable. Galaxy luminosity functions (see episode 3) are such a format; diagrams of number counts, in which the number of detected objects in a field is shown as a function of flux density or magnitude, are another (Figure 3.9).

---

[30] See Bessell (2005) and Chromey (2010). Starting with the Sloan Digital Sky Survey (SDSS), several large optical sky surveys have been calibrated using more sophisticated techniques inspired by radio astronomy (cf. Padmanabhan et al. 2008).

[31] Here it may be tempting to invoke Hanson's (1958) account of the theory-ladenness of observations and declare the resulting dataset to be phenomena-laden. Alternatively, since these astronomers used spectral (template) models to replicate phenomena and correct their data, we may consider the dataset as model-laden (Edwards 2010; Bokulich 2020, 2021). But given that the intertwining that I described also included the modification of practices (which I linked to Duhem's auxiliary hypotheses), this characterization would be incomplete. However, this is a case of what Collins calls the "data analysts' regress": "The only way to tell if one's data analysis is correct is to have it discover real effects, but the only way to find out if effects are real is to analyze data in a correct way" (Collins 2004, 668). In the research that I witnessed this regress was resolved through what philosophers of science call robustness reasoning, which dwells on the convergence of "multiple means of determination" (Wimsatt 2007, 43) toward a result (cf. Chapter 5). This process goes beyond what is commonly called the cross-calibration of datasets, which is common in astronomy (cf. Tsujimoto et al. 2011; Scolnic et al. 2015).

[32] See Wolf et al. (2001, 685) and Hogg et al. (2005, 57), but note Capak et al. (2007, 114).

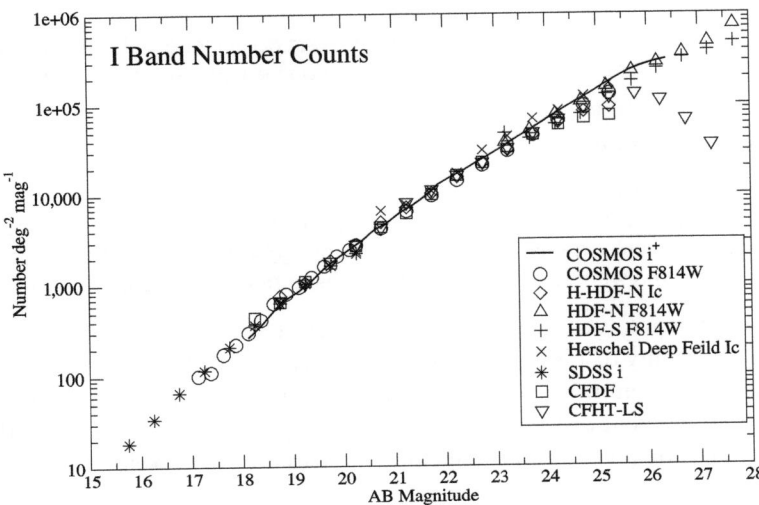

Figure 3.9   Journal articles accompanying the public release of deep field survey data often contain plots characterizing a new dataset and comparing it with existing ones. Number counts, showing the number of detected objects in a field (vertical axis) as a function of flux density or magnitude (horizontal axis), illustrate the degree of the datasets' "sameness." As such these diagrams assert and specify the reliability of new observations. (Figure 12 of Capak et al. 2007, 114; © American Astronomical Society. Reproduced with permission.)

They can be used to assess the similarity and difference of datasets visually. While cosmic variance affects and delimits "reasonable agreement" (Kuhn 1977, 185) in either format, astronomers deem data that have "withstood" being subjected to such diverse evidential contexts as more reliable than data that have not.[33]

Note, eventually, that engaging different contexts of accountability would have produced differently calibrated datasets, optimized, perhaps, for a better recognition of extended light or of galaxies that are merging, or for making measurements of weak gravitational lensing. In this way the researchers' interests are imprinted in a dataset.

A common sentiment among the astronomers I talked with is that one should only release higher-level data (such as catalogs) that have been used successfully for a scientific analysis. Says a senior astronomer:

---

[33] In successive data releases of the SDSS its photometric calibration was improved following a series of scientific projects.

Transcript 3.5
A <u>good</u> data release is something you can do <u>science</u> with. And if you've <u>done</u> science then those things that you've <u>used</u> should be your data release.

Another senior astronomer told me:

Transcript 3.6
My lesson from being in the survey business is that it's <u>only</u> when you do science with the data that you learn how <u>good</u> they are … or if there are problems with the data. Many mistakes appear only then.

"Doing science" in these views means successfully using data of relatively high externality to address specific evidential contexts. Note that neither of these two astronomers claim that a scientific result needs to be replicated for its constituent data to be releasable. Their point rather seems to be that researchers ought to inspect data and analyses for their "believability."

3.5.4   *Membership*

At the beginning of her project, when she encountered unfamiliar representational spaces, Nadine could not know herself what to count as "same" and "different," what was "good enough for now" and what had to be done differently.[34] Only after being exposed to various, diverse settings did she manage to share an order of, and for, practice, and make distinctions about sameness and difference with which members like Otfried, Otto, Oliver, and Peter agreed. Nadine's achievement was not solely "cognitive." Rather, with her becoming a user of a cosmology, cosmology's domain of accountability was extended to her and her work. Figuratively, this domain was a "meeting place" of her actions and the actions of those who were inducted earlier at the Institute and at other sites of extragalactic research. For these members, a shared "implicit cosmology" has become a "guide to perception" (Wieder 1974, 74).[35]

Nadine's successful use of a cosmology is not the only indicator of her achievement of membership in the culture and community of extragalactic astronomy. I witnessed how she participated in group and seminar discussions and laughed upon hearing puns like Owen's (Introduction,

---

[34] Douglas (1986, 55) argues that "similarity is a social institution." See also Barnes et al. (1996, 25–28, 53–57) on local cultural traditions and finitism in scientific instruction.

[35] It is not only in astronomy that instructed action links the performance of methods with the "substantive contents" of a field. Lynch and Jordan (1995, 228) observe this in their study of molecular biology.

Transcript I.1). Over time I kept noticing moments when, for Nadine, "the implicit" could eventually remain unsaid and backgrounded. When entering the MAMBO research group, Nadine's situation was not unlike that of an ethnographer entering a new field. Much of her learning happened without her noticing it, by immersing herself in a social setting. It included meetings with Otto and Otfried, discussions with Patrick and Peter, team meetings, lunch and coffee breaks, and travel to observatories and conferences. In various environments she had to learn how to ask questions and make practical sense of the responses she received.

I mentioned earlier that references to the reflexivity of accounting practices are characteristically absent in the methods sections of research publications. This includes the paper that Nadine wrote at the end of her work. Two years later, a new PhD student in the research group, who arrived after Nadine had gone, found it impossible to continue the calibrations and analyses that she had left behind straight away, but needed frequent consultations with Otfried, just as Nadine did early in her project.

It is tempting to define the achievement of membership in a scientific community as the achievement of becoming an author, a contributor to the scientific literature.[36] Episode 4 was part of this process for Nadine, but already episode 3 brought her data analysis in "contact" with the literature to which her paper was meant to contribute. Her data was about to become public along with her journal article or soon thereafter, and thus her work would soon be open to public scrutiny. That there is often no clear "correspondence relationship" (Sharrock and Anderson 1986, 58) between laboratory research and its description in a scientific article has been pointed out long ago (Medawar 1963). Early laboratory ethnographies dwelt on this and emphasized scientists' "literary reasoning" (Knorr Cetina 1981, 94) for rhetorical and argumentative purposes, for the benefit of securing resources, and as part of the process of "fact construction" (cf. Latour and Woolgar 1986, 75–88). While some forms of "literary reasoning" seem inevitable, the raised accountability of working with public data is bound to constrain data analyses and interpretations throughout a project, to which a journal article is reflexively tied.

As Nadine aspires to fulfill her dream of becoming a professional astronomer, her objective is biographical. As an author, her name is attached to her work, prompting her concerns over her reputation. In my account, reputation was alluded to only briefly in the third episode, where Otfried

---

[36] This view is challenged by the extension of authorship to contributors of various kinds (cf. Rennie et al. 1997).

consulted an article published by respected colleagues to assess Nadine's draft luminosity function, but scientists are obviously mindful of its significance and make decisions on its basis, as has been noticed in early sociological accounts and ethnographies.[37] As a visiting scientist at the Institute insisted, "science is self-correcting, but careers are not." Reputation, as this episode suggests, is a resource for accounting practices in data-rich research.

While focusing on the achievement of membership, I began this chapter with proposing to apply the tactics of Chapter 2 – take a problem of data-rich science, consider how it is "staffed" in a specific case, and follow its management ethnographically – to a different case: the common challenge of combining scientific datasets. This brought the reflexivity of data reductions and analyses as well as its resources (such as contexts of accountability), all typically omitted from published reports, into view. Members' social and cultural practices thus become scaffolds built into well-calibrated and well-combined datasets.

---

[37] For example, Latour and Woolgar (1986) and (Collins 1992).

CHAPTER 4

Diagrams
Spaces for Cultivating Data and Making Discoveries

4.1 This Chapter's Plan

We have seen in Chapter 3 that diagrams were central to Nadine's work, which oscillated between generating improved versions of her catalog (a table of measured and estimated galaxy properties) and representing it using various diagrams. Thus, her catalog episodically "surfaced" into a visible, inspectable form. In this chapter I build on this observation and examine how diagrams in use make private thoughts, models, and phenomena accessible intersubjectively and complex datasets surveyable. When designed and viewed in conventional ways, diagrams are bearers of tradition and culture. While this much has been discussed before, I aim to demonstrate that diagrams can also be resources for pruning datasets, for "cultivating" them, and for achieving social accountability. Diagrams materialize contexts of accountability. They are the ground on which scientists play and experiment with data. This play matters in making and assessing some discoveries – and unmaking others. As diagrams are standardized and used at many places, the resistance that their users experience can be ascribed to their efforts of being accountable to researchers elsewhere. Data, it seems, need makers and users who are members of a visual culture.

4.2 "Let's Start with the Figures": Using Diagrams to Prune a Dataset

Let us return to the last episode of Nadine's PhD project on distant galaxies in the field of the galaxy supercluster A2713, as described in Chapter 3. There she met Otfried and Peter to discuss her paper draft. This conversation marked a nexus in Nadine's project, as it assessed retrospectively if her work was properly done and, prospectively, how her intended readers – other researchers in the field – would understand it. Nadine, Otfried, and Peter have an hour or so to discuss a twenty-page draft that includes figures and tables. They meet in Otfried's office at a table that is soon covered with printouts, handwritten notes, plots, notebooks, pencils, a ruler, and a pocket calculator. As so often when scientists talk about science, they decide to focus on the figures first:[1]

> *Transcript 4.1*
> 1 Otfried: I would start with the <u>big</u> issues ... because ... ehm
> 2 Peter: Then I need to go through and think about them and <u>sort</u> them
> 3 Otfried: and then later I would go to the nitty gritty ... what is in the introduction ... what is ... for instance with this <u>histogram</u>
> 4 Peter: Let's start with the <u>histograms</u> ... let's start with the <u>figures</u> anyway ... let's start with the <u>figures</u>
> 5 Otfried: <u>Exactly</u> ... which you <u>criticized</u>!
> 6 Peter: Right. (...)

Diagrams are immediately visible to all participants in this conversation. They focus attention and can be pointed at. They are easier to survey than the twenty pages of Nadine's draft, not to mention the catalog or the tables used to generate the plots. The diagrams in Nadine's draft represent measurements, whereas the text describes their interpretation.

The first figure in Nadine's draft is a $n(z)$ plot, a histogram that describes her sample by representing the number of detected galaxies (n) in bins of increasing redshift (z) (Figure 4.1). This is the diagram that Peter is most concerned about. Prior to the meeting, he had annotated his printed copy with probing questions ("where did these go?," "fit plausible?," "selection too deep?," "really??," "m–z?") that he addresses in the discussion that follows.

> *Transcript 4.2*
> 6 Peter: Right. So when I looked at this histogram ((*Figure 4.1*)) I was <u>frightened</u> ... because ... I thought ... if <u>that's</u> the universe ... we've not known about it before ... so probably it is <u>not</u> the universe ... and that spells <u>trouble</u>. And I thought there are two alternative interpretations for this. And what I am specifically ... concerned about is this <u>dip</u> ... right? ((*He draws circles centering on the two peaks visible in the histogram, and connects them by tracing the histogram's depression in between; feature A in Figure 4.1*))
> 7 Nadine: Mm hm
> 8 Peter: where normally ... in exactly that place there should be something like <u>that</u> ((*He sketches feature B in Figure 4.1*))
> 9 Nadine: Mm hm

---

[1] See the Appendix for a complete list of the transcription conventions adopted.

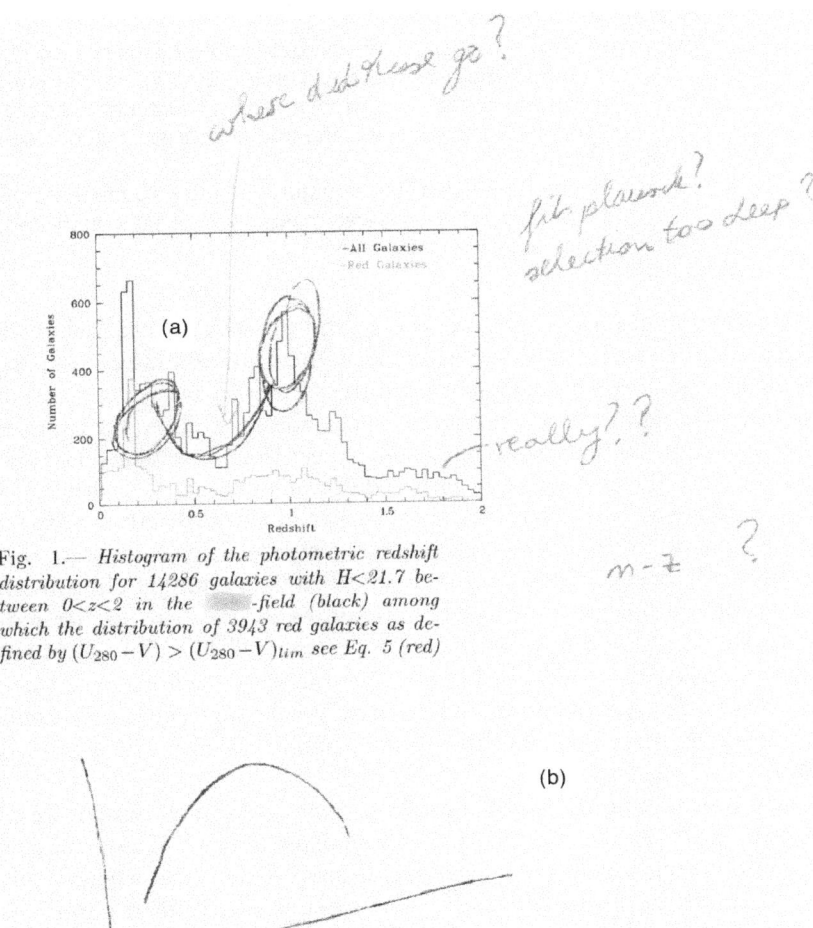

Fig. 1.— *Histogram of the photometric redshift distribution for 14286 galaxies with H<21.7 between 0<z<2 in the ▓▓▓-field (black) among which the distribution of 3943 red galaxies as defined by $(U_{280} - V) > (U_{280} - V)_{lim}$ see Eq. 5 (red)*

(b)

Figure 4.1   Histogram in Nadine's draft manuscript, showing the number of galaxies as a function of redshift for all objects detected in the A2713 field. This printout includes Peter's handwritten notes as made prior to the group meeting (unlabeled) as well as the marks he added during the discussion with Nadine and Otfried (labeled A and B).
See Transcript 4.2.
Note: The online version shows the colors of the original figure.

10 Peter: So I thought there is two possibilities. One possibility ... the more likely one ... ehhm ... because ... there is a <u>common</u> mistake that has happened to <u>myself</u> a lot of <u>times</u> and to various other people plotting such things various times ... is to choose a magnitude cut at which the sample is <u>not</u> <u>complete</u>.

11	Nadine:	Mm hm
12	Peter:	And so the shape that you get for the $n(z)$ is the <u>original</u> shape of the $n(z)$ in the universe <u>multiplied</u> by the completeness function … and if you go just deep enough almost all that you see is the completeness function itself.
13	Nadine:	Mm hm
14	Peter:	So you can't trust the <u>structure</u> anymore to mean something about the <u>universe</u> because it means something about your magnitude cut
15	Nadine:	Mm hm

By looking at the diagram and seeing "the universe," Peter acknowledges the processed data's high externality: these are calibrated and presented as instrument-independent measures.[2] Peter abstracts the shape of Nadine's histogram with the marks that I labeled A. This dip troubles him, as it conflicts with what one would expect from observing a homogenous distribution of galaxies with a detector of limited sensitivity. A deep field survey defines a cone that reaches out from Earth into space and widens with increasing redshift and distance. If galaxies were distributed homogenously in space, this so-called light cone should contain increasingly more galaxies per redshift bin as we move to higher redshifts. But after reaching a maximum at a certain redshift, the number of detected galaxies per redshift bin should ultimately decline, since these distant galaxies appear fainter and eventually fall below the survey's sensitivity limit. Peter sketches this expected pattern (which I have labeled feature B in Figure 4.1).

Alas, this is not what Nadine's histogram looks like. Where Peter expects a peak (B) there is a dip (A), whose depth seems like a measure of how concerning it is to him. Peter and Otfried disagree on whether this dip represents an underdensity of galaxies between redshift 0.3 and 0.9. Otfried believes that there is such a "hole in the universe." Peter rather suspects that the dip hints at an issue with the completeness of Nadine's sample, that is, which fraction of galaxies at a certain redshift the survey detects and includes in its catalog and which fraction it misses – causing a biased sample. Largely an onlooker, Nadine contributes affirmative utterances ("Mm hm") to the conversation.

Peter explains that a simple way to deal with the sample's incompleteness would be to define a "conservative" magnitude cut and include only

---

[2] See Chapter 3 for a discussion of Pinch's (1985) notions of externality and evidential specificity.

objects from the sample that are brighter than this limit. However, by doing so one would discard the sample's many faint galaxies, which are most interesting for Nadine's study. Peter, Otfried, and Nadine want to include as many objects in the sample as possible while not corrupting the signal and harming the team's credibility with readers:

Transcript 4.3

58 Peter: So the question is ... what do you want to <u>show</u> ... actually ... what <u>information</u> do you want to <u>convey</u> ... hence ... what do you need to <u>plot</u> ... hence ... what do you need to look <u>out</u> for ... for not plotting something that then looks <u>fishy</u>?

59 Nadine: Mm hm

60 Otfried: Yeah ... <u>exactly</u>

61 Peter: Ehm ... but this ... as it is ... as just a sort of global n(z) of your dataset is dominated by <u>incompleteness</u> issues ... rather than the physical <u>shape</u> of the histogram ... invites people to ... either <u>jump</u> on you ... or throw it away

62 Nadine: Mm hm

Thus far, this discussion has focused on Otfried's and Peter's printed and annotated copies of Nadine's draft. But now Peter uses his laptop computer to generate plots that illustrate the issues involved, using, however, not Nadine's latest "optical plus near-infrared" catalog, but Peter's older "optical-only" catalog. Peter prepares a scatterplot that shows the redshifts of galaxies over their red (R band) magnitudes, from 17 to 25 mag (Figure 4.2, fainter objects have larger magnitudes). It is useful for interpreting Nadine's histogram, which omits magnitude information:

Transcript 4.4

131 Peter: This <u>plot</u> ... probably makes clear what we are <u>talking</u> about

132 Nadine: ((*points to the dark horizontal feature that spans almost the entire width of the diagram near its bottom; Figure 4.2*)) This is A2713?

133 Peter: This is A2713

134 Nadine: Yeah yeah ... 24.5 ((*mag*)) is here ... and we have the hole there

135 Peter: Yeah ... and that is caused by <u>completeness</u> ... So if you look at the bright

136 Otfried: That's a <u>good</u> plot ... yeah

137 Peter: That's here ... and then things fan out ... <u>structures</u> fan out and get broader ... and more <u>points</u> as you go fainter ... this is why they look thicker

Figure 4.2   Peter explains a scatterplot that shows the redshifts of galaxies (vertical axis) over their red (R band) magnitudes (horizontal axis). See Transcript 4.4.
(Photograph: Götz Hoeppe)
Note: The online version shows the colors of the original figure.

138 Otfried: This plot is <u>perfect</u>

139 Peter: also fanning out with a bit of a redshift error … And so … if you look at … this part of the plot … higher luminosities … everything is <u>filled</u>

140 Nadine: Mm hm

141 Peter: except for a few <u>voids</u> … right … because of the ((galaxy)) clusters or things like that

142 Otfried: Mm hm

143 Nadine: Then it's thinning out

144 Peter: <u>But</u> … it already starts thinning out at 23 ((mag)) point and a bit … and you can make it more quantitative … but the plot illustrates it … There is a hole caused by <u>incompleteness</u>

145 Nadine: Mm hm

146 Peter: And most galaxies of this whole <u>plot</u> … this is 35.000 galaxies … and <u>90 percent</u> of them are in this section … between 23 ((mag)) and 25 ((mag))

147 Nadine: Mm hm

148 Peter: So almost all galaxies live <u>here</u> ... and hence the hole becomes very <u>prominent</u>. It is not just a second-order correction ... but it just <u>booms</u> through the histogram

As is typical for astronomical surveys, Nadine's catalog is more complete for brighter objects than for faint ones (which tend to be more distant). Peter's plot reminds Otfried and Nadine of how close to the detection limit most galaxies in the sample are (line 146), making sample completeness an issue. Peter argues that errors of the redshift estimation algorithm would also affect the distribution of galaxies in his plot and that these effects conspire for galaxies to cluster in the figure's upper right and lower right parts (the "two big bumps"; Transcript 4.5, line 184). Otfried agrees with this interpretation and concedes defeat, giving up on his claim that there is a "hole in the universe" in the field at this redshift range.

With the completeness issue confirmed, the challenge is how to use as many of the detected galaxies as possible for the analysis while keeping the sample sufficiently complete. Peter asks Nadine to prepare a scatterplot from her "optical plus near-infrared" catalog akin to the one that he made using his "optical-only" catalog and explore it in half-magnitude bins to recognize at which magnitude the artifactual "bumps" dominate the histogram.

Transcript 4.5
184 Peter: If you do the histogram ... for <u>example</u> ... cut at <u>20.5</u> ((*mag*)) and then separately 20.5 ((*mag*)) to <u>21.5</u> ((*mag*)) ... maybe this shows two big bumps and that shows more of a redshift structure. It could be all in the last magnitude bin where it comes from.
185 Otfried: <u>Yeah</u> yeah that's (   )
186 Peter: So one needs to <u>play</u> with these plots to see.

For Peter, "play" is an exploration using the histogram and the scatterplot to distinguish between artifactual "bumps" and real "redshift structure." He illustrates how this can be done by blocking parts of the diagram with one hand (Figure 4.3). Doing so involves making visual assessments:

Transcript 4.6
226 Peter: What I am saying is ... <u>because</u> we don't know what the completeness <u>is</u> ... and we don't have a <u>good</u> handle to produce a reliable completeness <u>map</u> on the <u>spot</u> ... we could try to <u>estimate</u> completeness on the basis of the

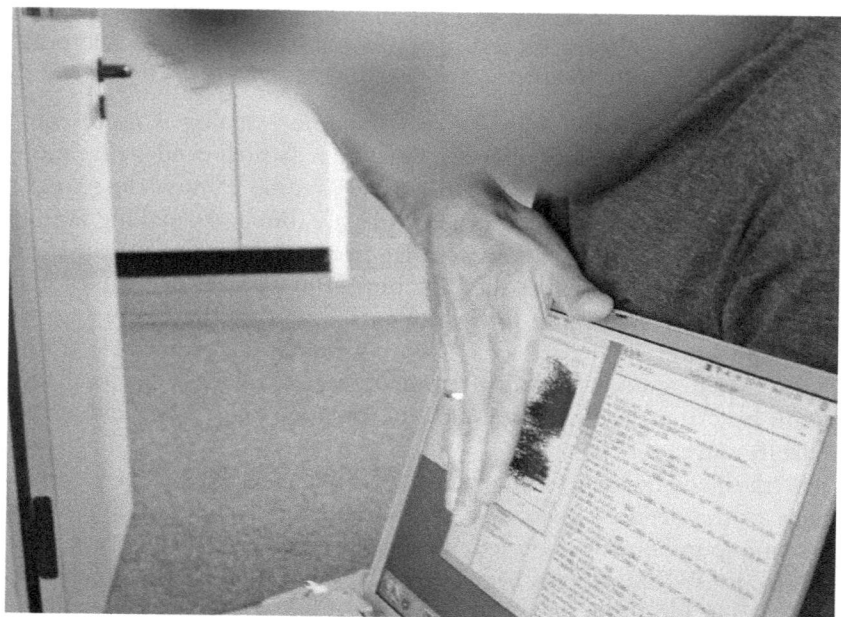

Figure 4.3   Peter demonstrates how Nadine may use the scatterplot to estimate the completeness of her galaxy catalog. See Transcripts 4.5 and 4.6.
(Photograph: Götz Hoeppe)
Note: The online version shows the colors of the original figure.

credibility of the histogram to your eye ... So you plot these histograms ... as long as they look healthy ... at brighter magnitudes ... you say "Everything that I know tells me that this is a reasonable histogram ... so I should believe it." ... And at some point it looks fishy and then you say "I have reasons not to believe that this is the universe." And then it is a judgment call where you make the cut.

Distinguishing between what looks "fishy" and what looks "healthy" in the histogram and the magnitude-redshift plot draws on visual skills specific to those who make photometric redshift surveys of galaxies. It requires an ability to assess "horizontal bands" of points that may be galaxy clusters, structures "fanning out" due to redshift errors, and "bumps" that may be due to redshift focusing, an artifact of the photometric redshift technique (see Chapter 3).

Whereas Otfried and others had previously guided Nadine to use diagrams to recognize mistakes and correct them, here Peter teaches her to use a diagram to "prune" her sample, taking out what would introduce biases into her sample. We may call this a "cultivation" of her dataset, for not only does this work make use of conventional diagram formats as well as conventional practices and units of measurement, such as astronomical magnitudes and colors. Their competent assessment also dwells on scientists' membership in an epistemic community, as suggested by Peter's references to other astronomers' evaluations of their work.[3] Embedded in scientists' uses, diagrams are a means for bringing data into a specific cultural realm. In the end, the sample used in the published paper consists of 10.692 galaxies instead of the 31.747 galaxies in Nadine's deep H band catalog. Besides their use in pruning the dataset, it was through their shared availability in this meeting that these diagrams became resources for instruction, accomplished agreements, and authorization. After all, Otfried (as Nadine's supervisor) had initially disagreed with Peter on how to interpret the $n(z)$ histogram, but changed his mind, affecting what Nadine had to do next.

By choosing to "look at the figures first," Peter and Otfried decided to use Nadine's draft in the way many scientists access the literature. In a manual advising graduate students on how to prepare graphs that Johns Hopkins University astronomy professor Nadia Zakamska posts on her website, we read:

> Figures are probably the most important part of the scientific paper: many readers of your paper will likely read the abstract and glance at the figures to decide whether the paper is worth reading / citing. Therefore, good selection and good presentation of figures is of outmost importance in conveying your results.

Continuing, Zakamska insists that "making figures is a major part [of] your overall research workflow." She adds remarks that point to the challenges that Nadine faced in her project:

> Do your figures make sense? Before showing your figures to anybody, ask yourself whether they make sense. Are your luminosities / masses / sizes reasonable, or orders of magnitude off? (If they are, this is a bug, not a new kind of astronomical object.) If your scatter plot is trending upwards, what would this mean and does that make sense? Interpreting your figures is often exactly what your research is about. Testing your figures with other figures will make you more confident of your results.[4]

Working out whether figures make sense is a continuing learning experience for scientists, restricted not only to novices like Nadine, but including senior scientists like Otfried, whom Peter convinced through his skilled use

---

[3] Note Sacks' (1992, vol. 1, 226–228, 245) remarks on "culture" as members' apparatus for doing and recognizing activities. See also Pinel and Svendsen (2024) on "domesticating data."

[4] zakamska.johnshopkins.edu/COMPUTING/graph_guide.html (accessed July 7, 2025).

of diagrams that there is no hole in the universe in the region they pondered. Note that Zakamska, in mentioning luminosities, masses, and sizes, refers to the absolute physical properties of objects and thus to data of high externality (Pinch 1985). Brought into the realm of known and previously agreed-upon phenomena, the plausibility of data can be assessed more easily.[5]

4.3   Thinking and Working in Diagrammatic Spaces

In the diagrams that Nadine, Peter, and Otfried make and discuss, an enormous amount of information – redshifts and magnitudes of thousands of galaxies – is condensed into a two-dimensional space on less than a single letter-sized page. Nadine can print these diagrams and place them on the table in their midst. Participants in the discussion can point to details and agree on what they see.[6] Diagrams are "fields for interaction" (Alač 2011). They literally enable discussants to "get on the same page." Of course, Nadine, Peter, and Otfried do not only point at their diagrams – they talk along with the pointing.[7] Doing so aids them in agreeing, prompting questions, eliciting requests for clarification, and expressing disagreement.

Then there is the operability of diagrams. Diagrams do not merely *show* something – one can *do* things with them, *operate* with them. Thus, by adding hand-drawn shapes to Nadine's histogram (Figure 4.1), Peter can abstract what he sees in it to illustrate a contrast with his expectations. By sequentially hiding parts of the scatterplot that he generated with his laptop computer, Peter can reason about, and demonstrate, what causes the dip in Nadine's histogram. This operability dwells on diagrams' curious "double life" in which the concreteness of their flat surface coalesces with an abstract space (Krämer 2022). When we point at the surface of a diagram, we often point at the material and the abstract at the same time.[8]

---

[5] See the discussion in Chapter 3 on calibration.

[6] In some ways this summarizes Latour's (1986) notion of "immutable mobiles." How essential diagrams are to interpretations of data is illustrated, for example, by Anscombe's (1973) famous quartet of four sets of points in a plane that, despite identical averages, linear regression line slope, error of this slope, and regression coefficients, suggest quite different functional relations (see also Tufte 1983, 13–14; Sainani 2016). Pearson (1956), Tukey (1962), and Tukey and Wilk (1966) provide influential early statements on visualization in data analysis. See Hullman and Gelman (2021) for a historical review.

[7] Enfield and Sidnell (2022, 107) note that when paired with pointing, "language becomes both an instrument and an object of accountability."

[8] Husserl (1970 [1954]) claimed that science is moving toward evermore abstract accounts of nature, but the embodiment and materiality of making and using diagrams implies that a move toward abstraction is not a one-way road: "Abstraction and concretion intertwine, they complement each other" (Krämer 2014, 347).

Many diagrams are the result of communal agreement and tradition: they are conventional. This includes that time is usually plotted along the x-axis, advancing to the right, and that north is shown at the top of most maps.[9] Nadine's work progressed from using photographic pixel exposures to individual objects' spectral energy distributions (SEDs) to representations of statistical properties of galaxy populations (cf. Figures 3.3, 3.8, and 3.9). These diagrams are specific to astronomy and common in galaxy evolution studies. Interpreting them properly is an acquired skill. Many researchers are experienced viewers and users of such diagrams, and this makes these diagrams resources for social accountability, as I will examine later in this chapter.

In Nadine's work, the SED of a single galaxy (such as in Figures 3.3 and 4.5b) is meaningful and potentially interesting, but, to represent a galaxy population's properties in a scatterplot,[10] the complexity of SED shapes must be reduced.[11] One means to do so is to define what astronomers refer to as colors. This notion is based on our visual perception, where, for example, an object looks blue if it radiates or reflects more light of visible short wavelengths than of longer wavelengths. In astronomy, colors are defined as the ratio of the flux density ("brightness") measured in different wavebands. Since magnitudes are defined as a logarithm of flux density, colors are the difference of magnitudes in two wavebands.[12] The color I − J is the difference of flux measured in the I and J bands. Thus defined, a color picks out one of the many bits of information contained in a SED.[13]

Well-chosen color differences can be suited to represent important properties of stellar and galactic populations. Color-magnitude diagrams (in which the brightness of objects is plotted over a characteristic color; see Figure 4.4) and color-color diagrams (in which measurements of two

---

[9] As Espeland and Stevens (2008, 424) point out, popular primers on graphical representation, like Tufte's (1983) *The Visual Display of Quantitative Information*, present lessons that are both technical and normative. Norms are relative to epistemic communities. In diagrams pertaining to cosmology and galaxy evolution, time is commonly plotted along the x-axis, but advancing to the left (since redshift – an observable – increases to the right and correlates with lookback time).

[10] Friendly and Wainer (2021, 121) argue that scatterplots, in which two different measurements of objects are plotted on perpendicular axes, "may be considered the most versatile and generally useful invention in the entire history of statistical graphics." See also Sainani (2016). In work with large datasets, density plots like Figure 4.4 are increasingly popular.

[11] This selection always comes along with a reduction of information. The ca. 35,000 galaxies represented in Figures 4.2 and 4.3, and the radiation they emit, have many other features besides their R band magnitudes and redshifts.

[12] This is because the logarithm of a fraction is the logarithm of the argument in the nominator minus the logarithm of the argument in the denominator.

[13] As colors reduce the complexity of data at the cost of a loss of transmitted information, they can be conceived as an example of a history of the compression of information using media that Sterne (2012) describes.

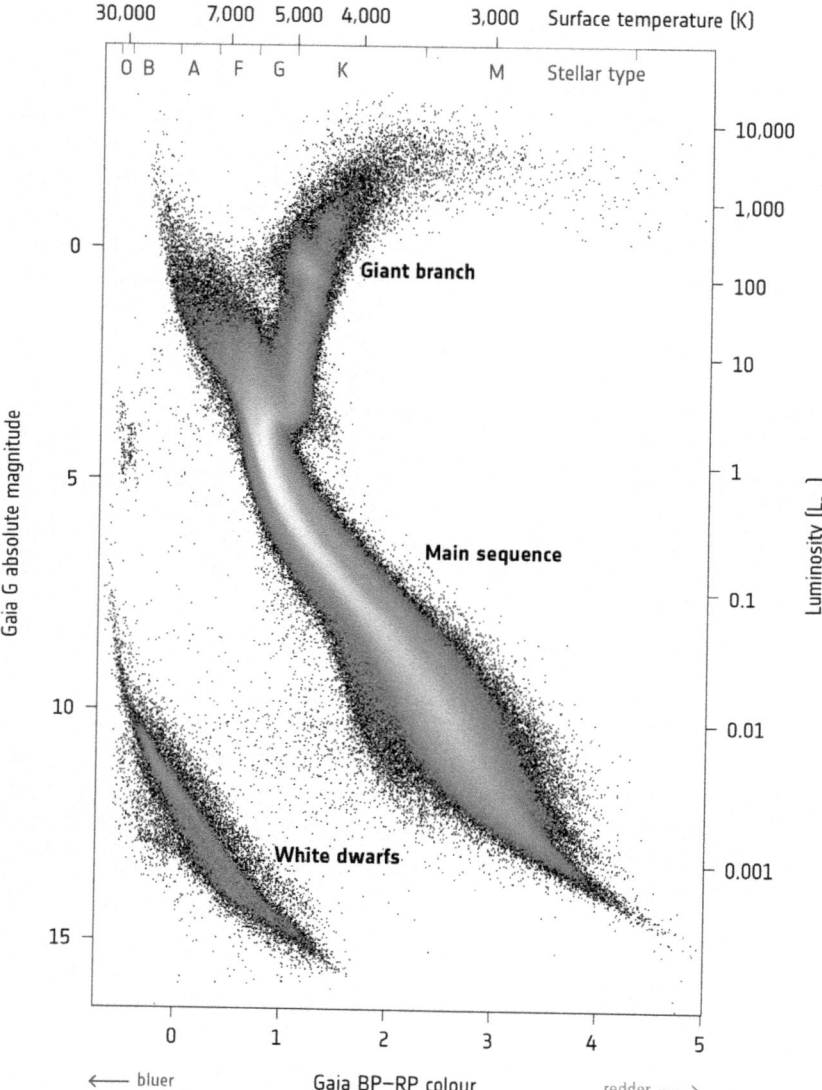

Figure 4.4   Hertzsprung–Russell Diagram of four million stars from measurements of the European Space Agency's Gaia spacecraft. Shown are the absolute magnitudes (a measure of luminosity) as a function of color (the ratio of flux measured in two optical wavebands). Here the scale does not represent the stars' physical colors but is a measure of the density of stars in the diagram: black dots represent individual stars, while shades of gray correspond to an increasing density of stars in the diagram. (© ESA/Gaia/DPAC 2018) Note: The online version shows the colors of the original figure.

different colors of stars or galaxies are plotted against each other, say I – J vs. J – H; see Figure 4.5a) reveal that measurements of stars and galaxies are not distributed randomly in these diagrammatic spaces. They cluster in "sequences," "branches," and "clouds," but seem lacking in "valleys" and "deserts." Astronomers interpret these distributions as clues to the effects of mass, chemical composition, evolutionary stage, and environment.[14] These diagrams mark representational spaces in and through which objects of scientific discourse are defined. As Michael Lynch and Steve Woolgar (1990, 13) argue, scientific objects and representations are "inextricably connected."[15] Diagrams materialize contexts of accountability (cf. Chapter 3). Diagrammatical accountabilities are social accountabilities.

Note, eventually, how sketches on paper and other media matter to discussions of diagrams and further computational uses of data. These include Peter's sketches in his printed copy of Nadine's draft (Figure 4.1) and Otfried's blackboard sketches (cf. Figure 5.4). Such sketches are often transient, wiped off the blackboard or discarded in a paper bin after their use in interaction.[16]

4.4 "Weird Objects in Color-Color Space": Discoveries as Resistance in Diagrams

While the dip in Nadine's $n(z)$ histogram inspired Otfried to argue for a "hole in the universe," the diagrams that Peter generated on his laptop computer made this interpretation unviable. Loosely speaking, the dip did not resist these researchers' scrutiny. Conversely, it seems that researchers would accept a discovery claim only when an anomalous feature in diagrammatic space resists efforts of its normalization or removal.

Let us examine this point further by considering a serendipitous, data-driven discovery in which the use of diagrams was critical. This episode

---

[14] The most widely known stellar color-magnitude diagram in astronomy is the Hertzsprung–Russell Diagram (Figure 4.4). Named after two early twentieth-century scientists, all astronomy students encounter it in their training and often use it to learn to make assessments of sameness, difference, and "reasonable agreement" (Kuhn 1961). See Spence and Garrison (1993) as well as Friendly and Wainer (2021, 149–151).

[15] Among a large literature, see Lynch (1985b) and Rheinberger (1997, 102–113) on representational spaces, Larkin and Simon (1987) as well as Alač (2011) on diagrammatic reasoning, and Wimsatt (1990) and de Regt (2017) on the use of visualizations for scientific understanding.

[16] As Ochs et al. (1994) observe, "contingently transient visual representations (...) are nevertheless an important means by which physicists work through problems of understanding and come to a consensus on matters of interpretation." It is possible to regard such sketches as continuous with scientists' gestures (Myers 2015).

focuses on the work of Arjen van der Wel, in 2011 a postdoctoral scholar and member of the Cosmic Assembly Near-IR Deep Extragalactic Legacy Survey (CANDELS) collaboration. CANDELS was an international team of researchers that used WFC3 (Wide-Field Camera 3), then a new camera on the Hubble Space Telescope (HST), to add deep near-infrared exposures in three wavebands (the I, J, and H bands) to existing data of GOODS-South, a much-observed deep field in the southern sky. In early 2011, the first CANDELS galaxy catalog of 34,930 objects became available to its team members.[17] Van der Wel used it to inspect what these new data could reveal about old massive galaxies at redshift 2, a class of objects that he had studied before and was now trying to examine at a higher angular resolution. To identify candidate objects, he searched the new catalog for entries with notable Balmer breaks, a marked discontinuity in the spectral continuum, which, for redshift 2 galaxies, is found between the I and J bands. Thus, van der Wel first selected objects of certain I − J colors from the catalog and then added more data, including the J − H colors, to assess their viability as candidate old massive galaxies at redshift 2. In an interview six years later, he reflects on this experience. A glossary of key terms follows the transcript (see Box 4.1).

> *Transcript 4.7*
> 1 Arjen van der Wel: I was looking for old galaxies ... old massive galaxies that also have a jump in ... say ... I − J. And then ... that is the Balmer break. It was the first time we had these data that we could ... So at redshift 2 we knew about old galaxies. But with this new camera ... the WFC3 on Hubble ((*Space Telescope*)) ... it was the first time we could get good insights into their structure and morphology. The previous camera NICMOS had <u>some</u> data ... but this ((*WFC3*)) was clearly the next big thing. With the initial dataset I was just curious ... what they would look like. So I didn't have SED fits or anything yet ... this was just a photometric catalog. So I tried this I − J color where galaxies in this redshift range around 2 would be <u>red</u> ... and then the J − H ... the redder color ... should be pretty <u>blue</u> ... again ... because SEDs are supposed to look like that.
>   And then I found these things that were <u>way</u> too blue in J − H. So the SED would look like <u>this</u>

---

[17] A refined version of this catalog was later published as Guo et al. (2013).

((draws into the air with his hand: a descending line with one peak)). It didn't look like that ((draws into the air with his hand: a descending line without the peak, but a drop at a certain point, indicating the Balmer break)). I thought that must be a mistake. So I started looking into these objects. It's not a sensible ... it is not a sensible SED. But there was nothing wrong with the photometry. So I looked at the images to see if there is something there. Yes ... it's <u>fainter</u> ((*laughs*)) to the surrounding ... that's where the light comes from. But now there is forty of them in the entire field.

2 Götz: So that was all first in the catalog? You didn't look at the images at first?

3 Arjen van der Wel: <u>First</u> the catalog and <u>then</u> the images ... to see if there is something <u>wrong</u> with the photometry ... right? If they all live on the edge of the image or if they all live next to a bright star ... right? Okay. You look at the images ... and it's ... Okay that's why these things are there and they're fake. Could also be the initial catalog with this new data ... so who knows what is wrong with it ... right? But it looked like they were real ... so then at some point you start thinking of outlandish explanations ... including that it could be an <u>emission</u> line that makes that one filter very <u>bright</u>. And that turned out to be the case.

Box 4.1 Glossary of terms (in order of appearance in the transcript)

I	I band (around 0.81 micrometer)
J	J band (around 1.25 micrometer)
H	H band (around 1.65 micrometer)
Balmer break	A feature in the spectra of galaxies that provides clues to the age and history of their stellar population
SED	Spectral Energy Distribution
SED fit	Fit of a galaxy model spectrum to flux measurements in various spectral bands, used to estimate the redshift and physical parameters of the galaxy
Photometric catalog	Table of photometric measurements of galaxies detected in the survey area

By querying the new CANDELS catalog, van der Wel thus found forty or so objects with I − J colors characteristic of old massive galaxies at redshift 2, but these objects had J − H colors unlike those galaxies. Their J band fluxes were unexpectedly high. This prompted van der Wel to inspect where in the processed photographs these objects are. If all these objects were near bright stars or at the edge of the field − notorious sources of image artifacts −, their photometry and colors would be questionable. But this is not what van der Wel found. Instead, he saw objects that appeared fainter and smaller than the massive galaxies for which he had searched.

Six years after this episode, van der Wel did not recall when he first used diagrams to make sense of these anomalous objects. He told me that "often I was just playing around by hand first … and I haven't saved that." But when he browsed through the computer scripts pertaining to this project, he noticed that "those color-color plots … they appear very early." He had prepared them for various combinations of colors as he explored these anomalous objects' properties.

After accepting that these curious objects were not artifactual, van der Wel gathered the CANDELS team's expertise and found additional data to compose a manuscript describing this discovery. At a CANDELS teleconference in July 2011, at which about fifteen team members were present, Arjen van der Wel presented an advanced draft. He opens the meeting with reviewing it. Figure 4.5 depicts the diagrams to which he refers. A glossary of key terms follows the transcript (see Box 4.2).

Transcript 4.8
I guess I'll talk for two minutes through the figures … basically. What's happening is here is that we have noticed weird objects in color-color space. In ((*Figure 4.5a*)) you see outliers in I − J versus J − H … ehm … just things with weird colors … and if you look at ((*Figure 4.5b*)) I show SEDs of those that are in ERS ((*Early Release Science*)) territory and have all similar SEDs … very flat in F(ν) … so β = − 2 in F(λ) … and they stick out in the J band. After thinking about that for a while we concluded that these must be bright emission lines that contribute pretty much the same amount of light in the J band as in the ((*spectral*)) continuum … implying very large equivalent widths … about 1000 ((*Ångstrom*)) or 1500 ((*Ångstrom*)) in the observed frame. That's quite crazy … ehm … so we checked what if a few of those objects might overlap with existing grism ((*spectra*)) data … so Amber ((*Straughn*)) and Ben ((*Weiner*)) looked at that and that's what's shown in ((*Figure 4.5c*)). Among the 52 candidates that I talk about in the current draft there are four that fall within grism exposures and all four are [OIII] emitters. You can see it's [OIII] because of the asymmetry of the [OIII] line … it has two components … that's

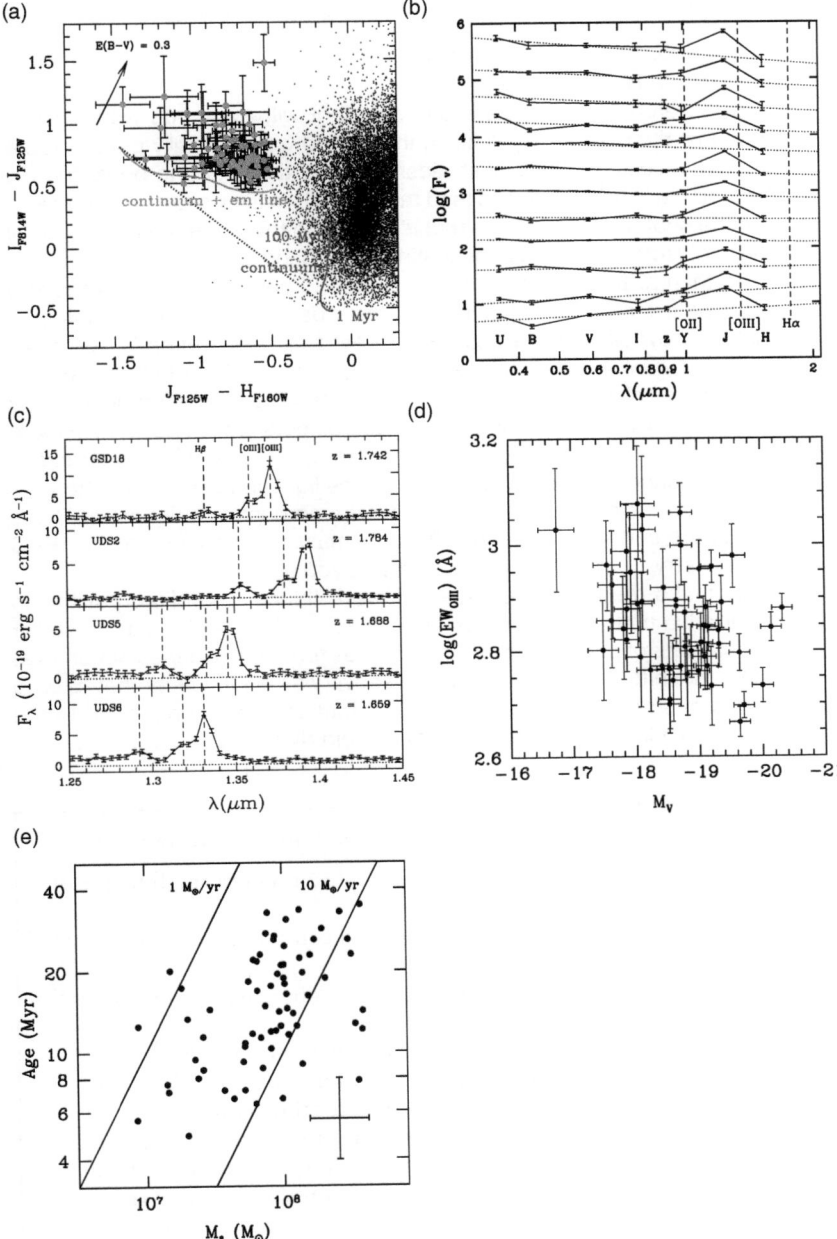

Figure 4.5   Figures of Arjen van der Wel's manuscript as discussed in the text.
Figure captions omitted. (© American Astronomical Society.
Reproduced with permission.)
Note: The online version shows the colors of the original figure.

4959 ((Ångstrom)) and 5007 ((Ångstrom)) ... and then in most cases there is a clear indication of Hβ.

So ... ehm ... this is perfectly consistent with what you would derive from just the photometry. [OIII] in the J band would usually put Hα in the H band unless the thing is at redshift higher than 1.6 and boost the Hα beyond the H band. You can read more details in the paper ... of course ... but the photometry suggests that it's [OIII]. So that's the premise ... for all these objects that [OIII] is dominating this J band excess light.

So then ... from the photometry alone ... I derive the luminosities and equivalent widths of the [OIII] line ... the V band continuum luminosity ... just to show what these objects ... what their distribution is ... I show that in ((*Figure 4.5d*)) ... this is also given in the table. And these are the basic properties that I use together with the Starburst99 model to say what these objects are. And what these objects are is shown in ((*Figure 4.5e*)). So they're typically 10^8 solar mass ... 10 to 50 million year old ... so very young ... starbursts ... Now all the light you see is from the star-burst and it is hard to really constrain the amount of older stars. These things are certainly less than 10^9 solar masses if you look at the IRAC photometry ... that's the best constraint you get.

So that's the basic properties of these things ... and we put this in a narrative that's more or less as follows ... The idea is that the stellar populations of present-day dwarf galaxies formed in a series of bursts at some redshift ... and we pitch this discovery as evidence for that. Strong bursts of star formation at redshift 1.7 that basically correspond to the stellar populations that we see today in old dwarf galaxies.

Box 4.2 Glossary of terms (in order of appearance in the transcript)

$F(\nu)$	Flux density of the spectral continuum as a function of the frequency of light
$F(\lambda)$	Flux density of the spectral continuum as a function of the wavelength of light
β	Exponent of the power law approximation of a spectral continuum
Grism	A grating prism that combines imaging and spectroscopy; the WFC3 camera on the HST has a grism mode that was used for this study
Equivalent width	Measure of the broadening of lines in galaxy spectra. Large equivalent widths indicate intense star formation
[OIII]	"Forbidden" twice ionized emission line of oxygen, at rest wavelengths 4959 and 5007 Ångstrom, a tracer of star formation in galaxies
Hβ	Hydrogen emission line, a tracer of star formation in galaxies

Hα	Hydrogen emission line, a tracer of star formation in galaxies
Starburst99	Computer model widely used to estimate star formation histories from observed spectra (Leitherer et al. 1999)
IRAC	Infrared Array Camera on board the NASA spacecraft Spitzer for measuring mid-infrared radiation
starburst	Period of intense star formation in a galaxy

Presenting the draft as a commentary on its figures, van der Wel does not mention his initial concern with image artifacts. Instead, he begins his report with noticing these "weird objects in color-color space." Represented as red dots with error bars in Figure 4.5a, their distance in the scatterplot from "normal" galaxies – visible as a "cloud" of black points – appears to be a measure of their "weirdness."

Van der Wel attributes this offset to the brighter-than-expected J band fluxes in these objects' SEDs (Figure 4.5b). He and his colleagues next suspect that the excess flux is due to a single emission line in the J band which adds to the light emitted by the galaxies' spectral continuum. To add the flux required to produce the excess J band light, such lines would need to be so bright and broad that van der Wel calls them "crazy," and this explanation "outlandish" (Transcript 4.7). However, so-called grism spectra are available for four of these objects (Figure 4.5c),[18] and these show that at least for them the excessive J band flux is indeed due to bright and broad emission lines characteristic of intense star formation events (starbursts). Surmising that this applies to all fifty-two anomalous objects in the sample, van der Wel plots the emission line widths versus the galaxies' luminosities, after using a cosmological standard model to infer distances from estimated redshifts (Figure 4.5d). Plugging the measured values into a model that simulates spectra of star bursting galaxies (Starburst99; Leitherer et al. 1999) yields absolute physical parameters and shows "what these objects are" (Figure 4.5e).

Van der Wel's draft did not include images of these galaxies, but only the diagrams shown in Figure 4.5. At the end of the teleconference, when edits to the draft were discussed, one participant remarked: "I'd think like we'd all like to see pictures of the galaxies … at least." Van der Wel responded: "They're little <u>dots</u>," prompting chuckling among participants and arguably

---

[18] Grisms are elements in a camera combining a grating with a prism to record spectra of sources in a photograph. The WFC3 camera on the HST is equipped with a grism.

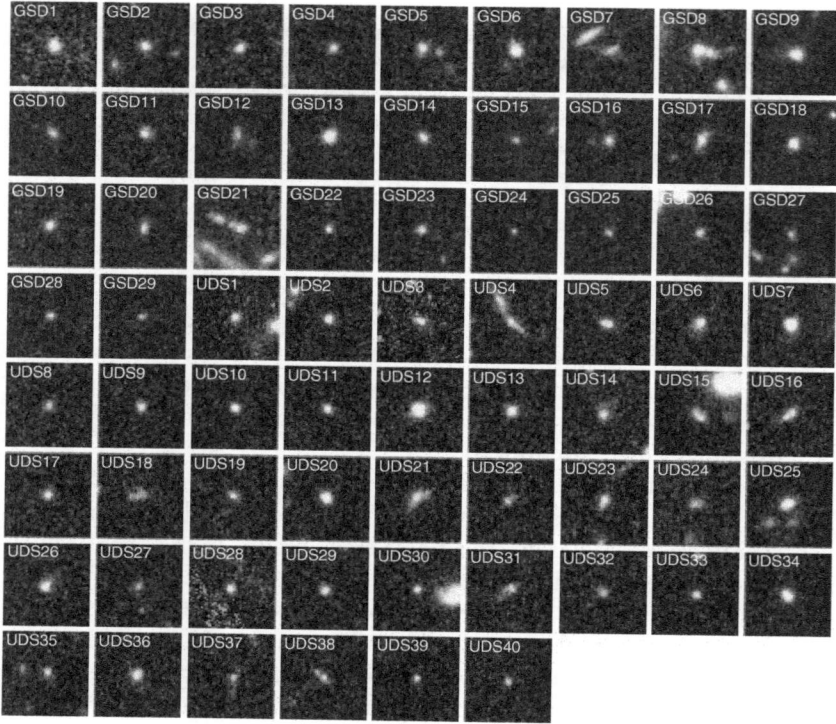

Figure 4.6   False color images of the galaxies in van der Wel's sample, made using Hubble Space Telescope I, J, and H exposures. This is Figure 2 of the published article (van der Wel et al. 2011), inserted between Figures 1 and 2 (Figures 4.5a and 4.5b) of the draft discussed in the text. Most galaxies seem to be compact, but some appear to be extended or have multiple components. (© American Astronomical Society/NASA/ESA/ Hubble Space Telescope. Reproduced with permission.)
Note: The online version shows the colors of the original figure.

implying that these objects look inconspicuous. But, subsequently, he and his coauthors agreed to include a panel of images of the sample's (by then) sixty-nine galaxies in the publication, cut out from the survey images (Figure 4.6).

Thus, it turned out that the "jump" between the I and J bands in these objects' SEDs does not indicate the Balmer break characteristic of old massive galaxies at redshift 2, but is due to bursts of star formation causing an emission line in low-mass dwarf galaxies at redshifts around 1.7. This is a serendipitous, data-driven discovery. Van der Wel's account turns surprisingly "weird" objects into reasonable ones by successively demonstrating that an unusual spectral feature is physically meaningful in an interpretation that locates these objects in a communally accepted narrative of galaxy evolution. Known to van der Wel and other CANDELS members, many nearby (low redshift) dwarf galaxies contain populations of what are now old stars that may well have formed at redshifts around 1.7.[19]

Note how this move from color differences to absolute physical properties is a move toward higher externality and greater evidential specificity (Pinch 1985; cf. Chapter 3). Only at high externality is the discourse on galaxy evolution liberated from specific observational detail, such that the Balmer break of redshift 2 galaxies is between the I and J bands. Thanks to this narrativization, these objects are no longer a conundrum to van der Wel and his colleagues. Instead, they confirm and strengthen an existing scenario of low-mass galaxy evolution.[20] Neither image artifacts nor questions of survey completeness (as in Peter's critique earlier) challenge this discovery and van der Wel and his coauthors introduce a name (Extreme Emission-Line Galaxies) and acronym (EELGs) for these objects that have been adopted in the literature since. But the strength of this narrative arguably is its tie with the diagrams. As Arjen van der Wel insists: "Diagrams are the <u>most</u> important things. I always make the figures first. If they don't <u>show</u> a story ... there <u>is</u> no story."

4.5 Playing with Data

Both Peter and Arjen van der Wel emphasize the importance of play in their work with data, and for both play is tied to using diagrams. Peter responds to Nadine's histogram, made late in her project, and suggests play to avoid incompleteness issues that may invalidate an interpretation. The play that Peter proposes is systematic: moving from bin to bin across the scatterplot (Figure 4.3) and assessing how their inclusion affects the $n(z)$ histogram's shape. Arjen van der Wel's play is more exploratory, as he constructs various color-color plots, hoping to get a better sense of anomalous objects. Peter and Arjen van der Wel both use play as they face

---

[19] Van der Wel et al. (2011). EELGs have been identified at redshifts from 0.2 (in the nearby universe, where they seem to be identical with the so-called Green Pea galaxies; Cardamone et al. 2009) to 9 (in the distant, early universe; Llerena et al. 2024).

[20] Note van der Wel's repeated use of the discourse marker "so" in Transcripts 4.7 and 4.8, which may mark the continuation of his storytelling, indicate preliminary conclusions, and initiate incipient consequential next actions which typically refer to diagrams and include, in line 1 of Transcript 4.7, graphical gestures. In Transcripts 4.2 to 4.6, Peter uses "so" similarly. See Bolden (2009) on various uses of "so," as well as Netz (1999) and de Freitas (2012) for links of (mathematical) diagrams with narrative structures.

uncertainty: "What is still acceptable?" (Peter). "What does this mean?" (van der Wel).

Play is an essential part of scientists' practical methodology. In their play, Peter and Arjen van der Wel do not pursue joy aimlessly or participate in a game that is inconsequential for life beyond its boundaries – aspects of play that philosophers have mostly pondered.[21] They rather explore possible alternative actions for deciding which among them to adopt and make consequential. Their play is set apart from ordinary, sequential courses of action by a metacommunicative frame (indicating that "this is play"; Bateson 1972), involving actions that are often deemed reversible (Huizinga 1955). By acknowledging that there are several alternatives of which one may be favored, play is an "intellectual insurance policy" (Nguyen 2022, 269).[22] Both Peter and Arjen van der Wel examine what they can get away with, that is, what other scientists will accept – presuming, conversely, that this is what they themselves find acceptable in others' work.

Play is tied to diagrams because diagrams make different alternatives visible and comparable. In data-rich science, they provide a sort of playground for exploratory work. Always done with somebody or something, and bounded spatially or by rules, play is often marked by movement in relation to a visual structure such as a field, board, or diagram. Thus, as psychologist F. J. J. Buytendijk observed, "the domain of play is the domain of the image" (1933, 129; my translation). How play will unfold is not knowable in advance. To play means to relinquish one's control: "one does not only play but is being played with" (Buytendijk 1933, 117). Employed when facing uncertainty, the outcome of play is not predictable. Surprises must be possible.[23]

Scientists play with data of various externalities and evidential specificities (Pinch 1985). This play includes early stages of data analysis. Consider

---

[21] Huizinga (1955), Suits (1978), Fink (2016), and Nguyen (2020).

[22] This resembles the "dirt gate" that Mody (2001, 26) observed in the work of materials scientists, where dirt in samples "seems to be an 'even though' gate; if the desired finding appears 'even though' dirt is present, then the finding will be more durable and, for practical reasons, more valuable." In astronomers' uses of machine learning, adversarial attacks play a similar role of introducing variations into data and models that allow assessing the robustness of interpretations (Huang et al. 2022).

[23] There is a resemblance of "playing with data" with "exploratory experimentation" (Steinle 1997; Franklin 2005) and "tinkering" (Lévi-Strauss 1966; Jacob 1977; Knorr Cetina 1981), but accounts of the latter two typically neglect uses of diagrams and visualizations, whereas descriptions of laboratory experimentation as "games" (Jacob 1982; Rheinberger 1997) and of board games as an analogy for scientific practice (Latour and Woolgar 1986, ch. 6; Sormani 2015) do not. Tukey and Wilk (1966, 696–697) already noticed that "data analysis is like doing experiments" and emphasized the role of visualization therein (see also Hullman and Gelman 2021).

the work of Patrick, a postdoctoral scholar in Otfried's group. Whereas Nadine worked on the A2713 dataset, Patrick was to analyze the MAMBO dataset of another galaxy cluster, A2714. New to the template-fitting technique and to data from the Omega near-infrared camera, Patrick was troubled that the slowness of his computer restricted his ability to "play" with the parameter settings in the data-reduction pipeline:

Transcript 4.9

1 Patrick: It took <u>forever</u> … you could not explore the parameter space in the reductions … for if every step takes several <u>hours</u> you have to think in advance if ((*the settings are*)) okay … and you cannot <u>play</u> around much. At first it took me some time … because I always made a mistake somewhere. I wasn't <u>familiar</u> with it … and so you play with it a bit more. And then … when you've played it through five times or so … and you <u>understand</u> the dataset … then it is … then you do the final data reduction and that's <u>it</u>.

2 Götz: Playing with what? The parameters?

3 Patrick: Well … I used to work with spectra and there are diverse possibilities. Here it is like that as well … and you wonder: Should I do another <u>superflat</u> correction? Should I subtract the <u>background</u>? How does it <u>look</u> like? Do I <u>improve</u> things? (…) You can think about much of this in advance … but in the end you want to see how it <u>looks</u> like.

His computer's apparent slowness invites Patrick to reason about what may be unremarkable otherwise: suspending sequential work for a period of play oriented toward deciding which action among potential alternatives to choose and make consequential for subsequent work. He is aware of the choices available to him in terms of procedures and the "parameter space," and he argues that it was through his play that he could properly "understand" the set of digital exposures constituting his data. Doing so involves assessments of previous actions. Patrick's mode of play is more interactive and faster paced than the play that Peter and Arjen van der Wel describe. But just like them, Patrick constructs alternatives that he assesses visually. His play is tied to diagrams as well, if we recognize digital photographic exposures as such.[24]

---

[24] Patrick's on-screen play arguably bears a resemblance with single-player video gaming (cf. Sudnow 1983; Reeves et al. 2017). For early remarks on astronomers' play with digital images, see Disney (1979). Note also Derrida's (1978) remarks on freedom and constraint in the play that certain (logical) structures enable (cf. Fortun 2009).

4.6 Accountable Exposures

So far, we have examined diagrams as resources for intersubjective action, for pruning a dataset, for surveying complex datasets, for making a scientific discovery, and as venues for doing so exploratively and playfully. In this work, diagrams are resources for holding others to account and this commonly happens far beyond face-to-face encounters. This accountability is not restricted to histograms and scatterplots but includes the photographic exposures (like Figure 4.6) on which the measurements they represent are based. It is at the micro-level of pixels that visual assessments meet the rigor and intersubjective force of mathematical notation.[25] Let me illustrate this with how individual exposures can be made accountable to globally accepted phenomena.

Remember that digital photographic exposures are two-dimensional "arrays of numbers" (Lynch 1991a; Chapter 1). Not only can one represent with diagrams how these exposures are processed arithmetically (Figure 4.7). If we adopt philosopher Charles Sanders Peirce's understanding of diagrams as "signs whose parts have analogous relations to those of their objects" (Alač 2011, 41), then we can recognize that many astronomers take digital pixel exposures to be diagrammatic in this sense.[26] Thus, a common way to make a completeness map for examining the limit sensitivity of a photographic galaxy survey – something that Peter wants, but cannot easily have, for Nadine's sample (Transcript 4.6, line 226) – is to randomly insert artificial digital galaxy images of various shapes, sizes, and magnitudes into a wide-field pixel image and examine which fraction of these an object detection code retrieves. This wide-field image is then treated like an image of the sky in which only natural objects are detected.[27]

---

[25] See Chapter 1 and compare Rotman (2000, 58), who insists that "without rigor, mathematics would vanish," since "rigor is not an externally enforced program of foundational hygiene, but rather an intrinsic and inescapable demand proceeding from writing." It is basic to transforming "mathematical intuition into an intersubjective writing/thinking practice." On visual evidence as a resource for accounting practices, see Neyland and Coopmans (2014).

[26] Peirce's notion of iconic signs is not exhausted by (photographic) images, which resemble their objects by looking like them. He also considered diagrams and metaphors as icons, the former because of resembling their objects in the analogous making-up of their parts, the latter because of other kinds of "parallelism" (Peirce 1931–1958 (1934), vol. 2, §277). Thus understood, iconicity reaches beyond what can be seen. Conceived as iconic signs, photographic exposures may likewise be regarded as diagrams which promise new insights into their objects by revealing otherwise hidden analogies when being experimented upon (Peirce 1933, vol. 4, §§530–531).

[27] Among many others, Giavalisco et al. (2004, L97–L98) employ this technique without referencing it, which suggests that it is not in need of being explained to members. See Hoeppe (2020b) for an examination of its use in contesting a discovery claim. Each pixel in a calibrated digital photograph is a measurement; an image is an array of measurements.

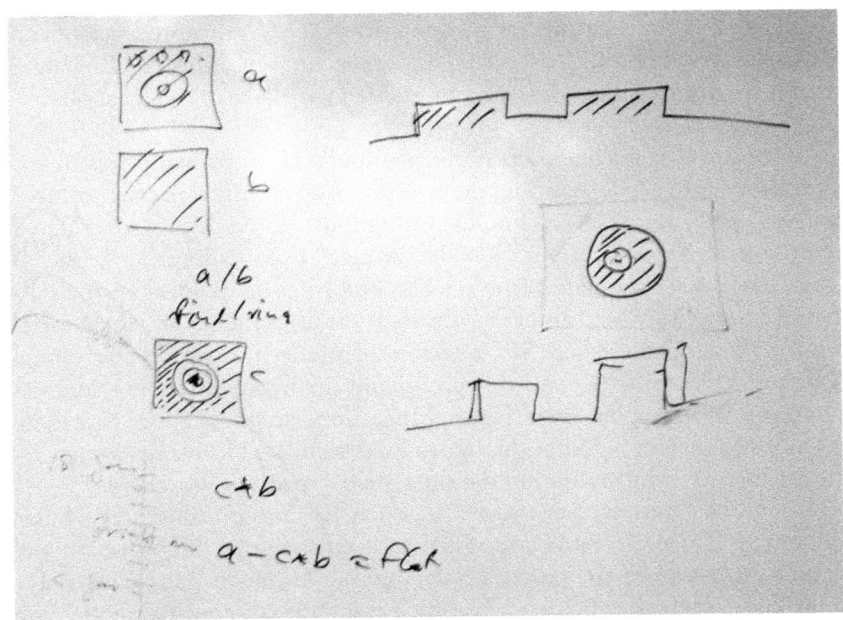

Figure 4.7   Otto's sketch of the sequence of arithmetic operations (left) that Nadine was to apply to remedy her flatfield issue. The outlines of a flatfield exposure (a), a noise pattern (b), and the modeled ring (c) are drawn schematically as square outlines of the infrared camera's 2048 pixels × 2048 pixels. The sketches at the right top and bottom represent cross-sections of the intensity of scattered light across the flatfield.
An arithmetic formula describes how scattered light is to be removed.
See also Figure 3.6. (Photograph: Götz Hoeppe)
Note: The online version shows the colors of the original figure.

Elsewhere I present episodes from the work of the MAMBO team to examine how stabilized, agreed-upon phenomena of astronomical discourse (such as the shapes of stellar and galaxy spectra) can serve as resources for the calibration of photographic exposures (Hoeppe 2019b). One of these episodes describes how Nadine removed the ring-like feature in her flatfield exposures that Otfried and his colleagues considered to be artifactual (cf. Chapters 3 and 5). These scientists oriented to flatfield calibration frames and science exposures in distinct ways. Taken during twilight before stars appear in the sky and lacking as such a referent external to the observing situation, flatfield exposures were not made accountable as images of celestial objects but were held to index a telescope and camera's optical performance only. Intended to help remedying local artifacts, flatfields were manipulated in a pixel-by-pixel way, sometimes by hand, conditional upon their further computational use. In this prospective and retrospective work, calibration frames were recursively adjusted. They were made visually and numerically accountable to artifacts of the local observing situation.

By contrast, team members never manipulated individual pixels in science exposures. Understanding them as indexing cosmic objects, they used science exposures as entire frames throughout. As such, they considered these exposures as "computationally distinct" from calibration frames.[28] They made science images (the science exposures as divided by the flat-field) numerically accountable, through measurements of their pixel values, to template galaxy SEDs (a sort of model) on which communal agreement, reaching beyond this group and involving different evidential contexts, had been achieved before. Thus understood, they shaped these science images as a medium that reproduces stabilized forms of extragalactic astronomy, while retaining the capacity to surprise researchers.[29]

In another episode, I witnessed how Patrick, the postdoctoral scholar quoted in Transcript 4.9, responded to a challenge in his work on the team's exposures of the galaxy cluster A2714. A known issue with stray-light in the camera, much as in Nadine's case, was complicated by the fact that several changes to the telescope's mechanical structure had been made over the four years in which the exposures of A2714 were recorded. Upon closer inspection of the exposures taken at different epochs, Patrick and his supervisor Otfried noticed that stars in the image's corners did not look round (as desired) but appeared to be more and more distorted the further they were away from the image's center. This effect appeared to grow worse over time. Otfried interpreted it as an optical error (astigmatism) caused by changes in the telescope's mechanical structure.

In discussion with Otfried, Patrick first considered using only the inner parts of exposures, where the distortions were small. However, since the cluster galaxies were distributed across the entire field, this would have curtailed the sample size in ways unacceptable for their project. The team's data-reduction software did not allow for consistently correcting artifacts whose shape varied across the images. Patrick next considered abandoning treating his exposures as a unit, but splitting them into a grid of 4 × 4 subfields and correcting the image distortions separately in each subfield.

[28] In flatfield division, science exposures are the dividend and flatfields the divisor, a divisor that is a unitless number (the relative sensitivity of pixels).

[29] In Hoeppe (2019b), I argue that Luhmann's (2012) distinction of medium and form can be brought into a domain of social accountability for describing how the replication of astronomical phenomena reflexively shapes the formatting of digital images as data suited for reuse.

He would then work with sets of sixteen exposures instead of single ones. Although technically feasible, doing so would have dramatically increased the number of choices for which they would have to account. This would have weakened whatever conclusion they could draw from these data. Troubled by this prospect, Otfried decided that Patrick should abandon work on this dataset.

Thus, salvaging the exposures of A2714 would have risked making the data "too soft" for discovery work, because scientists' capacity to attribute distinctions in them to epistemic novelty was compromised. The point is not that the computations involved could not possibly be made to match existing work and claim a discovery, but that only a certain effort to do so seemed legitimate to these researchers. This is a social accountability.

4.7 Discussion: Locality and Distance in Data-Rich Science

I conclude this chapter by pointing out some of these episodes' implications for claims made in science and technology studies about the localness of scientific work. Empirical studies of scientific practice by historians and ethnographers of science have emphasized the local origins of scientific knowledge in laboratories, observatories, and field sites.[30] Some of these studies have examined how such findings travel elsewhere, often only with considerable effort, through arranging public demonstrations and building infrastructure, as well as developing and enforcing calibrations and standards.[31] Leonelli's (2016, 69) notion of "data journeys" takes this image up and makes it productive as one way to consider data as "tools for communication."[32]

Historian Mario Biagioli (2006) takes issue with the "localist thrust" that he blames mostly on the sociology of scientific knowledge. Biagioli observes that the focus on the local has led to ascribing to distance a "central but negative role in recent interpretive models in science studies and the history of science" (Biagioli 2006, 22). It is exemplified, he claims, by Harry Collins' (1992, 145) notion that "[d]istance lends enchantment: the more distant in social space or time is the locus of creation of knowledge the more certain it is." Biagioli challenges negative assessments of distance with his study of Galileo Galilei, whom he portrays as a strategic actor

---

[30] See Garfinkel et al. (1981), and Shapin and Schaffer (1985), as well as Henke and Gieryn (2008).
[31] See, for example, Latour (1987) and Galison (2008).
[32] See also Leonelli and Tempini (2020). Borgman and Groth (2025) examine diverse kinds of "distance" in the reuse of scientific data.

who withheld data and delayed sharing it to increase his own authority and aura. Biagioli contends that this demonstrates the productive use of distance in the making not only of authority: "Once we consider the productive roles of distance, knowledge appears as something that is never completely local, not even at its so-called moment of origin" (Biagioli 2006, 74).

When we attend to the social accountabilities involved in data uses, the episodes discussed in this chapter add substance to Biagioli's claim. They show how scientists were oriented throughout toward other researchers and mindful that these would evaluate and assess their work. This was perhaps most clear with Peter's concern about Nadine's histogram, which can be read as a concern about the team's reputation (Transcript 4.3, line 61). But it also mattered to Arjen van der Wel's study, as well as to how Otfried guided Nadine and Patrick to use digital photographic exposures as "workable objects" whose usefulness was not guaranteed initially. Local work was oriented to potential reuses of images (as processed exposures) by researchers elsewhere, as demonstrated by concerns with the integrity of images and with ensuring that, with reasonable effort, their work can be described to others. These scientists display an awareness of being caught in a "web of inferences" regarding their actions (Levinson 1983, 321). Thereby, the distant was always present in work that was ostensibly local.[33]

---

[33] By focusing on "local production," ethnomethodology may appear to confine itself to spatially delimited face-to-face settings. However, as Lynch (1993, 125) insists, it is better understood as describing the production and reproduction of orderliness without "theoretically postulating a homogenous domain" like "panlinguistic structures, cognitive structures, *doxa*, or historical discourses." As described in Chapter 3, astronomers do use globally established phenomena and cosmological models as resources for the orderly production of data. But in many cases, the "production cohort" (Livingston 1987) of reusable digital images includes their possible future users, whose reciprocal perspective on their work data makers anticipate (see Chapter 8). For an extended meditation on the locality of data, see Loukissas (2019). See also Wittgenstein (1978), Warwick (1995), and Rotman (2000) on social accountabilities of notation and computation.

CHAPTER 5

World

Mundane Reason and the Relief
from Trust in Data Makers

5.1 This Chapter's Plan

This chapter examines "opportunistic" uses of "natural" objects and shared assumptions in scientific data analyses and explores what these imply for scientists' trust in the work of other researchers. Assuming that the world that her team observes is coherent helped Nadine to combine data (Chapter 3). As she did so, diagrams were essential tools for diagnosing trouble and for pruning her catalog (a table of measured and estimated galaxy properties; Chapter 4). These scientists resorted to what sociologist Melvin Pollner (1987) called "mundane reasoning": practices for resolving disjunctive experiences that assume a shared public and objective world. A common feature of ordinary social life, this is what Barry Barnes and coauthors (1996, 81) call a "realist strategy."[1]

This chapter examines mundane reasoning further by probing into its resources. I argue that, in data-rich science, a discipline's objects of inquiry are not only topics of research but may also function as resources for its conduct. These objects and their relations can be resources for intersubjective coordination that become available through practices of mediation and materialization. If recognized for their task-specific affordances, these objects can be resources for analyzing data.[2] There is a trade-off between epistemic uses of stable material objects and the placement of trust. In astronomical research, the sky (while not material) is not only an ordering device for assessing and using data of various origin – it is also a resource for the partial relief from trust in data makers.

---

[1] Note that, given my naturalistic approach, I am not taking a position on any philosophical version of "realism" and "world."

[2] Psychologist J. J. Gibson (1977, 67–68) argues that "the affordance of anything is a specific combination of the properties of its substance and its surface" for use in any perceiving animal's project (cf. Chapter 1).

5.2   "Now We Can Show Real Science!": Seeing the Same Things (Again)

Sociologist Harry Collins (1992, 19) once argued that replication is "the scientifically institutionalized counterpart to the stability of perception." According to a popular understanding, observations and experiments are properly scientific only when they are replicable – that is, if an experiment or observation yields the same result as that done by someone else who followed the same procedures. But in science there is no simple "looking" and "seeing" with the unaided eyes. Most scientists rather "look" with complexes of technology and "see" something in elaborately processed data.[3] Consider observations in astronomy. As astronomer David W. Hogg puts it, "[a]ll of astronomy and astrophysics is built on the observation and reobservation of sources on the sky."[4] Whether or not replication is their aim, new observations should improve on existing ones or add to them meaningfully, such as when variable objects are observed again. But for many astronomers there is not just one sky. Some of them use infrared telescopes and cameras to observe what they call the "infrared sky," others use radio telescopes to observe the "radio sky," and still others use x-ray telescopes to observe the "x-ray sky."[5]

One of the newest skies that astronomers study is the "microwave sky." Observed at millimeter and centimeter radio wavelengths, its dominant component is the cosmic microwave background (CMB), a thermal radiation from all directions whose flux density is not entirely uniform, but, when mapped, exhibits subtle fluctuations.[6] Cosmologists widely agree that these fluctuations were "imprinted" on the CMB soon after the Big Bang almost 14 billion years ago. Observations of their distribution, intensity, and polarization are rich sources of information about the early universe.

In March 2014, Princeton University astrophysicist David Spergel gave a talk on the state of CMB studies at New York University's Physics Department.[7] Early in his presentation, Spergel compared two grayscale pixel maps of the microwave background's fluctuation pattern in a patch

---

[3] These "lookings" and "seeings" are socially organized phenomena (cf. Coulter and Parsons 1991). "Lookers" and "seers" are culturally trained (Fleck 1979 [1935]).
[4] hoggresearch.blogspot.ca/2008/03/budavari-and-szalay.html (accessed July 7, 2025).
[5] See Cordes (2012) on the "radio sky," Moore and Kasliwal (2019) on the "infrared sky," Maselli et al. (2010) on the "x-ray sky," and Sehgal et al. (2010) on the "microwave sky."
[6] Durrer (2008), Peebles (2020, 2022), and Perović and Ćirković (2024).
[7] David Spergel, "Cosmology after Planck," lecture at New York University (NYU), March 27, 2014, youtube.com/watch?v=j3fHkQa6818 (accessed July 7, 2025).

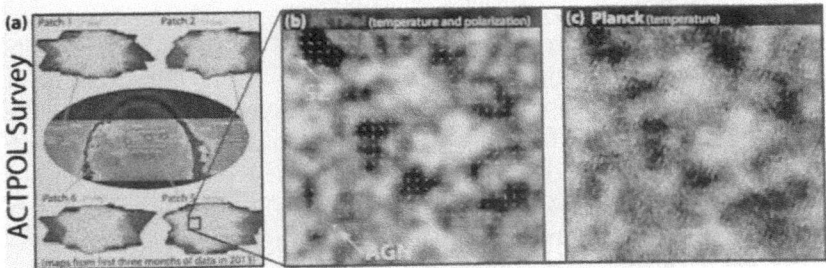

Figure 5.1   Presentation slide from David Spergel's lecture at New York University, showing two grayscale pixel maps of the microwave background fluctuation pattern of a patch in the sky. One is based on measurements taken with the Atacama Cosmology Telescope (ACT) in Chile using a transition-edge sensor, a sensitive quantum detector (center). The other map was made using a different detector design (a bolometer) onboard the Planck spacecraft (right). The left panel shows the location of this patch on a map of the sky. (© D. Spergel/Princeton University/ESA/Planck 2014)
Note: The online version shows the colors of the original figure.

of the sky (see Figure 5.1). One was based on measurements taken with the ACT in Chile using a transition-edge sensor (a sensitive semi-conducting detector); the other was made with a bolometer (a kind of sensitive thermometer) onboard the European Space Agency's Planck spacecraft. Using a laser pointer to highlight similarities in the grayscale patterns, Spergel explains:[8]

> Transcript 5.1
> These are completely different experimental set-ups ... and you see the same thing ... and this is true with a host of experiments ... One of the things I want you to take away from this is the remarkable agreement we have between independent experiments at this point ... making these measurements. (...) So if you actually look at the same part of the sky the agreement here is really remarkably good.[9]

Spergel is not surprised that the ACT and Planck teams managed to point their telescopes at the same part of the sky. Neither is he surprised that the microwave sky has not changed noticeably in between the ACT and Planck observations, which were presumably not made at the same time. Spergel thus assumes that the microwave sky is immutable, at least over

[8] See the Appendix for a complete list of the transcription conventions adopted.
[9] David Spergel, lecture at NYU, March 27, 2014, see footnote 7, ca. minute 6 and 10.

a few years.[10] What Spergel finds remarkable, though, is how closely the ACT and Planck measurements agree, depicting "the same thing" despite these detectors employing different physical processes.[11] This agreement is significant beyond these ACT and Planck measurements. Mapping the CMB is a relatively new field in which members often describe their work as "doing experiments." Until the early 2010s, these experiments did not usually enable researchers to "see the same things" on the sky. They were designed for measuring specific observables in single campaigns of observing patches on the sky that did not usually overlap.[12] By contrast, observatories now "observe and reobserve" signals from the microwave sky as an ambient environment again and again – viewed from the Earth and its vicinity as a shared vantage point. Spergel thus points to a step in the maturation of this scientific field.

Other astronomers shared Spergel's excitement. A month after his talk, at a workshop discussion on future observations of the microwave sky, McGill University astronomer Matt Dobbs addressed fellow panelist Barth Netterfield, a physicist from the University of Toronto, thus:

> *Transcript 5.2*
> We can make a measurement and other people can go out and <u>verify</u> that measurement and show <u>real</u> <u>science</u> ... <u>Barth</u>! ((*laughter*)) ... and <u>show</u> that that is a reproducible thing that is on the sky.[13]

Like Spergel, Dobbs regards the sky as fixed and immutable on the time-scale of these observations. And, as for Spergel, Dobbs' confidence does not seem to reside in either one of these maps alone, but from comparing them and finding them in agreement. Seeing "the same sky" again using different technologies appears to make these technologies robust.

While Spergel and Dobbs do not mention it here, robustness is a notion that astronomers use in much the same way as philosophers of science. Astronomers call a result "robust" if an independent trustworthy study confirms it, especially if the latter uses different instrumentation and is done at different observing conditions. Thus, when I asked Christina, a member of the MUWAGS collaboration (see Chapter 6), about her work on weak

[10] One may compare this with the immutability of the sky alluded to in Owen's pun in Transcript 1.1.
[11] Thus conceived, this is not a replication but rather a confirmation. As such, argues Collins (1992, 19), "if it is to be worth anything in its own right, [it] must be done in an elegant new way or in a manner that will noticeably advance the state of the art."
[12] For example, the fields that the ACT and the BICEP2 telescope (discussed later in this chapter) observed did not overlap.
[13] Discussion at the Perimeter Institute for Theoretical Physics, Waterloo (Ontario). See perimeterinstitute.ca/videos/prospects-future-measurements, ca. minute 38 (accessed January 11, 2020).

gravitational lensing (an approach used to map invisible cosmic dark matter) and mentioned a study of the "Bullet cluster" (commonly interpreted as a merger of two galaxy clusters) that described it as "direct empirical proof of the existence of dark matter" (Clowe et al. 2006), she responded:

Transcript 5.3
That is quite a <u>robust</u> analysis. There's been that … <u>lots</u> of different telescopes made the same ob… observed the cluster … <u>lots</u> of different ((atmospheric)) seeing conditions and they see that same offset. I mean … that … There was a paper back in 2003 which has <u>no</u> citations … but it's <u>exactly</u> the same result. But it was just <u>one</u> observation. And then the most recent one … with Maruša Bradač ((et al. 2008)) took more observations and is much more robust.

Christina's account implies that robustness goes together with the separability of artifacts from an observable's "real" features. She adopts a "realist strategy" (Barnes et al. 1996, 81).

Philosopher of science William Wimsatt (2007, 43) refers to robustness as the convergence of "multiple means of determination" toward one result. This relates to Ian Hacking's account of seeing, and recognizing, the "same" thing through different kinds of (optical, acoustic, scanning) microscopes. Confidence in its success emerges not only from understanding how these instruments rely on different physical principles, but also from the implausibility that such observations should converge accidentally.[14]

What Spergel and Dobbs "look at," "see," and "show" are data in different forms. The microwave sky is mediated, made manifest to these researchers through representations. For them, agreements and differences are not to be found in individual perceptions and memories, but in maps and diagrams like those shown in Figure 5.1. Note that Dobbs, like Spergel and Hogg (cited earlier), talks about things "on the sky," implicitly acknowledging the mediated nature of astronomical observation, where the "sky" is sometimes defined as "a two-dimensional distribution of intensity of electromagnetic radiation" (Léna 1989, 245).[15] It is through their uses of media that scientists regard the sky as something two-dimensional and operational, as we shall see now.

---

[14] Hacking (1983, 186–203). See Elder (2024) for more recent views on robustness in the philosophy of science.

[15] The "celestial sphere" is conceived as a two-dimensional surface. As Krämer (2016, 26) puts it poetically, "the sky is populated with constellations (German: Sternbilder – literally, 'star pictures') that transform the depth of space into a flat surface" (my translation).

5.3 Mundane Reason as a Resource for Working with Scientific Data

Viewed from ordinary life, where we routinely agree on seeing the same things, Spergel's and Dobbs' wonder about the similarity of the ACT and Planck maps may seem odd. After all, we never experience the world from the same place as others. That one's glasses are fogged, that fatigue affects someone's attention, and that another is colorblind are three more reasons for why our perceptions may differ. But this is not something we usually worry about. Instead, we routinely resolve what sociologist Alfred Schütz called the problem of intersubjectivity: "How can two or more actors share common experiences of the natural and social world and, relatedly, how can they communicate about them?" (Heritage 1984, 54). Schütz argued that social actors routinely resolve the problem of intersubjectivity by assuming they share a common world and that their perspectives are recip-rocal, that is, they assume that they would sense the world in the same way as another if they were in the other's place, and if their relevancies were congruent. This is what Schütz (1962, 11–13), following Edmund Husserl, calls the "natural attitude."

Many situations of conflicting perceptions and experiences may be resolved in this way, but there are cases when the natural attitude cannot accommodate divergent testimony: "puzzles" emerge that require "resolu-tions" (Pollner 1974b). This is often the case when the stakes are raised – such as in law courts, in psychiatric hospitals, or in scientific work.[16] As Schütz and others argued, actors could in principle adopt one of two stances: (1) that there is a single perceptible and ordered world that actors share, and that perceptual conflicts call for resolution; or that (2) there are multiple worlds, and there are no conflicts to be resolved when individual perceptions diverge.[17] Put loosely, the former is a realist stance and the latter a relativist one.

Drawing on a study of a municipal traffic court, sociologist Melvin Pollner (1974b, 1987) examined how actors maintain a shared world even when their perceptions, experiences, or memories come into conflict, lead-ing to a disjuncture. A driver's speed reading may differ from a police officer's measurement. While the driver may claim to have stayed within the speed limit, this disjuncture may be explained by the driver's car's tachometer being broken. Resolving such a disjuncture is contingent on

---

[16] See Coulter (1975) and Gilbert and Mulkay (1984).
[17] See Heritage (1984, 213).

participants' mutual orientation to the assumption of an "incorrigibly objective and commonly shared world" (Pollner 1974b, 53), which enables members of a practice to recognize and resolve disjunctive experiences. For doing so, documents are essential resources. Reality is assumed to be coherent, determinate, and noncontradictory.[18] When interpreting perceptions, a "realist strategy" distinguishes between what is deemed "real" and what is "artefactual," that is, what can be ascribed to issues with "the perceiving organ, instrument or apparatus" (Barnes et al. 1996, 81).

Mundane reasoners commonly rely on *ceteris paribus* clauses: the (often tacit) assumption that an observation or experiment is replicable only if "other things are equal." Embedded in members' reasoning, "incorrigible propositions" (Gasking 1955) are resources for reflexively preserving their own validity. This insight is inspired by Edward Evans-Pritchard's (1937) ethnographic study of the Azande (Central Africa), who used oracles for the diagnosis of misfortune. When operated properly, Azande specialists insisted, an oracle would be infallible. At times, however, Azande oracles produced outcomes that seemed contradictory to Evans-Pritchard, but his Azande interlocutors argued instead that the conditions for the oracle's proper use must not have been met. They employed what Evans-Pritchard (1937, 319) termed "secondary elaborations of belief," arguing, for instance, that the wrong plant had been chosen to prepare the oracular substance or that the oracle substance was too old and not efficacious anymore. Thus, they reflexively maintained the oracle's incorrigibility.

Scientists can be in a similar position. Chemist-philosopher Michael Polanyi observed: "In my laboratory I find the laws of nature formally contradicted at every hour, but I explain this away by the assumption of experimental error" (Polanyi 1964, 31). Arguably, at the end of Polanyi's days in his laboratory, the laws of nature were always again back in place. He appears to consider the laws of nature as incorrigible, at least for his ordinary lab work, and in doing so he relies on mundane reason. In Chapter 3 we have seen this kind of reasoning in action as Nadine was guided to employ what I called an "implicit cosmology" – a description of how we see what the universe looks like when using certain technologies and media in culturally specific ways.

Douglas Gasking (1955) takes the use of *ceteris paribus* clauses into the medium of numbers and addresses practices of counting, an elementary form of measurement in science (see also Warwick 1995). As a student of

---

[18] Pollner (1987, 26). Note that, similarly, the "uniqueness of the world" can be considered as many scientists' methodological maxim (Giere 2006, 35).

Ludwig Wittgenstein, Gasking is concerned with the relation of mathematics to the world. As it pertains to this book, the gist of Gasking's argument is to make mundane reason available for discussing calculation, measurement, and the uses of digital data. Performing and interpreting a calculation like "$7 + 5 = 12$" is not troublesome for most quotidian uses, Gasking argues, but if one decides to experimentally align such a calculation with real worldly materials one may be challenged. For example, if one tries to add 7 drops of mercury to 5 drops of mercury in a bowl, one may count less than 12 drops of mercury in the end. Drops may have merged while counting was in progress. Likewise, making calculations with observed data coherent may force one to invoke *ceteris paribus* clauses.[19]

Mundane reasoning is a linguistic practice, but stable features of the material world can be its resources. Pollner (1987, 40–45) alludes to Maurice Merleau-Ponty's (1968, 15) notion of the world as the "Great Object," an idealization of the perceptible world as a "finished explicit totality in which the relations are those of reciprocal determination." Kenneth Liberman (2013) demonstrates, in intriguing case studies of how students navigate with sketched maps and play board games, that people use various embodied, material, and representational means to organize and order their affairs, often utilizing features of a setting opportunistically. Edwin Hutchins (2005) argues that uses of what he calls "material anchors" blend conceptual structure with material structure and thus stabilize the former. He calls this "an old and pervasive cognitive strategy" (Hutchins 2005, 1555). Eric Livingston argues that the stability of the practices of playing checkers lies in the materiality of its culture, and he insists that different materials encountered in, say, laboratory chemistry or mathematical theorem proving, implicate different, specific forms of reasoning (Livingston 2006, 2008). Drawing on studies of girls' hopscotch play and archaeologists' uses of a Munsell color chart, Goodwin (2018) comes to a similar conclusion.

In data-rich science, the materiality of disciplinary objects becomes available to the virtuality of screenwork only through practices of representation and mediation. Astronomers conceive of the sky as immaterial, but it exhibits remarkably stable features that their predecessors interpreted as evidence for its materiality.[20] In screenwork its stable features become salient through their representation. Data of different origin may ostensibly be in conflict at any stage in research, and it is through media

---

[19] See Cartwright (1983) and Warwick (1995).

[20] Aristotle (1939). The apparent permanence of star patterns in the night sky exceeds that of most laboratory equipment.

that disjunctures and disagreements become perspicuous and available for repeated inspection.[21] Different materials and media offer distinct affordances for researchers' action, as the following two episodes illustrate.[22]

5.4   Using Mundane Reasoning to Recognize Mistakes in Data Analysis

David Spergel's March 2014 talk at New York University was scheduled as a review of recent studies of the CMB, but much of it became a commentary on a spectacular discovery that BICEP, a research collaboration led by Harvard University physicists, had announced twelve days earlier.[23] For three years, the BICEP team had operated a small radio telescope (BICEP2) and a detector array (the Keck Array) at the geographic South Pole to make sensitive measurements of the CMB and prepare maps of its intensity and polarization. Their polarization map had a greater sensitivity than any other such map made before. It revealed a swirl pattern that BICEP team members attributed to so-called B mode polarization, finding it to agree with models of inflation, a theorized phase of rapid expansion of the early universe. Its interpretation as observational evidence for inflation was a spectacular claim.

Engaging mundane reasoning, Spergel raises doubts about this interpretation. He acknowledges the importance of the discovery claim but emphasizes that, as such, it demands particular scrutiny. The BICEP2 map, of greater sensitivity than previous measurements of CMB polarization, could not be compared meaningfully with existing data. Spergel therefore turned to internal comparisons of the dataset and statistical tests that the BICEP team had presented in its discovery paper (Ade et al. 2014, table I). These tests were calculated using pixel maps of data generated from scans of the sky with the BICEP2 telescope. Spergel wondered about the consistency of these data considering possible artifacts such as those caused by scattered light in the telescope. To recognize such artifacts, the BICEP team had designed its telescope to be movable around three axes, allowing it to observe a given position on the sky (defined by its celestial coordinates) in four distinct orientations. This yielded four sub-datasets which could be scrutinized and compared for consistency. The BICEP

[21] Latour (1986). Recent accounts of scientific representation highlight researchers' interests and their purposeful choice-making as well as the unavoidable materiality of this work (Giere 2006; Coopmans et al. 2014).

[22] Both episodes are described in greater detail in Hoeppe (2019a).

[23] The acronym BICEP stands for Background Imaging of Cosmic Extragalactic Polarization. See Ade et al. (2014).

team did so using a so-called jackknife resampling technique.[24] It published its test statistic, presumably with the intention to demonstrate the reliability of its findings and the consistency of its subsamples.

Spergel, however, reads these statistics as hinting at problems in the BICEP2 analysis:

> **Transcript 5.4**
> You can look at the <u>sky</u> ... same part of the <u>sky</u> ... at four different ((*telescope*)) orientations and make four independent maps ... and ask ... Do I see the <u>same sky</u> at four different orientations? And that doesn't test <u>all</u> systematics ... but if there was something going on where scattered light was getting in you might expect to see something different. Well ... what's a little <u>worrying</u> is if they <u>do</u> that ... ((*points with laser pointer to a projected slide of Table I of Ade et al. 2014*)) here is their EE signal at four different orientations ((*of the telescope*)) ... the probability of finding that much <u>difference</u> between the two is at the 0.4 per cent level.[25]

Attending to statistical confidence levels, Spergel interprets this test as suggesting that the observations in the four configurations were inconsistent and did not see the "same sky." The BICEP team had allegedly missed this in their analysis.

Spergel next turns to examine the BICEP team's analysis of the similarity of the BICEP2 and the Keck Array maps. The BICEP team had computed cross-correlations of these data, a mathematical technique suited for assessing the similarity of series or arrays of adjacent measurements.[26] Spergel refers to these cross-correlation as "cross" in the transcribed talk.

> **Transcript 5.5**
> The amplitude of the B mean modes here ((*points at a diagram on a slide*)) are much <u>higher</u> than the theoretical prediction. And this is supposed to be due to ((*gravitational*)) lensing. Now some people say ... "<u>Oh</u> don't worry ... the Keck array ... the numbers get better" ... It's <u>not really fair</u> to play that game. I think it is better to ask ... Look at the consistency test and say ... they are looking at the same part of the sky. Why does the point ... why ... if I take <u>Keck</u> minus BICEP2 ... which should have no signal ... cross BICEP2 ... I see <u>shifts</u> ... of more than two sigma on most points ... which suggests they are not seeing a <u>consistent sky</u> between the two experiments.[27]

---

[24] The jackknife resampling technique is a method commonly used to estimate the variance and bias of samples (Tukey 1959).

[25] David Spergel, lecture at NYU, March 27, 2014, see footnote 7, ca. minute 49.

[26] Cross-correlations have been used also to calibrate measurements of the cosmic microwave background, including data from the ACT (Hajian et al. 2011).

[27] David Spergel, lecture at NYU, March 27, 2014, see footnote 7, ca. minute 54.

Interpreting differences of "more than two sigma" (standard deviations) as "not the same," Spergel concludes that the BICEP team did not used the sky as an organizational resource to recognize its own measurement uncertainties or, worse, inconsistencies in its data analysis. Working in a domain that is removed from any human's senses, David Spergel is persistently attentive to the sky and its uses as a diagnostic tool. In positing that the sub-datasets ought to be "the same" within statistical margins of significance he presumes an "incorrigibly objective and commonly shared world" (Pollner 1974b, 53). Spergel does not make use of any specific detail of the visible sky, but draws on idealizations available to all astronomers.

That Spergel's demand for the BICEP2 subsamples to exhibit the "same sky" was worth pointing out to fellow scientists is suggested by New York University astronomer David W. Hogg, who attended Spergel's talk and commented in his blog:

> One amusing thing about Spergel's talk was the repeated point (obvious, but often overlooked) that because all CMB experiments are observing the *same, single sky*, they ought to agree to better than one-sigma, especially on large scales where cosmic variance dominates.[28]

Hogg's view of Spergel's point as "obvious, but often overlooked" suggests an implicit agreement on the proper use of the (idealized) sky as a resource to assess processed data.[29]

5.5 Mundane Reasoning as a Resource for Repairing Data

Let us complement Spergel's critique of the BICEP2 result, which draws on idealizations of the sky's immutability and "self-sameness," with a case in which researchers used specific "objectual" properties of the sky to repair their data. The first reflexive moment in Nadine's PhD project (Chapter 3), in which her attempt of galaxy spectral energy distribution (SED) template fitting yielded "objects that do not exist" (Otfried), provides us with an example.

Otfried knew from his earlier work that Nadine's questionable template-fitting results could be due to artifacts in the flatfield – the exposure of the twilight sky used to correct for sensitivity variations of the charge-coupled device

---

[28] hoggresearch.blogspot.ca/2014/03/spergel-and-bicep2.html (accessed July 7, 2025; emphasis in the original).
[29] Flauger et al. (2014) subsequently published a more refined examination of the BICEP2 analysis. The BICEP2 discovery claim did not withstand this critique and has been widely dismissed since (Cho 2014).

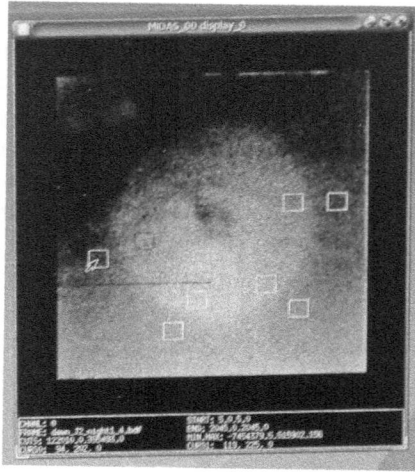

Figure 5.2   False-color image of one of Nadine's flatfields. The most conspicuous features in this flatfield are visible as a roundish structure at its center and a brightening toward the bottom of the exposure. The white rectangles denote areas of the pixel image in which she had measured the noise level. (Photograph: Götz Hoeppe)
Note: The online version shows the colors of the original figure.

chip in the digital camera. Lacking previous experience of working with such data and being new to the group's analysis techniques, Nadine could not possibly assess this herself. Otfried explained to her that there might be artifacts in the flatfield frames that had yet to be corrected for. Like other senior scientists, he insisted that such artifacts were either additive or multiplicative. Scattered light recorded in the flatfield frames during twilight, emerging perhaps from moonlight reflected in the dome, the telescope, or the camera, is considered an additive artifact and must be subtracted. Artifacts in science frames are multiplicative and are removed by division with a flatfield exposure.

Upon closer inspection, Nadine's flatfield seems to contain two artifacts that call for removal: a ring-like feature around the exposure's center and a gradient across the frame (see Figure 5.2). Otfried suspects that both features are due to scattered light. To remedy their effect on Nadine's data, she was to model the ring and the gradient and subtract them from the flatfield. To do so, Nadine needed to quantify these artifacts. Otto suggested that this might be accomplished through comparing Nadine's photometry of stars in the field with published data. The Two Micron All Sky Survey (2MASS) seemed particularly well suited for this task, as it included many (471 million) sources on the entire sky, including some in the A2713

Figure 5.3 Nadine briefing Otfried about her assessment of artifacts in the flatfield exposures, using paper printouts to summarize her findings. (Photograph: Götz Hoeppe) Note: The online version shows the colors of the original figure.

field that Nadine studied.[30] The 2MASS catalog includes measurements in the H band, in which Otfried and Nadine had noticed the flatfield's ring and gradient.

Instructed by Otto, Nadine searched the 2MASS catalog database in the field of her exposures and found thirty-one stars. Otto deemed this "not many" but "sufficient to try" comparing her photometry with those of the survey. After using the 2MASS website to generate an ASCII file of these stars' infrared fluxes, Nadine calculated the brightness differences that Otto had specified, as well as the noise variations in the flatfield frame. Once she was done with this, Otfried asked her to summarize her measurements on a map of the field. Thus equipped, she went to see him (Figure 5.3).

In their joint examination of the map, Otfried and Nadine agreed that the ring and gradient artifacts were noticeable as brightness differences of stars, which could be used to quantify these artifacts. Uncertain of how large a difference had to be to require correction, Nadine depended on Otfried's judgment. He asserted that differences of up to 0.03 mag were sufficiently "the same," whereas bigger differences had to be corrected

---

[30] See Skrutskie et al. (2006) and ipac.caltech.edu/2mass/ (accessed July 7, 2025).

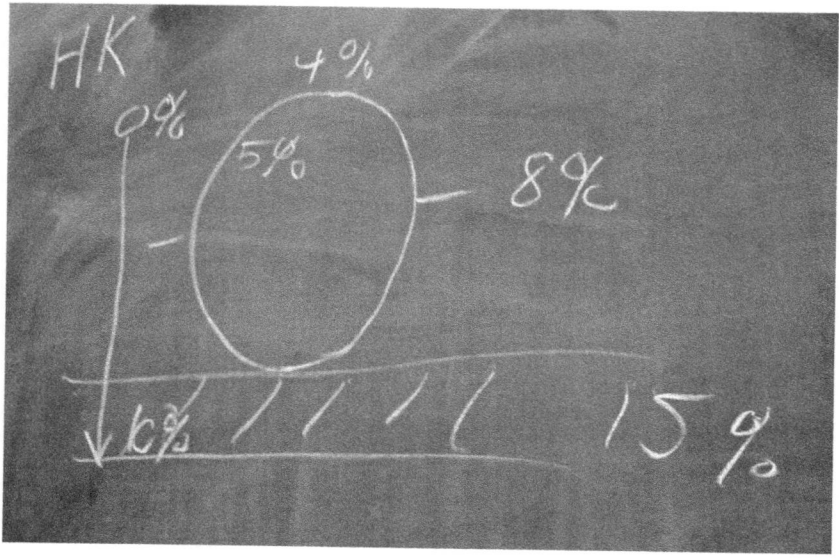

Figure 5.4   Otfried's schematic characterization and quantification of artifacts in the
flatfield frames on his office blackboard. (Photograph: Götz Hoeppe)
Note: The online version shows the colors of the original figure.

for.[31] Otfried tried to identify a structure that is both "simple enough" to
be described in a model and "good enough" to remove the artifact to proceed with the analysis.

Drawing on these assessments, Otfried proceeded to sketch and quantify
key elements of the flatfield model on his office blackboard (Figure 5.4). He
subsequently guided Nadine to make a model that consisted of a ring and
a gradient that was to be subtracted from the flatfield frames, which in turn
were used to divide all science exposures anew. This model later proved to
be "good enough" for Nadine's data to show "the same sky" as the measurements of the 2MASS. No further flatfield repair was considered necessary.

This is another case of mundane reasoning (Pollner 1974b, 1987) that
employs the sky as a stable structure available through uses of media. But
whereas Spergel used idealizations of the sky as a resource to shed doubt
on the BICEP2 analysis, Otfried, Otto, and Nadine used specific features
(the position and brightness of stars) as resources to improve their data

---

[31] This difference got inscribed into Nadine's photometric measurements without being explicated
anywhere in resulting publications.

calibration. They were "practical realists" who used the sky in ways not acknowledged in their subsequent publications.[32]

Note that these astronomers did not work with digital records only, but used a variety of media. Otto and Otfried first considered a set of numbers (redshifts and magnitudes), then inspected SEDs (on screen and on paper), and examined flatfield exposures represented as false-color images on Nadine's computer terminal (see Chapters 3 and 4). After specifying possible artifacts using the 2MASS catalog, Nadine summarized her findings on paper, before Otfried sketched the flatfield model on his blackboard (Figures 5.3 and 5.4). Not constrained by precise numerical values, uses of paper and the blackboard gave Otfried and Nadine room for approximations and schematic assessments that helped formulating a simple, but "good enough" model of the artifactual ring and gradient.[33]

5.6 Materiality and Mundane Reason as Resources for the Relief from Trust in Data Makers

We have examined two distinct uses of mundane reasoning engaging the mediated sky: one employing idealized properties, the other specific detail. The former provided David Spergel with resources to assess the BICEP2 data analysis beyond the information that the BICEP team had provided. The latter was Otto's, Otfried's, and Nadine's creative use of the 2MASS catalog as a resource for improving their data calibration. In both episodes the mediated sky was a resource for assessing and ordering research work. I now argue that, thanks to mundane reasoning, materiality and mediation can be resources for the partial relief from trust in the work of data makers.

That trust is foundational to doing science has become a commonplace in historical, philosophical, and sociological studies. Only a small part of our knowledge draws on our own experiences and so we need to rely on others' testimony. By placing trust, there is always a risk that one may be disappointed, but in science its promises are immense. As Steven Shapin (1994, 417) notes, "scientists know so much about the natural world by knowing so much about whom they can trust." With increasing complexity this dependence only increases (Simmel 1906), and it pertains as much

---

[32] Astronomers rarely acknowledge these practices' importance and widespread use. Hogg (2022, 16) is an exception. The idealization of the sky as an immutable two-dimensional structure can be regarded as an element of the "implicit cosmology" that I described in Chapter 3.

[33] This resembles an argument that Bachelard (2002 [1938], ch. 11) makes for quantification in science more generally.

to the data one uses as to the things one knows: "the relevant data and arguments are too extensive and too difficult to be had by any means other than testimony" (Hardwig 1991, 706). Although sociologists like Niklas Luhmann (2017) and Anthony Giddens (1990) have claimed that, in modern society, trust has shifted from personal relations to institutions, evaluations of persons continue to be highly important in scientific practice. But this trust is not blind. Scientists evaluate others' work by considering the reputation of individuals and their workplaces, their track records, and the awards and grants they receive.[34]

Some studies of the reuse of scientific data claim that trust in data commonly amounts to trust in data makers (Gregory et al. 2019; Yoon 2017). The reputation of data repositories and archives, as well as experiences with prior reuse, also affects users' trust in data (Faniel and Yakel 2017). Samuelle Carlson and Ben Anderson (2007) argue that, for one's data to be trusted, "making explicit their context of production and setting up appropriate systems of quality checks and assessment" are important (Carlson and Anderson 2007, 8; see also Yakel et al. 2019). When doing so, data makers demonstrate competence, honesty, and reliability – markers of trustworthiness (O'Neill 2014). One becomes trustworthy, argues philosopher Onora O'Neill (2014), by making oneself vulnerable to others. Well-placed trust, she insists, is a response to trustworthiness.

Studies of the reuse of scientific data have examined differences between disciplines. Kathleen Gregory and coauthors (2019) examine astronomy, Earth and environmental sciences, biomedicine, field archeology, and social sciences, and identify various criteria to assess the trustworthiness of data in use. They claim that in astronomy trust in data is contingent on "author reputation" and "source reputation," whereas in biomedicine trust in data is primarily contingent on the quality of "supporting documentation" and "social networks" (Gregory et al. 2019, 422).[35] Ixchel Faniel and Elizabeth Yakel (2017) examine archaeology, zoology, and social sciences to formulate a set of "trust markers" that members of the disciplines they consider share. But neither study addressed how discipline-specific objects and resources in use may partially relieve data reusers from trusting data makers.

David Spergel's assessment of the BICEP2 result and as Otfried and Nadine's use of the 2MASS catalog are exemplary uses of the sky as the

[34] See Latour and Woolgar (1986), MacKenzie (2001), as well as Collins and Evans (2007).
[35] Wynholds et al. (2011, 384) make a similar point about astronomers' "trust in sources," noting that they regard "extensively tested, vetted, and publicly reviewed data products" like the Sloan Digital Sky Survey as "valid, accurate, well documented, and trustworthy."

"object" that defines astronomy as a discipline. Conceptually, the sky is a resource at every astronomer's disposal for examining their peers' analyses and claims.[36] Spergel uses it without access to a telescope and data of his own. His assessment of the BICEP2 result does not involve personal evaluations, say, of trusting or not trusting BICEP team members or examining their reputation and track record.[37] Otto's suggestion to use the 2MASS catalog to formulate a model to repair the flatfield was a spontaneous act that puts to use what is to members an "obvious, but often overlooked" (Hogg) property of the sky. Otto and his colleagues, too, do not explicitly invoke personal trust or mistrust. Instead, they do what Lucy Suchman (2007, 67) describes in another context: "when practices become problematic, the world can be consulted for resolution." Different scientific disciplines have different means to do so.

In astronomy, the sky provides affordances not only to check others' work and use data in inventive ways (such as for improving calibrations), but also to partly relieve data users from trusting data makers. As they know that other astronomers share access to the sky and can exercise mundane reasoning, data makers are relieved in part from demonstrating their trustworthiness. Astronomers' joint access to the sky, if only as an idealization (as in Spergel's critique), makes them vulnerable to others, and, unsurprisingly, many astronomers expect that others will inspect their work. This may prompt particular care when releasing data (see Chapter 8 and Hoeppe 2020a). Conversely, junior astronomers like Nadine become equipped with tools and practices to examine other researchers' work and learn to demonstrate their own vulnerability (in O'Neill's sense).

That access to shared materialities can substitute for placing trust in people echoes David Graeber's (2011) history of money and debt. Graeber notices that, in Eurasian antiquity, periods in which credit money was widely accepted alternated with periods in which gold and silver were dominant as currency. A debt is a record of trust. Credit money is useful in a society that maintains reliable and stable records, which was possible only in times of relative peace. But "accepting gold or silver in exchange for merchandise, on the other hand, need trust nothing more than the accuracy of the scales, the quality of the metal, and the likelihood that

---

[36] Note that this disciplinary characteristic is needed to make "immutable mobiles" useful (Latour 1986).

[37] Spergel acknowledges that the BICEP team is making "extremely sensitive and difficult measurements" and emphasizes that his scrutiny of its result is a sign of respect. David Spergel, lecture at NYU, March 27, 2014, see footnote 7, ca. minute 39 and 45.

someone else will be willing to accept it" (Graeber 2011, 213). No wonder that mercenaries were commonly paid in gold. Gold and silver were, then, material reliefs from the challenges of trusting persons and fragile systems of accounting. There is a trade-off between uses of stable material objects and the placement of trust.[38]

In scientific practice, uses of materiality as resources for relieving trust in people extend from disciplinary objects to disciplinary tools. In today's observational astronomy, a diverse community of scientists shares a small number of telescopes, detectors, and data analysis software. Relying on their proper operation, calibration, and data management is an institutionalized form of trust (Giddens 1990; Luhmann 2017). Note that (unlike the specialist BICEP2 telescope and Keck Array) these telescopes generate data for diverse evidential contexts (Pinch 1985). This reflexively asserts their calibration. Within limits, one and the same dataset (such as that of the MUWAGS collaboration described in Chapters 6, 7, and 8) can be used for projects that examine different evidential contexts. This supports the robustness of this work, but it is also a resource for the relief from trust in data makers.

5.7   Conclusion

In all sciences, the stability of reference is ultimately achieved by social work, which includes practices of standardization (Wise 1995). Only some sciences can routinely draw on objects or environments that are widely accessible to community members. Of these, astronomy is arguably the foremost example. Musing about the origins of science, Gaston Bachelard (1985 [1934], 100) declared that "determinism descended from heaven to earth." Alexandre Koyré (1943, 333) argued that "modern physics takes its origin from the study of astronomical problems and maintains this tie throughout its history." And William Ivins (1953, 16) suggested that, besides geometry, in classical Greece only astronomy made progress, since "every clear night provides the necessary invariant image to all the world." But there are other sciences that access shared environments and objects,

---

[38] More discussed in the literature on trust in science and technology studies is a trade-off between uses of numbers and placing trust that historian Theodore Porter (1995) examined. Porter argued that traditional communities in which face-to-face interactions dominated were much less in need of "formal structures of objectivity" than complex European societies in the early eighteenth century: "reliance on numbers and quantitative manipulation minimizes the need for intimate knowledge and personal trust" (Porter 1995, ix). Porter's account is aligned with views that highlight the role of institutions in modern knowledge-making.

including geology and other Earth sciences. Still other sciences arguably engage models and taxonomies in broadly related, reflexive ways.[39]

Engaged to relieve data users' trust in data makers, disciplinary objects function in ways otherwise ascribed to institutions and infrastructures. Writing about the use of meteorological data for documenting climate change, Paul Edwards (2010, 19) notices: "Get rid of the infrastructure and you are left with claims you can't back up, facts you can't verify, comprehension you can't share, and data you can't trust." In attending to calibration practices I have considered infrastructure not as a noun, but as a verb (Star and Bowker 2006), and have foregrounded otherwise backgrounded work practices in what Geoffrey Bowker (1994) called "infrastructural inversion."

That the objects of scientific research can be used for work that is broadly infrastructural has been argued before. Thus, biological materials (Clarke and Fujimura 1992), *Drosophila* fruit flies (Kohler 1994), and laboratory mice (Rader 2004) became not only topics of research, but also resources for its conduct, as they embodied standards for comparison.[40] Made to serve as markers of pollution, a variety of West African insects became part of an infrastructure for ecotoxicological assessments (Tousignant 2013). Studies of these organisms' uses adhere to the notion that infrastructures are human-made and have network structures (of exchange, for example).

What I referred to in this chapter as "materiality" may be better called "objectivity," provided the latter is understood not as an observer-independent "view from nowhere" (Daston 1992), but as a capacity to object or resist. The German word *Gegenständlichkeit* ("standing-against-ness"), that Günter Figal (2006) advocates in a phenomenological study alert to Heidegger's probing examination of language, expresses this meaning (cf. also Liberman 2022). What is *gegenständlich* is not necessarily material in a physical sense.

In this chapter my objective was to assess how "opportunistic" uses of "natural" objects and structures (Hutchins 2005) matter to scientific work in which calibration and the stability of reference become topical. But properly viewed, "opportunistic" may be a misnomer in the cases that I described, since it posits a view from outside scientific practice, which inherently and essentially is about using disciplinary objects as resources for practical action.

---

[39] The distinction between *mathesis* and *taxinomia* that Foucault (1971) makes in *The Order of Things* could be a resource for reflecting on this (see also Mackenzie 2017).

[40] For the topic/resource distinction, see Garfinkel (1967, 31), Zimmerman and Pollner (1971), and Hoeppe (2019a).

CHAPTER 6

Organizing
Social, Medial, and Epistemic Orders
in Data-Centric Collaboration

6.1 This Chapter's Plan

This chapter examines data-centric collaborations in the natural sciences as "organizational experiments" (Sharrock 2011, 29). Distinct from collaborations that build and operate large facilities like high-energy physics particle detectors and space probes, many data-centric collaborations are relatively short-lived teams whose work centers on datasets produced at public facilities like observatories, research ships, field stations, spacecraft, and national laboratories. Researchers join together to submit proposals to these facilities and, if successfully reviewed, are granted time and opportunities to use their equipment. For a certain period of exclusive proprietary use, the data that such groups obtain and make are their epistemic and social "stuff" that members use to establish connections and collaborations. Other teams work with open data or combine open and proprietary datasets. Diverse in origin and structure, data-centric collaborations typically lack features of formal organization, such as organizational charts and legally binding contracts. They often emerge from ties of academic genealogy and friendship, but may also be instigated by meetings, such as at hack weeks.

I concentrate on how data-centric collaborations organize their work. As in previous chapters, I track social accountability and examine scientists' practical reasoning and its resources. These include medial formats, epistemic orders, and a team's joint orientation to a dataset's projected coherence. I will focus on what I refer to as the Multiwavelength Galaxy Survey (MUWAGS; a pseudonym), an international collaboration of around thirty astronomers, but consider less formal and spontaneous collaborations as well. This introduction to the MUWAGS team also serves as a background for the next two chapters, on normative expectations of data access in "open science" (Chapter 7) and attempts to encode a team's collective knowledge of its data (Chapter 8). But to locate the work of MUWAGS, we first need an overview of its epistemic and organizational context.

6.2 A Society of Collaborations? Complex Datasets, Large Teams, and "Open Science"

The increasing dominance of teamwork and large collaborations has been noticed in many sciences, raising issues of social organization, coordination, authorship, and identity.[1] Several studies examine long-lasting collaborations that have a privileged or even exclusive access to the data-generating facilities they build.[2] Some projects in astronomy are like this. More often, though, researchers do not build instruments themselves but form teams to use public facilities for limited, shorter-lived projects.[3]

In astronomy, the move to large teams is associated with surveys – observational censuses of object populations.[4] Many surveys observe galaxies to examine the universe's history and matter content. Such studies have been at the forefront of promoting the open access to data, assembling large datasets, as well as using computational techniques of data mining and machine learning. Deep field studies are a prominent kind of such projects.[5] Making long exposures of selected small fields on the sky at many wavelengths, they use the finite speed of light as a sort of time machine to infer the history of galaxies from observing populations of distant exemplars (cf. Chapter 3).

Deep field studies emerged from a conjunction of three technological developments: the availability of large charge-coupled devices to photograph substantial parts of the sky, the repair of the Hubble Space Telescope (HST) in 1994 (which enabled high-resolution optical and near-infrared imaging), and the availability of ground-based 8-meter telescopes (enabling deep, long exposures and sensitive spectroscopy). Robert E. Williams, then the director of the Space Telescope Science

---

[1] Hackett (2005), Shrum et al. (2007), Wuchty et al. (2007), Leahey (2016), and Wu et al. (2019).

[2] See Knorr Cetina (1999), Vertesi (2015, 2020), and Roy (2024).

[3] There are also intermediate cases, such as the Dark Energy Survey (Abbott et al. 2016) that built a dedicated camera for use at the 4-meter Blanco telescope at Cerro Tololo Inter-American Observatory in Chile, a tax-financed, national facility.

[4] Lahav (2001). Historically, the first large collaborations in astronomy were surveys, including the Carte du Ciel, a photographic sky atlas that used observatories in the northern and southern hemisphere (Jones 2000).

[5] In this chapter I use the term "deep field" inclusively as describing all fields on the sky observed with long exposures at multiple wavelengths for extragalactic studies. What follows is a condensed and partisan history. See Koo (1999) and Williams (2018) for earlier work.

Institute in Baltimore (Maryland, USA), decided to dedicate the entire annual "Director's Discretionary [Observing] Time" for 1995 on the HST to make series of long photographic exposures of a "blank field" (a region without bright stars) in the northern sky in four optical wavebands.[6] This so-called Hubble Deep Field (HDF) revealed an unexpectedly large number of faint and distant galaxies with unusual shapes and became a resource for many subsequent studies of galaxy evolution.[7] A team of sixteen postdoctoral scholars and staff scientists at the institute processed the data and released calibrated images and object catalogs (tables of the measured properties of detected objects) to the public less than six weeks after the last exposure had been taken – much shorter than NASA's usual one-year proprietary period for the exclusive use of unprocessed data (Williams 2018).

The late 1990s and early 2000s saw a sprawling development of deep field projects. Many institutions that had built a large telescope or detector selected and observed their own target field at a unique location on the sky. Examples are the Subaru Deep Field, observed with the National Astronomical Observatory of Japan's Subaru telescope, the FORS Deep Field, observed by the makers of the FORS (Focal Reducer and low-dispersion Spectrograph) instrument at the European Southern Observatory's (ESO's) Very Large Telescope, and the Chandra Deep Field South (CDFS), defined by a very long and sensitive x-ray exposure with NASA's Chandra spacecraft.[8] Astronomers soon realized that beginning new deep field projects all over the sky was not an optimal use of available resources. It seemed advisable to focus on selected fields and combine expertise and capacities to make deep (sensitive) exposures at many wavelengths to study detected object populations.[9] Thus, the deep x-ray exposure of the CDFS has attracted further observations at many other wavelengths ever since, making this one of the most observed parts of the sky. The two Hubble Deep Fields (HDFs; in the northern and southern sky) and the so-called COSMOS field have been much observed

---

[6] In 1995, the Director's Discretionary Time at the HST amounted to 10 percent of its annual observing time.

[7] Prior to the HST launch, Bahcall et al. (1990) had predicted that no new distant galaxy population would be found with this area, arguing against investing large amounts of telescope time for such a search. Mindful of this, Williams (2018, ch. 8) emphasizes that he is a risk-taker, arguably not unlike daring entrepreneurs (cf. Appadurai 2015).

[8] Riccardo Giacconi, a key figure in space x-ray astronomy, and his team chose the CDFS for their (successful) attempt to resolve the x-ray background radiation discovered in the 1960s (Giacconi 2008).

[9] This required forming teams with members of distinct "instrumental communities" (Mody 2011).

as well, being sometimes described as "magnets" that attract complementary datasets.[10]

This development is contingent both on what data are like (digital, additive, shared format; cf. Chapter 1) as well as on how astronomers conceive of the distant universe as an object of study. For many practical purposes it is stable over human lifetimes (one can add exposures taken at different times), as well as, on large scales, isotropic (the universe looks the same in all directions) and homogenous (it has a universal average density; cf. Chapter 3). Without these assumptions (and their observational support) astronomers could not make comprehensive claims about the universe's history from observing a few selected fields only. Medial and epistemic orders thus enable and shape the work in this domain.

Over the course of my fieldwork, conversations among researchers that I witnessed were punctured with acronyms that referred to various projects, including GOODS, VVDS, EDisCS, DEEP2, COSMOS, LEGA-C, CANDELS, CLASH, and, more recently, DES, DESI, JWST CEERS, JADES, COSMOS-Web, and RUBIES.[11] Such acronyms are not only shortcuts to avoid rehearsing long project names, to make projects recognizable, and their publications searchable on the internet, they are also markers of ownership, responsibility, and members' collective identity (cf. Chapters 7 and 8). Ideally, they help building a team's good reputation. The projects that these acronyms describe are organizations in the sense of having specific goals (that are described in observing proposals and on team websites) and a well-defined membership (as listed on team websites and author lists), assigning specific rights and duties (data access and work tasks), being organized hierarchically (led by a principal investigator whom a collaboration board may support), and being, within limits, autonomous in their decision-making.[12]

---

[10] Interview with Mark Dickinson, National Optical Astronomical Observatories, October 25, 2016.

[11] Here, CANDELS is the Cosmic Assembly Near-Infrared Deep Extragalactic Legacy Survey (Grogin et al. 2011), CLASH is the Cluster Lensing and Supernova Survey with Hubble (Postman et al. 2012), COSMOS is the Cosmic Evolution Survey (COSMOS, Scoville et al. 2007), COSMOS-Web is a JWST survey of the COSMOS field (Casey et al. 2023), DEEP2 is the Deep Extragalactic Evolutionary Probe 2 (Newman et al. 2013), DES is the Dark Energy Survey (Abbott et al. 2016), DESI is the Dark Energy Spectroscopic Instrument (Abdul-Karim et al. 2025), EDisCS is the ESO Distant Cluster Survey (White et al. 2005), GOODS is the Great Observatories Origins Deep Survey (Giavalisco et al. 2004), JADES is the JWST Advanced Deep Extragalactic Survey (Eisenstein et al. 2025), JWST CEERS is the James Webb Space Telescope Cosmic Evolution Early Release Science project (Ronayne et al. 2023), LEGA-C is the Large Early Galaxy Census (van der Wel et al. 2016), RUBIES is the Red Unknowns: Bright Infrared Extragalactic Survey (de Graaff et al. 2025), and VVDS is the VIMOS VLT Deep Survey (LeFèvre et al. 2005).

[12] According to Kühl (2011) these criteria define a formal organization.

Researchers are typically members of one collaboration or another.[13] As in Charles Perrow's (1991, 481) "society of organizations," it seems that, in this field, large collaborations have "absorbed society." Examined closer, many of these collaborations resemble each other in their organizational structure and work programs. This is the case for teams that assemble multiwavelength datasets, that is, observations in several distinct wavelength regimes like gamma rays, x-rays, ultraviolet, optical (visible light), infrared, and radio waves. Each of these wavelength regimes requires the use of specific kinds of detectors. Members of distinct "instrumental communities" (Mody 2011) make and calibrate these data. As the electromagnetic spectrum marks their division of labor, these collaborations' social organization mirrors their research's epistemic order and, indeed, the natural order that researchers in the field agree upon.

Collaborations in the field also divide labor according to specific tasks and scientific objectives that they broadly share. They usually include a group that estimates photometric redshifts (a measure of cosmic distance), one that conducts spectroscopy, and one that constructs a multiwavelength catalog (a table of measurements of objects sorted by celestial coordinates). Many datasets are used for a set of well-established research topics, such as measuring galaxy merger and star formation rates over cosmic time or mapping dark matter by observing distortions of background galaxy images due to weak gravitational lensing. Shared, as well, is the mandate to release datasets to the public. This may be done quickly, as with the HDF, or after periods of exclusive proprietary use. These periods introduce constraints on the temporality of teamwork. A sort of organizational isomorphism marks collaborations in this field.[14]

But collaborations must also signal being different from others in specific ways. To make the case for using large amounts of observing time at public facilities, applicants argue with metrics that demonstrate their unique advance over existing work, in terms of sensitivity, range and number of wavebands, observed sky area, or number of objects included in their sample.[15] As suggested earlier in this chapter, previous studies of deep

---

[13] Some astronomers are members of two or even more collaborations, even competing ones.
[14] I borrow this notion from DiMaggio and Powell's (1983) institutional isomorphism.
[15] Members' narratives cast relations between collaborations variously as complementary or competitive. When I asked members of a California-based team about its relation to the work of the MAMBO (pseudo-acronym) team, one astronomer argued that MAMBO had scooped it on key science, while another emphasized that their complementary techniques (MAMBO using photometric redshifts whereas the California team was using spectroscopic redshifts) yielded complementary insights.

fields could argue for the benefit of observing different locations on the sky to counter biases due to "cosmic variance," that is, deviations from cosmic isotropy and homogeneity. Mitigating effects of cosmic variance became an incentive for merging two deep field projects to concentrate yet more resources in one large team.[16]

The move to large collaborations is tied to the increasingly open access to large datasets. Most astronomers agree that there were two precedents for this development: the HDF and the Sloan Digital Sky Survey (SDSS). Robert E. Williams conceived the HDF as a critique of the "Balkanization of science" in the use of public facilities (like the HST), where time allocation committees allegedly try to split the available observing time into many small projects to "make everyone happy," instead of focusing resources on few significant, but possibly risky, observing projects.[17] Realizing that a broad range of new telescopes and digital detectors promised a new era of abundant data, Williams criticized many astronomers' secretiveness about their data and their hesitation to share it. The point, he argued, was to change the "culture" of astronomy.[18]

Williams insisted that large, complex datasets enable interesting projects for everyone and should therefore be openly available to all astronomers. The original HDF data were quickly complemented by other datasets, such as spectroscopic observations with the 10-meter Keck telescopes on Mauna Kea (Hawaii). Many makers of these complementary datasets followed the precedent that the HDF team had set and published their data soon after the observations. This novel openness to large datasets was also adopted in observations of the popular CDFS, arguably solidifying a normative expectation of data access in this domain (cf. Chapter 7).

Conceived in the early 1990s by James E. Gunn, the SDSS is an imaging and spectroscopic survey using the 2.5-meter telescope at Apache Point (New Mexico). It is not a deep field project but a panoramic survey that covers the northern and equatorial sky.[19] Begun by Gunn and his colleagues in the Department of Astrophysical Sciences of Princeton University, its complexity brought this project to the edge of failure until Fermilab (Chicago), a high-energy physics laboratory with previous

---

[16] This was an argument in the design of CANDELS (Grogin et al. 2011).

[17] Interviews with Ethan J. Schreier, October 7, 2008, and Robert E. Williams, October 7, 2007.

[18] Leonelli (2016, 144) notices that some open science projects in biology are associated with individuals that peers regard as charismatic. By many astronomers' accounts, Williams would match this characterization.

[19] The local galaxy population that the SDSS documents is often compared, as a "present-day view," to galaxy samples in deep fields observed in earlier stages of cosmic evolution.

experience in running large experiments, took over its management. The contact of university academics with the hierarchical management of a national laboratory turned out to be riddled with conflict, but it ultimately rescued the survey.[20] This is commonly described as a major learning experience for astronomers in terms of project management, dividing labor, tracking accountability, and budgeting costs. SDSS has been operating since 2000 in a series of five-year phases, financed and codeveloped by a variety of national and international partners who pay for their early access to its data, which have been subsequently made public in a series of releases. Scientists within SDSS and beyond have used these datasets for addressing a wide variety of scientific questions.

As with the HDF, astronomers within SDSS and beyond experienced the availability of its images, catalogs, and spectra as a sudden abundance of data that had a "civilizing" effect on how astronomers cooperate in using large datasets.[21] Gunn called for the SDSS to practice a sort of "open science" within the collaboration, where "any member could do any science he/she wanted. Nobody owned any data or any project." Members had to announce project ideas within the collaboration and allow interested members to join them. PhD projects, however, were protected, assuring early career scientists the exclusive use of SDSS data. Gunn argued that these rules "resulted in the natural growth of widespread collaborations of common interests across the world, and a very happy project." Much like Robert Williams with the HDF, Gunn argued that SDSS "changed the sociology" of astronomy.[22]

6.3   From Organizations to Organizing

This account suggests that, in studies of deep fields, collaborative work and organization is oriented to, and informed by, a field of other projects and organizations. I have used the notion of "field" casually.[23] But much of what I noticed resonates with field theories in the social sciences that examine "individual action by recourse to position vis-à-vis others" (Martin 2003, 1). Economic and organizational sociologists have adopted this viewpoint when examining competing businesses (Davis 2005) and

---

[20] Finkbeiner (2010), Szalay (2018), and Gunn (2020).

[21] By alluding to the "civilizing" effect of data I have Hirschman's (1977) study of early capitalism in mind.

[22] These quotations are from Gunn's award lecture at the 2019 Kyoto Prize celebration. See: youtube .com/watch?v=z657rXUIEus at minute 34 (accessed July 7, 2025).

[23] Perhaps confusingly, this would be a field of deep field studies.

it is tempting to compare scientific collaborations with firms: both operate in contexts where "isolated individuals hardly matter in the production of goods and services" (Granovetter 2005, 429) and both compete with similar units, mutually constituting their competitors' environment. I noticed the similarities of deep field collaborations in terms of their division of labor, calling this an example of organizational isomorphism. Some collaborations design their project to be comparable with others, thereby asserting a position in a field and making a claim for membership in it – arguably a case of organizational diffusion.[24]

Notions of field, isomorphism, and diffusion help to characterize important aspects of this domain of data-rich science. But that they describe the work of business firms equally well reminds us that invoking them ignores the specifics of either domain. For a naturalistic account such as mine this is unsatisfactory. I noticed earlier that discipline-specific medial and epistemic orders clearly matter to how these scientists work and cooperate. We can approach this by following Karl Weick and examine organizing as processes that interlock the actions of collaboration members through interpretive practices (Weick 1979; 1995). Egon Bittner suggested a related ethnomethodological approach, proposing to regard "the concept of organization as a common-sense construct" by studying how it is used in "real scenes of action by persons whose competence to use them is socially sanctioned" (Bittner 1965, 247).[25]

In the following, I speak of data-centric collaborations, since it is through the joint production and use of data that scientists develop "forms of togetherness and for-each-otherness" (Simmel 1992 [1908], 18–19; translated from German). Many data-centric collaborations in astronomy have idiosyncratic origins, beginning with small teams of supervisorand-student, friends, or colleagues, and growing through adding members or merging with other teams. These are "organizational experiments" (Sharrock 2011, 29) that typically lack organization charts, diagrams representing workflows, and legally binding contracts. But they are not without documents and other resources for coordination. Take observing proposals, for example. Although prepared for submission to time allocation committees, proposals are also resources for organizing. They document medial, epistemic, discursive, organizational, and regulatory conditions

---

[24] See Strang and Meyer (1993). Note how comparisons are essential for defining this field and for shaping and legitimating members' decisions (cf. Heintz 2016).

[25] See also Anderson et al. (1989, 63–64) and Anderson and Sharrock (2018).

and accountabilities: medial, since work with instrumentation and specific data formats shapes a project's "do-ability" (Fujimura 1987); epistemic, since the point of a project is to learn something new that justifies the proposed observing time; discursive, since peer reviewers unavoidably assess them in the context of competing proposals; organizational, since the do-ability of large projects hinges on team expertise and workforce; and regulatory, since proposals may specify promises about the release of data and data products (see Section 6.5).

Interesting as observing proposals are as organizational documents, the point of data-centric collaboration itself is to produce documents: digital image files, tables of measurements, other forms of data for addressing specific evidential contexts (Pinch 1985), and scientific publications. Going beyond Bittner, one may wonder whether a dataset, as an object of collaboration members' shared interest, may be an organizational resource even as it is being made. For examining this possibility, it is worthwhile to remember Harold Garfinkel's notion of accountability as the self-organization of social settings by its members who "make its properties as an organized environment of practical activities detectable, countable, recordable, reportable, tell-a-story-aboutable, analyzable – in short, *accountable*" (Garfinkel 1967, 33; emphasis in original).

In a study of the collaborative work of software engineers, Graham Button and Wes Sharrock (1998, 75) argue that this notion can be adopted in contexts where organizational accountability "involves describing how the engineers organize their work so that it is recognizable to relevant parties in the project's management and implementation as work-within-the-organization." The engineers that Button and Sharrock observed were members of teams that developed elements of software meant to be subsequently combined and operated. For this to succeed they "attempted to organize ways through which they could make their work visible to each other in the very course of its production" (Button and Sharrock 1998, 79). The orderliness of these engineers' collaborative work was commonly achieved not sequentially, but in "spheres of operation and accountability" (Anderson et al. 1990, 247). We can regard organizational accountability as a part of what Anselm Strauss (1988, 164) has termed "articulation work" in projects: "the specifics of putting together tasks, task sequences, task clusters – even aligning larger units such as lines of work and subprojects – in the service of work flow." It does not presume that organizational work is formally integrated (Schmidt 2011). These notions will help us to make sense of how the MUWAGS collaboration organized its work.

6.4 MUWAGS

MUWAGS was a collaboration of around thirty astronomers from ten countries, including tenured senior scientists, postdoctoral scholars, and PhD students. Its primary aim was to make and use a multiwavelength dataset to study the distribution of dark matter in a supercluster of galaxies and examine how its environmental conditions control the evolution of its member galaxies.

Active from 2004 to 2009, MUWAGS grew out of an optical multicolor imaging dataset that the MAMBO team had prepared (cf. Chapter 3). Made with the 2.2-meter telescope at La Silla Observatory (Chile) it provided classifications and photometric redshifts (measures of cosmic distance) for more than ten thousand objects in the field of the galaxy supercluster A2713. This then-unique dataset was a strong reason to award the MUWAGS team 80 orbits of observing time on the HST to make a mosaic of optical high-resolution images with its Advanced Camera for Surveys (ACS) that would allow detailed morphological studies of cluster galaxies. Once these observations were approved, the team successfully applied for deep mid-infrared imaging using the Multi-Band Imaging Photometer (MIPS) on the NASA Spitzer Space Telescope. These would give insights into the cluster galaxies' star formation rates and masses. Thus, the collaboration comprised three major sub-teams in charge of making three constituent datasets that were to be made consistent in a public data release. Additional data that the team acquired at x-ray, optical, and radio wavelengths were less central to its analyses.

By supplementing MAMBO data with an HST mosaic, MUWAGS was a follow-up project of SAMGES (Spectra and Morphologies for Galaxy Evolution Studies), which had already combined MAMBO data with an HST ACS mosaic of another deep field. Junior scientists who had done their PhDs in SAMGES assumed more senior positions in MUWAGS. Some now supervised PhD thesis projects themselves. Like SAMGES, MUWAGS was led by a principal investigator, but while SAMGES was hierarchical (with a principal investigator and two full professors at its head), decision-making in MUWAGS was more consensual. In part this was due to differences in funding. The principal investigator of SAMGES had funds to recruit PhD students and postdoctoral scholars to work on science full-time, whereas MUWAGS members described their collaboration as voluntary, lacking funding for salaries.[26] Most work of MUWAGS was

---

[26] This voluntary nature became critical when personal circumstances intervened in the life of a team member who was meant to do the basic calibrations of HST dataset, thus delaying teamwork for several months.

done in three regional clusters in Exeter (UK), Heidelberg (Germany), and Florida (USA), with individual members at Cambridge (UK), Portsmouth (UK), Bengaluru (India), Nanjing (China), Hamilton (Canada), Vienna (Austria), St. Louis (USA), and Göttingen (Germany).[27]

Senior SAMGES members had participated in the SDSS and GOODS projects. This inspired the MUWAGS management strategies, including the special protection granted to PhD projects. The broad outline of MUWAGS teamwork followed what the HST observing proposal had described, but it was refined at the first collaboration meeting following the completion of HST observations. A set of photographs of whiteboards, containing team members' agreements as reached in copresence, became a reference for the team's organizing and its publication policy. This was supplemented by agreements reached at teleconferences, as recorded in the principal investigator's meeting minutes. MUWAGS followed the SAMGES style of having annual or semi-annual in-person collaboration meetings as well as monthly or biweekly all-team teleconferences, apart from communications by email, telephone, video conferences, in-person meetings in sub-teams, and mutual visits of individual team members.

MUWAGS members consistently described their collaboration as a "happy family," "one friendly big family," a "group of friends," or a "gang."[28] When collaboration members became parents, they circulated photographs of their newborn children by email attachment to the team and these children were welcomed as new MUWAGS family members. Over the two years of my ethnography, I did not witness any significant conflict within the team but noticed a consistent orientation to mutual aid of work on the dataset. Abundant joking and common uses of irony marked conversations at team meetings (cf. Chapters 7 and 8).[29] When reviewing teamwork at a meeting four years into the project, Mallory, the principal investigator, remarked that "we're still a functioning and friendly collaboration and I think that's also an important thing. That's a fairly ... Götz ... that's a fairly rare thing!" This utterance prompted collective laughter and confirmatory nodding. It seemed to me that Mallory had a point with this

---

[27] These place names are pseudonyms.

[28] Occasionally these metaphors were invoked to mark a difference with other collaborations, that were deemed "armies," for example, or, ironically, "a group of generous people," when alluding to another collaboration's reputation of not sharing its data in a timely fashion.

[29] One could describe team members' shared exclusive access to data during the proprietary period, and perhaps their work on a shared dataset more generally, as a "gift of time" (Derrida 1992, 41) in which friendship is manifested and renewed. This includes a shared commitment to keeping secrets. On secrecy and friendship, see Simmel (1906, 464), who remarked that "what is withheld from the many appears to have a special value."

assessment. During the course of my ethnography I kept hearing gossip about conflict in other collaborations, such as fights over rights to use data for specific projects, competing interests, and complaints about the inadequate sharing of data between sub-teams or with other teams, often with the moral implication of not living up to the obligation of sharing what they had received as a gift from a public facility (cf. Chapter 7).

The shared experience of comfort in collaborating and the enjoyment of team meetings raised concerns among some MUWAGS members that their scientific analyses proceeded too slowly and that other researchers may use the team's data – openly available in unprocessed form one year after the observations – to scoop it on key science. This worry became acute when a research team based in Munich (Germany), known for its expertise in weak gravitational lensing, downloaded the MUWAGS HST mosaic, presumably for just such an analysis. Learning about this made Christina, the MUWAGS gravitational lensing expert, speed up her analysis and swiftly submit it to a journal (cf. Chapter 7). Concerns over being scooped flared up again when the team was about to release its core dataset, including the catalog. MUWAGS members recognized that it could be used to address several "low-hanging fruits"– projects that other astronomers could do in a "quick and dirty" way before MUWAGS members, stuck with their meticulous, time-consuming work practices, had time to do so themselves. Despite these concerns, team members decided not to delay the data release but use its publication to push themselves to speed up with their analyses before others did them.

Four and a half years after MUWAGS submitted its observing proposal and half a year after its data release, the principal investigator officially dissolved the team at its last collaboration meeting. By then ten journal articles and several conference proceedings had been submitted and more articles were still in progress. A core group around the principal investigator continued to work on the MUWAGS dataset, but after the team's official dissolution, the authorship of resulting papers became more selective. Two years after the dissolution of MUWAGS, this group began a follow-up project, now centered around a new spectroscopic survey of A2713, which soon chose a new name and acronym of its own.

6.5 The Proposal as Charter

In its members' narratives, MUWAGS began with a plan to develop an HST observing proposal. Collaboratively authored and submitted to peer-staffed time allocation committees, observing proposals can be curious objects. They list the names of principal applicants and co-applicants, make the case for using a telescope to address important questions or problems, specify the planned observations (including celestial coordinates, exposure times, etc.), and demonstrate the planned observations' "do-ability" (Fujimura 1987) and the applicants' capacity to analyze the data and publish results. Proposals sketch the planned data analysis as well as an applicant team's division of labor. Including prominent scientists as co-applicants can be read as demonstrating one's political endorsements, particularly when a team applies for considerable amounts of telescope time at public facilities that are in great demand. By defining medial, epistemic, discursive, organizational, and regulatory conditions and accountabilities, proposals can become data-centric collaborations' foundational documents – charters, so to speaks.[30] The successful SAMGES and MUWAGS HST proposals inform the following account.

Calls for proposals that observatories issue annually are common catalysts for new projects and collaborations. When the deadline to submit proposals for the next HST or JWST observing cycle is announced, many astronomers wonder: "What do we do for the next round of HST/JWST proposals?" Strong science cases for galaxy evolution surveys are often those that enable statistical explorations of regions in parameter space that promise important new insights. This may be possible by adding observations to existing datasets, thus extending the range of question that can be addressed. Both SAMGES and MUWAGS succeeded in this way by dwelling on the MAMBO team's set of photometric redshifts and spectral energy distributions of more than ten thousand galaxies in each field. (As mentioned, MAMBO members formed a core group of both SAMGES and MUWAGS.) In the early 2000s, such large samples of distant galaxies were unprecedented. The MUWAGS proposal also lists SAMGES as a complementary dataset. The proposed optical high-resolution images taken with HST's ACS would enable the team to link the galaxies' visible shapes to the physical parameters that MAMBO had measured already.

As with grant proposals submitted elsewhere, successful HST observing proposals sketch and promote a team's anticipated division of labor and its capability to do the proposed work. It lists the applicants' skillsets and their relevance for data analyses. For SAMGES and MUWAGS, these

---

[30] Survey description papers (like York et al. (2000) for the SDSS) can have a similar function, but they are usually published far into a collaboration's work.

included skills in reducing and calibrating HST images, automated object detection, modeling the light profiles of objects, and, of course, expertise in addressing various evidential contexts from tracing galaxy mergers to mapping cosmic dark matter. Leading team members had a track record of approved HST proposals and timely published results.

But to call a proposal a charter, as I suggest, it must also define rights and obligations. The SAMGES and MUWAGS teams used their proposals in this sense. Among the many documents that their members produced and worked with, the proposal stood out as a resource for organizing teamwork and reflecting on the scientific progress made. It marked the collaboration's boundary, defining its inside and, by implications, its outside. Those listed as co-investigators had a right to use the data and be coauthors of all resulting publications. This included co-applicants who ended up not contributing what the proposal had outlined. The SAMGES proposal exhibits a promissory character also in respect to outsiders by highlighting the team's decision to waive its period of exclusive proprietary access to the HST ACS raw data, making it immediately available to the public. Unable to work as swiftly as the SAMGES team, in which several team members were employed to work on the dataset full-time, the MUWAGS team decided not to do so.

6.6 Four Episodes in Organizing Data-Centric Collaboration

I have suggested considering data-centric collaborations as organizational experiments for the production and use of scientific datasets. For MUWAGS members, the proposal, photographs of whiteboards, and meeting minutes were resources for organizing their research. But these documents do not exhaust what they could, and did, use toward this end. In the following, I examine further resources, beginning with two episodes in the work of MUWAGS. At one moment the team used realist assumptions and mundane reasoning to settle a tension in its division of labor. At another, the team used its internal diversity of expertise to make their master catalog coherent. Then I move to smaller scales of social organization and consider friendship as a resource for mutual aid in accessing data. Eventually, I examine public hack weeks as venues for individual researchers to team up and learn how to use complex public datasets. In sum, I will have sketched elements of a continuum of size and formality in organizing research with large datasets.

6.6.1   The Projected Coherence of a Dataset as
an Organizational Resource

Along with organizational plans and documents, medial and epistemic orders can be resources for organizing collaborative work. What data are like (e.g., additive digital records) defines what a team can aspire to do (e.g., making highly sensitive records of deep fields), whereas scientists' shared understanding of the electromagnetic spectrum shapes many teams' division of labor, involving members of distinct "instrumental communities" (Mody 2011). But dividing labor for making a singular data product can lead to tensions in planning that require "articulation work" (Strauss 1988) for their resolution. The joint objective to make a coherent dataset can be one of its resources.

Much of the collaborative work in MUWAGS was dedicated to making a master catalog: a table of measured and estimated properties of galaxies detected in the A2713 field based on the team's ground-based optical data, the HST imaging mosaic, and the Spitzer MIPS infrared observations. This catalog was to be a resource for most team members' research projects.[31] As MUWAGS team members worked toward a consistent catalog, occasionally mutual dependencies between the three main constituent data subsets became a challenge. Some parts of the dataset did not depend on each other, such as measurements of galaxy images in the HST images and the Spitzer infrared photometry. But all absolute measures (galaxy luminosities, stellar masses, and star formation rates) depended on knowledge of galaxy distances, which the team derived from MAMBO photometric redshifts in conjunction with a cosmological model.

In March 2007, the detection of a mistake in the code that had been used to estimate the old (2003) photometric redshifts instigated the making of a revised draft MAMBO/HST catalog, called the J2007c catalog. It was circulated internally in late July 2007. Peter explained, in an email to the team,

> I have removed a bug in the photo-z software, which should make only a difference for rather faint objects. I also enlarged the redshift window considered – again, matters only for low-S/N objects. Should not matter for R<22 objects really much.

---

[31] Only Christina, the team's expert on weak gravitational lensing, needed a separate catalog for her work. In Chapter 8, I give a chronological account of how the MUWAGS team prepared its catalog for public release, focusing on a series of critical decisions.

Here "photo-z" stands for photometric redshift, the "redshift window" pertains to the (Bayesian) probabilistic approach used, "S/N" for signal-to-noise ratio, and "R<22 objects" designates a magnitude range that includes relatively bright objects in the field which were targets for most of the team's research on the galaxy cluster.

Peter's apparently minor correction of a bug in computer code meant trouble for another sub-team. Two days after Peter's message, Eddie, the infrared sub-team's head, responded to the team in an email with the subject line "doh!," expressing his exasperation that

> My ((*galaxy*)) masses, SFRs ((*star formation rates*)), etc ALL USE THE OLD REDSHIFTS. I.e. NOT the J2007c redshifts. Worse than that, I do not have the code which does the masses, so the timescale to make new masses is LONG. This is a big deal – it's a major SNAFU to change photoz version 1/2 way through a project (...)[32]

Eddie continued his message wondering if revised masses and values could be "piggybacked" somehow from other parameters listed in the catalog.

Three days later, and after conferring with Peter, Mallory, the team's principal investigator, circulated her assessment of the situation in an email. She noticed that the revised photometric redshifts did not change the results that the team had already published. In this respect, the revised redshifts were at most "mildly irritating." However, Mallory agreed that the implications for the computed values of galaxy masses and star formation rates appeared to be serious. There was no straightforward way to "piggyback" them. Furthermore, the new catalog's completeness would have to be reassessed, implying considerable additional work for Peter.

Following consultations with the team members involved, Mallory decided to return to the original 2003 redshifts, deeming Peter's effort to correct the redshifts "worthwhile but ultimately (...) not enough of an improvement to justify the effort involved to bring everything else to the same system." The J2007c catalog was abandoned and replaced by the J2007d catalog, which listed the redshifts of the J2007b catalog, but was refined in other ways.

This episode suggests that preparing the MUWAGS catalog gave progressively less and less room for reprocessing its constituent datasets. Improvements to one of these could affect others and endanger the catalog's coherence. Thus, at this late stage the catalog could not be completed

---

[32] SNAFU: "Situation Normal: All Fucked Up," cf. en.wikipedia.org/wiki/SNAFU (accessed July 7, 2025).

through a linear sequence of work. Rather, Mallory's coordination was attentive to what may be called a "sphere of accountability" (Anderson et al. 1990, 248) comprising the work of distinct MUWAGS sub-teams. Brokering an agreement with Peter and Eddie, Mallory was doing articulation work (Strauss 1988). It shows how, in this case, organizational accountability was an accountability to the catalog's coherence, its lack of apparent contradictions. By tying her assessment of the current catalog version to its agreement with the team's published work, Mallory exercised mundane reasoning and adopted a realist stance (cf. Chapters 3 and 5). Demanding the catalog be coherent and consistent with the team's earlier work is, here, a resource for the reflexive reproduction of a collaboration's social order.

6.6.2   A Collaboration's Diversity of Expertise as a Resource for Making a Complex Dataset Coherent

The previous episode was one of several retrospective efforts to maintain the MUWAGS catalog's coherence that followed the discovery of troubles. But the team also made prospective efforts to make its catalog coherent by engaging the team's diverse expertise.

The final MUWAGS master catalog assembled measurements in seventeen optical and one infrared wavebands and combined data made using one ground-based and two space observatories.[33] As a table of 88,000 rows and 200 columns, it was a remarkably complex object, made with a skillset that no single researcher possessed. It is practically impossible for any individual researcher to estimate photometric redshifts, process HST exposures, fit galaxy light profiles, combine mid-infrared observations with optical photometry, and estimate galaxy star formation rates.

When the team had merged the MAMBO, HST, and MIPS data into the first comprehensive MUWAGS catalog, Mallory asked its members in an email to "break" the catalog: "Please try to break it. Please recreate your earlier plots and make sure everything still works as it should." One afternoon I joined Antonio, a PhD student, in his effort to break the draft MUWAGS catalog. He began with uploading the catalog and selecting an object sample by specifying the celestial coordinates (Right Ascension and Declination) of the cluster field, explaining to me that "it is a good thing first to check RA and Dec." Antonio then plotted the positions of objects

---

[33] Additional constituent datasets, including optical spectra, ultraviolet, and x-ray images, as well as radio maps, were not used for the master catalog.

in the field, assessing whether the distribution of objects looked reasonable. He explained to me that a reasonable distribution was one that showed the familiar pattern of the cluster galaxies with a relatively smooth, seemingly random distribution of objects in the cluster's background. Finding this plot acceptable, Antonio next recreated plots pertaining to his own project that he had made using the older draft catalog. The new plots looked almost identical. He concluded this work after about two hours, telling me: "I would say that in general the catalog is right," and communicated this assessment in an email to Mallory.

Two months later, at a collaboration meeting, a "catalog-breaking session" was held. At this session, team members did not reconsider plots and scientific results, but the proper assignment of sample selection and quality flags. These are numerical or textual descriptors that help users to select samples from the catalog (such as "All galaxies in A2713" or "All galaxies detected in the infrared, but not in the optical") and to recognize potential issues with its entries ("Object contains one or more saturated pixels," "Object was too close to edge of frame").[34] The catalog-breaking session turned makers into users of their collective work. Their task was to impersonate fictional future users and approach the catalog "from the outside," as users would engage it. In doing so, team members' limited mutual familiarity with the measurements of sub-teams to which they did not belong became a resource for examining the catalog's coherence. Finding contradictory entries or inconsistent quality flags and sample selection flags are examples of "catalog breakings." A few additional mistakes were found and the specifications of sample selection flags corrected. When the possibilities of breaking it seemed exhausted, the catalog was declared completed. It was "frozen in," as Mallory put it.

Mallory's call to attempt breaking the catalog was a call for testing its usability. Attempts to "break" and "freeze" the catalog figuratively assert its achieved closure and "hardness," its materiality as an object, a singular product of teamwork. With each team member recreating their plots, they assessed the catalog's use for examining diverse evidential contexts (Pinch 1985). As such, the catalog became irreducible to any individual member's work. Team members' expertise on these topics was a fair sample of expertise in the community. That the final master catalog was usable for these diverse projects without apparent logical contradictions, delivering results that peer reviewers trusted, is what arguably made up its perceived

---

[34] An exemplary list of flags used in the SDSS EDR catalog is table 9 of Stoughton et al. (2002).

hardness.[35] Team members' expectation of working toward a catalog that would have these properties was driven by mundane reasoning (Pollner 1987) and their "realist strategy" (Barnes et al. 1996, 81). Their shared acceptance that a coherent catalog would result became an organizational resource for the team. As "catalog breaking" included all the team's projects on equal footing, it mirrored the team's flat hierarchy (cf. Rooksby 2009).

6.6.3   Mutual Aid and Relational Work in Accessing Data

Collaborations like SAMGES and MUWAGS are not facility builders, but groups of facility users with specific goals, rights, and duties, and defined membership, that are, within limits, autonomous in their decision-making. These features define a formal organization. But organizing data access matters beyond such an organizational form. In astronomy's diverse ecology of data production, many facilities accept observing proposals from researchers anywhere, but others restrict access to scientists working at institutions in member states. Networks of friends and ties of academic genealogy provide diverse ways of "mutual aid" to navigate such exclusions and organize access to data, assemble the expertise to analyze it, and establish coauthorship.

Let us consider Marcelo, during my fieldwork a postdoctoral scholar at the Heidelberg Institute. Hired to work mainly for COSMOS, a large collaboration, following his PhD at the University of Cambridge (UK), he also continued observational research on active galactic nuclei at multiple wavelengths (optical, infrared, millimeter radio waves) that he had begun in his PhD work. For him, this meant collaborating with former fellow graduate students, postdocs, and scientists in his supervisor's academic network. Marcelo explains:

> Transcript 6.1
> I guess I work in two groups. Here I work with COSMOS ... and then there are the people that I worked with in Cambridge. Well ... some of them are still in Cambridge ... most of them are in the UK and some are in the US. (...) The way we've worked until now with the people from the UK ... we write proposals ... normally relatively small ... in the sense of maybe one or two nights ... maybe a whole week ... but not months ... like ... They're not as big as things like COSMOS. And then ...

---

[35] This understanding of hardness resembles Wittgenstein's (1978, 84, 2009 [1953], §97) notion of the "hardness of the logical must." For more on the catalog's fixation and assessments of its "hardness," and how a catalog can be said to fixate a team's collective knowledge, see Chapter 8 and Hoeppe (2021).

if someone <u>gets</u> the time to do these projects ... but they have gaps ... for example at the beginning of the night or end of the night ... they come to observe their own objects ... then we give them other objects to <u>fill</u> in. And we try and help each other with data like that.

For Marcelo mutual aid is not limited to filling available telescope time with observations for friends and colleagues. It extends also to enabling them to use telescopes which they cannot access otherwise:

Transcript 6.2
So ... for example ... being in Germany I have access to certain millimeter telescopes that people in the UK <u>don't</u> have access to ... for example IRAM ((*a radio telescope in Spain*)). (...) When a colleague of mine who just finished his PhD (and) was studying a certain type of object I said: "<u>Look</u> ... we can look at them with a <u>millimeter</u> ((*telescope*))." So I write the proposal because it helps if the first person is from one of the countries that pays the telescope. If you're ... It kind of puts you into the normal time allocation committee. (...) But because it's <u>his</u> science ... we will go and observe together ... maybe ... and then if I can reduce the data very quickly for him then I will do it for him. Or if neither of us knows how to reduce it ... then one of the two would have to learn. But it's kind of <u>his</u> science ... so I will let him lead the work ... write the paper. So we <u>try</u> and help each other without stealing each other's work. (...) And it tends to lead to papers with maybe six or eight authors. And sometimes they help you and sometimes ... So it's a kind of mutual <u>help</u> that works very well ... but in a very informal way.

Marcelo's small, informal collaborations differ from teams like SAMGES and MUWAGS in lacking defined membership, formal organization, name, and acronym. Marcelo's teams may use observing proposals as charters that state rights and duties, but their participants are not in contractual relations, there is no website that list team members, and their structures do not mirror those of other teams.

A principal reason for Marcelo and his colleagues to collaborate resembles the now familiar incentive to form larger teams: the need to assemble a diverse set of technical expertise to process complex datasets. As Marcelo explains:

Transcript 6.3
If you go and use many bands ... this is the thing with photometric redshifts or with multi-wavelength catalogs ... <u>one</u> person cannot reduce twelve bands of data ... right? You need <u>teams</u> to observe it ... teams to reduce it. They are different ... optical data ... are different from mid-infrared. So you need different <u>expertise</u>. And that will inevitably ... the more bands ... the more hours you used ... the more <u>people</u> you will end up with in your paper.

That each article's author list differs alerts us to the inherent flexibility of this kind of mutual aid.[36] Its participants act in settings in which the rights and obligations characteristic of larger collaborations do not apply, enabling shorter-lived and often fluid forms of collaboration. These do not have formal contractual resources for holding others to account because they are based on different social relations – of friendship and academic genealogy – whose social accountabilities work differently. Human work lives are the characteristic timescale of these ties.[37]

6.6.4   Hack Weeks: Exploring Complex Datasets Collaboratively

Beginning with the Early Data Release (EDR) of the SDSS in 2002 (Stoughton et al. 2002), several facility-building collaborations have released large datasets to the public, including the European Space Agency's Gaia spacecraft's catalogs of the positions, proper motions, and spectra of more than a billion stars and galaxies.[38] In principle, such datasets allow individual researchers and small teams to do "cutting-edge" science. But because these datasets are so complex they can be hard to understand for those who did not make them. Using them properly can seem forbidding.

Hack weeks offer a remedy. In the words of regular organizers, hack weeks "combine structured, tutorial-style instruction with open-ended project work, providing opportunities for peer learning, networking, and building collaborations" (Huppenkothen et al. 2018, 8873). Groups of participants are recruited through open calls for meetings that never last more than five days. Hack weeks often follow the release of new large, public datasets. Participants are invited to bring and use their own code and data, provided they are willing to share access to them. Hack weeks are thus a social form contingent on openness, inclusiveness, and the abundance of data.

In May 2023, I joined a group of 35 astronomers at the "GaiaXPloration Workshop," a hack week at the Institute for Astronomy in Cambridge (UK) designed to train astronomers in using a recently released large and complex dataset that the Gaia Data Processing and Analysis

---

[36] Sophisticated practices of relationship-building and mutual aid have been documented among resource-poor actors in a variety of fields (cf. Collins et al. 2010).

[37] Several large data-centric collaborations in astronomy have developed from the friendship of actors in influential organizational roles. Thus, "old boys'" networks (McDonald 2011) certainly matter in this field.

[38] See Figure 4.4 for a representation of early Gaia measurements.

Consortium (DPAC), a team of around 450 scientists and engineers, had produced. In June 2022, the DPAC had published the third Gaia data release, which included 220 million low-resolution spectra of stars and galaxies measured with the spacecraft's two spectrophotometers (Gaia Collaboration 2023). Due to Gaia's idiosyncratic observing and data-processing modes, these so-called XP spectra were not published in the conventional format as wavelength-dependent radiation flux densities (such as the continuous curve in Figure 3.2), but as a set of fifty-five parameters, coefficients of a mathematical (Hermite) function. This made their use nonintuitive for many potential users. Along with these data, the Gaia DPAC published GaiaXPy, a Python software package for calibration, transforming the coefficients into the conventional format and computing so-called synthetic colors in various wavebands – a means to compare the Gaia measurements with those of other projects. In their workshop announcement, the organizers wrote that "[o]ur goal is to bring together the collaboration that made this data product with the community that benefits from it, to create new scientific opportunities, by encouraging brainstorming and collective work between DPAC members and Gaia data users."[39]

Three days of morning lectures and afternoon work sessions were followed by two days of hacking. The workshop began with a round of introductions. Each participant had to contribute a "pitch slide," rehearsing "Who I am," "What I want to learn," and "What I want to do" with the Gaia XP spectra. Lectures included Gaia DPAC members explaining how they had processed the XP spectra and how to use GaiaXPy. Researchers gave brief presentations on their current work and how it may benefit from the XP spectra. At lunch and in the afternoon work sessions, participants met to discuss, collaborate, and explore selected problems and opportunities of data and code. This continued over the days of the workshop, each day ending with a daily round of wrap-up reports including all participants.

The workshop concluded with a more formal wrap-up session at which each participant presented a slide on "What I learned," "What I did," and "What I plan to do next." It demonstrated participants' enthusiasm for the data (e.g., "XP is much richer than I thought!," "OMG there is still so much to do with and learn from XP!") and their praise for the Gaia DPAC and its work. Responses to "What I did" revealed a variety of relations, new and preexisting, among participants. At the hack week, most had

---

[39] See ast.cam.ac.uk/events/gaia-xploration-discovery-and-measurement-low-resolution-spectroscopy (accessed July 7, 2025).

worked with at least two other participants. They wrote: "Classification of WD [white dwarf star] samples (w/ Brigitte Nigellu)," "Devised stress tests for XP alpha measurements (w/ Zhuangzi Li),"[40] "Measured velocity dispersions in the ancient bulge (w/ Lilo Watkins),"[41] and "Quizzed the DPAC team members." On their "What I plan to do next" slide, several participants announced their intention to continue what they had begun together at the hack week.

Compared to the lifetimes of long-lasting formal collaborations and ties of friendship, this hack week was fleetingly short, but it gathered scientists with preexisting relations and ended with new connections. Whereas the MUWAGS team used its internal diversity of expertise in trying to "break" its catalog and assuring its coherence, at the hack week it was the diversity of participants' skills and experiences that helped them to discover new uses of the XP spectra and made their projects with this large and complex public dataset doable.

6.7   Conclusion

This chapter has defined and described a field of research with large datasets. Rather than focusing on types of organization, I have probed into organizing and its resources.[42] Many data-centric collaborations have formal resources to organize their collaborative work, but I took a broader view of their available resources, following the maxim that scientists, like all people, use whatever is available to them to organize their affairs (Liberman 2013). These resources include medial orders (such as the formatting of digital data) and epistemic orders (such as shared understandings of cosmology and the electromagnetic spectrum), which scientists engage through realist practices (cf. also Chapters 3 and 5). More than that, the MUWAGS team used its catalog-in-the-making reflexively as an organizational resource. Many of these resources are unavoidably discipline-specific, but ethnographers examining other disciplines can identify them by probing into the resources that realist practices engage.[43]

---

[40] In this context, "alpha" (α) is a measure of the abundance of chemical elements formed in stars by alpha process nucleosynthesis, including oxygen, neon, and magnesium.

[41] Work pertaining to the structure and dynamics of the inner Milky Way Galaxy.

[42] See Shrum et al. (2007) for a typology of scientific collaborations and Paine and Lee (2021) for a typology of data-intensive collaborations.

[43] Ankeny and Leonelli's (2016) notion of "repertoires" is useful to conceive of disciplinary-specific resources, but Ankeny and Leonelli do not address their role in uses of accounting practices and the ordering of work.

Organizing data-centric collaboration means to establish, maintain, and care for social relationships. As organizational experiments, such collaborations often begin with ties of academic genealogy (supervisor–student, fellow graduate students) and friendship (relations among peers who have established mutual trust).[44] But data-centric collaborations also operate, and organize their work, in view of their obligations. Producing large datasets with public, tax-financed facilities obliges teams to share their data and offer data products that others can use. Observing proposals for large programs commonly specify such commitments, like waiving one's period of exclusive proprietary access. Thus, there is a promissory element reminiscent of what anthropologists have observed in gift exchange (Mauss 2016 [1923–24]; see Chapter 7). The perspective of both relationships and obligations is "internalist," that is, scientists locate initiatives, actions, and accountabilities within their professional world, typically within their discipline or subfield.

Most data-centric collaborations in astronomy begin with developing an observing proposal. Then a team exists before its dataset. But in the novel "ecology" of large public datasets, this order may be reversed. Smaller and shorter-lived teams may form to use such data. In 2007 – at the beginning of my work on this project, when many astronomers who still worked in small teams noticed the rising dominance of large collaborations –, Alexander Szalay, an astronomy professor at Johns Hopkins University and one of the founders of the "Virtual Observatory," gave a talk in which he argued that large databases would be the only way to work in small teams in the 2020s.[45] When I attended the GaiaXPloration workshop in 2023, this assessment rang true to me. Working with large databases like the 220 million Gaia XP spectra calls for novel forms of data-centric sociality that events like hack weeks enable.

Hack weeks may be the latest in a history of precedents that have shaped astronomers' work with large datasets since 1995, when Robert Williams and his team presented the HDF, followed by the SDSS in 2002. In setting precedents of data sharing with the HDF and the SDSS,

---

[44] Note that joint graduate training and early career interactions are rich in opportunities for demonstrating competence, honesty, and reliability – markers of trustworthiness that inspire well-placed trust (O'Neill 2014).

[45] Heidelberg Astronomical Colloquium, May 22, 2007. The Virtual Observatory was originally conceived to make all existing astronomical dataset available through one portal (Szalay and Gray 2001) but has evolved into a set of standards that a variety of data centers uses. See ivoa.net (accessed April 26, 2025).

Robert Williams and James Gunn were both late in their careers and operated from influential, central positions in academic astronomy. Williams aimed to change astronomy's "culture" and Gunn its "sociology." But how should other astronomers act properly in either? Facing expectations of the open access to one's data makes normativity a practical problem for scientists that I examine in Chapter 7.

CHAPTER 7

Normativity
Inhabiting Statuses in "Open Science"

7.1 This Chapter's Plan

This chapter considers "open science" as a practical problem for scientists. The "open science movement" – a set of various governmental and organizational initiatives – has been described as aiming "to foster the wide dissemination, scrutiny and reuse of research components for the good of science and society" (Leonelli 2023, 1), but "open science" has also been identified as "an ambiguous and deeply political concept" (Ross-Hellauer et al. 2022, 13).[1] In the naturalistic spirit of my inquiry, I confine myself to what is arguably central to it: the extended access to research data. I consider how researchers evaluate the social and moral accountabilities of the open access to data and the tensions that result from them. I focus on astronomy, where the access to research data has been remarkably open (see Chapter 6).[2] Most large scientific datasets are made by collaborations and thus I examine two exemplars. I begin with the ALLSKY (pseudo-acronym) consortium and then return to the MUWAGS (Multiwavelength Galaxy Survey; a pseudonym) collaboration described in Chapter 6. As members of both teams prepared datasets for public release, they became both inquirers into, and actors in, what many astronomers refer to as their discipline's "culture of open data access." I witnessed these teams being groups of "practical methodologists" (Garfinkel 1967, 180) who used their "inner dialogues" to explore the normative expectations and tensions of this domain, seeking to inhabit a proper status in it. I argue that examining scientists' understanding of status and its achievement offers resources for a refined critique of "open science" that is considerate of the context sensitivity of

---

[1] See also Mirowski (2018) and Beck et al. (2022).
[2] There are also remarkable communal open software developments in astronomy, such as the work of the Astropy collaboration (2013, 2018, 2022).

data production and use. Along the way, we will examine some methods of how scientists, as members, are doing ethnography.

7.2 "What Do We Owe to Others?"

Let us begin with a discussion of the public release of a large dataset among members of ALLSKY, an international collaboration that was to build and operate a dedicated telescope for a novel photographic sky survey. This survey would revisit the same parts of the sky every two weeks to detect variable sources in the "dynamic sky," including asteroids that could hit the Earth. Adding these exposures would disattend from variations and produce very deep images of the "static sky," particular in its deep and medium deep survey components. The survey would include the y band (around 960 nanometer), a waveband missing in most other projects but useful for detecting distant quasars (active galactic nuclei) and brown dwarfs (substellar objects). This made ALLSKY distinct from existing projects like the Sloan Digital Sky Survey (SDSS, cf. Chapter 6). The ALLSKY consortium comprised 130 scientists working at 36 institutes in 6 countries, who contributed to the building and operating costs for early access to its data.

It had been decided at the outset that ALLSKY would make a comprehensive public data release after its completion, but this was far in the future. In the meantime, fellow astronomers could become envious of the consortium's data. This was a concern for the ALLSKY team. When Henry (pseudonym), the director of a member institute, returned from an ALLSKY board meeting and reported about it to a group of local ALLSKY researchers, he addressed this issue. An important context for this discussion is the institute's earlier involvement in the SDSS, which had published an Early Data Release (EDR) two years into its first five-year observing phase.[3]

> Transcript 7.1
> 1 Henry: Another relevant point was that the ((ALLSKY)) board
>   at least talked about that we need to do something
>   else about making the data public to the world. At
>   the moment it says there will be one data release just
>   exactly one year after the whole affair is <u>done</u>. That
>   means ... in five years down the road there will be
>   a data dump. <u>Sloan</u> ((Digital Sky Survey)) and other

---

[3] See the Appendix for a complete list of the transcription conventions adopted.

experience has shown that this just makes the project <u>unpopular</u> with the community ... which if you write follow up telescope proposals ... if you write grant proposals ... if you write this and that ... just always ... you know ... the envy factor ... just always <u>kills</u> the proposals. So ... ehm ... <u>one</u> of the specific things that was actually thought about was to have ... a year after the survey starts ... to release a multi-color dataset that covers one percent of the sky to a medium depth. Perhaps even <u>popular</u> parts of the sky. But there is probably also something where at the April meeting input will be solicited.

2	Eddie:	That sounds like a <u>really</u> bad idea.
3	Henry:	Hmm?
4	Eddie:	That sounds like a really bad idea.
5	Francesca:	Did you say just <u>one</u> per cent?
6	Henry:	[Yeah.
7	Joe:	[Yeah.
8	Eddie:	Aha ... HA-HA-HA-HA ... let's just release the first <u>byte</u> ... the first <u>bit</u> to everybody.
9	( ):	(EDR)
10	Henry:	Well ... that's what ((the SDSS)) EDR ((*Early Data Release*)) was.
11	(Group):	((*intense cross-talking*))
12	Joe:	But EDR was a different motivation ... EDR was to prove to the funding ... to the funders that they can actually <u>publish</u> ... you know ... process and <u>publish</u> data. That was different. That wasn't for the community ... that was to keep the money flowing.
13	Henry:	That's true ... but if you ... for example ... ( )
14	Joe:	I know ... if it was <u>full</u> depth ... like ... if you ... you know ...no ... well we need to discuss ... obviously.
15	( ):	That sounds like
16	Henry:	That is obviously to be discussed.
17	Eddie:	ha-ha-ha-ha-ha If I was on a National Science Foundation panel ... I wouldn't buy that. I'd be like ... "<u>forget</u> <u>it</u>!"
18	Henry:	Ehm ... You know ... it's not my ...
19	Eddie:	I know.
20	Joe:	Is this <u>a</u> suggestion ... or is this the official <u>board</u> suggestion?
21	Henry:	<u>No</u> ... the board said ... for example ... one could consider a near real time release of ALLSKY data covering <u>one</u> percent of the sky. It's just ... you know ...
22	Nour:	Ehm ... what's <u>specific</u> with ALLSKY?

23	Francesca:	Its depth …
24	Joe:	Its y band
25	Henry:	Its time dependence
26	Joe:	Yeah
27	Eddie:	Its time dependence in ((sky)) area.
28	Keira:	So … an area pre-release is obviously not useful?
29	Joe:	And a time dependence pre-release?
30	Kristin:	That is difficult.
31	Henry:	Why? I mean three hundred … you know … three hundred or a thousand square degrees with … time <u>sampling</u> is a dataset that doesn't <u>exist</u>.
32	Joe:	Yeah … but it's also the dataset that everybody in the science consortium <u>paid</u> to get first. So …
33	Henry:	Ah::: … so <u>now</u> you're saying it's already <u>too</u> much! You see … this is how the number came about. I've heard this is ridiculously <u>little</u>.
34	Eddie:	I think it makes no sense to release … something so small as a first data release. The point is that the three interesting things about ALLSKY are <u>area</u> … <u>depth</u> in the medium deep survey … and a <u>time</u> sampling. And … so … if … no … the first data release the community needs to have all three aspects in it. ehm … and it's okay if that comes two years after the start of observations. But the point is we do have to make something <u>useful</u> available for the community … because otherwise it will just be viewed as an insult.

The conversation documents these scientists' expectation that fellow researchers would hold them accountable for releasing their data. Henry reports the board's concern that astronomers beyond the collaboration, unable to access ALLSKY's data in a timely fashion, could become envious and may, when serving on review panels, punish ALLSKY members by rejecting their follow-up observing or grant proposals. This sort of retaliation, Henry argues, was likely. To preempt this, a certain amount of data could be released early. But Eddie, a tenured staff scientist, rejects the proposed amount as insufficient and emerges as a thoroughly critical voice. His critique (in lines 2 and 4) opens the floor for a collaborative exploration of what is specific about the new dataset and how much of it could be shared without violating the interests of the consortium that pays for the survey. Francesca's question of clarification (line 5) is followed by Eddie's apparently ironic suggestion to share an unusably small amount of data (line 8), comparisons with the SDSS EDR (lines 10 and 12), reminders of the provisional state of discussion (line 16), Eddie's impersonation (using reported direct speech) of an imagined peer reviewer (line 17), as well as a request about the offer's author (line 20). Eventually, participants turn to review the ALLSKY dataset's unique value (lines 22 to 27), which team members felt obliged to share, at least in part, and in a timely manner (lines 28 to 34).

Transcript 7.1 demonstrates how ALLSKY members anticipated their peers' expectations, but it also suggests that we need to know more about it and its context to understand the team's decision-making. ALLSKY's regular survey operation was not to begin for another two years after this discussion, a period in which a series of constraints to its conduct emerged that derailed the options that team members had discussed. One of these was that a significant part of ALLSKY's funding came from the United States Air Force. Wary that EDRs may reveal the orbits of secret military satellites, it initially blocked the sharing of some data even within the collaboration. Another constraint was the lack of funding to prepare a partial data pre-release. As a result, a comprehensive data release was published only two years after the end of survey operations. Collaboration members shared these reasons with their peers external to the team.

7.3 Norms and Statuses

These later developments do not affect this conversation's exploratory character, which is worth examining in more detail. With nobody refusing to release some data early, it marked the beginning of a joint search for what an adequate quality and amount of data to release early would be like, informed by an understanding of the survey's specifics and the consortium's self-interest. There was no rule or written document that specified the apparently normative expectations they sought to meet. As Nick Enfield (2013, 22; emphasis in original) defines them, norms are "learned patterns of behavior that are consistent in a community not because it is explicitly stated anywhere that they be followed like rules, but because *not* behaving in a manner consistent with those patterns will attract special attention in the form of surprise or sanction." That peer reviewers will reject future ALLSKY proposals if the consortium refuses to pre-release data may be a sanction. But are there norms that Henry and his colleagues can follow to preempt this threat?

Norms in everyday life, such as the expectation for a greeting to be returned, are typically unproblematic and routinely understood by interlocutors. While most greetings are not consciously interpreted, Henry and his colleagues cannot but interpret and argue about what an adequate ALLSKY data pre-release would be like. They may or may not come to an agreement and it is possible that not all external scientists will agree that ALLSKY will have adequately shared its data. In fact, there may not be a unique communal assessment of the team's conduct. Philosopher Robert Brandom (1994, 38; emphasis in original) notes in a discussion of normativity that "the idea of communal performances, assessments, or verdicts (...) is a fiction," since "assenting, endorsing, accepting, and regarding as right are in the first instance things done by *individuals*." The normativity of sharing data is not like the normativity of responding to a greeting or that of using linguistic practices correctly.[4] But note that Henry's expression of concern (in line 1) lacks a reference to personal names and explicitly references "the community." It pertains to every astronomer who could be on a peer-evaluation committee, a marker of membership in the community of professional astronomers. This is how Henry and his fellow ALLSKY board members appear to conceive of, and acknowledge, communal assessments.

But what about the use of precedents? In line 9, an unidentified speaker appears to suggest the SDSS's EDR as a precedent for an ALLSKY data pre-release. Even though Joe points out that the SDSS EDR had been made to assure its funding and not to avoid community members' blame (in line 12), precedents have been important in this domain. After all, as described in Chapter 6, many astronomers regard the Hubble Deep Field (HDF) and the SDSS as precedents that transformed communal attitudes and practices toward data sharing.[5] Brandom (1979, 189) argues that "[s]ocial practices evolve the way case-law does – an issue may be resolved very differently depending upon where in a chain of precedents it comes up for adjudication."[6] Precedents can be invoked, but do not prescribe how this adjudication is to unfold; they are resources for its conduct.

---

[4] Except, perhaps, for a hypothetical rule for all researchers to make all research data public immediately after their production, it seems impossible to formulate a universal norm for releasing data publicly. This provides scientists with options and reasons to navigate demands for access to their data and other resources. Thus, Hilgartner (2017, 72) argues that scientific work entails a "dialectic of revelation and concealment through which knowledge is selectively made available and unavailable." Developing this insight in an interview-based study, Levin and Leonelli (2017, 280) conceive of openness as "a dynamic and highly situated mode of valuing the research process and its outputs." On discipline-specific differences in openness, see Velden (2013).

[5] See, for instance, Almeida et al. (2023, 3).

[6] Barnes (1995, 55) points out that following a rule or norm means to act "in a way learned by familiarity with previous accepted instances or examples. The intention is to act in proper analogy with those examples."

Participants in the discussion examine ALLSKY's rights and duties. In so doing, they probe into what we may call its status. Paul Kockelman (2007, 57) follows Ralph Linton (1936) in defining a person's status as a "collection of rights and responsibilities attendant upon inhabiting a certain position in the social fabric."[7] These rights and responsibilities are not necessarily fixed once and for all but are often contestable and negotiable. Statuses are hard to pin down because they are objects in semiotic processes. They are never directly observable but always interpreted through uses of signs. ALLSKY, however, is not a human person. It is a large project run by an internationally distributed team that is a "unit of accountability" (Kockelman 2007, 154). Through its organization, name, and acronym it resembles a firm or juridical person. To outsiders it is a unit with a singular observing program and dataset that it will publish as a collective author. Henry and his colleagues leave little doubt that it inhabits a certain position in astronomy's "social fabric."[8]

If inhabiting a status is a work-in-progress,[9] then how do collaboration members manage their incumbency? To examine this question naturalistically we can take inspiration from Harold Garfinkel's study of how Agnes, a person undergoing sex-reassignment surgery, sought to pass as a properly gendered person. Garfinkel (1967, 180) describes Agnes as a "practical methodologist" who investigates "everyday activities as members' methods for producing correct decisions about normal sexuality in ordinary activities." Agnes does so for her own uses. Elsewhere, Garfinkel remarks that "members doing sociology" ought to "treat the rational properties of practical activities as 'anthropologically strange'" (Garfinkel 1967, 9). He notices that it is in "doing, recognizing, and using ethnographies" that members accomplish the "analyzability of actions-in-context." Considering that this is "for members a commonplace phenomenon" (Garfinkel 1967, 10), it would seem that "doing ethnography" is a routine task and achievement for members. In Garfinkel's view, every social actor, as member, is an ethnographer, and here we ought to include Agnes (who made visible to Garfinkel and his readers what "properly gendered persons" routinely do).

---

[7] Like Kockelman and Linton, I do not understand status as signifying prestige or an element in a social hierarchy. Enfield (2013, 57) points out that status resembles the notion of membership category in conversation analysis and ethnomethodology, whose practitioners likewise examine its contextual and sequential production in specific cases (cf. Sacks 1992; Housley and Fitzgerald 2009; Fitzgerald and Housley 2015).

[8] How the collaboration acts collectively appears to shape its identity in its social environment (cf. Blommaert 2019).

[9] In Linton's (1936) terminology, this pertains to achieved statuses (that are inhabited through intentional acts; cf. Kockelman 2007), as contrasted with ascribed statuses (that one is born into).

We may also include these astronomers, who seek to pass as scientists who make their data adequately accessible.[10] While Agnes manages what are, to her, novel gender expectations, these scientists seek to manage what are, to them, novel expectations of a public data release. Neither Agnes nor these scientists can act unreflectively as in returning an everyday greeting.

Note how Henry and his colleagues locate practices of releasing data and their assessment within their professional world, their academic discipline. Many astronomers know, of course, that public policies and institutional conditions and accountabilities shape the domain in which they work, including, for example, NASA's data policies and initiatives for interdisciplinarity promoted since the 1990s.[11] But in this discussion such organizational constraints are mentioned only once, in Eddie's impersonation of a United States National Science Foundation reviewer (line 17). This agency mandates that the outputs of its funded projects are made "publicly available to the greatest extent" in a timely fashion.[12]

Many astronomers express their understanding of this "internalism" in cultural terms as a contrast with the alleged closure of high-energy physics, where the measurements produced by particle accelerators are not shared beyond instrument-centered collaborations that tend to keep their data and analysis software secret.[13] Thus, one astronomer, in his early thirties, told me:

Transcript 7.2

These are simply different cultures. For us it is clear that data ought to be open … and for them ((the high-energy physicists)) it is obvious that it is stupid to publish data … since other people can't know how to deal with them. That is the most common argument … "It is so complicated to get from our raw data to our data products. Nobody else would have a chance to get it right."

But not all uses of the term "culture" are so clear-cut. When I asked Robert Williams about the HDF as a precedent for changing astronomers' attitudes of access to their data (cf. Chapter 6), he responded that "it seemed

---

[10] Compare how Hester and Eglin (2017, 200) call any social actor "an inquirer into the practical circumstances that confront the member going about the business of everyday life, an ethnographer of its culture." Ethnography, as these ethnomethodologists understand it, does not involve a critical step back from acting in context. Garfinkel glosses over the distinction of "doing ethnography" and its products – typically written accounts. See also Section 7.5 and Chapters 2, 3, and 8.

[11] See Genova (2018) and Borgman and Wofford (2021) on astronomy as a model of open data access.

[12] See nsf.gov/public-access (accessed July 7, 2025).

[13] See also White (2007). The attitude here ascribed to high-energy physicists appears to have changed. Laboratories such as CERN in Geneva (Switzerland) have made much of their data public, cf. opendata.cern.ch (accessed May 13, 2025). With the involvement of the US Air Force in its funding and operation, ALLSKY was to meet a very different culture.

to me really important to change this whole … <u>culture</u>." Note the slight pause before Williams utters the word "culture," as if he was searching for a word that better expressed his intended meaning, but finding none. Utterances like these suggest that these scientists invoke the notion of "culture" for general accounts of data access practices in astronomy – that data somehow become openly accessible at all. But to understand its practical implications for researchers we need to examine their conduct's finer granularity.

7.4 Doing "Being 'Open Scientists'"

Equipped with these considerations, let us return to the MUWAGS collaboration that I discussed in Chapter 6. Remember that MUWAGS was an international team of astronomers that made a multiwavelength dataset of the galaxy supercluster A2713 to investigate its dark matter content and its environmental impact on galaxy evolution. Much of MUWAGS's collaborative work was oriented toward making a master catalog: a table of measured and estimated properties of ca. 88.000 objects detected in the A2713 field based on the team's ground-based optical data, the Hubble Space Telescope (HST) imaging mosaic, and the Spitzer Multi-Band Imaging Photometer infrared observations. This catalog was a resource for most team members' research projects. It was also the central element of the public data release that the team published at the end of its core science work.

As successful applicants for observing time at major observatories, including the HST, senior MUWAGS scientists' membership in professional astronomy was established beyond doubt. But how could they "do being 'open scientists'" together?[14] How could they act to produce a data release that was adequate for the team, as its authors, and usable for scientists beyond the team? And how do these questions point to methodological issues of an ethnographic kind?

Let us ponder these questions by examining a discussion at a MUWAGS collaboration meeting a few months before the data release. At this moment the catalog was already finished – "frozen in" as Mallory, the principal investigator, called it (cf. Chapters 6 and 8). The team now considered options for how to release it and how to formulate instructions for users that were to be posted on the archive website. Besides Mallory – who is gathering ideas for this text –, Christina, Mike, Ken, and Ben are

---

[14] Here I imitate Sacks's (1992, vol. 2, 215) title, "Doing 'Being Ordinary.'"

the speakers in the following discussion, at which Elias and three other team members, as well as me (GH) as an ethnographer, were also present. IMAGS and LENSURV (pseudo-acronyms) are the names of broadly similar collaborations that used public observatories and prepared data releases, whereas GalaxFit and REDCOR (pseudo-acronyms) are the names of open-access computer codes for data analysis.

Transcript 7.3

1   Christina: Now IMAGS has an interesting eh … so … <u>data</u> use policy in that you can download and use the data for anything but if you want to <u>publish</u> it you have to contact … them.

2   ((*3 second pause*))

3   Mallory: For <u>permission</u>?

4   Christina: For <u>permission</u> … yeah. This is a new one only. I never heard people doing this before.

5   Mallory: And are they are they … is there <u>authorship</u> … eh issues there as well?

6   Christina: I … eh eh so we've been looking at different models for authorship for the LENSURV because … we've had various problems with people using the archive data but … <u>anyway</u> … ehm but we've been looking at different models and that's the one that I'm <u>personally</u> interested in and that's the IMAGS model. So I don't propose we have any of that but … we <u>cou::ld</u> if we wanted … if we were worried about our <u>ke::y</u> science being taken by other people.

7   Mallory: Well I think I think we've made a decision when we made it public that … eh … we weren't gonna wait so <u>long</u> that everything has been <u>done</u> by us … ehh … but we and we weren't gonna release things … for which we put in a <u>ton</u> of work and never had a <u>chance</u> to have … ehmm … reap the rewards. But for the <u>rest</u> of it I think it's it's kind of the <u>other</u> side of the coin is the incentive for <u>us</u>.

8   Christina: Yes no I think we should

9   Mallory: So I don't think we can release it and then say you <u>can't</u> use it for the science (area).

10   Christina: No:: but we could have something saying "we … we're really keen to hear about what you are doing

11   Mallory: <u>Yeah</u>!

12   Christina: with the <u>data</u>."

13   Mallory: Oh yeah definitely. "Tell us" … <u>OR</u> "If you don't wanna do it on your own if you want to collaborate with us that's fine as well."

14	Christina:	Yeah
15	Mike:	Mm hm
16	Mallory:	Yeah. And I think a friendly note saying "Please keep us informed as to how you <u>use</u> these data." ... That would be a way out of it.
17	Ken:	<u>Or</u> directions on (how) to use the data ... like with GalaxFit ... Don't you have to register or give your email so you can download it? So that you can
18	Mike:	GalaxFit? <u>No!</u>
19	Ken:	Who <u>did</u> that? Somebody did that with an application you know
20	Mallory:	<u>Ye::ah!</u>
21	Ken:	I don't want I don't want to ... basically they were saying it was for <u>updates</u>.
22	Christina:	Yeah.
23	Ken:	I just want to [keep a list of people that are
24	Ben:	[CHUANG
25	Ken:	<u>interested</u>.
26	Ben:	<u>Chuang</u> <u>asks</u> people to send him an email but he ... because he ... constantly sends around upgrades on the on the pro-gram but it's not a <u>need</u>
27	Mike:	Aguirre does that for REDCOR
28	Ken:	That <u>could</u> be that you just don't get to the download page ... unless you put an email address. You know [( )
29	Mike:	[when he asks up to ... ehh ... what? ... certain to <u>reference</u> certain papers of his ... if you're using his work and to send him an email if you're using the code ... But you can still <u>download</u> them and not do anything.
30	Christina:	Yeah that's not bad.
31	Mallory:	I think I'll put that on <u>top</u> of the page that ... you know ... "A few things" ... "please read before you download" ... "please send us your email" ... you know ... "please reference"
32	Ken:	"Please (put in your email address and) ( )"
33	Ben:	Put put <u>check</u> <u>boxes</u> ... like that
34	Ken:	"I've read [the
35	Ben:	["the terms and conditions"
36	Mallory:	haha
37	(Group):	HA-HA-HA-HA-HA-ha-ha-ha ((*collective laughter*))
38	Mallory:	Yeah
39	Ken:	A statement ... "<u>Billing</u> address ... please add your credit card here"
40	Ben:	hhh[( )

41 (Group):   [HA-HA-HA-HA-HA-ha-ha-ha ((*explosive collective laughter*))
42 Ken: Not that we'll use it of course
43 (Group):   uhuhuhuh
44 Ken: but we <u>need</u> it.
45 (Group):   ha-ha-ha-ha ((*collective laughter subsiding*))
46 Mike: It's always good to have that information.
47 Mallory: A <u>deposit</u>
48 Ken: A deposit
49 Mallory: [A deposit
50 Mike: [he-he-he-he
51 Mallory: "If you <u>misuse</u> the data we will charge you."
52 Ben: ha-ha-ha
53 Christina: Anything new might be less worth if it is just internet-based that people submit their (internet)( ) e-mail but I'm not very sure how many people would do that ... there is only a handful ( ) not to worry
54 Ken: But it would be easier for people to just put in ... to fill in a field before they press the download button

Whereas the conversationalists in Transcript 7.1 examined duties and responsibilities, here the focus is on the balance of credit and responsibility characteristic of authorship.[15] These astronomers' concern is to be recognized as the authors of data, while not being "scooped" for scientific results and blamed for misuses of their data. Christina's description of the IMAGS data release policy as a possible precedent, a model for how MUWAGS could proceed (line 1), turns into an exercise in the collaborative formulation of instructions for users of the MUWAGS data release. It begins with Christina formulating a request to users, hearable through her use of syntax and prosody as quoting a text (lines 10 and 12). Mallory continues in the same style (lines 13 and 16). Ken, Mike, and Ben supplement Christina's account of the IMAGS model with their knowledge of how other researchers share their open-access data analysis software – two possible models for MUWAGS (lines 17 to 29). Instead of making data or software available unconditionally to anonymous users, these discussants seek to identify user identities and explore measures to hold them to account. Mallory uses these suggestions to formulate written instructions. As before it is her use of syntax and prosody that makes her utterance hearable as the quotation of a text (line 31).

---

[15] On authorship as credit and responsibility see Foucault (1977), Rennie et al. (1997), Biagioli (2003, 2006), Galison (2003), and O'Neill (2022).

Ken and Ben build on Mallory's formulation, continuing with similar prosody indicating textual quotation, but invoking the language of legal contracts and payments (lines 32 to 39). Unlike Christina's and Mallory's formulations (in lines 10, 12, 13, and 16), their playful and apparently ironic remarks elicit loud collective laughter (in lines 37 and 41), initiated, respectively, by Mallory (line 36) and Ben (line 40), and subsequently petering out (in lines 43 and 45). This laughter appears to edit, or even negate, the literal meaning of these contractual terms. With her suggestion for users to leave a monetary deposit, Mallory (in lines 47 and 49) continues to invoke the language of legal contracts and again uses syntax and prosody to mark a textual quotation (line 51). Her formulation instigates Ben's and Mike's laughter (line 50 and 52). Christina subsequently returns (in line 53) to speech with normal prosody. She does not continue to laugh, nor does she build on the formulation, thus marking a return to a non-ironic mode.

These invocations of the language of legal contracts can be heard as being ironical and playful.[16] This irony is invoked and sustained, and thereby apparently understood, by those who participate in this formulating and in the subsequent laughter.[17] References to users committing to a contractual agreement can be heard as expressing these scientists' concern about the proper use of their data and their desire to hold users accountable for their actions in a legal sense. Although these suggestions were dismissed, they arguably point to what these scientists would like but cannot have in astronomy's regime of open access. Christina's return to non-ironic speech (in line 53) marks a return to assessing what one could, after all, do as "open scientists": asking data users for their email addresses and formulating written instructions for them.

Note that by invoking the language of legal contracts ("terms and conditions"), uses of bank accounts and credit cards, these scientists are borrowing from the everyday culture that these young astronomers from Western Europe, the USA, and Canada partly share, and translating from it to a novel domain of open data access. These junior scientists seek to act adequately in this domain. Their joking and playful uses of irony seem to be conscious and deliberate as they examine what can be expected of them and what they could get away with as they inhabit a status in this domain of open access.

[16] Compare this with line 8 in Transcript 7.1, where Eddie likewise adds laughter to an utterance and thus makes it hearable as being ironic.
[17] Compare Sidnell (2010a, 70). See also Hutchby and Drew (1995) and Clift (1999).

7.5 Ethnography, Translation, and Irony

As these scientists use terms from one domain for exploring how to act in another, translation and irony are two of their "methods of social inquiry" (Garfinkel 1967, 104). Examining them further helps refine the notion of "scientists doing ethnography" that I began considering in Chapters 2 and 3. Translation has been deeply implicated in how sociocultural anthropologists have conceived of ethnography. It was often understood, sometimes tacitly, as the translation of systems, not only of language, but also of "cultures as an assemblage of texts" (Geertz 1973, 448) and "modes of thought" (Lienhardt 1954, 95), particularly in British social anthropology (Asad 1986). Thus conceived, its currency has reached beyond the writing of ethnographies into debates on relativism and to Thomas Kuhn's view of scientific change.[18] Notably, Kuhn (1970, 175) argues that communities of scientists are "language communities." As Susan Gal (2015) observes, sociologists' and anthropologists' more recent understandings of translation point to a wide range of semiotic processes. These include approaches like Actor-Network Theory (Latour 2005), which dwells on a metaphorical understanding of translation, as well as what is essential to ethnography as a method: "[l]anguage learning, note-taking, interaction, transcription, and the effort to make findings intelligible to colleagues all require translations of various kinds" (Gal 2015, 228).

William Hanks and Carlo Severi (2014, 2) insist that people from all walks of life translate by means of what they, as linguistic anthropologists, call "code switching, blending, crossing, paraphrasing, reported speech, and giving accounts."[19] They argue that "understanding is itself a matter of translation" (Hanks and Severi 2014, 2), or, as Hanks (2014, 21; emphasis in original) puts it yet more poignantly, "the intralingual translation of an expression quite simply *is its meaning*." It is not only that translation is prevalent in monolingual speech. Rather, "translation is not only productive but at the heart of language as a social form, and society as the dynamic product of self-interpretation" (Hanks 2014, 33). This insight may well be gained from Harvey Sacks' lectures on conversation,[20] but Hanks and Severi take inspiration from Roman Jakobson's (1959) essay "On

---

[18] See, for example, Hollis and Lukes (1982).

[19] Note that translation harks back to early concerns of ethnomethodology, whose central notion of indexicality was inspired by considering troubles in early efforts of machine translation (Garfinkel and Sacks 1970, 349).

[20] See especially Sacks' lecture on "patients with observers" as "performers with audience" (Sacks 1992, vol. 2, 104–113).

Linguistic Aspects of Translation." For Jakobson, intralingual translation is one of three kinds of translation besides the more familiar cross-language translation and the cross-modal translation of speech into gestures.[21]

An alternative formulation of the generativity of translation is Michael Silverstein's (2003) notion of transduction. Silverstein questions that one term, translation, adequately describes what is in fact a continuum of practices, of which purely denotational "word-by-word" translation is one extreme and at the same time a caricature, since there may never be a complete and specifiable correspondence of grammatical-categorial spaces in source and target languages. Silverstein proposes the notion of transduction as a mode that takes translation seriously as an unavoidably indexical and interactional practice.[22]

Consonant with Silverstein's reasoning, Hanks and Severi (2014, 2) note that "[i]ronically, the process of successive failed translation may be our best tool in discerning what is specific to any object society or to any 'original.' In other words, it becomes a method (…)." A method, one may add, for analysts and members. A method, too, for exploring unfamiliar worlds, such as, for these junior scientists, the open access to their data. Christina, Mallory, Ben, Ken, and Mike, it seems, attempted to translate between two domains. But compared to the practices of translation that Silverstein (2003) describes – from the "other's language" to one's own –, theirs was a translation in the opposite direction, as they playfully adopted terms and actions from their quotidian culture to describe actions in astronomy's "culture of open data access."[23]

By addressing the "simultaneous presence of two dimensions of meaning" (Clift 1999, 533) irony shares some aspects with translation, but, rather than seeking to reveal "sameness-in-difference" (Gal 2015, 226), it arguably projects "an attitude of disbelief along with the 'outer' meaning of their words" to "convey a contrary, 'inner,' meaning to those who can catch the cue." As such, it can express a "questioning attitude" or "critical stance"

---

[21] Each of these kinds draws on Charles Sanders Peirce's notions of the sign and chain-like semiosis, which precipitate open-ended processes of interpretation and communication (cf. Peirce 1932, 135; Daniel 1984, 19; and Parmentier 1994, 5; see also the discussion in Hoeppe 2020a).

[22] For Silverstein, who (like Jakobson) draws on Peirce, transduction is intermediate between translation (narrowly conceived) and the transformation of meaning: "there is always something of the transformational in every attempted translation" (Silverstein 2003, 93).

[23] This direction of translation was common in early ethnographic accounts which projected elements of Euro-American culture, history, and mythology onto the societies investigated. This is recognizable, for example, in the title of Edward Evans-Pritchard's (1937) book *Witchcraft, Oracles, and Magic among the Azande*, that projects ritual notions from European history onto the practices of an African society.

(Fernandez and Huber 2001, 1). In Transcript 7.3, I see it as consonant with playfulness as an exploration of possible alternative actions.[24] Yet, as Hayden White (1973, 37) argues, irony may also signal "the ascent of thought in a given area of inquiry to a level of self-consciousness on which a genuinely 'enlightened' – that is to say, self-critical – conceptualization of the world and its processes has become possible."

7.6　A Theft of Data?

Participants in the discussions described in Transcripts 7.1 and 7.3 considered their duties and rights in sharing their data prospectively. Let us refine our inquiry and consider retrospective assessments of duties and rights in a case that sheds further light on the open access to data as a moral issue. When MUWAGS was about to publish its data release, the standard one-year period of the team's exclusive proprietary use of HST observations had ended and its "raw data" (processed not by the team but by observatory staff in standard ways unspecific to any scientific use) had become available to anyone who wished to download and work with them. This was a grave concern for Christina, who learned that a competing group based in Munich (Germany) had downloaded the MUWAGS data, presumably for just the kind of analysis that she worked on herself, but had not completed yet. Consequently, she rushed to finish her analysis of the A2713 galaxy supercluster.

In Transcript 7.4, Christina has wrapped up an account of mapping dark matter in A2713, when Mallory, the team's principal investigator, asks her about the work of the Munich group (line 1). Like Christina and Mallory, Elias is a member of MUWAGS, whereas Albert, Andrew, and Anthony are (absent) members of "the Munich group," known (by Christina) and referred to by their first names. Mentioned already in Transcript 7.3, LENSURV is a large weak lensing survey with a ground-based telescope of which Christina is a member. I use quotation marks to transcribe what I heard as reported direct speech.

Transcript 7.4
1　Mallory:　　Hmm … (are there) any news from the <u>Munich</u> group (what about) <u>their</u> analysis?

---

[24] See also Chapter 4 on exploratory uses of playfulness. In an instructive anthropological study, Basso (1979) links irony to playfulness. Taken to its extreme, however, irony may amount to a suspension of seriousness and a retreat from much human social life (Nguyen 2022, 276).

2	Christina:	They <u>stole</u> our LENSURV data instead and started working on that which I've [( )
3	Elias:	[huhuhuh[hu
4	Mallory:	[hehe[he
5	Christina:	[HA-HA
6	Elias:	You have some (<u>thieves</u> following you)[( )
7	(Mallory):	[HA-HA-HA
8	Christina:	Ha they <u>steal</u> my HST ((*Hubble Space Telescope*)) data and then <u>steal</u> my ground-based data it's <u>ri::ght</u>! ... haHA haHA ... yeah
9	Elias:	Ah:::
10	Christina:	They're like "oh you wouldn't need some of the HST data ... we're taking it" so .... hh-ha-ha-ha-ha-ha
11	Elias:	No::: heh
12	Christina:	I think they (would be in that) mood
13	Elias:	Have they (started the data analysis)( )
14	Christina:	Ehm ... well I see Albert end of <u>May</u> so we did we we we also spoke about it we said "we should really do some comparisons" and (I don't know) ... ehm ... I wrote to <u>Andrew</u> and Anthony yesterday who are doing a 3D analysis and haven't heard <u>back</u> ... so ... I don't know how that's going but Andrew also has the Munich catalog so he's the ... sort of most ... eh ... <u>likely</u> person to do ... that sort of analysis but ... they don't have the redshifts so there is not much they can do ... until the data release anyway ... ehh
15	Mallory:	Can you take the Munich catalog?
16	Christina:	Yeah yeah yeah ... if we <u>wanted</u> to ... it's not that bad an idea because they've got a much better PSF ((*Point Spread Function*)) correction scheme

Asked by Mallory about the competing team's work (line 1), Christina, a native speaker of English, responds that instead of using the MUWAGS data to "scoop" her on the analysis of A2713, as she had feared they might do, they "stole" her other dataset (line 2). As she emphasizes the verb "stole," her voice exhibits a raise in pitch, a prosodic shift. Elias and Mallory react with contained laughter (lines 3 and 4), to which Christina (in line 5) herself responds with louder laughter. Elias then interprets Christina's statement and builds on it, responding to her reference to "stealing" with a statement on "thieves" (line 6). Someone, probably Mallory, reacts with laughter (line 7), upon which Christina raises her voice in a noticeable prosodic shift (line 8), thereby animating imagined direct reported speech (line 10). Referring to members of the Munich group by their first names, she indicates that those who "stole" her data are no strangers to her and the others present, and would presumably even share their work ("the Munich catalog") with Christina and her colleagues (lines 14 to 16).

A notable feature of this exchange is Christina's report on the alleged theft of data and her subsequent laughter. What she presents is "troubles-talk" and one may well hear her laughter as exhibiting "troubles-resistance" (Jefferson 1984, 351), that is, her demonstration that these troubles are not getting the better of her. If so, her laughter edits, and possibly negates, the accusation's literal meaning. Since her laughter was joined by that of other collaboration members (lines 3, 4, and 7), who conceive of these data as collectively theirs, they may experience trouble as well. More specifically, this exchange can be heard as an instance of irony, where what Christina meant is not literally expressed by her words, but subverts the words' literal meaning. In using data that had become public already, the "Munich group" acted legitimately and did not breach any formal rule. Participants in this conversation certainly knew this. Recipients of irony commonly treat it as humor and react with laughter, or they build on it and thereby sustain it.[25] Here Elias, at least, does both (lines 3 and 6). But subsequently he retracts from this position (in line 11) and initiates a return to talk in a non-ironic mode (line 13).

Two days later, on a bus traveling home from the meeting, I had the opportunity to talk with Christina. As she elaborated on what she regarded as challenges in organizing the team's workload, I asked her about the alleged theft of data. In her response she specifies its moral dimension:

Transcript 7.5

1 Christina: And that's why I think we have a problem with our team that we ... we're not getting the <u>science</u> results out because ... nobody is spending one hundred percent of their research time on it. And so ... but with the <u>competition</u> I hurried up.

2 Götz: The Munich collaboration ... you said they kind of <u>stole</u> your data?

3 Christina: They've done it again yeah he-he-he-he-he ... so yeah ... so yeah I I sent them a copy of the paper when we submitted it

4 Götz: Yeah

5 Christina: and then they stopped working on the MUWAGS data because there was nothing more they could do without photometric redshifts. And then ... then they looked around which other data was available on the archive and

---

[25] Hutchby and Drew (1995), Clift (1999), and Sidnell (2010a).

now they've downloaded the LENSURV data ... which is the other data set I am working with.

6 Götz: It is also public?

7 Christina: It is a:lso public. So ... I mean it's ... <u>yeah</u> ... and in fairness to them they always ... they tell us what they are doing ... so

8 Götz: So they write to you an email that they're downloading it?

9 Christina: So I mean they ... yeah it's it's ... they are they are being fair but it's still ... a bit ... a bit <u>tiresome</u>. You work really hard to <u>get</u> the data. And then people who don't spend any time writing proposals just take it from the archive and ... so ... it's:::: it's <u>fair</u>. The archive is there for a reason but ... it's difficult when people download archive data to do the key science that you were planning to do with it. What you want is them to do things that you wouldn't have thought of or ... aren't your key science. But when they're ... in direct competition that's tough. It happens he-he-he-he-he. But <u>now</u> I have an ... I mean ... this meeting is the first time I thought about MUWAGS in a long time so ... I guess I will be advisor on <u>papers</u> that come out in the next round but until we get them I won't be working any more scientifically on MUWAGS.

When transcribing this conversation, I realized that, by saying "kind of <u>stole</u> your data" (line 2) I may have unwittingly invited Christina to conceive of the Munich team's use of the data in the same way as she had done two days ago. Remarkably enough, though, she again adds laughter to her verbal response (in line 3) as well as to her account of what led to this situation (line 9). More clearly than before she acknowledges that the Munich team had not acted illegitimately and breached any formal rule in downloading the public MUWAGS data, despite her concerns about them doing so (line 9). Her reference to fairness alludes to their adherence to formal regulations.

Christina's answer and her laughter, which largely echo Transcript 7.4, support the interpretation of her utterance being ironic. Doing so questions "stealing" as the literal meaning to describe an action in the domain of open data access with the English-language vocabulary of Euro-American academics. Christina uses it to translate intralingually (in Jakobson's sense), as she rephrases and interprets an observation in her everyday language. Christina points to a concern about the regulation of data access, that is, to the possibility of competitors doing one's own key science after the proposal authors' one-year period of exclusive proprietary access has ended. She appreciates that data become public, but bemoans that the research goals described in the proposal are not protected for longer than the proprietary period, despite the MUWAGS team's scarcity of resources. Her complaint, then, is about the context-insensitive application of a data release policy as well as fellow researchers' ignorance of her circumstances. Unrecognizable in the transcript, Christina is one of several MUWAGS members on nonpermanent, untenured positions, making her particularly vulnerable.

By notifying Christina about downloading the data, members of the Munich group had arguably acknowledged her and her team's right to know of it, even though to do so may have been solely out of courtesy considering their personal acquaintance (cf. Transcript 7.4, line 14). Yet, for Christina, it seems to be just this familiarity of the Munich team with herself and her two projects, MUWAGS and LENSURV, that makes their uses of "her" data questionable. After all, members of the Munich team are not about to access and reuse data from an anonymous or unrelated source. These scientists know that they obtained data produced for Christina to address her key science. Thus, she regards a mere notification of these uses as insufficient. To her, fairness and properly ethical uses are not the same. These scientists' understanding of irony and translation thus points to an ethical tension in open data access. Inhabiting a status in it, Christina may want to have the right to sanction data users' actions in a context-specific way.

If the improperness of "stealing data" hinges on the familiarity of "perpetrator" and "victim" one could suspect that using data that strangers have made would be less contentious and not be regarded as a theft. However, in the circumscribed domain of this collaboration's work (as throughout astronomy), with its shared access to major facilities like the HST, there are few, if any, strangers.

Let us consider another instance of where the access to open data is being described as an act of theft, this time by a scientist who recounts his own team's actions. The following is an excerpt from a conversation I had with Norman, a PhD student in the MUWASHH project (unrelated to MUWAGS). Like Christina, he is a native English speaker.

Transcript 7.6

1 Norman: MUWASHH is the MUlti Wavelength Survey by Harvard and Hawaii and in this particular field to call that a survey is a bit of a cheat ... because ah ... so it's an optical plus infrared survey ... so it's got 6 optical bands ... or it's 7 optical bands and 3 near infrared.

2 Götz: Right.

3 Norman: Of those we stole <u>all</u> of the optical imaging ... and we stole
            <u>one</u> of the near infrared bands. So we've in fact ... oh
            that's not quite true ... we stole all but <u>one</u> of the optical
            bands from the archives. So we didn't actually <u>take</u> these
            data ourselves ... they were publicly available. And in fact
            we didn't even re-<u>reduce</u> these data he-he-he-he-he. We
            didn't even steal them from the archive ... someone <u>else</u>
            went ... so Albert went ... as part of ... he called his survey
            MDS ... what is just the Munich Deep Survey. They went to
            the archive ... <u>they</u> took all the data for a bunch of different
            fields including the Chandra Deep Field South. Then they
            re-reduced the data ... and then they gave it to us ... and
            then we added the near-infrared. You get the point. We
            stole someone else's data and we added this stuff to it.

Norman adds light laughter to his verbal description of "stealing data from the archives." This laughter, however, does not follow mentions of the verb "stole" closely and thus its sequential import appears to differ from that of Christina's laughter in Transcripts 7.4 and 7.5. Rather, Norman frames his entire account as a series of thefts, presumably counting on my understanding of his irony. After all, data that are publicly available from an archive cannot be literally "stolen" if their use is properly referenced. Norman's point rather seems to be that doing so does not seem to give adequate credit to these data's makers. He signals a tension with an evaluative sensibility that is morally troubled by this way of acquiring scientific data.

I do not mean to suggest with these three transcripts that perceptions of data being "stolen" are pervasive in astronomy or among junior astronomers. It is noteworthy, however, that two junior scientists with little prior experience in releasing data publicly chose this wording. As such, they are, perhaps, more prone to describing it in terms of their competence of English and notions of property and ownership in the Euro-American culture with which they are familiar. The regime of open access in astronomy – shaped by institutional demands, made practicable by the digitality of its data, enabled by network infrastructures and archives, and marked by periods of exclusive proprietary access – thus instigates scientists to problematize what is owned and ownable and how it is recognizable, recognized, and limited, as owned or ownable, if only temporarily.[26] Their

---

[26] Note in this context Sacks' lectures on possessables and possessitives (Sacks 1992, vol. 1, 382–388, 605–609).

considerations point to the limits of abstracting the value of data in view of personal investments and interests.

7.7   Conclusions

Normative concerns have pervaded the work that I described in earlier chapters, from agreements on standard data formats and the achievement of membership, to uses of diagrams and the composition of research teams. This chapter takes such concerns to "open science," a domain in which norms have changed swiftly, partly because of organizational policies, but also because of the internal development of disciplinary practices. I focused on two research collaborations, ALLSKY and MUWAGS. Their members' "inner dialogues" may well be described as a "perspicuous setting" (Garfinkel and Wieder 1992, 181) in which "participants must routinely and repeatedly 'place their understandings on view'" (Koschmann 2011, 436). I identified translation and uses of irony as methods for addressing and criticizing tensions in the use of open-access data and as means to extend the scope of collaborative deliberation. For members, issues of data access and authorship are enduring concerns, specifically views of its temporality and the limitations of formal rules, with which moral assessments can be in tension (as in Christina's case).

Both cases demonstrate participants' attention to fellow scientists and their sensibilities. All cited researchers locate practices of data sharing and their assessment within their professional world. In the case of the ALLSKY discussion in Transcript 7.1, Eddie seems to adopt a "reciprocity of perspectives" (Schütz 1962; 1964) with other scientists to formulate a reasonable critique of the collaboration board's suggestion. Henry delimits the community's boundary as including potential peer reviewers. The MUWAGS discussion in Transcript 7.2 identifies membership through considering comparable projects, whereas Christina's critique (in Transcripts 7.4 and 7.5) specifies ethical expectations of members' conduct. Thus, we witness in either case how members define their communities from within. We do not need to rely on what analysts claim. However, to grasp the moral issues informing these interactions we need more than transcripts of conversations and have to add ethnographic and contextual detail.

That "open access" and "open science" are moral matters has been widely acknowledged, with some authors arguing that these are "moral economies."[27] But these studies leave open how these "economies" are brought

---

[27] See, for example, Bacevic and Muellerleile (2018) as well as König et al. (2024).

about and sustained by their members as "moral" affairs.[28] For examining this, the notion of status can be a useful tool. Robert Merton's (1973, Part 3) understanding of the "normative structure of science," including the norm of "communism" (that scientific knowledge is owned communally), is often invoked as anticipating the "open science movement" (Leonelli 2023, 13). Merton's view of norms has been rightly criticized, not least since "norms cannot fix how people apply them" (Barnes 2003, 128–129) – they are resources, much like the precedents that the conversationalists invoked earlier in this chapter. But Merton builds on an account of academic scientific communities as "status groups" (Weber 1978) that is more defensible. As Max Weber conceives of them, status groups are moral communities defined by their specific lifestyle and practices of honoring (Barnes 2003). If we examine these practices as interactional and subject to social accountabilities, we come to understand statuses as works-in-progress. Invoking precedents and conversational uses of translation and irony are means to explore, define, and challenge statuses while attending to ethical concerns.

Note that all references to statuses that I identified were bound to these scientists' academic discipline, astronomy. They were context-sensitive and entailed views of status incumbency that were mindful of a dataset's intended uses. Accounting practices are unavoidably context-sensitive (cf. Chapter 3). Universal demands for the open access to data sacrifice this context sensitivity. This matters not only when data users "scoop" data makers to their scientific results. Equally important for many scientists is the risk of attracting blame from other researchers when they use someone's published data wrongly, and the effort to assure to properly transmit one's knowledge through a dataset, as I examine in Chapter 8.

---

[28] To some anthropologists' dismay, moral economies are all too often conceived as collectives in which the moral is naively identified with the social (Hann 2010; Laidlaw 2014; Keane 2016). Moral economies are frequently invoked when contrasting a community's long-term good with individuals' short-term profit-seeking (Thompson 1991; Kohler 1994, 1999; Strasser 2019).

Encoding Knowledge
Can Data Be Made to Speak for Themselves?

8.1 This Chapter's Plan

How can scientists pass on what they have learned not only *from*, but *about* their data? This chapter proposes to answer this question by considering data as a form of writing and examining its social uses. I argue that scientific datasets do not merely represent information, but can be structured and presented to have a pragmatic function oriented to enable users' understanding. I demonstrate this by describing how the Multiwavelength Galaxy Survey (MUWAGS; a pseudonym) collaboration, discussed in Chapters 6 and 7, designed its catalog – a table of the measured and estimated properties of galaxies –, to guide users to self-correct wrong uses and delimit being held accountable for misuses. Some astronomers argue that catalogs encode their makers' collective knowledge of their data. I examine this claim based on what I witnessed ethnographically, suggest elements of a pragmatics of data reuse, and end with a reflection on socio-computational orders, that is, entanglements of the social and the computational in data-rich science.[1]

As in Chapter 7, witnessing a collaboration's "inner dialogues" allows us to explore otherwise unarticulated assumptions about how data makers and users think and act as practical methodologists. This is another example of taking a problem of data-rich science – here that of making a user-friendly data release while maintaining a balance of securing credit and demonstrating accountability –, considering its "staffing" with people, and following its management ethnographically.

---

[1] Here I refer to linguistic pragmatics, which is "centrally concerned with how speakers and hearers achieve understanding in and through language" (Koschmann 2011, 435). I informally seek to transpose its program to address scientists' communication with measurements that are typically numerical. Note the distinction between linguistic pragmatics and philosophical pragmatism (e.g., Misak 2016).

8.2 Makers and Users, Writers and Readers

A frequent observation in studies of the reuse of scientific data is that aspiring reusers commonly miss what they consider necessary information about the data, putting its uses at stake. Conversely, data makers worry about the misuse of their data.[2] Finding existing data and making them usable can be challenging, since data reusers often need to know more than metadata ("data describing data") provide. Making the diverse contextual information that reusers desire explicit can overwhelm data producers.[3] Paul Edwards and his coauthors (2011) note that where proper infrastructures are not established, users often understand others' data only through elaborate communications with data makers, a process they call "data friction." They recognize the parallel of this process to everyday social interaction, in which "common ground" – shared understandings fundamental to mutual sensemaking – is typically provisional and contingent, being coproduced by the interactants themselves (Clark 1996). In this view, data need someone to speak for them.

"If only data could speak for themselves," one feels tempted to respond. Putting it this way echoes Socrates' despair about writing, then (ca. 420 BCE) relatively new as a communication medium in Athenian society. In a famous passage of the dialogue *Phaedrus* (Plato 2005), Socrates compares reading a piece of writing with looking at a painting. Much like paintings are unable to respond to questions viewers ask, Socrates finds written words to "point to just one thing, the same each time" (Plato 2005, 63, 275d5). Writing, like a painting, "trundles about everywhere in the same way" and "does not know how to address those it should address and not those it should not" (276e1). These, of course, are concerns of a philosopher whose favorite mode of instruction is spoken dialogue.

One can define scientific data inclusively as "any product of research activities (…) that is collected, stored, and disseminated *in order to be used as evidence for knowledge claims*" (Leonelli 2016, 77; emphasis in original), but when conceived as digital photographs ("arrays of numbers") or machine-generated "inscriptions" (Latour and Woolgar 1986), digital data may appear to be text-like, as forms of writing.[4] This would make

---

[2] Zimmerman (2008), Brewer (2017), Gregory et al. (2019), and Pasquetto et al. (2024). Note, however, that data reuses in astronomy are often successful (cf. Plant and Hanisch 2020).
[3] Compare Faniel et al. (2019) and Yakel et al. (2019). On conflicting definitions of data reuse, see van de Sandt et al. (2019).
[4] Bokulich and Parker (2021, 6) notice that, as per Leonelli's definition, "a mice colony could constitute data, if it is taken as potential evidence for claims about a link between genes and behaviour." They prefer to define data as records that are separate from the system or phenomenon under study.

data users the readers of texts who may well experience Socrates' despair. Media scholar John Durham Peters (1999) argued that the transmission of writing is fundamentally distinct from dialogical exchanges in copresence. Philosopher Sybille Krämer (2015, 23) concurs when she writes that "[t]ransmission is precisely not dialogical: the goal of technical communication is emission or dissemination, not dialogue. We can thus clearly distinguish between the personal principle of understanding and the postal principle of transmission." In written discourse there appears to be a "lack of recipient accountability" (Deppermann 2015, 61).

The contrast between transmission and dialogue is stark,[5] but various studies suggest a congruence. Mikhail Bakhtin (1986, 165) muses that "the listener (reader, viewer)" is included "in the system (structure) of the [literary] work." Umberto Eco (1979, 7) argues that, to "make his text communicative, the author has to assume that the ensemble of codes he relies upon is the same as that shared by his possible reader." Wolfgang Iser (1980; 1989) notices that the meaning of texts (and not only literary ones) is found not simply in the words, but in the interaction between text and reader. Ethnomethodological studies that regard readers as hermeneutical practitioners who use documentary methods of interpretation support this view (McHoul 1982; Livingston 1995). Historical studies of science supplement this picture, finding that scientists dominantly used letters well into the eighteenth century to communicate data and results (Daston 1991). These letters were often "simulations of conversations" (Bohn 1999). Jumping to the twenty-first century and moving beyond science, social media users routinely bridge the chasm between text and talk-in-interaction that Krämer identifies. Thus, Patricia Bou-Franch and coauthors (2012) identify interactional coherence, a notion of linguistic pragmatics, in commentaries on YouTube videos, whereas David Giles and coauthors (2015, 2017) use conversation analysis to identify sequential structures in blog postings, chatrooms, and YouTube commentaries. William Housley and coauthors (2017) adopts Erving Goffman's (1983) notion of the interaction order in interpreting sequences of messages on Twitter.

More relevant for a study of data reuse in science is Dorothy Smith's (2001, 175–176) suggestion to conceive of the social, organizational, and institutional uses of texts, especially of printed materials, as

---

By following Hacking (1992a, 48) and considering only the products of data generators as data, my view is yet narrower and more specific.

[5] Arguably, it is even meaningless, since it sets up a false contrast. Thanks to Grey Gundaker for this alert. I describe Peters' (1999) and Krämer's (2015) arguments for illustrative purposes.

text–reader conversations in which, unlike real-life conversations, one side of the conversation is fixed and unresponsive to the other's responses. (...) However the reader takes it up, the text remains as a constant point of reference against which any particular interpretation can be checked. It is the constancy of the text that provides for the standardization effect. (...) Text–reader conversations are embedded in and organize local settings of work. (...) In standardizing one "party" to every text–reader conversation, the terms of all conversations with the "same" text are standardized. Among participants, an open-ended chain is created: text–reader–reader–reader–.

Smith explores the consequences of the spread of "identical copies" to multiple sites. This resembles Bruno Latour's (1986) account of "immutable mobiles." But Smith goes beyond Latour by focusing also on the sequentiality of "text–reader conversations" and by examining organizational and institutional uses, which provide contexts of (social) accountability.[6] This, after all, is a key point in scientific data reuse: that readers are users. What they do with others' data will itself be open for assessment.

As an elementary form of scientific data, measurements are generated procedurally and are, as such, resources for the achievement of intersubjectivity. Data makers and users – as members of a discipline – commonly agree, in principle, on how those measurements are to be made.[7] Remember how, in measuring the luminosities and redshifts of a sample of distant galaxies, specific contexts of accountability mattered to the fixation of Nadine's dataset and how an invisible public of absent evaluators seemed to be curiously present in Nadine's and Otfried's conversations (Chapters 3 and 4). In turn, Nadine was guided to present her measurements in a "statistical language," a "technology of intersubjectivity" (Hacking 1992b, 152).

Scientists typically supplement public data releases by journal articles that describe the data production, processing, and analysis. These papers are meant to instruct users. But can such instructions ever be complete and will data users follow them? After all, studies of technology use have

---

[6] Harper (1998). Smith argues, furthermore, that there is a movement between what is "locally historic" (Garfinkel et al. 1981) – that is, sequential, reflexive, possibly interactional, and intersubjective – and textually mediated discourse. When "out of action, [textual materials] exist in potentia but their potentiating is in time and in action, whether in ongoing text–reader conversations or in how the 'having read' enters into the organization of what is to come" (Smith 2001, 174).

[7] For example, measuring the position of a star in a pixel image requires finding its center coordinates, whereas measuring its brightness requires adding the amount of its light recorded in several pixels. Both operations follow discipline-specific methods and protocols, including calibrations. They involve assessments of what is "good enough" to complete a measurement and to share it meaningfully.

provided ample demonstrations that many users do not consult manuals when setting out to operate new devices or turn to them only at last resort.[8] Such attitudes have inspired designers to develop artifacts that aspire to be "self-explanatory," that is, "their operation should be discoverable without extensive training, from information provided on or through the machine itself" (Suchman 2007, 43). Yet even when users try to follow such instructions they are bound to be challenged. Revisiting her influential study of how users of a photocopy machine interact with its support system, Lucy Suchman (2007, 4–5) concludes that "human–machine communications take place at a very limited site of interchange," whose asymmetries "profoundly limit possibilities for interactivity, at least in anything like the sense that it proceeds between persons in interaction." Suchman builds on, and illustrates, Harold Garfinkel's (2002) insight that all instructions are essentially incomplete and context-dependent. This finding extends to scientific practice (Lynch and Jordan 1995) and it seems likely that it pertains to data reuses as well.

8.3   Fixating a Catalog, Encoding Collective Knowledge?

Conceived as a form of writing, data can be formatted in diverse ways, from single numbers to lists, tables, matrices in several dimensions, and various relational structures.[9] In astronomy, catalogs are a dominant form of data. At the time of writing this, in August 2025, the Centre des Données astronomiques de Strasbourg (France), a major astronomical data center, provided digital access to 26,503 astronomical catalogs.[10] Many catalogs are tables that list information for one object per row. Columns typically begin with object identifiers (such as the object number) and continue with the celestial coordinates Right Ascension (which resembles geographic longitude) and Declination (which resembles geographic latitude). These are typically followed by columns of specific measurements and their errors, such as the brightness (magnitude) in certain wavelength bands, the shape of objects, radial velocities, photometric redshifts, and so on. Figure 8.1 shows an excerpt of George Abell's (1958) catalog of 2,712 galaxy clusters in the northern and equatorial sky. Abell spent many months visually inspecting the Palomar Observatory Sky Survey's 879 pairs of photographic plates

---

[8] See Novick and Ward (2006) and Blackler et al. (2016).

[9] For an overview of the variety of data structures, see McKinney (2017) and en.wikipedia.org/wiki/ List_of_data_structures (accessed July 7, 2025).

[10] See Genova (2018) and cds.unistra.fr/fr/ (accessed July 7, 2025).

No.	R. A. (1855) Decl.		Precession R. A. (1900) Decl.		l	b	Mag. Dist. Rich.		
1	00 00.1	15 43	0.512	3.34	75.6	−45.4	17.1	5	1
2	00 01.0	−20 27	0.512	3.34	35.9	−78.2	17.3	6	1
3	00 01.8	03 14	0.512	3.34	71.1	−57.6	17.0	5	1
4	00 01.9	05 59	0.512	3.34	72.6	−54.9	17.8	6	1
5*	00 02.8	32 18	0.514	3.34	80.6	−29.2	17.1	5	1
6	00 03.0	16 54	0.513	3.34	77.0	−44.4	17.5	6	2
7	00 04.2	31 37	0.515	3.34	80.8	−30.0	17.1	5	1
8	00 04.7	−12 00	0.511	3.34	59.3	−72.0	17.2	5	1
9	00 04.9	08 40	0.513	3.34	74.9	−52.5	18.0	6	1
10	00 05.4	−06 48	0.511	3.34	65.9	−67.3	17.2	5	2
11	00 05.4	−17 15	0.511	3.34	49.5	−76.6	17.2	5	2
12	00 05.9	−08 25	0.511	3.34	64.6	−68.9	17.2	5	2

Figure 8.1 The first entries of George Abell's (1958) catalog of 2,712 galaxy clusters in the northern and equatorial sky, based on his visual inspection of the photographic plates of the Palomar Observatory Sky Survey. For each object the columns list the catalog number (column 1), celestial coordinates and positional information (columns 2 to 7), the visually estimated magnitude of the tenth brightest cluster galaxy (columns 8), as well as coarse estimates of the cluster distance (column 9), and of the number of galaxies it contains (column 10). (© American Astronomical Society. Reproduced with permission)

of the northern and equatorial sky.[11] His catalog was printed on forty-three pages in an issue of the *Astrophysical Journal's Supplement Series*.

If Abell's catalog is remarkable for having been made by a single astronomer, then the catalogs of the Sloan Digital Sky Survey (SDSS) are noteworthy for being the joint work of a large team. The SDSS Early Data Release (EDR), which records measurements of 14 million detected objects, was accompanied by a data release paper published by 192 authors (Stoughton et al. 2002). Thirty-two of these can be identified as lead authors, the core team of catalog makers.[12] (The SDSS catalogs cannot be shown as the Abell catalog, as they are accessed by database queries specific to user interests; Figure 8.2 illustrates instead the formatting of a recent, less complex catalog.) SDSS users can access the survey's "raw" data, such as digital photographic exposures, and process these data "from scratch" according to the specific requirements of their research project. Indeed, doing so is what David W. Hogg, a member of the SDSS collaboration, recommends, in principle, to users who want to exploit the information content of the

[11] Each field "was photographed twice, once on a [blue-sensitive Kodak] Eastman type O emulsion and once on a type E emulsion through a red Plexiglass filter" (Abell 1958, 121).
[12] The author list of Stoughton et al. (2002) is strictly alphabetical only from the thirty-third listed author, suggesting that the first thirty-two authors were particularly involved in the catalog's creation.

2MRS Catalog

(1) 2MASS ID	(2) R.A. (deg)	(3) Dec. (deg)	(4) l (deg)	(5) b (deg)	(6) K_P^0	(7) H_P^0	(8) J_P^0	(9) K_M	(10) H_M^c	(11) J_M^c	(12) $\sigma(K_P^0)$	(13) $\sigma(H_P^0)$	(14) $\sigma(J_P^0)$	(15) $\sigma(K_M^c)$	(16) $\sigma(H_M^c)$	(17) $\sigma(J_M^c)$	(18) E_{BV} (mag)	(19) r_{iso}	(20) r_{ext}	(21) b/a	(22) flags	(23) Type	(24) L.src	(25) v (km/s)	(26) $\sigma(v)$	(27) cat	(28) Bibcode	(29) Catalog ID
00424433+4116074	10.68471	41.26875	121.17430	−21.57319	0.797	0.929	1.552	0.743	0.881	1.497	0.016	0.016	0.015	0.017	0.017	0.016	0.683	3.208	3.491	0.473	Z11	3A2s	ZC	−300	4	N	1991RC3.9.C...000od	MESSIER 031
00473313−2517196	11.88806	−25.28880	97.36301	−87.96452	3.815	4.132	4.858	3.765	4.077	4.798	0.016	0.016	0.015	0.017	0.016	0.016	0.019	2.799	2.965	0.264	Z11	5X s	ZC	243	2	N	2004AJ....128...16K	NGC 0253
09553318+6903549	148.88826	69.06526	142.09190	40.90022	3.898	4.131	4.784	3.803	4.043	4.690	0.016	0.016	0.015	0.018	0.018	0.017	0.080	2.688	2.878	0.517	Z11	2A2s	ZC	−34	4	N	1991RC3.9.C...000od	MESSIER 081
13252775−4301073	201.36565	−43.01871	309.51639	19.41761	3.948	4.244	4.931	3.948	4.203	4.876	0.015	0.016	0.015	0.016	0.016	0.016	0.115	2.445	2.613	0.957	Z11	−2 P	ZC	547	5	N	1978PASP..90..237G	NGC 5128
13052727−4928044	196.36366	−49.46790	305.27151	13.34007	4.471	4.790	5.508	4.421	4.735	5.444	0.016	0.016	0.015	0.017	0.017	0.016	0.176	2.627	2.772	0.308	Z11	6B s	ZC	563	3	N	2004AJ....128...16K	NGC 4945
01335090+3039057	23.46210	30.65994	133.61024	−31.33081	4.477	4.697	5.346	4.087	4.329	5.003	0.016	0.016	0.015	0.020	0.017	0.017	0.041	2.699	3.032	0.792	Z11	5A4s	ZC	−179	3	N	1991RC3.9.C...000od	MESSIER 033
03464851+6805459	56.70214	69.67970	141.40953	40.56710	4.636	5.003	5.744	4.610	4.973	5.704	0.015	0.015	0.015	0.015	0.015	0.015	0.156	2.357	2.542	0.396	Z11	0	ZC	203	4	N	1991RC3.9.C...000od	MESSIER 082
13370091−2951567	204.25383	−29.86576	314.58353	10.57999	4.682	4.952	5.494	4.362	4.682	5.169	0.020	0.018	0.016	0.018	0.019	0.018	0.033	2.571	2.676	0.858	Z11	6X2T	ZC	31	3	N	1999PASP..111..438F	IC 0342
12395949−1137230	189.99789	−11.62307	298.46094	5.14923	4.991	5.228	5.897	4.944	5.177	5.841	0.015	0.015	0.015	0.017	0.015	0.015	0.058	2.495	2.709	0.825	Z11	5X2s	ZC	513	5	N	2004AJ....128...16K	MESSIER 083
00424182+4051546	10.67427	40.86517	121.14999	−21.97652	5.084	5.301	6.171	5.040	5.275	6.142	0.015	0.015	0.015	0.025	0.019	0.015	0.067	2.305	2.473	0.682	Z11	1 A P	ZC	1024	6	N	2000MNRAS.313..469S	MESSIER 104
12505314+4107125	192.72145	41.12016	123.36211	76.00777	5.163	5.408	6.068	5.100	5.344	6.010	0.015	0.015	0.015	0.017	0.016	0.015	0.155	2.168	2.360	0.913	Z11	−6	ZC	−200	6	N	2000UZC....C....0F	MESSIER 032
12564369+2140575	194.18207	21.68266	315.68127	84.42287	5.381	5.623	6.300	5.315	5.558	6.231	0.015	0.015	0.016	0.016	0.016	0.015	0.018	2.236	2.414	0.847	Z11	2A3R	ZC	308	1	N	1993AAA..272...63M	MESSIER 094
20345233+6009132	308.71805	60.15368	95.71873	11.67289	5.424	5.821	6.147	5.424	5.711	5.971	0.018	0.017	0.015	0.017	0.016	0.016	0.041	2.332	2.490	0.583	Z11	2AT	ZC	408	4	N	1991RC3.9.C...000od	MESSIER 064
12294679+0800014	187.44499	8.00041	296.92224	70.19597	5.498	5.732	6.370	5.498	5.732	6.370	0.08	0.07	0.017	0.034	0.029	0.025	0.342	2.402	2.680	0.770	Z11	6X1T	ZC	40	2	N	2008MNRAS.388..500E	NGC 6946
13295264+4711429	202.46957	47.19926	104.85159	68.56064	5.589	5.796	6.486	5.569	5.796	6.484	0.017	0.016	0.016	0.025	0.021	0.019	0.022	2.253	2.496	0.913	Z33	2AT	ZC	997	7	N	2000MNRAS.313..469S	MESSIER 049
12185761+4718133	184.74008	47.30372	138.31865	68.84251	5.592	5.947	5.632	5.592	5.632	6.370	0.016	0.016	0.016	0.022	0.021	0.017	0.035	2.296	2.549	0.902	Z11	4A1P	ZC	463	3	N	1991RC3.9.C...000od	MESSIER 106
03224178−3712295	50.67412	−37.30920	240.16275	−56.68984	5.831	5.681	6.498	5.681	5.706	6.361	0.016	0.015	0.015	0.022	0.017	0.017	0.058	2.421	2.662	0.495	Z33	4X s	ZC	448	3	N	1991RC3.9.C...000od	NGC 1316
13154932+4201454	198.95554	42.02929	105.99706	51.93508	5.681	5.947	5.806	5.681	5.860	6.427	0.016	0.016	0.015	0.019	0.018	0.017	0.021	2.220	2.470	0.792	Z33	−2X P	ZC	1760	10	N	2008MNRAS.388..500E	MESSIER 063
02424077−0000478	40.66988	−0.01329	172.10397	−57.04243	5.806	6.266	6.995	5.776	6.238	6.937	0.015	0.015	0.016	0.016	0.016	0.016	0.033	1.978	2.162	0.880	Z11	3A T	ZC	1137	45	6	1999ApJS..121..287H	MESSIER 077
12434000+1133093	190.91670	11.55261	295.87354	74.31767	5.816	6.094	6.740	5.730	5.984	6.647	0.016	0.016	0.015	0.016	0.017	0.017	0.026	2.166	2.383	0.891	Z11	−5	ZC	1117	6	N	2000AJ....119.1645T	MESSIER 060
03171659−4106290	49.32750	−41.10907	247.52402	−67.04243	5.847	6.093	6.731	5.653	5.958	6.512	0.016	0.015	0.015	0.024	0.021	0.019	0.013	2.157	2.513	0.891	Z11	0B s	ZC	801	3	6	2009GGF...C...000oJ	g0317186-410629
11054869−0002092	166.45247	−0.03590	255.53194	52.82921	5.848	6.094	6.731	5.847	5.866	6.099	0.016	0.015	0.016	0.021	0.018	0.021	0.057	2.216	2.432	0.693	Z11	4X3T	ZC	788	6	N	2000AJ....128...16K	NGC 3521
00404289+4141070	10.09198	41.68530	120.71631	−21.13871	5.866	6.099	6.662	5.815	5.866	6.374	0.020	0.019	0.017	0.045	0.040	0.029	0.085	2.450	2.760	0.594	Z11	−5	ZC	−241	3	N	1991A&A...246..349B	MESSIER 110
12304942+1223279	187.70593	12.39110	283.77777	74.49174	5.896	6.144	6.806	5.804	6.060	6.699	0.016	0.016	0.015	0.019	0.018	0.017	0.023	2.134	2.368	0.990	Z11	−4 P	ZC	1307	7	N	2000MNRAS.313..469S	MESSIER 087

Figure 8.2   Structure of the 2MASS Redshift Survey (2MRS) catalog, which contains data on 44,599 nearby galaxies selected from the catalog of 2MASS, a near-infrared all-sky survey, and is supplemented with spectroscopic observations by John Huchra and his collaborators. For each object the columns list an identity number (column 1), celestial and galactic coordinates (columns 2 to 5), measured magnitudes in six infrared bands and their errors (columns 6 to 17), the galactic reddening (column 18), angular size and orientation (columns 19 and 21), flags (column 22), galaxy type (column 23), redshift and redshift uncertainty (columns 24 and 25), as well as additional information (columns 26 to 29). This is not a regular excerpt of the catalog but a portion shown "for guidance regarding its format and content" (Huchra et al. 2012, 6).

SDSS's photographic exposures maximally. But for most users the SDSS catalogs have an inestimable benefit, as Hogg explains:[13]

> *Transcript 8.1*
> The <u>most</u> important thing about catalogs is ... they <u>encode</u> the collective knowledge of the people who make the data. So the Sloan catalog is the <u>only</u> place ((*where*)) we really encoded what we think the noise model of Sloan is ... what we think the point-spread function is ... what we think the data artifacts are. Because the catalog has been made <u>sensitive</u> to those things. (...) We shouldn't be passing forward these important metadata through the catalog. But the reality is ... <u>we</u> <u>are</u> ... this <u>is</u> how we propagate these <u>metadata</u>![14]

Hogg's claim, that catalogs "encode the collective knowledge of the people who make the data," may, in one sense, appear to be self-evident and uncontroversial. Of course, scientists ought to have made the best possible use of their knowledge in processing and analyzing their data. They are most familiar with the detectors and procedures they used. They collaborate in teams to make these data, and divide their labor, so would they not use their collective knowledge for everything they release? Furthermore, many astronomers agree that it is virtually impossible to describe all decisions that led to a final catalog. Peter made this point in Transcript I.2 (Introduction), and Otfried concurs when he explains:

> *Transcript 8.2*
> You just cannot document all ... individual steps ... ehm ... so that you could give someone the raw data ... and she gets the same catalog in the end. That is ... ehm ... there are too many steps in between that remain undocumented. It's just like that. And that ... you cannot really <u>avoid</u> that because this work would grow unfathomably ... so to say ... I mean the work of documenting what you have done.

In this sense, the practical circumstances of catalog production challenge the distinction between data and metadata ("data describing data") that

---

[13] See the Appendix for a complete list of the transcription conventions adopted.
[14] David W. Hogg, "Probabilistic Catalogs and 'Catalog Space,'" Space Telescope Science Institute, Baltimore (Maryland), June 16, 2011. See realserver4.stsci.edu/t/data/2011/06/2642/DavidHogg061611.mp4 at minute 12 (accessed February 5, 2013). Noise models (which quantify the effects of the length of exposure time and detector properties on the image quality), point-spread functions (which quantify the blurring of starlight due to atmospheric turbulence and telescope and camera optics), and image artifacts (present in any astronomical exposure) are specific to the processing of digital exposures, such as those generated by the charged-coupled devices of the SDSS telescope at Apache Point in New Mexico (USA). The SDSS catalog's metadata ("data describing data") only include basic general information on exposure times, column headings, etc. Users find more detailed, but not exhaustive, information on SDSS data processing in the data release papers which accompany every new release.

is essential to many discussions of data reuse and "open science" (cf. Mayernik 2019).

But Hogg's remarks, although made informally, seem profound in yet another sense and worthy of further reflection: Would "collective knowledge" – an elusive and controversial topic of philosophical debate – here become conceivable, consequential, and meaningful through its materialization in a digital object? Much of the philosophical debate revolves around whether the notions of "knowledge" and "knowing" can be applied not only to individuals, but also to collectives. Another question is whether "knowledge" should be conceived as a proposition, as most philosophers of science maintain, or as a capability, as those following Ludwig Wittgenstein (2009 [1953]) and Gilbert Ryle (1949) argue. To examine these questions empirically, let us first consider some key episodes in the fixation of the MUWAGS catalog.

8.4   Steps in the Collaborative Fixation of an Astronomical Catalog

We know from Chapters 6 and 7 that MUWAGS was an international team of astronomers that made a multiwavelength dataset of the galaxy supercluster A2713 to investigate its dark matter content and its environmental impact on galaxy evolution. Much of MUWAGS's collaborative work was oriented to making a master catalog: a table of measured and estimated properties of around 88.000 objects detected in optical images of the A2713 field. In its production, three main constituent datasets were to be combined: the MAMBO team's optical ground-based data, the Hubble Space Telescope (HST) Advanced Camera for Surveys (ACS) team's measurements of galaxy shapes, and the infrared team's Spitzer Multi-Band Imaging Photometer (MIPS) observations. The final MUWAGS data release included the master catalog and the processed images, as well as maps of weak gravitational lensing in the A2713 field. The catalog was presented as a FITS (Flexible Image Transport System; see Chapter 1) table and accompanied by a data release paper in a leading journal. The data were made available through the Space Telescope Science Institute's archive, the Centre de données astronomiques de Strasbourg (France), and the collaboration's website.[15]

In the following, I give a chronological account of how the MUWAGS team agreed on the final version of its master catalog for public release. Prior to these episodes, the team had resolved dependencies between

---

[15] See archive.stsci.edu and cds.unistra.fr/fr/ (accessed July 7, 2025).

constituent data subsets, as described in Section 6.6.1. None of the following episodes resulted in a return to data calibrations and analyses. They rather specify some methods of "packaging" data (cf. Leonelli 2016).

The following episodes are particularly rich in specific detail necessary to identify and describe these scientists' methods and accounting practices. Readers may wish to jump to Section 8.5 and return for details thereafter.

8.4.1 Guiding Catalog Users by Introducing and Structuring Redundancies

One way to counteract potential misuses of a catalog is to introduce opportunities for instructing users beyond the prescriptive information provided in the data release publication. Introducing redundant catalog entries are one means to do so.

In the work of MUWAGS, a major step in moving toward the first catalog version merging the MAMBO (pseudo-acronym), HST ACS, and Spitzer MIPS data was the assemblage of the so-called J2007d catalog.[16] This table of around 88,000 rows (one for each detected object) contained the outputs of diverse algorithms – including optical positions, radiation fluxes, and redshifts – and their error estimates. It included duplicate information and various cross-checks, many comprehensible only to their makers. With 709 columns per object, this draft catalog was too big to be shared meaningfully with any user beyond the team. At a collaboration meeting the number of columns was to be reduced to about 200 and the catalog was to be made more user-friendly.

Peter, the main author of the MAMBO catalog, argued that users working with the flux measurements and their "galactic reddening" would benefit from a redundancy in the catalog. Astronomers agree that dust and gas in our Milky Way Galaxy scatter the light of distant objects and "redden" it. The amount of reddening depends on where distant objects are on the sky relative to the band of the Milky Way, the plane of our (spiral) galaxy. Objects behind the Milky Way band are reddened most strongly. This galactic foreground reddening can be estimated and subtracted from flux measurements.[17] In astronomical terms, de-reddening "delocalizes"

---

[16] Catalog version names with an initial J are playful allusions to the epoch of celestial coordinates, such as the commonly used epoch J2000. Celestial coordinates change over time due to shifts in the orientation of the Earth's axis.

[17] Since the MUWAGS field is relatively small (about the size of the full moon), one singular galactic reddening correction could be applied to the measured radiation fluxes of all objects in the field.

the data, yielding the radiation fluxes one would measure when, hypothetically, observing extragalactic objects from outside our own galaxy. This makes it easier to compare the fluxes and colors of objects observed at different positions on the sky. Every practicing astronomer should be able to calculate de-reddened and re-reddened fluxes; this is taught in introductory laboratory courses for undergraduate students. Thus, team members could have simply listed the dust reddening correction that they had applied in the data release paper, which is what they did. But here, as elsewhere throughout the discussion, there is the lingering expectation that catalog users will not read the data release paper carefully, be prone to make mistakes, and "pester" the team with inquiries and requests. Consider this exchange between Peter and Mallory, the team's principal investigator:

Transcript 8.3

1 Peter: So ... um ... I thought ... it would be <u>best</u> ... to make it ... as <u>easy</u> and non-confusing as possible for the <u>public</u> ... uhh ... by giving them something that is <u>de-reddened</u> ... and ... uh ... well ... the calibrations are completely consistently corrected and so on ... so it's a dataset where you don't need to understand ... <u>any</u> of the intricacies ... I thought that would be the <u>best</u> because that way we <u>avoid</u> a lot of discussion ... but we were also saying

2 Mallory: You avoid people <u>pestering</u> you

3 (Group): hhhhh *((chuckling))*

4 Peter: Sorry?

5 Mallory: You avoid people <u>pestering</u> you *((chuckling))*

6 Peter: <u>Exactly</u>! yeah ... no ... <u>seriously</u> ... I mean ...

7 (Group): haha hhhh

8 Peter: whenever there's a source of confusion it reduces ... uh ... the motivation of people to use the data ... it it it it causes ... a lot of ... uh ... <u>questions</u> ... via email from people who are <u>persistent</u> in ... in their <u>attempt</u> to use them and it just creates work for everyone ... at a potentially <u>perpetual</u> level ... and if we can just preempt all of that ... that would be the <u>best</u> ... and an and ... I'd be happy to do this in in very little ... <u>time</u> I believe ... um ... but I think we still need to give them ... some ... um ... we'll need to give them a <u>prescription</u> ... prescription of how to ... how to <u>re-redden</u> the data

Peter wants to list de-reddened fluxes to make uses of the catalog "as easy and non-confusing as possible" (line 1). Mallory suggests that by doing so he seeks to preempt being "pestered" by users (lines 2 and 5), which Peter confirms and formulates as the catalog makers' and users' shared concern (lines 6 and 8). Peter and Mallory worry about catalog users' potential mistakes. Interactions with users seem possible, but, worried about their "potentially perpetual level," Peter rejects them in the pursuit of achieving the project's closure.

After agreeing as a team that the catalog would list de-reddened optical fluxes, Peter suggests also including a column with the uncorrected ("un-de-reddened" or "re-reddened") fluxes in the R band, the deepest image of the optical dataset, even though this information was redundant:

Transcript 8.4

1 Peter: (...) and ... so ... we need one magnitude that is somehow in common or is translatable

2 Mallory: Mm hm

3 Peter: and ... uh ... the <u>best</u> thing would ... be ... to ... well ... look ... oh no ... it's actually not a problem because I've just suggested we give them two sets of ... no ... I said ... I ... we ... I suggested we give them one set of magnitudes <u>de-reddened</u> and a prescription how to ... <u>re-redden</u> them ... uhm ... what if we give them this prescription ... but one additional actual <u>column</u>

4 Mallory: Mm hm

5 Peter: which is ... the <u>re-reddened</u> ... R-band magnitude ... as observed

6 Mallory: Yep

7 Peter: because that is the cut that we use in our ... em ... I mean the ... variable that we ... use to define cuts on our own and then people can use that same <u>variable</u> ... they can do an R equals 24 ((*magnitude*)) cut or something ... and if that means 23.786 in R for de-reddened ... then ... well ... so be it ... um ... at least they would have a <u>column</u> to straightforwardly <u>use</u> ... and ... and they could see ... for the example of this column as well ... if their re-reddening procedures with the reddening law ... although it'll be a very simple one ... has actually <u>worked</u> ... they could confirm with this column ... "Yes ... I'm not doing something ... I'm not doing multiplication instead of division or something <u>stupid</u>" ... So that would be an extra <u>column</u> ... Mm hm

8 Mallory: Uh ... okay ... so ... I think that sounds reasonable ... my ... my strongest motivation is that ... we ... are internally consistent ... I mean ... are consistent with

9 Peter: Right

10 Mallory: what we already <u>published</u>

By including both the de-reddened and the uncorrected fluxes in the catalog, Peter aims to give catalog users the opportunity to assess their calculations with catalog entries. Peter makes this explicit when (in line 7), using reported direct speech, he takes an imagined user's perspective. Mallory approves of including this extra column (lines 8 and 10), emphasizing her concern for the consistency of the catalog with the team's published work. Including the extra column did not affect this.

This was one of several exchanges in which team members pondered introducing redundancies into the catalog. Eliciting a response generates a sequence of actions. Including the extra column enables, and arguably invites, catalog users to perform a three-part sequence: (1) being instructed to re-redden galaxy magnitudes; (2) using these to calculate specific re-reddened magnitudes; and (3) being afforded the opportunity to self-assess their results for one waveband (the R band). This sequence accommodates users' projectable actions. It is reminiscent of a common feature of instructional sequences in classroom talk: a teacher asking a student a question, the student responding with an answer, followed by the teacher's subsequent assessment of this response. This is the I-R-E (Initiation-Response-Evaluation) sequence, or Question with Known Answer (Mehan 1979).[18] Unlike classroom interaction, of course, catalog makers and users are typically not copresent, users' "response" is in writing, and users would self-evaluate their computations.

As Peter did here, MUWAGS team members commonly adopted the perspective of imagined users in their discussions. Given that these astronomers themselves used other scientists' data, this is hardly surprising. Peter told me:

Transcript 8.5
Every now and then I use other people's data and want to do <u>science</u> with them ... want to write papers ... and there are factors that <u>interest</u> me as a catalog user. I have caught myself thinking ... "Gosh ... now it's getting too complicated with this catalog. What all do I have to know to use it properly and not come up with nonsensical interpretations ... biased results?" Perhaps the <u>catalog</u> makers have provided lots of descriptive knowledge or whatever ... but for <u>me</u> the situation may become uncertain as I don't know how to use this knowledge and use the catalog to transform it into the product that I wanted to have. And then I sit there and wonder: "Isn't what I am actually looking for there somewhere on the web?" And then I use it and <u>that's</u> it. Or I let this paper go because the effort is getting too big.

---

[18] See also Macbeth (2003) and Lindwall et al. (2015).

Peter describes himself as being an impatient reader of other scientists' catalog descriptions, arguably missing the guidance of the (numerical) catalog entries themselves. A written description alone, it seems, leaves open too many ways of going astray.

8.4.2 Numerical Order as a Resource for Making Nonsensical Data Uses Perspicuous

Let us now turn from anticipated sequential orders of action to uses of numerical order for structuring catalog users' experience. A few months prior to MUWAGS's public data release, when team members had made a comprehensive draft catalog, some of the catalog's entries could not be filled. Some objects were too close to bright stars or the edge of an exposure, challenging precise photometric measurements, and others were affected by cosmic ray hits and other artifacts. But due to formatting requirements, table cells could not remain empty. Thus, blanking values – a sort of placeholder – had to be adopted for them. One MUWAGS sub-team had chosen –99 as a blanking value, a number that, they believed, would not be confused with astronomical measurements. Another sub-team had used NaN ("Not a Number") as the blanking value.[19] Users could search for this text string, such as when aiming to delete questionable table entries from an application. Now striving for a consistent catalog that employed a unique blanking value, Peter, the maker of the ground-based optical catalog, sent an email to the team, requesting ideas for how best to pick a single, consistent blanking value for the entire catalog. His message elicited a lively exchange: over two days, nine team members sent twenty-three messages, from which I quote in what follows.

Ben and Mike, in charge of the optical HST catalog, were mostly concerned with their code's operability and argued for a blanking value of –99 because IDL (Interactive Data Language), popular for data analysis, could not easily process NaNs. By contrast, Susheela and Mallory emphasized that catalog users ought to be able to recognize their mistakes, such as when accidentally calculating with a numerical blanking value like –99. Susheela writes:

> I prefer "NaN" as it limits possibility of error from the user, with absolute mag ((*magnitude*)) cuts and a global replace by the user to his/her blanking

---

[19] In the Institute of Electrical and Electronics Engineer (IEEE) standard for floating-point arithmetic (IEEE 754), NaN is a number type for undefined or unrepresentable values. See MacKenzie (1993) for a historical sociology of the IEEE 754 standard.

value is clean and unambiguous. I agree with Mike that we should not mix blanking values.

Mallory writes:

> Although I am used to the −99 values I would prefer NaN in this case. Users not realizing the convention can get easily caught out, e.g. with a magnitude selection such as R<24. NaN avoids this so seems better practice to me, and can be easily globally replaced if required.

Susheela and Mallory are both alert to the dangers of confusing blanking values with physically meaningful table entries (in this case astronomical magnitudes). Both argued that NaNs, because of not being numbers, would lead computer code to crash, thereby making wrong uses recognizable. This seemed clearly preferable to introducing unrecognized mistakes. However, Chuang notices that this is not always the case when using NaNs as a blanking value. He realized that some code converts NaNs into numbers that would be difficult to trace, making it challenging to recognize mistakes:

> I have a slight preference for −99 because it won't cause any *algorithmic* difficulties for unwary programmers now and in the future. If you program outside of IDL, MIDAS,[20] or what not, you won't have to worry about it causing your program to crash. I do nearly all my programming in C, for example, and C will convert NaN into a float (*(floating point number)*) or int (*(integer number)*), depending on the conversion string you choose, but it will not otherwise complain that NaN is not a number. What then happens is that NaN becomes some number that gets operated on. It'll likely produce a nonsensical result when that happens. But depending on C or other languages to produce a nonsensical result is quite dangerous, when the sense of the nonsense is not in our control (does this make sense?). So if we're exporting the catalog to the outside world, we ought to keep this in mind.
>
> My feeling is that mathematical operations on −99 would produce numerical nonsense that is in our control and would be easy to flag. Otherwise, choosing an even more unrealistic number, e.g. −1e99, should solve any chance of confusion.

Here −1e99 = −10^{99} is an immensely large negative number, far outside the range of astronomical quantities measured or calculated in this team's work. Its mistaken use would be easily spotted in any calculation.

---

[20] MIDAS, the Munich Image Data Analysis System, is a software package for astronomical data analyses that the European Southern Observatory provides for researchers; see eso.org/sci/software/esomidas/ (accessed July 7, 2025).

Writing independently of Chuang, Otfried came to a similar conclusion and proposed to pick a blanking value "outside the range of all possible data", that is, an "unrealistic number":

> I understand that NaN is not perfect for some packages (especially those, that use ASCII as input) So a VERY negative number seems preferable. But I would strongly argue for a number which is not just outside the magnitude range, but well outside the range of all possible data (for instance distance vectors between two objects in arcsec could be about –1800.) So I suggest something more substantial: –99999 or so.

But even such a large blanking value could be problematic, as Mike points out in response to Chuang and Otfried. Mike argued that globally replacing a table entry would depend on which number formats users would choose. It would produce values that may not be recognized easily. Rounding errors could make it hard to recognize them as well:

> When doing a global replace the maximum allowed data range is specified by the "smallest" data type, in our case integer. So using –99999 will produce –32768 e.g. for NR [the catalog object number]. We should keep that in mind in the choice of our value. Or we would have to consider introducing several values (–9999 for INT [integers], –999999999 for LONG, FLOAT, DOUBLE). Also, keep in mind that for large numbers round-off errors might occur (float(–1e22) = –1.00000e+22; double(–1e22) = –9.9999998e+21).

Mike, who had initially rejected using NaN as a blanking value, now changed his mind, noticing that the popular IDL data analysis code he preferred could, after all, process NaNs:

> On second thought, for IDL users NaN is not that much of a nuisance. If encountering a –99 the plot range has to be adjusted anyway, so filtering has to be done and then one could also use finite() to remove NaNs. NaN also has the advantage that after removal plots can be made without interfering with the plot range at all (min and max has now a sensible value).

Mike's suggestion moved critics like Chuang to accept NaN as the catalog blanking value. Mallory, the principal investigator, subsequently endorsed this with the team's approval. The "README file," a brief users' manual released along with the data, was supplemented to give instructions for how to best find and replace the NaN entries in the MUWAGS catalog.

This discussion illustrates how MUWAGS members were mindful of how imagined users would work with the catalog: doing calculations, checking their results, and noticing what makes astronomical sense and what does not. The team considered, but ultimately rejected, dwelling on a

numerical order that catalog makers and users share as professional astronomers: "the range of all possible data" as Otfried called it.[21] This is a "realist strategy" that distinguishes between what is deemed "real" and what
is "artefactual" (Barnes et al. 1996, 81). It provides users with a resource
to self-correct their work. As in the previous episode, it is reminiscent of
the classroom I-R-E sequence. But in this case the formal constraint of
how numbers are represented in the catalog, set by the IEEE 754 standard, thwarted the team's efforts to do so. Any specific numerical blanking
value represents a choice for which the MUWAGS team could be blamed.
Employing the nonnumerical NaN blanking values arguably shifts the
responsibility of using catalog entries properly to users.

8.4.3   Guiding Catalog Users by Selectively
Deleting Information and Defining Flags

Besides introducing redundancies to enable catalog users to cross-check
their work, catalog makers may delete information that is prone to mistaken uses or mark catalog entries with flags – numerical or textual descriptors that alert users to possible issues with certain entries.

Late in the assembly of the MUWAGS catalog, the infrared-derived
galaxy masses and star formation rates, previously listed separately, were
merged with the optical MAMBO/HST catalog. Before doing so, Eddie,
the head of the Spitzer MIPS infrared sub-team, decided to delete what
he regarded as confusing information and applied flags to mark them as
not being contained in the survey's area. At a teleconference, his decision
became the topic of an exchange between Mallory, Peter, and Eddie:

Transcript 8.6

1 Mallory: Oh … actually … we didn't talk about the star formation
rates (hhhh) for MUWAGS … Eddie … you want to say a
bit about that … briefly?

2 Eddie: Ah::: … not really. Just to say that they're … they're
<u>almost</u> the same as before … you know … so anyone
using star formation rates will have to look at it … ahm
… I'm assuming that … there'll be <u>some</u> small amount of
documentation … if … if not I can send an email … ahhhm
… but basically what happened is that there are now total
star formation rates for galaxies with infrared detections
that are in the <u>high</u> signal-to-noise part of the image …

---

[21] In Hoeppe (2020b), I examine how some astronomers employed the visual order of digital photographs as a resource for the reuse of data.

and I've cleaned up all the <u>low</u> significance detections and all the ... detections in ... messy parts of the image by simply <u>killing</u> them ... ahm ... and saying ... ahm ... and just saying that there is <u>no</u> information in those parts of the images ... so ...

3 Peter: Can I just <u>ask</u> and confirm? ... so when you have a ... a low signal-to-noise part of the image or something ... ahmm ... do you give them flag zero "outside of the area" or do you give them flag two meaning "not detected"?

4 Eddie: I gave them flag zero meaning "outside of the area" and I set

5 Peter: Okay

6 Eddie: I set their ... all their infrared-based data to <u>zero</u>

7 Peter: Yeah ... okay

8 Eddie: Ahm ... so I have gotten rid of it ... which is not necessarily the ... ahh ... the <u>best</u> thing to do for those who are interested in <u>all</u> the <u>data</u> but ... I thought that if I did ... I mean ... I had confused Susheela by doing the other thing ... so I figured

9 Peter: Yes. ( ) (complete sample) now

10 Eddie: I choose something simple ... ahhh ... ahmmm ... and should make everyone happy

Invited by Mallory to update the team on his work on the star formation rates, Eddie reports the changes he made to a previous version (line 2). The potentially contentious nature of his action – the "killing" of information derived from "messy" parts of the image – becomes noticeable through Peter's request for explanation (in line 3), which Eddie answers and continues to address (in lines 8 and 10) despite Peter repeatedly acknowledging his understanding and acceptance (in lines 5, 7, and 9). Mallory remains silent throughout this exchange.

When Peter and Eddie talk about "flags" in this exchange, they refer to sample selection and quality flags.[22] Quality flags can be assigned manually to catalog entries or generated automatically by algorithms like the source detection code SExtractor (Bertin and Arnouts 1996) and the GALAPAGOS pipeline (Barden et al. 2012). The MUWAGS collaboration defined quality flags for each of the constituent "sub-catalogs." These flags were refined while fixating the data release and writing the data release paper. At this stage in the discussion the MIPS catalog had three sample selection flags: 0 ("source not covered," that is, not in the MIPS "footprint" on the sky), 1

---

[22] Table 9 of Stoughton et al. (2002) lists the quality flags adopted by the SDSS's EDR, a model for other survey projects.

("source covered and detected"), and 2 ("source covered, but not detected" – that is, a flux density below the detection limit).

As the head of the infrared sub-team, Eddie was entitled to set all entries for "messy parts of the image" (line 2) to zero. What is a "messy" part of an infrared image was not for the members of other sub-teams to judge. However, what Eddie describes as "killing" has a moral connotation. Setting numerical values of the table to zero can be heard as disregarding the epistemic and economic value of these data, obtained as they were using the particularly precious observing time of a space telescope. Eddie acknowledges that deleting entries is not the best thing to do, but he emphasizes his orientation to avoid confusing catalog users, maintaining that even Susheela, a team member, had been confused (in line 8). For Eddie, this concern for cooperation and intelligibility, among team members and beyond, overrides the effort to maximize the catalog's information content. Note that Susheela appears to have made visible to Eddie what he could not presume to be an unquestioned background.

Reflecting on the formulation of quality flags, a collaboration member told me:

> *Transcript 8.7*
> You know ... we insert a column for the <u>dumb</u> ones. This sounds arrogant ... but what I mean is this ... Let's <u>pretend</u> the public is dumb. And what we do is to tell them "Look ... this is a column for <u>you</u> ... and if you find this number there then just ignore this thing and use the rest only ... before it's getting too complicated ... where too much can go wrong ... where you have to know too much as a user ... or where we would have to communicate <u>too</u> much <u>too</u> precisely ... and we are not willing to make that effort." ... We try to simplify the <u>situation</u>. In that way you cannot use <u>one</u> <u>hundred</u> percent of the power of the catalog ... but they can ... let me just make up a number ... it can be used by <u>eighty</u> or <u>ninety</u> percent by the dumbest possible user. At least nothing will go wrong. That is the point. Better leave opportunities untouched than to let users produce nonsense.

Thus conceived, the resort to flags is a shortcut to account for operations that are difficult to describe and prone to mistaken uses. Eddie's assignment of flags marks the closure of work on the infrared data. These were not processed further.

8.4.4   Turning Makers into Users: Testing the Catalog by Trying to Break It

The end of the team's work on the master catalog was marked by several efforts to "break" it, that is, to check its entries' coherence and logical consistency and impersonate catalog users beyond the team to identify remaining inconsistencies in need of correction. In Section 6.6.2, I reviewed this work through the lens of organizational practice. After several trials, the team arrived at a catalog that allowed diverse uses coherently, was logically consistent, and was accountable to the various evidential contexts (Pinch 1985) that members investigated. At this point it was "frozen in," as Mallory declared, and became a singular digital object. Given the compromises that fixating the catalog entailed (cf. Episode 3), it was irreducible to any individual team member's work.

8.4.5   Contemplating Additional Possibilities
for Users' Sequential Engagement

After the MUWAGS catalog was "frozen in," team members kept pondering further opportunities to engage and instruct users, but the team's discussion also turned to possibilities of holding users to account. At the last collaboration meeting before the data release, team members considered additional means for preempting wrong uses of the catalog. I use quotation marks to transcribe what I heard as quoted fictional text.

Transcript 8.8

1	Mallory:	But I mean we did have discussions on how to … on <u>defensive</u> things … how to guard against lazy and stupid people and possibly making some quantities negative … thinking that that would be <u>very</u> obvious … but it's not necessary. So all we could do is explicitly write down what these quantities are
2	Ken:	Yeah
3	Mallory:	and explain them very well … and point people to everything
4	Ken:	That's a good idea. We can <u>test</u> … you know … fill out a multiple-choice test. "If you want to create … if you want to create … stellar mass versus … something … for cluster members
5	Ben:	<u>Aha</u>!
6	Ken:	which column do you use?"
7	Ben:	The <u>MUWAGS</u> <u>catalog</u> <u>driver's</u> <u>license</u>!
8	(Group):	<u>HA-HA-HA-</u>HA-HA-ha-ha-ha ((*laughter and mumbling*))
9	Mallory:	But that's in light … but it's <u>not</u> necessarily a bad idea … again in the README a few obvious examples … to say … "If you want … what are the obvious things for … stellar masses for confirmed galaxies … or

		star formation rates for detected galaxies?" We could actually put that ... in as little
10	Elias:	and give references to where these things are explained in detail
11	Ken:	and say why the other ones are wrong. We could say "Do not use that one because ... under your assumptions ... don't use that"
12	Elias:	Will there be references where this is explained?
13	Mallory:	Well ... it's all going to be explained in the data release paper. That is going to have everything in there. It's going to be like twenty pages.
14	Elias:	Yeah ... yeah. It's good as a reference paper. So again ... just balance between being comprehensive and then people not reading it because it's too much stuff.
15	Christina:	Twenty pages!
16	Mallory:	Uh huh. It's not done yet.

In line 1, Mallory alludes to the discussion on blanking values summarized in Episode 2. While she argued for explaining questionable catalog entries in the data release paper, Ken jokingly suggests letting potential users take an online quiz before granting them access to the data (lines 4 and 6). Mallory instead opts for written instructions in the README file, a document that can be downloaded along with the catalog (line 9; cf. Ochsenbein et al. 2000). Much like the "MUWAGS catalog driver's license" (line 7) it would instruct users. In lines 10 and 11, Ken and Elias continue a sentence that Mallory began in line 9, transforming it into a collaborative formulation. Elias expresses the concern, previously made, that users would not read the data release paper with sufficient care (line 14).

This discussion continues the team's playful and exploratory mood of the conversation excerpted in Transcript 7.2 (Chapter 7). There, team members pondered users' signing and acknowledging the "terms and conditions" of the data release as well as requiring them to deposit their credit card numbers for financial compensation in cases of misuse. Somewhat like the introduction of redundant columns in Episode 1, the multiple-choice test that Ken suggests in line 4 is meant to elicit users' responses. It projects users' actions, unavailable for correction in copresence, and seeks to prompt them to self-correct their understanding. References to users passing a driver's license test and committing to a contractual agreement, although made jokingly, can be heard as pointing to team members' desire to hold users legally accountable for their actions.

8.5 Discussion

I began this chapter by wondering whether data can be made to "speak for themselves." I examined data as forms of writing that can be "more-than-evidential" when they are structured and presented to have a pragmatic function oriented to users' sensemaking and understanding, with the caveat that writing and written instructions can never substitute for talk-in-interaction. They cannot determine users' actions. Five episodes of the MUWAGS team's "inner dialogues" illustrate how its members aimed to produce an astronomical catalog that was acceptable to all of them, that was coherent with their diverse projects, and that would preempt at least some mistaken uses. In the following, I draw on these episodes to discuss how a data object can instruct potentially unruly users, what they tell us about the claim that a catalog encodes a team's collective knowledge, and how socio-computational orders become a worthwhile topic of ethnographic inquiry.

8.5.1 Making an Instructing Data Object for Potentially Unruly Users

Although it would have been possible for MUWAGS team members to consult with potential users and design their data release accordingly, they did not do so. But real and imagined users (and imagined uses) featured prominently in team discussions, in which members commonly represented users' actual and presumed actions and intentions with reported direct speech (such as in Transcripts 8.4 and 8.5) or referenced them otherwise (such as in the online discussion on blanking values in Episode 2). Imagined users were described as potentially "pestering" catalog makers (Transcript 8.3), as not reading instructions carefully (Transcript 8.8), and as being prone to make mistakes for which they could hold the team accountable (Transcript 8.6). In sum: viewed through their (imagined) actions, users were deemed potentially unruly – and so were (potential) uses of the released data. A closer look reveals that these characterizations draw on team members' self-reflection of their own conduct as professional astronomers. They assume a "reciprocity of perspectives" (cf. Schütz 1962; 1964).

The designers that Steve Woolgar (1991) studied considered users as generic subjects that were to be configured, Madeline Akrich (1992) observed how users were "scripted" into a design, Wes Sharrock and Robert Anderson (1994) witnessed users being typified as "scenic features in design," whereas David Martin and coauthors (2007) witnessed potential users as the "context" for design. But for these astronomers, data makers and anticipated data users were agents who act in recognizably structured ways as members of the same epistemic community. MUWAGS team members were themselves users of other scientists' data (cf. Transcript 8.5) and they drew on this experience as they assembled their catalog. In a certain sense, team members became (auto-)ethnographers of their own culture, a stance now familiar from Chapters 2, 3, and 7.

Since team members could not draw on resources available for repair in face-to-face interaction, their challenge was to structure the data release to make it an object that guides its users beyond the instructions provided by the data release paper. The episodes described in this chapter reveal some methods for doing so: introducing and structuring redundancies (Episode 1), choosing specific blanking values (Episode 2), selectively deleting table entries and defining flags (Episode 3). Yet other methods could certainly be identified. To speak of methods here may seem exaggerated. After all, little of this was particularly noteworthy for these scientists themselves. Yet it is just their apparent "common sense" that makes these ways of acting a part of extragalactic astronomy's form of life.

Redundancies may, at first, seem odd as a means for communication in science. In a manual for science writers, Silvia M. Rogers (2014, 59) states that "[r]edundancies are common troublemakers in scientific communication." But the diverse uses of redundancies in coding, data storage, cryptography, and communications challenge this view.[23] An instructive case is the use of notation in mathematical writing, such as when formulating exercises. Donald Knuth and coauthors (1987, 19) explain:

> Exercises are some of the most difficult parts of a book to write. Since an exercise has very little context, ambiguity can be especially deadly; a bit of carefully chosen redundancy can be especially important.

Much as students who try to solve textbook problems, data users often lack the experience of using data makers' detectors, algorithms, and analysis procedures. Redundancies are not merely duplicating information but afford users a variety of sequential engagements to assess their understanding. That repetitions of utterances in talk-in-interaction are not meaningless is a central lesson of pragmatic understandings of language. In Episode 1, I noticed team members' aspiration to design redundancies meant to instigate users to go through a three-part sequence for self-correcting mistaken uses. I found this to be reminiscent of student–teacher interaction in classrooms.[24] This triadic structure builds on what Harvey Sacks,

---

[23] Shannon (1948) and MacKay (2003).
[24] Mehan (1979), Macbeth (2003), and Lindwall et al. (2015).

Emanuel Schegloff, and Gail Jefferson (1974, 728–729) refer to as a "proof procedure" for the analysis of turns in conversation, whereby speakers' responses to a previous utterance display their understanding of the utterance to coparticipants of a conversation.[25]

I wondered at the beginning of this chapter if we could formulate elements of a pragmatics of data reuse. Here I understand "pragmatics" inclusively as the study of "meaning in context" (Chapman 2011, 1), and of "how speakers and hearers achieve understanding in and through language" (Koschmann 2011, 435), transposing it to scientists' uses of (numerical) measurements. Sequential engagements with catalog entries, as elicited by means of redundancies, could be one of its topics. Intersubjective uses of measurements, uses of statistical language, statistical descriptors, and the formatting of data could be others. After all, lists and tables afford specific uses and help reducing ambiguity.[26] Their structure, order, and notational characteristics afford diverse uses which are "foundational for coordinating activity distributed in time and space" (Bowker and Star 1999, 138). But, when engaged through accounting practices, other formats afford pragmatic uses as well, including digital pixel images.[27]

8.5.2 Does a Catalog Encode a Team's "Collective Knowledge" of its Data?

Inspired by astronomer David W. Hogg's claim that astronomical catalogs "encode the collective knowledge of the people who make the data" (Transcript 8.1), I wondered if "collective knowledge," a topic of philosophical debate, becomes conceivable, consequential, and meaningful (only) through its materialization in a digital object. I now attempt to formulate an anthropological response to this question.

Let me begin by making two distinctions. One is whether "knowing" should be conceived as propositional – that it "consists in possessing the right sort of belief in the right sort of propositions" (Chang 2017, 103) –, which is what most philosophers of science seem to assume, or as a capability, as Wittgenstein (2009 [1953]) and Ryle (1949) argued.[28] The other

---

[25] See also Moerman and Sacks (1988). Lynch (2011, 554) argues that rather than "offer[ing] a guarantee that a conversation analyst who uses a tape recording to get access to what co-participants' 'understand' from each other's talk will get it right" it only "narrows the field of relevancies" for such analysis.

[26] Goody (1977), Schmidt and Wagner (2004), and Dourish (2017).

[27] See Chapter 4 and Hoeppe (2019b).

[28] Hasok Chang insists that science needs both knowledge-as-ability and knowledge-as-information. Chang quotes Philip Kitcher, who argues that "a crucial feature of propositional knowledge is that

is to distinguish summative views of collective knowledge from those that insist on its irreducibly collective nature. Let me begin with the latter pair, which presumes that knowledge is propositional. The summative view asserts that "a collective knows p iff [if and only if] each member knows p" (de Ridder 2014, 38). Thus conceived, collective knowledge is reducible to the knowledge of individuals and so there is nothing distinctively collective about it. Views that consider collective knowledge as irreducible to that of individuals are of greater interest. For example, a committee could arrive at a certain position without each, or any, individual member subscribing to it (Wray 2017). If one adopts the commonly held philosophical notion of knowledge as "justified true belief" – as all these accounts do or at least set out from – one is led to regard human collectives as "epistemic subjects" that can hold beliefs collectively. This is what Margaret Gilbert (2000) argues for in her "plural subject theory."

Brad Wray (2007; 2017) objects to Gilbert's view by arguing that ascribing shared acceptance to a collective is more plausible than positing a shared belief. He reformulates knowledge as "justified true acceptance." In either case, the collectivity of knowers is delineated by those who believe or accept a claim. Whereas Gilbert extends collective beliefs to disciplines and adherents of Kuhnian paradigms, Wray (2007) confines collective acceptance to research teams and committees, arguing that only these have specifiable decision procedures. Probing another part of the definition of knowledge as "justified true belief," Jeroen de Ridder (2014) suggests attending to the unavoidably collective justification of knowledge in science. It is, for example, beyond any individual scientist's capacity to justify or evaluate findings of elaborate experiments. Questions of collective knowledge then turn into questions of justification and ultimately into questions of trust (Hardwig 1991; cf. also Wagenknecht 2016, ch. 8).

These considerations can inform an interpretation of the MUWAGS catalog's fixation. One may accept both Wray's (2007; 2017) replacement of "belief" by "acceptance" and de Ridder's (2014) unavoidably collective justification of its contents. The data release paper's collective authorship signals the collective acceptance of the dataset that it describes. My five episodes illustrate how the justification of catalog entries and quality flags relied on members of distinct sub-teams. That the final catalog became irreducible to individuals' knowledge is suggested by the diverse evidential contexts engaged by team members as well as the compromises made in its completion.

---

it is the most suitable form of knowledge for public communication" (Chang 2022, 17). As this chapter suggests, this may not hold for scientists communicating knowledge through data.

However, for the naturalistic position that I adopt, the propositional view of knowledge as a form of belief is disappointing. After all, scientists' "[s]hared beliefs are much less common than shared practices" (Netz 1999, 2).[29] It is more interesting to follow Gilbert Ryle (1949, 133–134) and consider "know" as a "capacity verb (…) that is used for signifying that the person described can bring things off, or get things right." By contrast, for Ryle, "believe" is a "tendency verb and one which does not connote that anything is brought off or got right." Ascribing knowledge to someone therefore presumes the witnessability of this person's actions, or of these actions' products. Harold Garfinkel turned Ryle's and Wittgenstein's (2009 [1953]) problems of mutual understanding into topics for empirical study. Responding to fellow sociologist Aaron Cicourel in a discussion on researching children's acquisition of language skills, Garfinkel (in Hill and Crittenden 1968, 47) put it pithily:

> "know" here has to do not with what one might have in mind in some secret place. It is not a case of your having to calm a respondent or seduce him in order for him really to tell you. Then you would be illuminated on what he had been hiding all along. Instead, "know" consists really in a structure of activity. That is what the "know" consists of.

Note that, in holding this view, Garfinkel explicitly counters arguments that locate knowledge in the mind or in the brain – arguably the root cause of the philosophical controversy on collective knowledge. Garfinkel (1967, 30–31) insists that the "appropriate image of a common understanding is therefore an operation rather than a common intersection of overlapping sets." He is concerned with "a *procedural* sense of common or shared, a set of practices by which actions and stances could be predicated on and displayed as oriented to 'knowledge held in common' – knowledge that might thereby be reconfirmed, modified, and expanded" (Schegloff 1991, 152; emphasis in original).

In the MUWAGS team's catalog making, only their shared data analysis skills and practices of agreement may be collective in this sense, since otherwise its members' skills (capacities) were clearly differentiated and irreducible, as the five episodes above and the two episodes in Chapter 6 have shown. It is then the catalog's singularity, its unity, and "thingness"

---

[29] See also Rouse (2003) and Chang (2017; 2022). Otfried, Nadine's supervisor (Chapter 3), repeatedly expressed to me his belief that the standard Lambda cold dark matter (ΛCDM) cosmology was wrong. The Hubble constant, he believed, must be much lower than the commonly accepted value. Nevertheless, he used the latter in all of his publications. Using a different value may not have passed peer review at important journals and reduced his readership.

in its published, materialized, fixated form, that is most interesting for a discussion of "collective knowledge."[30] In this "frozen" form, the catalog is a "means of forgetting" (de Certeau 1984, 97), leaving no trace of the discussions and agreements involved in its closure, a product of its makers' analyses and the team's negotiations. It may properly instruct only users familiar with the evidential contexts, to address which the catalog was designed for, and may be contingent, as well, on shared accounting practices. In its users' data analyses, the catalog makes the team's knowledge of its data actionable, but it does so without developing users' capacity to "bring things off, or get things right" (Ryle 1949, 133) beyond specific applications.[31]

8.5.3   Socio-Computational Orders

Learning from data is the point of making and using them. But how to pass on what has been learned not only *from* data, but about *them*? A "frozen" catalog has "frozen" the knowledge of its makers about their data without specifying it.[32] This, after all, is how its fixation is a "means of forgetting." One way to learn is to change one's beliefs, but "belief" need not be something hidden in a private mind (cf. Ryle 1949). Computational scientists rather use it as in Bayesian inference, where it stands for the prior distribution as an estimate of the probability of a hypothesis. According to Bayes' theorem, a prior is updated by multiplying it with the likelihood – the "measure of the evidential support provided by data for particular parameter values" (Spiegelhalter 2019, 392) –, resulting in the posterior probability distribution. "In a sense," argues Sivia (2006, 6), "Bayes' theorem encapsulates the process of learning." It is a principle foundational not only to the spectral template-fitting technique that Nadine used (Chapter 3), but also to machine learning and generative artificial intelligence.

[30] The philosophical literature has little to say on how the materiality of writing shapes conceptions of collective knowledge, an exception being when Wray (2017) discusses Beatty's (2006) example of how an expert committee arrived at an assessment of radiation safety, which prominently involved the use of documents. By contrast, discussions of collective authorship commonly focus on documents – the authored publications (e.g., Hardwig 1991; Galison 2003; Huebner et al. 2017).
[31] See Ribes and Bowker (2009) for an alternative view of encoding the knowledge of communities, focusing on communally shared and explicable classifications and descriptions (ontologies). Another view is to conceive of a collaboration as the group to which knowledge about its data properly belongs (cf. Sharrock 1974).
[32] See Hogg and Lang (2008, 2010) for intriguing ideas on how to transmit makers' knowledge of their data not through catalogs, but via imaging data and computer code. However, at least in 2025, catalogs were still widely used in astronomy. Transmitting knowledge through code also hinges on the maintenance of the code's usability, which can be challenging in the long run (Cohn 2019).

Updating beliefs with Bayes' theorem can appear to be a purely mechanical operation, but it is also deeply social. Not only are Bayesian priors unavoidably subjective, but every inquiry must begin somewhere and where to begin is a human choice. Social agreements, shared assumptions, and normative considerations are the ground on which data are usable and meaningful. Measuring, and agreeing on the adequacy of measurements, is about sharing "common ground."[33] Thomas Kuhn (1970) argued that scientific disciplines are "language communities" bound by "concerted agreements on theories, measuring techniques, and characteristic modes of demonstration" (Lynch 1991b, 105fn 1). As we have seen in Chapter 3, learning to make proper measurements is a key element of achieving membership in such a community. Their social and epistemic orders are aligned, and so is the numerical order of the measurements central to their work (cf. Section 8.4.2). Measurements are presented in a "statistical language" that serves as a "technology of intersubjectivity" (Hacking 1992b, 152).

The collaborative production of a catalog (and other forms of processed data) may encode a team's knowledge about noise models and artifacts, but it also serves future users as a shared reference. It brings them "on a page" and allows them to compare their analyses and assess these analyses' robustness.[34] In each of the SDSS's five-year phases, subsequent annual data releases were meant improve earlier ones, but all data releases are still available online. As Alexander Szalay, a long-term SDSS collaboration member, put it: "A data release is like a book. You cannot take it down. People use old editions."[35] This adds another view to the uses of writing in research with large datasets that this chapter has explored.

---

[33] Lewis (1969), Clark (1996), and Enfield (2013).

[34] Key elements of many astronomical catalogs are produced with computer code that is widely shared, including the SExtractor source identification code (Bertin and Arnouts 1996) that Nadine used (cf. Chapter 3). In recent years, code intercomparison projects, in which the output of different codes in processing the same dataset is compared, have aimed at agreeing on best practices (e.g., Kitching et al. 2013 and references therein). See also Sundberg (2011) and Mayernik (2021).

[35] Heidelberg Astronomical Colloquium, Heidelberg (Germany), May 22, 2007. Note that subsequent phases of the SDSS do not simply improve on earlier observations but use new instrumentation and observe different targets.

Outlook
Scientific Data, Artificial Intelligence, and People

My aim in this book has been to examine how scientific data not only represent information but are also implicated in social accountabilities and social action. I argued that, more than ever before, data have become a peculiarly epistemic and social stuff that scientists make, use, and circulate to learn about nature, instruct students, build connections, transmit knowledge, grow trust, and evaluate the work of others. I have considered scientists, students, and technicians as people: embodied, cognizant, social, and cultural human beings. By attending to participants' accounting practices and their resources I focused on matters that are elementary and common and took them very seriously (cf. Munger 2023). I have aimed to stay true to Peter Winch's (1958, 84) observation that "to understand the activities of an individual scientific investigator we must take account of two sets of relations: first, his relation to the phenomena which he investigates; second, his relation to his fellow-scientists." I have refrained from separating "the epistemic" and "the social" and argued that proceeding this way promises insights that are both foundational and transferable beyond the settings that I have examined. But how can this approach contribute to make sense of transformations in data-rich science due to machine learning (ML) and generative artificial intelligence (AI)? In the following, I make the case for the benefits of considering this question at the refined granularity of social interaction, consider how scientists themselves are social inquirers who do ethnography, and attend to emergent socialities and their ethics.

Speculations about, and expectations of, the impact of ML and generative AI in the sciences reach from novel possibilities of discovery and changes to the division of labor, to concerns over the trustworthiness of results, the unsettling nature of AI systems as "black boxes," humans' potential marginalization in creative work, illusions of understanding, and problems of responsible uses, as well as concerns over the credit and authorship of data and results. Although ML and generative AI are related conceptually (such as in automatizing probabilistic inference), many scientists regard them as distinct technologies. Diverse forms of ML have been part of scientific work for more than a decade and include widely accepted methods like artificial neural networks and Gaussian processes (Ting 2025). By contrast, uses of generative AI, conceived as Large Language Models (LLMs) and related technologies, have attracted scientists' attention since the publication of the transformer algorithm in 2017 and its uses in chatbots. Many forms of ML and AI have humans "in the loop" to improve their performance, such as in supervised learning or reinforcement learning (Ting 2025). These uses add a contemporary example to *How Data Need People*. But this is not what I address in the following.

Continuing my naturalistic stance, I propose to consider researchers as people – embodied, social human beings – who use ML and generative AI in data-rich science. Some authors focus on ML and AI applications in the sciences without explicitly addressing the sociality of their participants (Wang et al. 2023; Hogg and Villar 2024), others attend to researchers as individuals that interact with machines (Krenn et al. 2022; Collins et al. 2024),[1] and still others consider communal aspects in abstract terms (Messeri and Crockett 2024).[2] From the perspective that I adopt in this book, doing science is unavoidably both an individual and a collective endeavor. Much of what is interesting and consequential happens between the individual and the collective and comes into focus only when we attend to situated interactions. Doing so may also be our best way to identify backgrounded assumptions and to avoid abstractions that may easily turn out to be misplaced. Furthermore, a naturalistic ethnographic approach attends not to fixed relations and situations, but to members' methods that are by necessity open to novel and likely unexpected developments that lie ahead. Communities may be the sites where social norms are enacted, but their members are social actors – users of methods who live lives and thus have biographies.

Like anyone in society, scientists use accounting practices in their social and professional lives. In this book two distinct notions of accountability have been in play. Both are described in the Introduction. One is ethnomethodological accountability. Situated in lived practice, it is reflexive

---

[1] By invoking a sort of Turing test to examine the scientific understanding of AI systems, Krenn et al. (2022) go beyond individualist assumptions.

[2] For example, Messeri and Crockett (2024, 50) ponder illusions of understanding, due to uses of AI, of "communities of knowledge," defined as "groups of individuals with distributed knowledge and understanding that allow individual community members to benefit from expertise held by others."

in the sense that "the describing of social activities is part and parcel of the activities so described" (Sharrock and Anderson 1986, 57). The point is to "study the ways in which [people] organize themselves so that they can tell us about the things they do" (Sharrock and Anderson 1986, 57). In Chapters 2 to 8, I have traced ethnomethodological accountability through an observatory's control room, graduate student training, uses of diagrams and mundane reason in data analyses and interpretations, organizing collaborative work, achieving proper membership in "open science," and encoding the team's knowledge of its data in the dataset itself. These episodes show how epistemic and social orders are entangled in scientific work with large datasets. As scientists seek to agree on uses of ML and generative AI, they are unavoidably going to use accounting practices, but what these are, and which resources they involve, are questions for empirical study. Scientists will remain evaluative, accounting practices will shape the achievement of membership, diagrammatic practices and mundane reasoning are bound to remain fundamentally important, and normative orders will emerge.

The other accountability, of second order, that this book has considered is the "tyranny of accountability," the "ever-present possibility of being noticed, praised, blamed, questioned, called out, and judged" (Enfield and Sidnell 2022, 21), a reflective stance that requires language to become socially salient. Its relevance in view of the emergence of ML and generative AI may be recognizable more readily than ethnomethodological accountability. In science, peer review is a central "system of accountability" (Douglas 1980, 35) where authorship and its balancing of credit and responsibility come to the fore. This is where communal standards and norms, legitimate practices and resources, and issues of membership are adopted and sanctioned. Its changes deserve close attention. Journal articles are units of the scientific literature and, as such, also units of accountability. As Chapters 3, 4, 5, and 8 show, the accountability of authorship is reflexive throughout on the research process, including data analyses, which leads us back to the accounting practices that ethnographic studies can identify and describe.

During my study I found that it was not just I, the visiting anthropologist, who worked ethnographically, but that scientists and technicians, too, were social inquirers who did a sort of ethnography themselves, albeit one that is distinct from the anthropologist's (cf. Chapters 2, 3, 7, and 8). It is no surprise that rapid technological and conceptual changes prompt people to inquire into how fellow members adopt them, ponder the limits of acceptable or agreeable uses, and shape new norms. Anthropologists have documented how swiftly uses of new media lead to the adoption of new norms (Miller and Horst 2012). Astronomers' reflections on the impact of ML and generative AI have many sites, from lunch conversations and seminar discussions to conferences and hack weeks. Some astronomers have probed into their community's practices, composed reports of their findings, and posted them on the arXiv preprint server, making them widely accessible.

Considering ML, Daniela Huppenkothen and her coauthors (2023) assembled a team of astronomers at a hack week to formulate a "primer to the astronomical community, including authors, reviewers, and editors, on how to implement machine learning models and report their results in a way that ensures the accuracy of the results, reproducibility of the findings, and usefulness of the method." Examining uses of LLMs, Morgan Fouesneau and his coauthors (2024) "conducted a study involving 13 astronomers at different career stages and research fields to explore LLM applications across diverse tasks over several months and to evaluate their performance in research-related activities." This was followed up by a survey and led to the formulation of recommendations to ensure that "these tools serve as aids rather than substitutes for rigorous scientific inquiry." In proposing best practices and formulating recommendations, both studies have a normative bent.[3]

These "members' studies" are not ethnographic, but one may consider them as one part of a spectrum of scientists' social inquiries, of which a collaboration's "ethnographic" exploration of how to act properly in the uncommon domain of "open science" is another (Chapter 7). The latter translated elements of a shared lifeworld (uses of credit cards, contracts, lawsuits, and other means of sanctioning) into the domain of open data access. Exploring a novel domain and describing it with a certain vocabulary may be consequential in that the terms used to describe it may end up defining its practices. Given how easily and swiftly generative AI, in the form of chatbots, is integrated into diverse scientific workflows and is designed to be interactive, an interactional ethnographic perspective appears almost inevitable. But an ethnographic approach is also called for to discover ethical issues that can remain hidden from analysts otherwise.

My notion of data-centrism – that making, using, and publishing data causes humans to interact and engage in specifiable ways – is inspired by Georg Simmel's explorations of the diversity of social forms in the early

---

[3] Related earlier studies include surveys of astronomers' use of software (like Momcheva and Tollerud 2015) that informed the work of the Astropy Collaboration (2013, 2018, 2022).

twentieth century. As I wrote in the Introduction, Simmel realized when writing his *Sociology* (1992 [1908]) that many forms of sociation awaited discovery – not least by means of more detailed, "microscopic" studies –, but also because new forms keep coming-to-be while others pass away. And so it will be in the twenty-first century. The large-scale impacts of ML and generative AI will unavoidably be tied to microscopic, granular interactions, whose study, I hope, will continue to be a reminder of human agency and responsibility.

Appendix
Transcription Conventions

In order to capture pragmatically consequential aspects of talk I transcribe recorded conversations using conventions that are mostly adopted from Gail Jefferson's (2004) scheme, but simplified to make them readable by nonexperts in conversation analysis.

Lines are numbered for reference.

Emphasis

Underscoring indicates emphasis:

> 5 Peter: which is ... the <u>re-reddened</u> ... R-band magnitude ... as observed

Intervals within and between Turns

An ellipsis marks an interval or pause of various length in time:

> 5 Otfried: So ... it seems that we make some progress

Jefferson's (2004) scheme times intervals more precisely, but this detail is not needed for my purposes in this book.

Intonation

A full stop indicates a fall in tone at the end of a meaningful unit:

> 16 Henry: That is obviously to be discussed.

A question mark indicates a raise in intonation:

> 1 Olli: How's the wind doing?

An exclamation mark indicates speech that is exceptionally animated:

> 5 Otfried: <u>Exactly</u> ... which you <u>criticized</u>!

Uncertain and Incomprehensible Sounds
and Speaker Ascriptions

Where I was unable to recognize verbal sounds confidently, I include candidate transcriptions in parentheses:

        12 Christina: I think they (would be in that) mood

Empty parentheses mark the approximate length of indecipherable sounds:

        13 Henry: That's true … but if you … for example … (   )

Parentheses also indicate uncertain speaker ascriptions:

        7   (Mallory):   [HA-HA-HA

Empty parentheses indicate unidentified speaker ascriptions:

        15 ( ):   That sounds like

Simultaneous Turns

Left side brackets on consecutive lines indicate where simultaneous turns begin:

        6   Henry: [Yeah.
        7   Joe: [Yeah.

Overlapping Talk

Left side brackets on consecutive lines indicate where overlapping talk begins:

        6   Elias: You have some (<u>thieves</u> following you)[( )
        7   (Mallory):   [HA-HA-HA

Volume

Upper case letters mark increased volume:

        24 Ben: [CHUANG

Note that – unlike in the Jefferson (2004) scheme – I generally list project, software, and instrument names referenced in the text – like MUWAGS, REDCOR, and GROND – in capitals (as scientists do), at the risk of confusion with sounds louder than their surroundings.

Sound Stretches

A colon marks a stretched sound:

    7   Christina: It is a:lso public.

Added colons indicate longer stretched sounds:

   11 Elias: no::: heh

Laughter

Series of h's signify the outbreath characteristic of chuckling or giggling:

    1   Otfried: and tonight hhhh the first observations of A2713 for more than a year hhhhh have <u>happened</u> hhhhh

A series of ha-ha- marks laughter, its length indicates the length of laughter:

   17 Eddie: ha-ha-ha-ha-ha If I was on a National Science Foundation panel

A series of he-he- marks laughter as well:

    3   Christina: They've done it again yeah he-he-he-he-he … so yeah

HA-HA-HA marks loud laughter:

    6   (Group):   HA-HA-HA-HA-HA-HA-HA-HA-HA-HA-HA

Verbal Descriptions

Double parentheses contain descriptions of context, witnessed actions, and the delivery of talk:

    2   Mary: ((*looks at current weather data on the La Silla MeteoMonitor*)) It says stable at eleven … on this one
    7   Otto: ((*whispers*)) It has drifted away

Words Omitted from the Transcript

An ellipsis in parentheses marks the omission of words from the transcript:

The <u>first</u> thing is to <u>upload</u> the exposures … check the FITS headers and do all that. (…) The <u>next</u> steps are bias subtraction … <u>correcting</u> for nonlinear effects and some other small

Reported Direct Speech and Quoted Text

I indicate what I heard as reported direct speech using quotation marks:

Cristina: We were having dinner ... and it was raining. And then the astronomer tells me: "I am going to the ..." That was when we were observing in the dome.

Likewise, I indicate what I heard as reported quoted text using quotation marks:

39 Ken: a statement ... "Billing address ... please add your credit card here"

References

Abbott, T., Abdalla, F. B., Aleksić, J., et al. (2016). The Dark Energy Survey: More than Dark Energy: An Overview. *Monthly Notices of the Royal Astronomical Society*, 460, 1270–1299.

Abdul-Karim, M., Adame, A. G., Aguado, D., et al. (2025). Data Release 1 of the Dark Energy Spectroscopic Instrument. *arXiv:2503.14745*.

Abell, G. O. (1958). The Distribution of Rich Clusters of Galaxies. *Astrophysical Journal Supplements*, 3(2), 211–288.

Ade, P. A. R., Aikin, R. W., Barkats, D., et al. (2014). Detection of B-Mode Polarization at Degree Angular Scales by BICEP2. *Physical Review Letters*, 112, 241101 (26pp).

Agar, M. (1995). Ethnography. In J. Verschueren, J.-O. Östman & J. Blommaert, eds. *Handbook of Pragmatics: Manual*, Amsterdam: John Benjamins, 583–590.

Akrich, M. (1992). The De-Scription of Technical Objects. In W. Bijker & J. Law, eds., *Shaping Technology / Building Society*. Cambridge, MA: MIT Press, 202–225.

Alač, M. (2011). *Handling Digital Brains: A Laboratory Study of Multimodal Semiotic Interaction in the Age of Computers*. Cambridge, MA: MIT Press.

Alač, M. (2020). Beyond Intersubjectivity in Olfactory Psychophysics, I: Troubles with the Subject. *Social Studies of Science*, 50(3), 440–473.

Almeida, A., Anderson, S. F., Argudo-Fernandez, M., et al. (2023). The Eighteenth Data Release of the Sloan Digital Sky Surveys: Targeting and First Spectra from SDSS-V. *Astrophysical Journal Supplement Series*, 267, 44.

Anderson, R. J., Hughes, J. A., & Sharrock, W. W. (1989). *Working for Profit: The Social Organisation of Calculation in an Entrepreneurial Firm*. Aldershot: Avebury.

Anderson, R. J. & Sharrock, W. W. (2018). *Action at a Distance: Studies in the Practicalities of Executive Management*. London: Routledge.

Anderson, R. J., Sharrock, W. W., & Hughes, J. A. (1990). The Division of Labour. *Réseaux. Communication – Technologie – Société*, 8(2), 237–252.

Ankeny, R. A. & Leonelli, S. (2016). Repertoires: A Post-Kuhnian Perspective on Scientific Change and Collaborative Research. *Studies in History and Philosophy of Science*, 60, 18–28.

Anscombe, F. J. (1973). Graphs in Statistical Analysis. *American Statistician*, 27(1), 17–21.

Appadurai, A. (2015). *Banking on Words: The Failure of Language in the Age of Derivative Finance*. Chicago, IL: University of Chicago Press.

Aristotle. (1939). *On the Heavens*, transl. W. K. C. Guthrie. Loeb Classical Library, vol. 338. Cambridge, MA: Harvard University Press.

Arthur, W. B. (2009). *The Nature of Technology: What It Is and How It Evolves*. New York: Free Press.

Asad, T. (1986). The Concept of Cultural Translation in British Anthropology. In J. Clifford & G. E. Marcus, eds., *Writing Culture: The Poetics and Politics of Ethnography*. Berkeley: University of California Press, 141–164.

Astropy Collaboration. (2013). Astropy: A Community Python Package for Astronomy. *Astronomy & Astrophysics*, 558, A33.

Astropy Collaboration. (2018). The Astropy Project: Building an Open-Science Project and Status of the v2.0 Core Package. *Astronomical Journal*, 159, 123.

Astropy Collaboration. (2022). The Astropy Project: Sustaining and Growing a Community-oriented Open-source Project and the Latest Major Release (v5.0) of the Core Package. *Astrophysical Journal*, 935, 167.

Baccus, M. D. (1986). Sociological Indication and the Visibility Criterion of Real World Social Theorizing. In H. Garfinkel, ed., *Ethnomethodological Studies of Work*. London: Routledge and Kegan Paul, 1–19.

Bacevic, J. & Muellerleile, C. (2018). The Moral Economy of Open Access. *European Journal of Social Theory*, 21(2), 169–188.

Bachelard, G. (1985 [1934]). *The New Scientific Spirit*, transl. A. Goldhammer. Boston, MA: Beacon Press.

Bachelard, G. (2002 [1938]). *The Formation of the Scientific Mind: A Contribution to a Psychoanalysis of Objective Knowledge*, transl. M. M. Jones. Manchester: Clinamen Press.

Bahcall, J. N., Guhathakurta, P., & Schneider, D. P. (1990). What the Longest Exposures from the Hubble Space Telescope Will Reveal. *Science*, 248 (4952), 178–183.

Bakhtin, M. M. (1986). *Speech Genres and Other Late Essays*, transl. V. W. McGee. Austin, TX: University of Texas Press.

Barden, M., Häußler, B., Peng, C. Y., McIntosh, D. H., & Guo, Y. (2012). GALAPAGOS: From Pixels to Parameters. *Monthly Notices of the Royal Astronomical Society*, 442, 449–468.

Barley, S. & Bechky, B. (1994). In the Backrooms of Science: The Work of Technicians in Science Labs. *Work and Occupations*, 21(1), 85–126.

Barnes, B. (1995). *The Elements of Social Theory*. Princeton, NJ: Princeton University Press.

Barnes, B. (2003). Thomas Kuhn and the Problem of Social Order in Science. In T. Nickles, ed., *Thomas Kuhn*. Cambridge: Cambridge University Press, 122–141.

Barnes, B., Bloor, D., & Henry, J. (1996). *Scientific Knowledge: A Sociological Analysis*. Chicago, IL: University of Chicago Press.

Basso, K. H. (1979). *Portraits of "The Whiteman": Linguistic Play and Cultural Symbols Among the Western Apache*. Cambridge: Cambridge University Press.

Bateson, G. (1972). A Theory of Play and Fantasy. In G. Bateson, ed., *Steps to an Ecology of Mind*. Chicago, IL: University of Chicago Press, 177–193.

Baum, W. A. (1955). Counting Photons – One by One. *Sky and Telescope*, 14, 264–267, 330–334.

Baum, W. A. (1962). Photoelectric Magnitudes and Red-Shifts. In G. McVittie, ed., *Problems of Extragalactic Research*. New York: Macmillan, 390–400.

Baum, W. A. (1964). Photosensitive Detectors. *Annual Review of Astronomy and Astrophysics*, 2, 165–184.

Baxandall, M. (1972). *Painting and Experience in Fifteenth-Century Italy: A Primer in the Social History of Pictorial Style*. Oxford: Oxford University Press.

Bear, L. (2014). For Labour: Ajeet's Accident and the Ethics of Technological Fixes in Time. *Journal of the Royal Anthropological Institute*, 20(S1), 71–88.

Beatty, J. (2006). Masking Disagreements among Experts. *Episteme*, 3(1–2), 52–67.

Beaulieu, A. (2002). Images Are Not the (Only) Truth: Brain Mapping, Visual Knowledge, and Iconoclasm. *Science, Technology, and Human Values*, 27(1), 53–86.

Beck, S., Bergenholtz, C., Bogers, M., et al. (2022). The Open Innovation in Science Research Field: A Collaborative Conceptualisation Approach. *Industry and Innovation*, 29(2), 136–185.

Benacchio, L. (1997). Astronomical Data Archives and the Next Ground-Based Telescopes. *Experimental Astronomy*, 7, 391–397.

Benvenuti, P. (1994). Archives of Space-Borne and Ground-Based Observatories: Where Are They Different? In M. A. Albrecht & F. Pasian, eds., *Handling and Archiving Data from Ground-based Telescopes*. Garching: European Southern Observatory, 1–3.

Bergmann, J. (2011). Von der Wechselwirkung zur Interaktion – Georg Simmel und die Mikrosoziologie heute. In H. Tyrell, O. Rammstedt & I. Meyer, eds., *Georg Simmels große "Soziologie": Eine kritische Sichtung nach hundert Jahren*. Bielefeld: transcript, 125–148.

Bertin, E. & Arnouts, S. (1996). SExtractor: Software for Source Extraction. *Astronomy and Astrophysics Supplement Series*, 117(2), 393–404.

Bessell, M. S. (2005). Standard Photometric Systems. *Annual Review of Astronomy and Astrophysics*, 43, 293–336.

Bhattacharyya, G. & Bodner, G. M. (2014). Culturing Reality: How Organic Chemistry Graduate Students Develop into Practitioners. *Journal of Research in Science Teaching*, 51(6), 694–713.

Biagioli, M. (2003). Rights or Rewards? In M. Biagioli & P. Galison, eds., *Scientific Authorship: Credit and Intellectual Property in Science*. New York: Routledge, 253–279.

Biagioli, M. (2006). *Galileo's Instruments of Credit: Telescopes, Images, Secrecy*. Chicago, IL: University of Chicago Press.

Birnholtz, J. P. & Bietz, M. J. (2003). Data at Work: Supporting Sharing in Science and Engineering. In M. Pendergast, ed., *Proceedings of the 2003 International*

ACM SIGGROUP Conference on Supporting Group Work (GROUP'03). New York: Association for Computing Machinery, 339–348.

Bittner, E. (1965). The Concept of Organization. *Social Research*, 32(3), 239–255.

Blackler, A. L., Gomez, R., Popovic, V., & Thompson, M. H. (2016). Life Is Too Short to RTFM: How Users Relate to Documentation and Excess Features in Consumer Products. *Interacting with Computers*, 28(1), 27–46.

Blanchette, J.-F. (2011). A Material History of Bits. *Journal of the American Society for Information Science and Technology*, 62(6), 1042–1057.

Bland-Hawthorn, J., Shopbell, P. L., & Malin, D. F. (1993). Deep Sky Surveys: A Motivation for Stacking Digitized Photographic Plates. *Astronomical Journal*, 106(5), 2154–2160.

Blanton, M. R., Evans, J. D., Norman, D., et al. (2023). The Future of Astronomical Data Infrastructure: Meeting Report. *arXiv:2311.04272v1*.

Blommaert, J. (2019). From Groups to Actions and Back in Online-Offline Sociolinguistics. *Multilingua*, 38(4), 485–493.

Blommaert, J. & Jie, D. (2020). *Ethnographic Fieldwork: A Beginner's Guide*. Bristol: Multilingual Matters.

Blumenberg, H. (1987). *The Genesis of the Copernican World*, transl. R. M. Wallace. Cambridge, MA: MIT Press.

Blumer, H. (1969). *Symbolic Interactionism: Perspective and Method*. Berkeley: University of California Press.

Bogen, J. & Woodward, J. (1988). Saving the Phenomena. *Philosophical Review*, 97(3), 303–352.

Bohn, C. (1999). Schnittstellen: Konversation und Schriftlichkeit im Übergang zur Moderne. *Berliner Journal für Soziologie*, 9, 213–233.

Boksenberg, A. (1976). University College London Image Photon Counting System. In M. Duchesne & G. Lelievre, eds., *Astronomical Applications of Image Detectors with Linear Response*. Proceedings of the I. A. U. Colloquium n° 40, Paris: Observatoire Paris-Meudon, 13-1–13-16.

Bokulich, A. (2020). Towards a Taxonomy of the Model-Ladenness of Data. *Philosophy of Science*, 87(5), 793–806.

Bokulich, A. (2021). Using Models to Correct Data: Paleodiversity and the Fossil Record. *Synthese*, 198(Supplement 24), S5919–S5940.

Bokulich, A. & Parker, W. (2021). Data Models, Representation and Adequacy-for-Purpose. *European Journal for Philosophy of Science*, 11, 31 (26pp).

Bolden, G. B. (2009). Implementing Incipient Actions: The Discourse Marker "So" in English Conversation. *Journal of Pragmatics*, 41, 974–998.

Borgman, C. L. (2015). *Big Data, Little Data, No Data: Scholarship in the Networked World*. Cambridge, MA: MIT Press.

Borgman, C. L. & Groth, P. (2025). From Data Creator to Data Reuser: Distance Matters. *Harvard Data Science Review*, 7(2). doi.org/10.1162/99608f92.35d32cfc

Borgman, C. L., Wallis, J. C., & Mayernik, M. S. (2012). Who's Got the Data? Interdependencies in Science and Technology Collaborations. *Computer Supported Cooperative Work*, 21(6), 485–523.

Borgman, C. L. & Wofford, M. F. (2021). From Data Processes to Data Products: Knowledge Infrastructures in Astronomy. *Harvard Data Science Review*, 3(3). doi.org/10.1162/99608f92.4e792052

Boroson, T. A. (1996). Discussion Session. In T. A. Boroson, J. K. Davies & E. I. Robson, eds., *New Observing Modes for the Next Century*, ASP Conference Series, vol. 87. San Francisco: Astronomical Society of the Pacific, 245–260.

Bou-Franch, P., Lorenzo-Dus, N., & Blitvich, P. G.-C. (2012). Social Interaction in YouTube Text-Based Polylogues: A Study of Coherence. *Journal of Computer-Mediated Communication*, 17, 501–521.

Bourdieu, P. (2000). *Pascalian Meditations*, transl. R. Nice. Stanford, CA: Stanford University Press.

Bowker, G. C. (1994). *Science on the Run: Information Management and Industrial Geophysics at Schlumberger, 1920–1940*. Cambridge, MA: MIT Press.

Bowker, G. C. (2005). *Memory Practices in the Sciences*. Cambridge, MA: MIT Press.

Bowker, G. C. & Star, S. L. (1999). *Sorting Things Out: Classification and Its Consequences*. Cambridge, MA: MIT Press.

Boyce, P. B. (1977). Low Light Level Detectors for Astronomy. *Science*, 198(4313), 145–148.

Boyd, N. M., De Bardemaekers, S., Heng, K., & Matarese, V., eds. (2023). *Philosophy of Astrophysics: Stars, Simulations, and the Struggle to Determine What Is Out There*. Cham: Springer.

Bradač, M., Allen, S. W., Treu, T., Ebeling, H., Massey, R., Morris, R. G., von der Linden, A., & Applegate, D. (2008). Revealing the Properties of Dark Matter in the Merging Cluster MACS J0025.4–1222. *Astrophysical Journal*, 687, 959–967.

Brandom, R. B. (1979). Freedom and Constraint by Norms. *American Philosophical Quarterly*, 16(3), 187–196.

Brandom, R. B. (1994). *Making It Explicit: Reasoning, Representing, and Discursive Commitment*. Cambridge, MA: Harvard University Press.

Brewer, P. (2017). Do You Expect Me to Just Give Away My Data? *Eos, 98*. doi.org/10.1029/2018EO081175

Brooker, P., Sharrock, W., & Greiffenhagen, C. (2019). Programming Visuals, Visualizing Programs. *Science and Technology Studies*, 32(1), 21–42.

Butler, J. (2005). *Giving an Account of Oneself*. New York: Fordham University Press.

Button, G., Crabtree, A., Rouncefield, M., & Tolmie, P. (2015). *Deconstructing Ethnography: Towards a Social Methodology for Ubiquitous Computing and Interactive Systems Design*. Cham: Springer.

Button, G. & Sharrock, W. (1998). The Organizational Accountability of Technological Work. *Social Studies of Science*, 28(1), 73–102.

Buytendijk, F. J. J. (1933). *Wesen und Sinn des Spiels*. Berlin: Kurt Wolff Verlag.

Campbell, R. A. (2003). Preparing the Next Generation of Scientists: The Social Process of Managing Students. *Social Studies of Science*, 33(6), 897–927.

Capak, P., Aussel, H., Ajiki, M., et al. (2007). The First Release COSMOS Optical and Near-IR Data and Catalog. *Astrophysical Journal Supplement Series*, 172, 99–116.

Cardamone, C. N., Schawinski, K., Sarzi, M., et al. (2009). Galaxy Zoo Green Peas: Discovery of a Class of Compact Extremely Star-Forming Galaxies. *Monthly Notices of the Royal Astronomical Society*, 399, 1191–1205.

Carlson, S. & Anderson, B. (2007). What Are Data? The Many Kinds of Data and Their Implications for Data Re-use. *Journal of Computer-Mediated Communication*, 12(2), 635–651.

Cartwright, N. (1983). *How the Laws of Physics Lie*. Stanford, CA: Stanford University Press.

Casey, C. M., Kartaltepe, J. S., Drakos, N. E., et al. (2023). COSMOS-Web: An Overview of the JWST Cosmic Origins Survey. *Astrophysical Journal*, 954, 31 (32 pp).

Chang, H. (2011). The Philosophical Grammar of Scientific Practice. *International Studies in the Philosophy of Science*, 25(3), 205–221.

Chang, H. (2017). Operational Coherence as the Source of Truth. *Proceedings of the Aristotelian Society*, 67(2), 103–122.

Chang, H. (2022). *Realism for Realistic People: A New Pragmatist Philosophy of Science*. Cambridge: Cambridge University Press.

Chapman, S. (2011). *Pragmatics*. London: Bloomsbury.

Chau, A. Y. (2006). *Miraculous Response: Doing Popular Religion in Contemporary China*. Stanford, CA: Stanford University Press.

Cho, A. (2014). Blockbuster Big Bang Result May Fizzle, Rumor Suggests. science.org/content/article/blockbuster-big-bang-result-may-fizzle-rumor-suggests (accessed October 17, 2025).

Chromey, F. S. (2010). *To Measure the Sky: An Introduction to Observational Astronomy*. Cambridge: Cambridge University Press.

Cimatti, A., Fraternali, F., & Nipoti, C. (2019). *Introduction to Galaxy Formation and Evolution*. Cambridge: Cambridge University Press.

Clark, H. H. (1996). *Using Language*. Cambridge, MA: MIT Press.

Clarke, A. & Fujimura, J. H., eds. (1992). *The Right Tools for the Job: At Work in Twentieth-century Life Sciences*. Princeton, NJ: Princeton University Press.

Clift, R. (1999). Irony in Conversation. *Language in Society*, 28(4), 523–553.

Clowe, D., Bradač, M., Gonzalez, A. H., et al. (2006). A Direct Empirical Proof of the Existence of Dark Matter. *Astrophysical Journal*, 648, L109–L113.

Cohn, M. L. (2019). Keeping Software Present: Software as a Timely Object for STS Studies of the Digital. In J. Vertesi & D. Ribes, eds., *digitalSTS: A Field Guide for Science & Technology Studies*. Princeton, NJ: Princeton University Press, 423–446.

Collins, D., Morduch, J., Rutherford, S., & Ruthven, O. (2010). *Portfolios of the Poor: How the World's Poor Live on $2 a Day*. Princeton, NJ: Princeton University Press.

Collins, H. M. (1992). *Changing Order: Replication and Induction in Scientific Practice*. Chicago, IL: University of Chicago Press.

Collins, H. M. (2004). *Gravity's Shadow: The Search for Gravitational Waves*. Chicago, IL: University of Chicago Press.

Collins, H. M. & Evans, R. (2007). *Rethinking Expertise*. Chicago, IL: University of Chicago Press.

Collins, K. M., Sucholutsky, I., Bhatt, U., et al. (2024). Building Machines that Learn and Think with People. *Nature Human Behaviour*, 8, 1851–1863.

Comerón, F. (2004). Observing in Service Mode: The Experience at the European Southern Observatory. In A. Heck, ed., *Organizations and Strategies in Astronomy 5*. Dordrecht: Kluwer, 141–158.

Coopmans, C., Vertesi, J., Lynch, M., & Woolgar, S. eds. (2014). *Representation in Scientific Practice Revisited*. Cambridge, MA: MIT Press, 37–59.

Corbin, J. & Strauss, A. (2014). *Basics of Qualitative Research: Techniques and Procedures for Developing Grounded Theory*, 4th ed. Los Angeles: Sage Publications.

Cordes, J. M. (2012). The Dynamic Radio Sky. In R. E. M. Griffin, R. J. Hanisch & R. Seaman, eds., *New Horizons in Time-Domain Astronomy*. Cambridge: Cambridge University Press, 49–54.

Coulter, J. (1975). Perceptual Accounts and Interpretive Asymmetries. *Sociology*, 9(3), 385–396.

Coulter, J. & Parsons, E. D. (1991). The Praxiology of Perception: Visual Orientations and Practical Actions. *Inquiry*, 33(3), 251–272.

Crabtree, A., Tolmie, P., & Rouncefield, M. (2013). "How Many Bloody Examples Do You Want?" Fieldwork and Generalisation. In O. W. Bertelsen et al., eds., *ECSCW 2013: Proceedings of the 13th European Conference on Computer Supported Cooperative Work*. London: Springer, 1–20.

Crabtree, D. R., Durand, D., Gaudet, S., Hill, N. & Morris, S. (1996). Scientific Archives and New Observing Modes in the 21st Century. In G. H. Jacoby & J. Barnes, eds., *Astronomical Data Analysis Software and Systems V*. San Francisco, CA: Astronomical Society of the Pacific, 207–214.

Cyranoski, D. (2016). The Sequencing Superpower. *Nature*, 534 (23 June 2016), 462–463.

Daniel, E. V. (1984). *Fluid Sign: Being a Person the Tamil Way*. Berkeley: University of California Press.

Darwall, S. (2006). *The Second-Person Standpoint: Morality, Respect, and Accountability*. Cambridge, MA: Harvard University Press.

Daston, L. (1991). The Ideal and Reality of the Republic of Letters in the Enlightenment. *Science in Context*, 4(2), 367–386.

Daston, L. (1992). Objectivity and the Escape from Perspective. *Social Studies of Science*, 22(4), 597–618.

Daston, L. (2009). Science Studies and the History of Science. *Critical Inquiry*, 35(4), 798–813.

Davies, D. (2005). Medium in Art. In J. Levinson, ed., *The Oxford Handbook of Aesthetics*. Oxford: Oxford University Press, 181–191.

Davis, G. F. (2005). Firms and Environments. In N. J. Smelser & R. Swedberg, eds., *Handbook of Economic Sociology*. Princeton, NJ: Princeton University Press, 478–502.

de Certeau, M. (1984). *The Practice of Everyday Life*. Berkeley: University of California Press.

de Freitas, E. (2012). The Diagram as Story: Unfolding the Event-Structure of the Mathematical Diagram. *For the Learning of Mathematics*, 32(2), 27–33.

de Graaff, A., Brammer, G., Weibel, A. et al. (2025). RUBIES: A Complete Census of the Bright and Red Distant Universe with JWST/NIRSpec. *Astronomy and Astrophysics*, 697, A189 (21 pp).

de Regt, H. W. (2017). *Understanding Scientific Understanding*. Oxford: Oxford University Press.

de Ridder, J. (2014). Epistemic Dependence and Collective Scientific Knowledge. *Synthese*, 191(1), 37–53.

De Stefani, E. & Mondada, L. (2025). Navigating Ethical Issues Through Conversation Analysis's Fundamental Principles. *Research on Language and Social Interaction*, 58(2), 121–128.

Delamont, S. & Atkinson, P. (2001). Doctoring Uncertainty: Mastering Craft Knowledge. *Social Studies of Science*, 31(1), 87–107.

Dennis, A. (2024). Secondary Ethnographic Analysis: Thinking about Things. *Qualitative Research*, 24(1), 99–115.

Deppermann, A. (2015). Retrospection and Understanding in Interaction. In A. Deppermann & S. Günthner, eds., *Temporality in Interaction*. Amsterdam: Benjamins, 57–94.

Derrida, J. (1978). Structure, Sign, and Play in the Discourse of the Human Sciences. In *Writing and Difference*, transl. A. Bass. Chicago, IL: University of Chicago Press, 278–293.

Derrida, J. (1992). *Given Time: I. Counterfeit Money*, transl. P. Kamuf. Chicago, IL: University of Chicago Press.

DiMaggio, P. J. & Powell, W. W. (1983). The Iron Cage Revisited: Institutional Isomorphism and Collective Rationality in Organizational Fields. *American Sociological Review*, 48(2), 147–160.

Disney, M. (1979). Concluding Remarks. In G. Sedmak, M. Cappaccioli, R. J. Allen, et al., eds., *Image Processing in Astronomy*. Trieste: Osservatorio Astronomico, 495–500.

Dodd, N. (2014). *The Social Life of Money*. Princeton, NJ: Princeton University Press.

Doing, P. (2009). *Velvet Revolution at the Synchroton: Biology, Physics, and Change in Science*. Cambridge, MA: MIT Press.

Dor, D. (2015). *The Instruction of Imagination: Language as a Social Communication Technology*. Oxford: Oxford University Press.

Douglas, M. (1975). *Implicit Meanings: Essays in Anthropology*. London: Routledge.

Douglas, M. (1980). *Edward Evans-Pritchard*. Glasgow: Fontana.

Douglas, M. (1986). *How Institutions Think*. Syracuse, NY: Syracuse University Press.

Douglas, M. (1992). Rightness of Categories. In M. Douglas & D. Hull, eds., *How Classification Works: Nelson Goodman among the Social Sciences*. Edinburgh: Edinburgh University Press, 239–271.

Dourish, P. (2017). *The Stuff of Bits: An Essay on the Materialities of Information.* Cambridge, MA: MIT Press.

Duhem, P. (1954 [1914]). *The Aim and Structure of Physical Theory*, transl. P. Wiener. Princeton, NJ: Princeton University Press.

Durkheim, É. (1915 [1912]). *The Elementary Forms of the Religious Life*, transl. J. W. Swain. London: G. Allen & Unwin.

Durkheim, É. (1982 [1895]). *Rules of Sociological Method and Selected Texts on Sociology and Its Method*, ed. S. Lukes, transl. W. D. Halls. New York: Free Press.

Durranti, A. & Goodwin, C., eds. (1992). *Rethinking Context: Language as an Interactive Phenomenon.* Cambridge: Cambridge University Press.

Durrer, R. (2008). *The Cosmic Microwave Background.* Cambridge: Cambridge University Press.

Earman, J., Glymour, C., & Mitchell, S., eds. (2002). *Ceteris Paribus* Laws. *Erkenntnis*, 57(3).

Eco, U. (1979). *The Role of the Reader: Explorations in the Semiotics of Texts.* Bloomington: Indiana University Press.

Edwards, P. N. (2010). *A Vast Machine: Computer Models, Climate Data, and the Politics of Global Warming.* Cambridge, MA: MIT Press.

Edwards, P. N., Mayernik, M. S., Batcheller, A. L., Bowker, G. C., & Borgman, C. L. (2011). Science Friction: Data, Metadata, and Collaboration. *Social Studies of Science*, 41(5), 667–690.

Eisenstein, D. J., Willott, C., Alberts, S., et al. (2025). Overview of the JWST Advanced Deep Extragalactic Survey. arXiv:2306.02465v2.

Eisenstein, E. (1979). *The Printing Press as an Agent of Change: Communication and Cultural Transformations in Early Modern Europe.* Cambridge: Cambridge University Press.

Elder, J. (2024). Independent Evidence in Multi-Messenger Astrophysics. *Studies in History and Philosophy of Science*, 104, 119–129.

Enfield, N. J. (2013). *Relationship Thinking: Agency, Enchrony, and Human Sociality.* New York: Oxford University Press.

Enfield, N. J. & Levinson, S. C. (2006). Introduction: Human Sociality as a New Interdisciplinary Field. In N. J. Enfield & S. C. Levinson, eds., *Roots of Human Sociality: Culture, Cognition, and Interaction.* Oxford: Berg, 1–35.

Enfield, N. J. & Sidnell, J. (2017). *The Concept of Action.* Cambridge: Cambridge University Press.

Enfield, N. J. & Sidnell, J. (2022). *Consequences of Language: From Primary to Enhanced Intersubjectivity.* Cambridge, MA: MIT Press.

Espeland, W. N. & Stevens, M. L. (2008). A Sociology of Quantification. *Archives Européennes de Sociologie*, 44(3), 401–436.

Evans-Pritchard, E. E. (1937). *Witchcraft, Oracles, and Magic among the Azande.* Oxford: Clarendon Press.

Fabian, J. (1983). *Time and the Other: How Anthropology Makes Its Object.* New York: Columbia University Press.

Fabian, J. (1995). Ethnographic Misunderstanding and the Perils of Context. *American Anthropologist*, 97(10), 41–50.

Falk, J., Nolte, A., Huppenkothen, D., et al. (2024). The Future of Hackathon Research and Practice. *IEEE Access*, 12, 133406–133425.

Faniel, I. M., Frank, R., & Yakel, E. (2019). Context from the Data Reuser' Point of View. *Journal of Documentation*, 75, 1275–1297.

Faniel, I. M. & Yakel, E. (2017). Practices Do Not Make Perfect: Disciplinary Data Sharing and Reuse Practices and Their Implications for Repository Data Curation. In L. R. Johnson, ed., *Curating Research Data, Volume 1: Practical Strategies for Your Digital Repository*. Chicago, IL: Association of College and Research Libraries, 103–125.

Fellgett, P. B. (1955). Photo-Electric Devices in Astronomy. *Vistas in Astronomy*, 1, 475–490.

Fernandez, J. W. & Huber, M. T. (2001). Introduction: The Anthropology of Irony. In J. W. Fernandez & M. T. Huber, eds., *Irony in Action: Anthropology, Practice and the Moral Imagination*. Chicago, IL: University of Chicago Press, 1–37.

Figal, G. (2006). *Gegenständlichkeit: Das Hermeneutische und die Philosophie*. Tübingen: Mohr Siebeck.

Fink, E. (2016). *Play as Symbol of the World and Other Writings*, transl. I. A. Moore & C. Turner. Bloomington, IN: Indiana University Press.

Finkbeiner, A. (2010). *A Grand and Bold Thing: An Extraordinary New Map of the Universe Ushering in a New Era of Discovery*. New York: Free Press.

Fitzgerald, R. & Housley, W., eds. (2015). *Advances in Membership Categorisation Analysis*. Los Angeles, CA: SAGE.

Flauger, R., Hill, J. C., & Spergel, D. N. (2014). Toward an Understanding of Foreground Emission in the BICEP2 Region. *Journal of Cosmology and Astroparticle Physics*, August 2014(39) (11pp).

Fleck, L. (1979 [1935]). *Genesis and Development of a Scientific Fact*, transl. T. Trenn. Chicago, IL: University of Chicago Press.

Floridi, L. & Taddeo, M. (2016). What Is Data Ethics? *Philosophical Transactions of the Royal Society A*, 374, 20160360 (5 pp).

Ford, W. K. (1979). Digital Imaging Techniques. *Annual Review of Astronomy and Astrophysics*, 17, 189–212.

Fortun, K. (2009). Figuring Out Ethnography. In J. D. Faubion & G. E. Marcus, eds., *Fieldwork Is Not What It Used to Be: Learning Anthropology's Method in a Time of Transition*. Ithaca, NY: Cornell University Press, 167–183.

Foucault, M. (1971). *The Order of Things: An Archaeology of the Human Sciences*. New York: Pantheon Books.

Foucault, M. (1977). What Is an Author? In D. Bouchard, ed., *Language, Counter-Memory, Practice: Selected Essays and Interviews*. Ithaca, NY: Cornell University Press, 113–138.

Fouesneau, M., Momcheva, I. G., Chadayammuri, U., et al. (2024). What Is the Role of Large Language Models in the Evolution of Astronomy Research? *arXiv:2409.20252v*.

Francis, D. & Hester, S. (2004). *An Invitation to Ethnomethodology*. London: SAGE.

Franklin, A. (1997). Calibration. *Perspectives on Science*, 5(1), 31–80.

Franklin, L. R. (2005). Exploratory Experiments. *Philosophy of Science*, 72(5), 888–899.

Freedman, W. L. & Madore, B. F. (2010). The Hubble Constant. *Annual Review of Astronomy and Astrophysics*, 48, 673–710.

Friedman, T. L. (2005). *The World Is Flat: A Brief History of the Twenty-First Century*. New York: Farrar, Straus and Giroux.

Friendly, M. & Wainer, H. (2021). *A History of Data Visualization and Graphic Communication*. Cambridge, MA: Harvard University Press.

Fujimura, J. H. (1987). Constructing "Do-Able" Problems in Cancer Research: Articulating Alignment. *Social Studies of Science*, 17(2), 257–293.

Gadamer, H. G. (1960). *Wahrheit und Methode: Grundzüge einer philosophischen Hermeneutik*. Tübingen: Mohr Siebeck.

Gaia Collaboration (2023). Gaia Data Release 3: The Galaxy in Your Preferred Colours: Synthetic Photometry from Gaia Low-Resolution Spectra. *Astronomy and Astrophysics*, 674, A33 (58pp).

Gal, S. (2015). Politics of Translation. *Annual Review of Anthropology*, 44, 225–240.

Galison, P. (1997). *Image and Logic: A Material Culture of Microphysics*. Chicago, IL: University of Chicago Press.

Galison, P. (2003). The Collective Author. In M. Biagioli & P. Galison, eds., *Scientific Authorship: Credit and Intellectual Property in Science*. New York: Routledge, 325–355.

Galison, P. (2008). Ten Problems in History and Philosophy of Science. *Isis*, 99, 111–124.

Garfinkel, H. (1956). Some Sociological Concepts and Methods for Psychiatrists. *Psychiatric Papers*, 6, 181–195.

Garfinkel, H. (1963). A Conception of, and Experiments with, "Trust" as a Condition for Stable Concerted Actions. In O. J. Harvey, ed., *Motivation and Social Interaction*. New York: Ronald Press, 187–238.

Garfinkel, H. (1967). *Studies in Ethnomethodology*. Englewood Cliffs, NJ: Prentice-Hall.

Garfinkel, H. (2002). *Ethnomethodology's Program: Working Out Durkheim's Aphorism*, ed. A. W. Rawls. Lanham, MD: Rowman & Littlefield.

Garfinkel, H. (2022). *Studies of Work in the Sciences*, ed. M. Lynch. London: Routledge.

Garfinkel, H., Lynch, M., & Livingston, E. (1981). The Work of a Discovering Science Construed with Materials from the Optically Discovered Pulsar. *Philosophy of the Social Sciences*, 11(2), 131–158.

Garfinkel, H. & Sacks, H. (1970). On Formal Structures of Practical Actions. In J. C. McKinney & E. A. Tiryakian, eds., *Theoretical Sociology: Perspectives and Developments*. New York: Appleton-Century-Crofts, 337–366.

Garfinkel, H. & Wieder, L. D. (1992). Two Incommensurable, Asymmetrically Alternate Technologies of Social Analysis. In W. Graham & R. Seiler, eds., *Text in Context: Contributions to Ethnomethodology*. London: SAGE, 175–206.

Gasking, D. (1955). Mathematics and the World. In A. Flew, ed., *Logic and Language (Second Series)*. Oxford: Basil Blackwell, 204–221.

Gebauer, G. (2009). *Wittgensteins anthropologisches Denken*. Munich: C. H. Beck.

Geertz, C. (1973). *The Interpretation of Cultures: Essays in Interpretive Anthropology*. New York: Basic Books.

Gell, A. (1998). *Art and Agency: An Anthropological Theory*. Oxford: Clarendon Press.

Genova, F. (2018). Data as a Research Infrastructure: CDS, the Virtual Observatory, Astronomy, and Beyond. *EPJ Web of Conferences*, 186, Article 01001.

Giacconi, R. (2008). *Secrets of the Hoary Deep: A Personal History of Modern Astronomy*. Baltimore, MD: Johns Hopkins University Press.

Giavalisco, M., Ferguson, H. C., Koekemoer, A. M., et al. (2004). The Great Observatory Origins Deep Survey: Initial Results from Optical and Near-Infrared Imaging. *Astrophysical Journal*, 600, L93–L98.

Gibson, J. J. (1977). The Theory of Affordances. In R. Shaw & J. Bransford, eds., *Perceiving, Acting, and Knowing: Toward an Ecological Psychology*. Hillsdale, NJ: Lawrence Erlbaum, 67–82.

Giddens, A. (1990). *The Consequences of Modernity*. Stanford, CA: Stanford University Press.

Giere, R. (2006). *Scientific Perspectivism*. Chicago, IL: University of Chicago Press.

Gilbert, M. (2000). *Sociality and Responsibility: New Essays on Plural Subject Theory*. Lanham, MD: Rowman and Littlefield.

Gilbert, N. & Mulkay, M. J. (1984). *Opening Pandora's Box: A Sociological Analysis of Scientists' Discourse*. Cambridge: Cambridge University Press.

Giles, D., Stommel, W., & Paulus, T. M. (2017). The Microanalysis of Online Data: The Next Stage. *Journal of Pragmatics*, 117, 37–41.

Giles, D., Stommel, W., Paulus, T. M., Lester, J., & Reid, D. (2015). Microanalysis of Online Data: The Methodological Development of 'Digital CA'. *Discourse, Context and Media*, 7, 45–51.

Gitelman, L., ed. (2013). *"Raw Data" is an Oxymoron*. Cambridge, MA: MIT Press.

Goffman, E. (1963). *Stigma: Notes on the Management of Spoiled Identity*. New York: Simon & Schuster.

Goffman, E. (1964). The Neglected Situation. *American Anthropologist*, 66(6), 133–136.

Goffman, E. (1983). The Interaction Order. *American Sociological Review*, 48(10), 1–17.

Goodwin, C. (1987). Forgetfulness as an Interactive Resource. *Social Psychology Quarterly*, 50(2), 115–130.

Goodwin, C. (2013). The Co-operative, Transformative Organization of Human Action and Knowledge. *Journal of Pragmatics*, 46(1), 8–23.

Goodwin, C. (2018). *Co-operative Action*. New York: Cambridge University Press.

Goody, J. (1977). *The Domestication of the Savage Mind*. Cambridge: Cambridge University Press.

Goody, R. & Massey, H. (1976). *An International Discussion of Space Observatories. Report of a Conference Held at Williamsburg, Virginia, January 26–29, 1976*, Washington, DC: National Academy of Sciences.

Graeber, D. (2011). *Debt: The First 5000 Years*. Brooklyn, NY: Melville House.

Graham, B. J., Greenfield, P., & Dencheva, N. (2023). ASDF – Advanced Science Data Format. In *Data, Analysis and Software in Heliophysics* (DASH) 2023 Conference Proceedings. doi.org/10.5281/zenodo.8415578

Granovetter, M. (2005). Business Groups and Social Organization. In N. J. Smelser & R. Swedberg, eds., *Handbook of Economic Sociology*. Princeton, NJ: Princeton University Press, 429–450.

Greenfield, P., Droettboom, M., & Bray, E. (2015). ASDF: A New Data Format for Astronomy. *Astronomy and Computing*, 12, 240–251.

Gregory, K., Groth, P., Cousijn, H., Scharnhorst, A., & Wyatt, S. (2019). Searching Data: A Review of Observational Data Retrieval Practices in Selected Disciplines. *Journal of the Association for Information Science and Technology*, 70(5), 419–432.

Greisen, E. W. (2003). FITS: A Remarkable Achievement in Information Exchange. In A. Heck, ed., *Information Handling in Astronomy–Historical Vistas*. Dordrecht: Springer, 71–87.

Grogin, N., Kocevski, D. D., Faber, S. M., et al. (2011). CANDELS: The Cosmic Assembly Near-Infrared Deep Extragalactic Legacy Survey. *Astrophysical Journal Supplement Series*, 197(35) (39pp).

Gundaker, G. (1998). *Signs of Diaspora – Diaspora of Signs: Literacies, Creolization, and Vernacular Practice in African America*. New York: Oxford University Press.

Gunn, J. E. (2020). Jack of All. *Annual Review of Astronomy and Astrophysics*, 58, 1–25.

Guo, Y., Ferguson, H. C., Giavalisco, M., et al. (2013). CANDELS Multi-Wavelength Catalogs: Source Detection and Photometry in the GOODS-South Field. *Astrophysical Journal Supplement Series*, 207, 24 (23pp).

Gurwitsch, A. (1964). *The Field of Consciousness*. Pittsburgh, PA: Duquesne University Press.

Hackett, E. J. (2005). Essential Tensions: Identity, Control, and Risk in Research. *Social Studies of Science*, 35(5), 787–826.

Hacking, I. (1983). *Representing and Intervening: Introductory Topics in the Philosophy of the Natural Sciences*. Cambridge: Cambridge University Press.

Hacking, I. (1992a). The Self-Vindication of the Laboratory Sciences. In A. Pickering, ed., *Science as Culture and Practice*. Chicago, IL: University of Chicago Press, 19–64.

Hacking, I. (1992b). Statistical Language, Statistical Truth and Statistical Reason: The Self-Authentification of a Style of Scientific Reasoning. In E. McMullin, ed., *The Social Dimensions of Science*. Notre Dame, IL: University of Notre Dame Press, 130–157.

Hahn, C., Hoffman, A. S., Slota, S. C., Inman, S., & Ribes, D. (2018). Entangled Inversions: Actor/Analyst Symmetry in the Ethnography of Infrastructure. *Interaction Design and Architecture(s)*, 38, 124–139.

Hajian, A., Acquaviva, V., Ade, P. A. R., et al. (2011). The Atacama Cosmology Telescope: Calibration with the Wilkinson Microwave Anisotropy Probe Using Cross-Correlations. *Astrophysical Journal*, 740, 86 (9pp).

Hanisch, R. J., Farris, A., Greisen, E. W., Pence, W. D., Schlesinger, B. M., Teuben, P. J., Thompson, R. W., & Warnock III, A. (2001). Definition of the Flexible Image Transport System (FITS). *Astronomy and Astrophysics*, 376, 359–380.

Hanks, W. F. (2014). The Space of Translation. *Hau: Journal of Ethnographic Theory*, 4(2), 17–39.

Hanks, W. F. & Severi, C. (2014). Translating Worlds: The Epistemological Space of Translation. *Hau: Journal of Ethnographic Theory*, 4(2), 1–16.

Hann, C. (2010). Moral Economy. In K. Hart, J.-L. Laville & A. Cattani, eds., *The Human Economy: A Citizen's Guide*. Cambridge: Polity Press, 187–198.

Hanson, N. R. (1958). *Patterns of Discovery*. Cambridge: Cambridge University Press.

Harding, S. (1995). "Strong Objectivity": A Response to the New Objectivity Question. *Synthese*, 104(3), 331–349.

Hardwig, J. (1991). The Role of Trust in Knowledge. *Journal of Philosophy*, 88(12), 693–708.

Harper, R. H. R. (1998). *Inside the IMF: An Ethnography of Documents, Technology and Organisational Action*. San Diego, CA: Academic Press.

Harper, R. H. R. (2000). The Organisation in Ethnography. *Computer Supported Cooperative Work*, 9(2), 239–264.

Hart, K. (2001). *The Money Bank: Money in an Unequal World*. New York: Texere.

Hart, K. (2016). Introduction. In K. Hart, ed., *Money in a Human Economy*. New York: Berghahn, 3–14.

Hartlap, J., Schrabback, T., Simon, P., & Schneider, P. (2009). The Non-Gaussianity of the Cosmic Shear Likelihood or How Odd Is the Chandra Deep Field South? *Astronomy & Astrophysics*, 504, 689–703.

Hearnshaw, J. B. (1996). *The Measurement of Starlight: Two Centuries of Astronomical Photometry*. Cambridge: Cambridge University Press.

Heintz, B. (2007). Zahlen, Wissen, Objektivität: Wissenschaftssoziologische Perspektiven. In Mennicken, A. & Vollmer, H., eds. *Zahlenwerk: Kalkulation, Organisation und Gesellschaft*. Wiesbaden: Verlag für Sozialwissenschaften, 65–85.

Heintz, B. (2016). "Wir leben im Zeitalter der Vergleichung." Perspektiven einer Soziologie des Vergleichs. *Zeitschrift für Soziologie*, 45(5), 305–323.

Helmreich, S. (2016). Gravity's Reverb: Listening to Space-Time, or Articulating the Sounds of Gravitational-Wave Detection. *Cultural Anthropology*, 31(4), 464–492.

Henke, C. R. & Gieryn, T. F. (2008). Sites of Scientific Practice: The Enduring Importance of Place. In E. J. Hackett, O. Amsterdamska, M. Lynch & J.

Wajcman, eds., *The Handbook of Science and Technology Studies*. Cambridge, MA: MIT Press, 353–376.

Heritage, J. (1984). *Garfinkel and Ethnomethodology*. Cambridge: Polity Press.

Heritage, J. C. & Watson, D. R. (1979). Formulations as Conversational Objects. In G. Psathas, ed., *Everyday Language*. New York: Irvington Publishers, 123–162.

Herzfeld, M. (2001). *Anthropology: Theoretical Practice in Culture and Society*. Malden, MA: Blackwell.

Hester, S. & Eglin, P. (2017). *A Sociology of Crime*, 2nd ed. London: Routledge.

Hilgartner, S. (1995). Biomolecular Databases: New Communication Regimes in Science? *Science Communication*, 17(2), 240–263.

Hilgartner, S. (2017). *Reordering Life: Knowledge and Control in the Genomics Revolution*. Cambridge, MA: MIT Press.

Hill, R. J. & Crittenden, K. S., eds. (1968). *Proceedings of the Purdue Symposium on Ethnomethodology*. West Lafayette, IN: Institute for the Study of Social Change.

Hine, C. (2008). *Systematics as Cyberscience*. Cambridge, MA: MIT Press.

Hirschman, A. O. (1977). *The Passions and the Interests: Political Arguments for Capitalism Before Its Triumph*. Princeton, NJ: Princeton University Press.

Hoeppe, G. (2012). Astronomers at the Observatory: Place, Visual Practice, Traces. *Anthropological Quarterly*, 85(4), 1141–1160.

Hoeppe, G. (2014). Working Data Together: The Accountability and Reflexivity of Digital Astronomical Practice. *Social Studies of Science*, 44(2), 243–270.

Hoeppe, G. (2018a). Tensions of Accountability: Scientists, Technicians and the Ethical Life of Data Production in Astronomy. *Science as Culture*, 27(4), 488–512.

Hoeppe, G. (2018b). Practical Cosmologies. *Ethnologies*, 40(2), 75–92.

Hoeppe, G. (2019a). Mediating Environments and Objects as Knowledge Infrastructure. *Computer Supported Cooperative Work*, 28(1–2), 25–59.

Hoeppe, G. (2019b). Medium, Calculation, Play: On Digital Images in Scientific Practice. *Social Studies of Science*, 49(5), 758–784.

Hoeppe, G. (2020a). Members Doing Ethnography? On Some Uses of Irony and Failed Translation, Witnessed in an Episode of Data Sharing in Open Science. *Ethnographic Studies*, 17(1), 1–20.

Hoeppe, G. (2020b). Sharing Data, Repairing Practices: On the Reflexivity of Astronomical Data Journeys. In S. Leonelli & N. Tempini, eds., *Data Journeys in the Sciences*. Cham: Springer, 171–190.

Hoeppe, G. (2021). Encoding Collective Knowledge, Instructing Data Reusers: The Collaborative Fixation of a Digital Scientific Data Set. *Computer Supported Collaborative Work*, 30(4), 463–505.

Hoeppe, G. (2023). Learning from Harold Garfinkel's Studies of Work in the Sciences. *Soziologische Revue*, 46(2), 120–129.

Hoeppe, G., Brinks, E., Klein, U., et al. (1994). Radio Continuum and Far-Infrared Observations of Low Surface Brightness Galaxies. *Astronomical Journal*, 108(2), 446–455.

Hogg, D. W. (2022). Magnitudes, Distance Moduli, Bolometric Corrections, and So Much More. *arXiv:2206.00989v2 [astro-ph.IM]*.

Hogg, D. W., Eisenstein, D. J., Blanton, M. R., Bahcall, N. A., Brinkmann, J., Gunn, J. E., & Schneider, D. P. (2005). Cosmic Homogeneity Demonstrated with Luminous Red Galaxies. *Astrophysical Journal*, 624, 54–58.

Hogg, D. W. & Lang, D. (2008). Astronomical Imaging: The Theory of Everything. arXiv: 0810.3851v1 [astro-ph].

Hogg, D. W. & Lang, D. (2010). Telescopes Don't Make Catalogues! In C. Turon, F. Meynadier & F. Arenou, eds., *Gaia: At the Frontiers of Astrometry*, EAS Publications Series, vol. 45. Les Ulis Cedex: EDP Sciences, 351–358.

Hogg, D. W. & Villar, S. (2024). Is Machine Learning Good or Bad for the Natural Sciences? In Proceedings of the 41st International Conference on Machine Learning. *arXiv:2405.18095 [stat.ML]*.

Hollis, M. & Lukes, S., eds. (1982). *Rationality and Relativism*. Cambridge, MA: MIT Press.

Housley, W. & Fitzgerald, R. (2009). Membership Categorization, Culture and Norms in Action. *Discourse & Society*, 20(3), 345–362.

Housley, W., Webb., H., Edwards, A., Procter, R., & Jirotka, M. (2017). Digitzing Sacks: Approaching Social Media as Data. *Qualitative Research*, 17(6), 627–644.

Hoyningen-Huene, P. (2013). *Systematicity: The Nature of Science*. New York: Oxford University Press.

Huang, N. T., Hogg, D. W., & Villar, S. (2022). Dimensionality Reduction, Regularization, and Generalization in Overparametrized Regressions. *SIAM Journal on Mathematics of Data Science*, 4(1), 126–152.

Huchra, J. P., Macri, L. M., Masters, K. L., et al. (2012). The 2MASS Redshift Survey – Description and Data Release. *Astrophysical Journal Supplement Series*, 199, 26 (22 pp).

Huebner, B., Kukla, R., & Winsberg, E. (2017). Making an Author in Radically Collaborative Research. In T. Boyer-Kassem, C. Mayo-Wilson & M. Weisberg, eds., *Scientific Collaboration and Collective Knowledge: New Essays*. Oxford: Oxford University Press, 95–116.

Huizinga, J. (1955). *Homo Ludens: A Study of the Play-Element in Culture*. Boston, MA: Beacon Press.

Hullman, J. & Gelman, A. (2021). Designing for Interactive Exploratory Data Analysis Requires Theories of Graphical Inference. *Harvard Data Science Review*, 3(3). doi.org/10.1162/99608f92.3ab8a587

Huppenkothen, D., Arendt, A., Hogg, D. W., Ram, K., VanderPlas, J. T., & Rokem, A. (2018). Hack Weeks as a Model for Data Science Education and Collaboration. *Proceedings of the National Academy of Sciences*, 115(36), 8872–8877.

Huppenkothen, D., Ntampaka, M., Ho, M., et al. (2023). Constructing Impactful Machine Learning Research in Astronomy: Best Practices for Researchers and Reviewers. *arXiv:2310.12528v1*.

Husserl, E. (1970 [1954]). *The Crisis of the European Sciences and Transcendental Phenomenology*, transl. D. Carr. Evanston, IL: Northwestern University Press.

Hutchby, I. & Drew, P. (1995). Conversation Analysis. In J. Verschueren et al., eds., *Handbook of Pragmatics*. Amsterdam: Benjamins, 182–189.

Hutchins, E. (1995). *Cognition in the Wild*. Cambridge, MA: MIT Press.

Hutchins, E. (2005). Material Anchors for Conceptual Blends. *Journal of Pragmatics*, 37, 1555–1577.

Hutchins, E. & Hazlehurst, B. (1995). How to Invent a Shared Lexicon: The Emergence of Shared Form-Meaning Mappings in Interaction. In E. Goody, ed., *Social Intelligence and Interaction: Expressions and Implications of the Social Bias in Human Intelligence*. Cambridge: Cambridge University Press, 53–67.

Hymes, D. H. (1996). *Ethnography, Linguistics, Narrative Inequality: Toward an Understanding of Voice*. London: Taylor & Francis.

Illingworth, G. & Butcher, H. (1980). The Detector Program at Kitt Peak. In P. Crane & K. Kjär, eds., *Proceedings of the ESO Workshop on Two-Dimensional Photometry*. Geneva: European Southern Observatory, 99–118.

Ingold, T. (2018). *Anthropology: Why It Matters*. Cambridge: Polity Press.

Iser, W. (1980). *The Act of Reading: A Theory of Aesthetic Response*. London: Routledge and Kegan Paul.

Iser, W. (1989). *The Implied Reader: Patterns of Communication in Prose Fiction from Bunyan to Beckett*. Baltimore, MD: Johns Hopkins University Press.

Ivezić, Ž., Connolly, A. J., VanderPlas, J. T., & Gray, A. (2020). *Statistics, Data Mining, and Machine Learning in Astronomy: A Practical Python Guide for the Analysis of Survey Data*. Updated Edition. Princeton, NJ: Princeton University Press.

Ivins, W. M. (1953). *Prints and Visual Communication*. Cambridge, MA: Harvard University Press.

Jacob, F. (1977). Evolution and Tinkering. *Science*, 196(4295), 1161–1166.

Jacob, F. (1982). *The Possible and the Actual*. Seattle, WA: University of Washington Press.

Jakobson, R. (1959). On Linguistic Aspects of Translation. In R. A. Brower, ed., *On Translation*. Cambridge, MA: Harvard University Press, 232–238.

Jay, M. (2000). The Speed of Light and the Virtualization of Reality. In K. Goldberg, ed., *The Robot in the Garden: Telerobotics and Telepistemology in the Age of the Internet*. Cambridge, MA: MIT Press, 144–162.

Jaynes, E. T. (2003). *Probability Theory: The Logic of Science*. Cambridge: Cambridge University Press.

Jefferson, G. (1984). On the Organization of Laughter in Talk about Troubles. In J. M. Atkinson & J. Heritage, eds., *Structures of Social Action: Studies in Conversation Analysis*. Cambridge: Cambridge University Press, 346–369.

Jefferson, G. (2004). Glossary of Transcript Symbols with an Introduction. In G. Lerner, ed., *Conversation Analysis: Studies from the First Generation*. New York: John Benjamins, 13–31.

Jones, D. (2000). The Scientific Value of the Carte du Ciel. *Astronomy & Geophysics*, 41(5), 16–20.

Jones, T. C. & Dugdale, D. (2001). The Concept of an Accounting Regime. *Critical Perspectives on Accounting*, 12(1), 35–63.

Joyce, K. A. (2006). From Numbers to Pictures: The Development of Magnetic Resonance Imaging and the Visual Turn in Medicine. *Science as Culture*, 15(1), 1–22.

Kaiser, D. (2005). Introduction: Moving Pedagogy from the Periphery to the Center. In D. Kaiser, ed., *Pedagogy and the Practice of Science: Historical and Contemporary Perspectives*. Cambridge, MA: MIT Press, 1–8.

Kanipe, J. (2007). *Chasing Hubble's Shadow: The Search for Galaxies at the Edge of Time*. New York: Hill & Wang.

Keane, W. (2014). Affordances and Reflexivity in Ethical Life: An Ethnographic Stance. *Anthropological Theory*, 14(1), 3–26.

Keane, W. (2016). *Ethical Life: Its Natural and Social Histories*. Princeton, NJ: Princeton University Press.

Kellermann, K., Bouton, E. N., & Brandt, S. S. (2020). *Open Skies: The National Radio Astronomy Observatory and Its Impact on US Radio Astronomy*. Cham: Springer.

Kessler, E. A. (2012). *Picturing the Cosmos*. Minneapolis, MN: University of Minnesota Press.

Kinzel, K. P. (2012). Geschichte ohne Kausalität: Abgrenzungsstrategien gegen die Wissenschaftssoziologie in zeitgenössischen Ansätzen historischer Epistemologie. *Berichte zur Wissenschaftsgeschichte*, 35, 147–162.

Kitching, T. D., Rowe, B., Gill, M., et al. (2013). Image Analysis for Cosmology: Results from the GREAT10 Challenge. *Astrophysical Journal Supplement*, 205, 12 (11 pp).

Klein, U. (2003). *Experiments, Models, Paper Tools: Cultures of Organic Chemistry in the Nineteenth Century*. Stanford, CA: Stanford University Press.

Knorr Cetina, K. (1981). *The Manufacture of Knowledge: An Essay on the Constructivist and Contextual Nature of Science*. Oxford: Pergamon Press.

Knorr Cetina, K. (1999). *Epistemic Cultures: How the Sciences Make Knowledge*. Cambridge, MA: Harvard University Press.

Knuth, D., Larrabee, T., & Roberts, P. M. (1987). Mathematical Writing. http://jmlr.csail.mit.edu/reviewing-papers/knuth_mathematical_writing.pdf (accessed June 19, 2025).

Kockelman, P. (2007). From Status to Contract Revisited: Value, Temporality, Circulation and Subjectivity. *Anthropological Theory*, 7(2), 151–176.

Kockelman, P. (2017). *The Art of Interpretation in the Age of Computation*. Oxford: Oxford University Press.

Kockelman, P. (2025). *Mathematical Models of Meaning: A Dynamical Systems Approach to Possible World Semiotics*. Cambridge, MA: MIT Press.

Kohler, R. (1994). *Lords of the Fly: Drosophila Genetics and the Experimental Life*. Chicago, IL: University of Chicago Press.

Kohler, R. (1999). Moral Economy, Material Culture, and Community in Drosophila Genetics. In M. Biagioli, ed., *The Science Studies Reader*. London: Routledge, 243–257.

König, T., Vilain, E., & LoTempio Jr., J. E. (2024). Open Science? Conceptualizing Openness as an Emerging Moral Economy of Science. irihs.ihs.ac.at/id/

eprint/6832/7/koenig-vilain-lotempio-2024-open-science-conceptualizing-openness.pdf (accessed June 3, 2025).

Koo, D. C. (1999). Photometric Redshifts: A Perspective from an Old-Timer on Their Past, Present and Potential. In R. J. Weymann, L. J. Storrie-Lombardi, M. Sawicki & R. J. Brunner, eds., *Photometric Redshifts and High Redshift Galaxies*. San Francisco, CA: Astronomical Society of the Pacific, 3–12.

Korczynski, M. & Macdonald, C. L. (2009). Critical Perspectives on Service Work: An Introduction. In M. Korczynski & C. L. Macdonald, eds., *Service Work*. New York: Routledge, 1–10.

Koschmann, T. (2011). Understanding Understanding in Action. *Journal of Pragmatics*, 43, 435–437.

Koschmann, T. (2019). Tracing the Seminal Notion of Accountability across the Garfinkelian OEuvre. *Human Studies*, 42, 239–252

Koschmann, T. & Zemel, A. (2014). Instructed Objects. In M. Nevile, P. Haddington, T. Heinemann & M. Rauniomaa, eds., *Interacting with Objects: Language, Materiality, and Social Activity*. Philadelphia, PA: John Benjamins Publishing Company, 357–377.

Koyré, A. (1943). Galileo and the Scientific Revolution of the Seventeenth Century. *Philosophical Review*, 52(4), 333–348.

Krämer, S. (2007). Was also ist eine Spur? Und worin besteht ihre epistemologische Rolle? Eine Bestandsaufnahme. In S. Krämer, W. Kogge & G. Grube, eds., *Spur: Spurenlesen als Orientierungstechnik und Wissenskunst*. Frankfurt am Main: Suhrkamp, 11–33.

Krämer, S. (2014). Mathematizing Power, Formalization, and the Diagrammatical Mind or What Does "Computation" Mean? *Philosophy of Technology*, 27, 345–357.

Krämer, S. (2015). *Medium, Messenger, Transmission: An Approach to Media Philosophy*, transl. A. Enns. Amsterdam: Amsterdam University Press.

Krämer, S. (2016). *Figuration, Anschauung, Erkenntnis: Grundlinien einer Diagrammatologie*. Berlin: Suhrkamp.

Krämer, S. (2019). Epistemologie der Medialität: Eine medienphilosophische Reflexion. *Deutsche Zeitschrift für Philosophie*, 67(5), 833–850.

Krämer, S. (2022). Reflections on "Operative Iconicity" and "Artificial Flatness." In D. Wengrow, ed., *Image, Thought, and the Making of Social Worlds*. Heidelberg: Propylaeum, 251–272.

Krenn, M., Pollice, R., Guo, S. Y., et al. (2022). On Scientific Understanding with Artificial Intelligence. *Nature Reviews Physics*, 4, 761–769.

Kriesberg, A., Frank, R. D., Faniel, I. M., & Yakel, E. (2013). The Role of Data Reuse in the Apprenticeship Process. *Proceedings of the American Society for Information Science and Technology*, 50(1), 1–10.

Kubler, G. (1962). *The Shape of Time: Remarks on the History of Things*. New Haven, CT: Yale University Press.

Kühl, S. (2011). *Organisationen: Eine sehr kurze Einführung*. Wiesbaden: VS Verlag für Sozialwissenschaften.

Kuhn, T. S. (1961). The Function of Measurement in Modern Physical Science. *Isis*, 52(2), 161–193.

Kuhn, T. S. (1970). *The Structure of Scientific Revolutions*, 2nd ed. Chicago, IL: University of Chicago Press.

Kuhn, T. S. (1977). *The Essential Tension: Selected Studies in Scientific Tradition and Change*. Chicago, IL: University of Chicago Press.

Lahav, O. (2001). Large Surveys in Cosmology: The Changing Sociology. arXiv: astro-ph/0105351.

Laidlaw, J. (2014). *The Subject of Virtue: An Anthropology of Ethics and Freedom*. Cambridge: Cambridge University Press.

Lambek, M. (2015). *The Ethical Condition: Essays on Action, Person, and Value*. Chicago, IL: University of Chicago Press.

Larivière, V. (2012). On the Shoulders of Students? The Contribution of PhD Students to the Advancement of Knowledge. *Scientometrics*, 90, 463–481.

Larkin, J. & Simon, H. (1987). Why a Diagram Is (Sometimes) Worth Ten Thousand Words. *Cognitive Science*, 11(1), 65–99.

Latour, B. (1986). Visualization and Cognition: Thinking with Eyes and Hands. *Knowledge and Society*, 6(1), 1–40.

Latour, B. (1987). *Science in Action: How to Follow Scientists and Engineers Through Society*. Cambridge, MA: Harvard University Press.

Latour, B. (2005). *Reassembling the Social*. Oxford: Oxford University Press.

Latour, B. & Woolgar, S. (1986 [1979]). *Laboratory Life: The Construction of Scientific Facts*, 2nd ed. Princeton, NJ: Princeton University Press.

Lave, J. & Wenger, E. (1991). *Situated Learning: Legitimate Peripheral Participation*. Cambridge: Cambridge University Press.

Law, J. & Akrich, M. (1994). On Customers and Costs: A Story from Public Sector Science. *Science in Context*, 7(3), 539–561.

Leahey, E. (2016). From Sole Investigator to Team Scientist: Trends in the Practice and Study of Research Collaboration. *Annual Review of Sociology*, 42, 81–100.

Lee, A. (1927). *Sociality: The Art of Living Together*. London: Holborn Publishing House.

LeFèvre, O., Vettolani, G., Garilli, B., et al. (2005). The VIMOS VLT Deep Survey. *Astronomy and Astrophysics*, 439(3), 845–862.

Leitherer, C., Schaerer, D., Goldader, J. D., et al. (1999). Starburst99: Synthesis Models for Galaxies with Active Star Formation. *Astrophysical Journal Supplement Series*, 123(1), 3–40.

Lempert, M. (2013). No Ordinary Ethics. *Anthropological Theory*, 13(4), 370–393.

Léna, P. (1988). *Observational Astrophysics*. Berlin: Springer.

Léna, P. (1989). Images in Astronomy: An Overview. In I. Appenzeller, H. J. Habing & P. Léna, eds, *Evolution of Galaxies. Astronomical Observations. Proceedings of the Astrophysics School Organized by the European Astrophysics Doctoral Network at Les Houches*. Berlin: Springer-Verlag, 243–282.

Leonelli, S. (2016). *Data-Centric Biology: A Philosophical Study*. Chicago, IL: University of Chicago Press.

Leonelli, S. (2023). *Philosophy of Open Science*. Cambridge: Cambridge University Press.

Leonelli, S. & Tempini, N., eds. (2020). *Data Journeys in the Sciences*. Cham: Springer.

Leroi-Gourhan, A. (1993 [1964]). *Gesture and Speech*. Cambridge, MA: MIT Press.

Leung, G. C. K., Bagley, M. B., Finkelstein, S. L., et al. (2023). NGDEEP Epoch 1: The Faint End of the Luminosity Function at $z \sim 9–12$ from Ultradeep JWST Imaging. *Astrophysical Journal Letters*, 954, L46 (17 pp).

Lévi-Strauss, C. (1966). *The Savage Mind*. Chicago, IL: University of Chicago Press.

Levin, N. & Leonelli, S. (2017). How Does One "Open" Science? Questions of Value in Biological Research. *Science, Technology, & Human Values*, 42(2), 280–305.

Levinson, S. C. (1983). *Pragmatics*. Cambridge: Cambridge University Press.

Lewis, D. (1969). *Convention: A Philosophical Study*. Cambridge, MA: Harvard University Press.

Liberman, K. (1999). From Walkabout to Meditation: Craft and Ethics in Field Inquiry. *Qualitative Inquiry*, 5(1), 47–63.

Liberman, K. (2013). *More Studies in Ethnomethodology*. Albany, NY: SUNY Press.

Liberman, K. (2022). *Tasting Coffee: An Inquiry into Objectivity*. Albany, NY: State University of New York Press.

Lienhardt, G. (1954). Modes of Thought. In E. Evans-Pritchard, ed., *The Institutions of Primitive Society*. Oxford: Basil Blackwell, 95–107.

Lin, H., Yee, H. K. C., Carlberg, R. G., et al. (1999). The CNOC2 Field Galaxy Luminosity Function. I. A Description of Luminosity Function Evolution. *Astrophysical Journal*, 518, 533–561.

Lindwall, O., Lymer, G., & Greiffenhagen, C. (2015). The Sequential Analysis of Instruction. In N. Markee, ed., *Handbook of Classroom Discourse and Interaction*. Hoboken, NJ: Wiley, 142–157.

Linton, R. (1936). *The Study of Man: An Introduction*. New York: Appleton-Century-Crofts.

Livingston, E. (1987). *Making Sense of Ethnomethodology*. London: Routledge & Kegan Paul.

Livingston, E. (1995). *An Anthropology of Reading*. Bloomington, IN: Indiana University Press.

Livingston, E. (2006). Ethnomethodological Studies of Mediated Interaction and Mundane Expertise. *Sociological Review*, 54(3), 405–425.

Livingston, E. (2008). *Ethnographies of Reason*. Aldershot: Ashgate.

Llerena, M., Amorín, R., Pentericci, L., et al. (2024). Physical Properties of Extreme Emission-line Galaxies at $z \sim 4–9$ from the JWST CEERS survey. *Astronomy & Astrophysics*, 691, A59 (18 pp).

Locke, J. (1988 [1690]). *Two Treatises of Government*, ed. P. Laslett. Cambridge: Cambridge University Press.

Lockman, F. J. (2005). Can Remote Observing Be Good Observing? Reflections on Procrustes and Antaeus. arXiv: astro-ph/0507140v1.

Loukissas, Y. A. (2019). *All Data Are Local: Thinking Critically in a Data-Driven Society*. Cambridge, MA: MIT Press.

Luhmann, N. (2012). *Theory of Society*, vol. 1, transl. R. Barrett. Stanford, CA: Stanford University Press.

Luhmann, N. (2017). *Trust and Power*, transl. C. Morgner & M. King. Cambridge: Polity Press.

Lupton, R. H., Gunn, J. E., & Szalay, A. S. (1999). A Modified Magnitude System that Produces Well-Behaved Magnitudes, Colors, and Errors Even for Low Signal-To-Noise Ratio Measurements. *Astronomical Journal*, 118, 1406–1410.

Lynch, M. (1985a). *Art and Artifact in Laboratory Science: A Study of Shop Work and Shop Talk in a Research Laboratory*. London: Routledge & Kegan Paul.

Lynch, M. (1985b). Discipline and the Material Form of Images: An Analysis of Scientific Visibility. *Social Studies of Science*, 15(1), 37–66.

Lynch, M. (1991a). Laboratory Space and the Technological Complex: An Investigation of Topical Contextures. *Science in Context*, 4(1), 51–78.

Lynch, M. (1991b). Method: Measurement – Ordinary and Scientific Measurement as Ethnomethodological Phenomena. In G. Button, ed., *Ethnomethodology and the Human Sciences*. Cambridge: Cambridge University Press, 77–108.

Lynch, M. (1993). *Scientific Practice and Ordinary Action: Ethnomethodology and Social Studies of Science*. Cambridge: Cambridge University Press.

Lynch, M. (2001). Ethnomethodology and the Logic of Practice. In T. R. Schatzki, K. Knorr Cetina & E. von Savigny, eds., (2001). *The Practice Turn in Contemporary Theory*. London: Routledge, 131–148.

Lynch, M. (2011). Commentary: On Understanding Understanding. *Journal of Pragmatics*, 43, 553–555.

Lynch, M. (2022). Editor's Introduction. In M. Lynch, ed., *Harold Garfinkel: Studies of Work in the Sciences*. London: Routledge, 1–15.

Lynch, M. & Jordan, K. (1995). Instructed Action in, of and as Molecular Biology. *Human Studies*, 18(2/3), 227–244.

Lynch, M., & Woolgar, S. (1990). Sociological Orientations to Representational Practice in Science. In M. Lynch & S. Woolgar, eds., *Representation in Scientific Practice*. Cambridge, MA: MIT Press, 1–18.

Macbeth, D. (1994). Classroom Encounters with the Unspeakable: "Do You See, Danelle?" *Discourse Processes*, 17(2), 311–335.

Macbeth, D. (2003). Hugh Mehan's *Learning Lessons* Reconsidered: On the Differences between the Naturalistic and Critical Analysis of Classroom Discourse. *American Educational Research Journal*, 40(1), 239–280.

Macbeth, D. (2007). Sequential Analysis in an Ethnomethodological Key: Order without Theory. In N. Lawrence, ed., *Theoretical Approaches to Dialogue Analysis: Selected Papers from the IADA Chicago 2004 Conference*. Berlin: De Gruyter, 199–213.

MacKay, D. J. C. (2003). *Information Theory, Inference and Learning Algorithms*. Cambridge: Cambridge University Press.

Mackenzie, A. (2017). *Machine Learners: Archaeology of a Data Practice*. Cambridge, MA: MIT Press.

MacKenzie, D. (1993). Negotiating Arithmetic, Constructing Proof: The Sociology of Mathematics and Information Technology. *Social Studies of Science*, 23(1), 37–65.

MacKenzie, D. (2001). *Mechanizing Proof: Computing, Risk, and Trust.* Cambridge, MA: MIT Press.

MacWhinney, B. (2025). Understanding Language through TalkBank. *Current Directions in Psychological Science*, 34(2), 75–81.

Madianou, M. & Miller, D. (2013). Polymedia: Towards a New Theory of Digital Media in Interpersonal Communication. *International Journal of Cultural Studies*, 16(2), 169–187.

Maher, M. A., Wofford, A. M., Roksa, J., & Feldon, D. F. (2020). Finding a Fit: Biological Science Doctoral Students' Selection of a Principal Investigator and Research Laboratory. *CBE – Life Science Education*, 19, 31 (15 pp).

Mair, M., Greiffenhagen, C., & Sharrock, W. (2016). Statistical Practice: Putting Society on Display. *Theory, Culture & Society*, 33(3), 51–77.

Mannheim, K. (1952). *Essays on the Sociology of Knowledge.* New York: Oxford University Press.

Manning, P. (2008). Barista Rants about Stupid Customers at Starbucks: What Imaginary Conversations Can Teach Us about Real Ones. *Language & Communication*, 28(1), 101–126.

Manovich, L. (2001). *The Language of New Media.* Cambridge, MA: MIT Press.

Marres, N. & Stark, D. (2020). Put to the Test: For a New Sociology of Testing. *British Journal of Sociology*, 71, 423–443.

Martin, D., Rooksby, J., & Rouncefield, M. (2007). Users as Contextual Features of Software Product Development and Testing. In *GROUP '07: Proceedings of the 2007 ACM International Conference on Supporting Group Work.* New York: Association for Computing Machinery, 301–310.

Martin, J. L. (2003). What Is Field Theory? *American Journal of Sociology*, 109(1), 1–49.

Marx, K. (1990 [1867]). *Capital*, vol. 1, transl. B. Fowkes. London: Penguin.

Maselli, A., Cusumano, G., Massaro, E., et al. (2010). The Blazar Content in the Swift-BAT Hard X-Ray Sky. *Astronomy and Astrophysics*, 520, A47 (6 pp).

Matarese, V. & McCoy, C. D. (2024). When "Replicability" Is More than Just "Reliability": The Hubble Constant Controversy. *Studies in History and Philosophy of Science*, 107, 1–10.

Maurer, B. (2021). Data Forward: An Afterword. *Journal of the Royal Anthropological Institute*, 27(S1), 171–175.

Mauss, M. (2016 [1923–24]). *The Gift*, transl. J. Guyer. Chicago, IL: Hau Books.

Mayernik, M. S. (2017). Open Data: Accountability and Transparency. *Big Data & Society*, 4(2), 1–5.

Mayernik, M. S. (2019). Metadata Accounts: Achieving Data and Evidence in Scientific Research. *Social Studies of Science*, 49(5), 732–757.

Mayernik, M. S. (2021). Credibility via Coupling: Institutions and Infrastructures in Climate Model Intercomparisons. *Engaging Science, Technology, & Society*, 7(2), 10–32.

McCray, W. P. (2000). Large Telescopes and the Moral Economy of Recent Astronomy. *Social Studies of Science*, 30(5), 685–711.

McCray, W. P. (2014). How Astronomers Digitized the Sky. *Technology & Culture*, 55(4), 908–944.

McCray, W. P. (2017). The Biggest Data of All: Making and Sharing a Digital Universe. *Osiris*, 32(1), 243–263.

McDonald, S. (2011). What's in the "Old Boys" Network? Accessing Social Capital in Gendered and Racialized Networks. *Social Networks*, 33(4), 317–330.

McHoul, A. (1982). *Telling How Texts Talk: Studies in Reading and Ethnomethodology*. London: Routledge.

McKinney, W. (2017). *Python for Data Analysis*, 2nd ed. Sebastopol, CA: O'Reilly.

McLean, I. S. (2008). *Electronic Imaging in Astronomy: Detectors and Instrumentation*, 2nd ed. Berlin: Springer.

McLuhan, M. (1964). *Understanding Media: The Extensions of Man*. New York: McGraw-Hill.

McMullan, D. (1980). Review of Electronographic Systems. In P. Crane & K. Kjär, eds., *Proceedings of the ESO Workshop on Two Dimensional Photometry*. Geneva: European Southern Observatory, 13–23.

Mead, G. H. (1934). *Mind, Self and Society from the Standpoint of a Social Behaviorist*. Chicago, IL: University of Chicago Press.

Medawar, P. B. (1963). Is the Scientific Paper a Fraud? *The Listener*, 70(1798), 377–378.

Mehan, H. (1979). *Learning Lessons: Social Organization in the Classroom*. Cambridge, MA: Harvard University Press.

Mennicken, A. & Vollmer, H., eds. (2007). *Zahlenwerk: Kalkulation, Organisation und Gesellschaft*. Wiesbaden: Verlag für Sozialwissenschaften.

Merleau-Ponty, M. (1968). *The Visible and the Invisible*, transl. A. Lingis. Evanston, IL: Northwestern University Press.

Merton, R. K. (1973). *The Sociology of Science*. Chicago, IL: University of Chicago Press.

Messeri, L. & Crockett, M. J. (2024). Artificial Intelligence and Illusions of Understanding in Scientific Research. *Nature*, 627(7 March 2024), 49–58.

Miller, D. (2015). The Tragic Denouement of English Sociality. *Cultural Anthropology*, 30(2), 336–357.

Miller, D. & Horst, H. A. (2012). The Digital and the Human: A Prospectus for Digital Anthropology. In D. Miller & H. A. Horst, eds., *Digital Anthropology*. London: Bloomsbury, 3–35.

Mink, J. D. (2015). Astronomical Data Formats: What We Have and How We Got Here. *Astronomy and Computing*, 12, 128–132.

Mirowski, P. (2018). The Future(s) of Open Science. *Social Studies of Science*, 48(2), 171–203.

Misak, C. (2016). *Cambridge Pragmatism: From Peirce and James to Ramsey and Wittgenstein*. Oxford: Oxford University Press.

Mody, C. C. M. (2001). A Little Dirt Never Hurt Anyone: Knowledge-Making and Contamination in Materials Science. *Social Studies of Science*, 31(1), 7–36.

Mody, C. C. M. (2011). *Instrumental Community: Probe Microscopy and the Path to Nanotechnology*. Cambridge, MA: MIT Press.

Moerman, M. & Sacks, H. (1988). On "Understanding" in the Analysis of Natural Conversation. In M. Moerman, *Talking Culture: Ethnography and Conversation Analysis*. Philadelphia: University of Pennsylvania Press, 180–186.

Momcheva, I. & Tollerud, E. (2015). Software Use in Astronomy: An Informal Survey. *arXiv:1507.03989v1*.

Moore, A. & Kasliwal, M. M. (2019). Unveiling the Dynamic Infrared Sky. *Nature Astronomy*, 3(1), 109.

Mountain, M. (2014). Commentary: Flattening the Astronomy World. *Physics Today*, 67(2), 8–9.

Munger, C. (2023). *Poor Charlie's Almanack: The Essential Wit & Wisdom of Charles T. Munger*, ed. P. D. Kaufman. 4th ed. San Francisco, CA: Stripe Press.

Munro, R. (2001). Calling for Accounts: Numbers, Monsters and Membership. *Sociological Review*, 49(4), 473–494.

Myers, N. (2015). *Rendering Life Molecular: Models, Modelers, and Excitable Matter*. Durham, NC: Duke University Press.

Nasim, O. W. (2013). *Observing by Hand: Sketching the Nebulae in the Nineteenth Century*. Chicago, IL: University of Chicago Press.

Nasim, O. W. (2021). *The Astronomer's Chair: A Visual and Cultural History*. Cambridge, MA: MIT Press.

Nersessian, N. J. & MacLeod, M. (2022). Rethinking Ethnography for Philosophy of Science. *Philosophy of Science*, 89, 721–741.

Netz, R. (1999). *The Shaping of Deduction in Greek Mathematics: A Cognitive History*. Cambridge: Cambridge University Press.

Newman, J. A., Cooper, M. C., Davis, M. et al. (2013). The DEEP2 Galaxy Redshift Survey: Design, Observations, Data Reduction, and Redshifts. *Astrophysical Journal Supplement Series*, 208, 5 (57 pp).

Newman, J. A. & Gruen, D. (2022). Photometric Redshifts for Next-Generation Surveys. *Annual Review of Astronomy and Astrophysics*, 60, 363–414.

Neyland, D. & Coopmans, C. (2014). Visual Accountability. *Sociological Review*, 62(1), 1–23.

Nguyen, C. T. (2020). *Games: Art as Agency*. New York: Oxford University Press.

Nguyen, C. T. (2022). Playfulness versus Epistemic Traps. In M. Alfano, C. Klein & J. de Ridder, eds., *Social Virtue Epistemology*. London: Routledge, 269–290.

Nicol, M.-H., Meisenheimer, K., Wolf, C., & Tapken, C. (2011). Red-Sequence Galaxies at High Redshift by the COMBO-17+4 Survey. *Astrophysical Journal*, 727, 51 (11 pp).

Norman, D. A. (2002). *The Design of Everyday Things*. New York: Basic Books.

Novick, D. G. & Ward, K. (2006). Why Don't People Read the Manual? In *ACM SIGDOC'06: Proceedings of the 24th ACM International Conference on Design of Communication*. Myrtle Beach, SC: Association for Computing Machinery, 11–18.

Ochs, E., Gonzales, P., & Jacoby, S. (1996). "When I Come Down I'm in the Domain State": Grammar and Graphic Representation in the Interpretive Activity of Physicists. In E. Ochs, E. E. Schegloff & S. A. Thompson, eds., *Interaction and Grammar*. Cambridge: Cambridge University Press, 328–369.

Ochs, E., Jacoby, S., & Gonzales, P. (1994). Interpretive Journeys: How Physicists Talk and Travel through Graphic Space. *Configurations*, 1, 151–171.

Ochs, E. & Solomon, O. (2010). Autistic Sociality. *Ethos*, 38(1), 69–92.

Ochsenbein, F., Bauer, P., & Marcout, J. (2000). The VizieR Database of Astronomical Catalogues. *Astronomy & Astrophysics Supplement Series*, 143(1), 23–32.

O'Neill, O. (2014). Trust, Trustworthiness, and Accountability. In N. Morris & D. Vines, eds., *Capital Failure: Rebuilding Trust in Financial Services*. Oxford: Oxford University Press, 172–190.

O'Neill, O. (2022). *A Philosopher Looks at Digital Communication*. Cambridge: Cambridge University Press.

Padmanabhan, N., Schlegel, D. J., Finkbeiner, D. P., et al. (2008). An Improved Photometric Calibration of the Sloan Digital Sky Survey. *Astrophysical Journal*, 674, 1217–1233.

Padmapriya, S. T. & Parthasarathy, S. (2024). Ethical Data Collection for Medical Image Analysis: A Structured Approach. *Asian Bioethics Review*, 16, 95–108.

Paine, D. & Lee, C. P. (2021). Coordinative Entities: Forms of Organizing in Data Intensive Science. *Computer Supported Cooperative Work*, 29(3), 335–380.

Pang, A. (2002). *Empire and the Sun: Victorian Solar Eclipse Expeditions*. Stanford, CA: Stanford University Press.

Parmentier, R. J. (1994). *Signs in Society: Studies in Semiotic Anthropology*. Bloomington: Indiana University Press.

Pasquetto, I., Cullen, Z., Thomer, A., & Wofford, M. (2024). What Is Research Data "Misuse"? And How Can It Be Prevented or Mitigated? *Journal of the American Society for Information Science and Technology*, 75(12), 1413–1429.

Pearson, E. S. (1956). Some Aspects of the Geometry of Statistics: The Use of Visual Presentation in Understanding the Theory and Application of Mathematical Statistics. *Journal of the Royal Statistical Society. Series A (General)*, 119(2), 125–146.

Peebles, P. J. E. (2020). *Cosmology's Century: An Inside History of Our Modern Understanding of the Universe*. Princeton, NJ: Princeton University Press.

Peebles, P. J. E. (2022). *The Whole Truth: A Cosmologist's Reflections on the Search for Objective Reality*. Princeton, NJ: Princeton University Press.

Peirce, C. S. (1906). Prolegomena to an Apology for Pragmaticism. *The Monist*, 16(4), 492–546.

Peirce, C. S. (1931–1958). *Collected Papers*, 8 vols. Cambridge, MA: Harvard University Press.

Pepe, A., Goodman, A., Muench, A., Crosas, M., & Erdmann, C. (2014). How Do Astronomers Share Data? Reliability and Persistence of Datasets Linked in AAS Publications and a Qualitative Study of Data Practices among US Astronomers. *PLoS ONE*, 9(8), e104798 (11 pp).

Perović, S. & Ćircović, M. M. (2024). *The Cosmic Microwave Background: Historical and Philosophical Lessons*. Cambridge: Cambridge University Press.

Perrow, C. (1991). A Society of Organizations. *Theory and Society*, 20, 725–762.

Peters, J. D. (1999). *Speaking into the Air: A History of the Idea of Communication*. Chicago, IL: University of Chicago Press.

Pichler, F. B. & Turner, S. J. (2007). The Power and Pitfalls of Outsourcing. *Nature Biotechnology*, 25, 1093–1096.

Pickering, A. (1995). *The Mangle of Practice: Time, Agency, and Science*. Chicago, IL: University of Chicago Press.

Pinch, T. J. (1985). Towards an Analysis of Scientific Observation: The Externality and Evidential Significance of Observational Reports in Physics. *Social Studies of Science*, 15(1), 3–36.

Pinch, T. J. & Bijker, W. E (1984). The Social Construction of Facts and Artefacts: Or How the Sociology of Science and the Sociology of Technology Might Benefit Each Other. *Social Studies of Science*, 14(3), 399–441.

Pinel, C., Prainsack, B., & McKevitt, C. (2020). Caring for Data: Value Creation in a Data-intensive Research Laboratory. *Social Studies of Science*, 50(2), 175–197.

Pinel, C. & Svendsen, M. N. (2024). Domesticating Data: Traveling and Value-making in the Data Economy. *Social Studies of Science*, 54(3), 429–450.

Planck Collaboration (2020). Planck 2018 Results: VI. Cosmological Parameters. *Astronomy & Astrophysics*, 641, A6 (67pp).

Plant, A. L. & Hanisch, R. J. (2020). Reproducibility in Science: A Metrology Perspective. *Harvard Data Science Review*, 2(4). doi.org/10.1162/99608f92.eb6ddee4

Plato (1997). *The Complete Works*, ed. J. M. Cooper. Indianapolis, IN: Hackett Publishers.

Plato (2005). *Phaedrus*, transl. C. Rowe. London: Penguin.

Polanyi, M. (1964). *Science, Faith and Society*, 2nd ed. Chicago, IL: University of Chicago Press.

Pollner, M. (1974a). Sociological and Common-Sense Models of the Labelling Process. In R. Turner, ed., *Ethnomethodology*. Harmondsworth: Penguin Books, 27–40.

Pollner, M. (1974b). Mundane Reasoning. *Philosophy of the Social Sciences*, 4(1), 35–54.

Pollner, M. (1987). *Mundane Reason: Reality in Everyday and Sociological Discourse*. Cambridge: Cambridge University Press.

Pollner, M. (2012). Ethnomethodology from/as/to Business. *American Sociologist*, 43(1), 21–35.

Pomerantz, A. (1980). Telling "My Side": "Limited Access" as a "Fishing" Device. *Sociological Inquiry*, 50, 186–198.

Poole, A. (2023). Data Flourishing: Developing Human-Centered Data Science through Communities of Ethical Practice. *Proceedings of the Association for Information Science and Technology*, 60(1), 338–352.

Porter, T. M. (1995). *Trust in Numbers: The Pursuit of Objectivity in Science and Public Life*. Princeton, NJ: Princeton University Press.

Pössel, M. (2020). A Beginner's Guide to Working with Astronomical Data. *arXiv:1905.13189v2*.

Postman, M., Coe, D., Benítez, N., et al. (2012). The Cluster Lensing and Supernova Survey with Hubble. *Astrophysical Journal Supplement Series*, 199, 25 (23 pp).

Primack, J. R. (2005). Precision Cosmology. *New Astronomy Reviews*, 49(2–6), 25–34.

Primas, F., Tacconi-Garman, L., Marteau, S., et al. (2014). Fifteen Years of Service Mode Operations: Closing the Loop with the Community. *The Messenger (European Southern Observatory)*, 158, 8–15.

Quine, W. V. O. (1970). Grades of Theoreticity. In L. Foster & J. W. Swanson, eds., *Experience and Theory*. Boston: University of Massachusetts Press, 1–17.

Rader, K. A. (2004). *Making Mice: Standardizing Animals for American Biomedical Research, 1900–1955*. Princeton, NJ: Princeton University Press.

Ramirez-i-Olle, M. (2020). *Into the Woods: An Epistemography of Climate Change*. Manchester: Manchester University Press.

Rawls, A. W. (2002). Editor's Introduction. In H. Garfinkel, *Ethnomethodology's Program: Working Out Durkheim's Aphorism*. Lanham, MD: Rowman & Littlefield, 1–64.

Rawls, A. W. & Lynch, M. (2024). Ethnography in Ethnomethodology and Conversation Analysis: Both, Neither, or Something Else Altogether? *Qualitative Research*, 24(1), 116–144.

Reeves, S., Greiffenhagen, C., & Laurier, E. (2017). Video Gaming as Practical Accomplishment: Ethnomethodology, Conversation Analysis, and Play. *Topics in Cognitive Science*, 9(2), 308–342.

Rejkuba, M., Hainaut, O. R., Bierwirth, T., Pruemm, M., & Weiss, A. (2024). Time Allocation and Long-Term Scheduling of ESO Telescopes at La Silla Paranal Observatory. *arXiv:2407.15470 [astro-ph.IM]*.

Rejkuba, M., Tacconi-Garman, L. E., Mieske, S., Anderson, J., Gadotti, D., Marteau, S., & Patat, F. (2018). Should I Stay, or Should I Go? Service and Visitor Mode at ESO's Paranal Observatory. *The Messenger*, 173, 2–6.

Rennie, D., Yank, V., & Emanuel, L. (1997). When Authorship Fails: A Proposal to Make Contributors Accountable. *Journal of the American Medical Association*, 278(7), 579–586.

Rheinberger, H.-J. (1997). *Toward a History of Epistemic Things: Synthesizing Proteins in the Test Tube*. Stanford, CA: Stanford University Press.

Rheinberger, H.-J. (2011). Infra-Experimentality: From Traces to Data, from Data to Patterning Facts. *History of Science*, 49(3), 337–348.

Rheinberger, H.-J. (2023). *Split and Spice: A Phenomenology of Experimentation*. Chicago: University of Chicago Press.

Ribes, D. & Bowker, G. (2009). Between Meaning and Machine: Learning to Represent the Knowledge of Communities. *Information and Organization*, 19(4), 199–217.

Robinson, L. B. & Wampler, E. J. (1972). The Lick Observatory Image-Dissector Scanner. *Publications of the Astronomical Society of the Pacific*, 84(497), 161–166.

Rochberg, F. (2016). *Before Nature: Cuneiform Knowledge and the History of Science*. Chicago, IL: University of Chicago Press.

Rogers, S. M. (2014). *Mastering Scientific and Medical Writing*. Berlin: Springer Verlag.

Ronayne, K., Papovich, C., Yang, G., et al. (2023). CEERS: 7.7μm PAH Star Formation Rate Calibration with JWST MIRI. *Astrophysical Journal*, 970, 61 (16 pp).

Rooksby, J., Rouncefield, M., & Sommerville, I. (2009). Testing in the Wild: The Social and Organisational Dimensions of Real World Practice. *Computer Supported Cooperative Work*, 18(5–6), 559–580.

Rose, A. (1946). A Unified Approach to the Performance of Photographic Film, Television Pickup Tubes and the Human Eye. *Journal of the Society of Motion Picture and TV Engineers*, 47, 273–294.

Ross-Hellauer, T., Reichmann, S., Cole, N. L., Fessl, A., Klebel T., & Pontika, N. (2022). Dynamics of Cumulative Advantage and Threats to Equity in Open Science: A Scoping Review. *Royal Society Open Science*, 9, 211032 (22 pp).

Roth, W.-M. & Bowen, G. M. (2001). "Creative Solutions" and "Fibbing Results": Enculturation in Field Ecology. *Social Studies of Science*, 31(4), 533–556.

Rotman, B. (2000). *Mathematics as Sign: Writing, Imagining, Counting*. Stanford, CA: Stanford University Press.

Rouse, J. (2003). Kuhn's Philosophy of Scientific Practice. In T. Nickles, ed., *Thomas Kuhn*. Cambridge: Cambridge University Press, 101–121.

Roy, A. (2024). *Unfinished Nature: Particle Physics at CERN*. New York: Columbia University Press.

Rutherford, D. (2025). *Beautiful Mystery: Living in a Wordless World*. Durham, NC: Duke University Press.

Ryle, G. (1949). *The Concept of Mind*. London: Hutchinson.

Sacks, H. (1992). *Lectures on Conversation*, ed. G. Jefferson. Malden, MA: Blackwell.

Sacks, H., Schegloff, E., & Jefferson, G. (1974). A Simplest Systematics for the Organization of Turn-taking for Conversation. *Language*, 50, 696–735.

Sainani, K. L. (2016). The Value of Scatter Plots. *Physical Medicine and Rehabilitation*, 8(12), 1213–1217.

Schaffer, S. (1994). *From Physics to Anthropology – And Back Again*. Cambridge: Prickly Pear Press.

Schegloff, E. A. (1991). Conversation Analysis and Socially Shared Cognition. In L. B. Resnick, J. M. Levine & S. D. Teasley, eds., *Perspectives on Socially Shared Cognition*. Washington, DC: American Psychological Association, 150–171.

Schegloff, E. A. (2006). Interaction: The Infrastructure for Social Institutions, the Natural Ecological Niche for Language, and the Arena in Which Culture Is Enacted. In N. J. Enfield & S. Levinson, eds., *Roots of Human Sociality: Culture, Cognition and Interaction*. Oxford: Berg, 70–96.

Schick, F. (1984). *Having Reasons: An Essay on Rationality and Sociality*. Princeton, NJ: Princeton University Press.

Schmidt, K. (2011). *Cooperative Work and Coordinative Practices*. London: Springer Verlag.

Schmidt, K. & Wagner, I. (2004). Ordering Systems: Coordinative Practices and Artifacts in Architectural Design and Planning. *Computer Supported Cooperative Work (CSCW)*, 13(3–4), 349–408.

Schröter, J., Ernst, C., & Warnke, M. (2022). Quantum Computing and the Analog/Digital Distinction. *Grey Room*, 86, 28–49.

Schütz, A. (1962). *Collected Papers, Volume 1: The Problem of Social Reality*, ed. M. Natanson. The Hague: Martinus Nijhoff.

Schütz, A. (1964). *Collected Papers, Volume 2: Studies in Social Theory*, ed. A. Brodersen. The Hague: Martinus Nijhoff.

Schwartz, H. (1976). On Recognizing Mistakes: A Case of Practical Reasoning in Psychotherapy. *Philosophy of the Social Sciences*, 6(1), 55–73.

Scolnic, D., Casertano, S., Riess, A., et al. (2015). Supercal: Cross-Calibration of Multiple Photometric Systems to Improve Cosmological Measurements with Type Ia Supernovae. *Astrophysical Journal*, 815, 117 (15pp).

Scoville, N. Z., Aussel, H., Brusa, M., et al. (2007). The Cosmic Evolution Survey (COSMOS): Overview. *Astrophysical Journal Supplement Series*, 172(1), 1–8.

Scroggins, M. & Boscoe, B. M. (2020). Once FITS, Always FITS? Astronomical Infrastructure in Transition. *IEEE Annals of the History of Computing*, 42(2), 42–54.

Sehgal, N., Bode, P., Das, S., et al. (2010). Simulations of the Microwave Sky. *Astrophysical Journal*, 709, 920–936.

Sellen, A. J. & Harper, R. H. R. (2002). *The Myth of the Paperless Office*. Cambridge, MA: MIT Press.

Shannon, C. (1948). A Mathematical Theory of Communication. *Bell Systems Technical Journal*, 27(3), 379–423.

Shapin, S. (1994). *A Social History of Truth*. Chicago, IL: University of Chicago Press.

Shapin, S. (1995). Cordelia's Love: Credibility and the Social Studies of Science. *Perspectives on Science*, 3(3), 255–275.

Shapin, S. & Schaffer, S. (1985). *Leviathan and the Air-Pump: Boyle, Hobbes, and the Experimental Life*. Princeton, NJ: Princeton University Press.

Sharrock, W. W. (1974). On Owning Knowledge. In R. Turner, ed., *Ethnomethodology*. Harmondsworth: Penguin Books, 45–53.

Sharrock, W. W. (2011). The Project as an Organisational Environment for the Division of Labour. In M. Rouncefield & P. Tolmie, eds., *Ethnomethodology at Work*. Burlington, VT: Ashgate, 19–35.

Sharrock, W. W. & Anderson, R. J. (1986). *The Ethnomethodologists*. Chichester: Ellis Horwood.

Sharrock, W. W. & Anderson, R. J. (1991). Epistemology: Professional Skepticism. In G. Button, ed., *Ethnomethodology and the Human Sciences*. Cambridge: Cambridge University Press, 51–76.

Sharrock, W. W. & Anderson, R. J. (1994). The User as a Scenic Feature of the Design Space. *Design Studies*, 15(1), 5–18.

Sharrock, W. W. & Coulter, J. (1998). On What We Can See. *Theory & Psychology*, 8(2), 147–164.

Shibayama, S. (2019). Sustainable Development of Science and Scientists: Academic Training in Life Science Labs. *Research Policy*, 48(3), 676–692.

Shrum, W. C., Genuth, J., & Chompalov, I. (2007). *Structures of Scientific Collaboration*. Cambridge, MA: MIT Press.

Sidnell, J. (2010a). *Conversation Analysis: An Introduction*. Chichester: Wiley-Blackwell.

Sidnell, J. (2010b). The Ordinary Ethics of Everyday Talk. In M. Lambek, ed., *Ordinary Ethics: Anthropology, Language, and Action*. Bronx, NY: Fordham University Press, 123–139.

Silverstein, M. (2003). Translation, Transduction, Transformation: Skating 'Glossando' on Thin Semiotic Ice. In P. G. Rubel & A. Rosman, eds., *Translating Cultures: Perspectives on Translation and Anthropology*. Oxford: Berg, 75–105.

Simmel, G. (1906). The Sociology of Secrecy and of Secret Societies. *American Journal of Sociology*, 11(6), 441–498.

Simmel, G. (1992 [1908]). *Soziologie: Untersuchung über die Formen der Vergesellschaftung*. Frankfurt am Main: Suhrkamp.

Simmel, G. (2004 [1900]). *The Philosophy of Money*, transl. T. Bottomore & D. Frisby. London: Routledge.

Sivia, D. S. (2006). *Data Analysis: A Bayesian Tutorial*. Oxford: Oxford University Press.

Skrutskie, M. E., Cutri, R. M., Stiening, R., et al. (2006). The Two Micron All Sky Survey (2MASS). *Astronomical Journal*, 131(2), 1163–1183.

Smith, D. E. (1990). *Texts, Facts, and Femininity: Exploring the Relations of Ruling*. London: Routledge.

Smith, D. E. (2001). Texts and the Ontology of Organizations and Institutions. *Studies in Cultures, Organizations and Societies*, 7(2), 159–198.

Smith, D. R. (2015). The Outsourcing and Commercialization of Science. *EMBO Reports*, 16(1), 14–16.

Smith, R. W. & Tatarewicz, J. N. (1985). Replacing a Technology: The Large Space Telescope and CCDs. *Proceedings of the IEEE*, 73(7), 1221–1235.

Smith, R. W. & Tatarewicz, J. N. (1994). Counting on Invention: Devices and Black Boxes in Very Big Science. *Osiris*, 9(1), 101–123.

Sormani, P. (2014). *Respecifying Lab Ethnography: An Ethnomethodological Study of Experimental Physics*. Farnham: Ashgate.

Sormani, P. (2015). Fun in Go: The Timely Delivery of a Monkey Jump and Its Lingering Relevance to Science Studies. *Human Studies*, 38(2), 281–308.

Spence, I. & Garrison, R. F. (1993). A Remarkable Scatterplot. *American Statistician*, 47(1), 12–19.

Spergel, D. N., Verde, L., Peiris, H. V., et al. (2003). First-Year Wilkinson Microwave Anisotropy Probe Observations: Determination of Cosmological Parameters. *Astrophysical Journal Supplement Series*, 148(1), 175–194.

Spiegelhalter, D. (2019). *The Art of Statistics: Learning from Data*. London: Pelican Books.

Squibb, G. F. & Cheung, C. Y. (1988). NASA Astrophysics Data System (ADS) Study. In A. Heck & F. Murtagh, eds., *Astronomy from Large Databases*,

ESO Conference Workshop Proceedings, No. 28. Garching: European Southern Observatory, 489–496.

Star, S. L. & Bowker, G. C. (2006). How to Infrastructure. In L. A. Lievrouw & S. Livingstone, eds. *Handbook of New Media. Updated Student Edition.* London: SAGE, 230–245.

Star, S. L. & Strauss, A. (1999). Layers of Silence, Arenas of Voice: The Ecology of Visible and Invisible Work. *Computer Supported Cooperative Work,* 8(1), 9–30.

Steinle, F. (1997). Entering New Fields: Exploratory Uses of Experimentation. *Philosophy of Science,* 64(Supplement), S65–S74.

Sterne, J. (2012). *MP3: The Meaning of a Format.* Durham, NC: Duke University Press.

Sterzik, M., Dumas, C., Grothkopf, U., et al. (2015). The Scientific Return of VLT Programmes. *The Messenger (European Southern Observatory),* 162, 2–8.

Stetter, C. (1997). *Schrift und Sprache.* Frankfurt am Main: Suhrkamp.

Stoughton, C., Lupton, R. H., Bernardi, M., et al. (2002). Sloan Digital Sky Survey: Early Data Release. *Astronomical Journal,* 123, 485–548.

Strang, D. & Meyer, J. W. (1993). Institutional Conditions for Diffusion. *Theory and Society,* 22(4), 487–511.

Strasser, B. J. (2019). *Collecting Experiments: Making Big Data Biology.* Chicago, IL: University of Chicago Press.

Strathern, M. (1988). *The Gender of the Gift: Problems with Women and Problems with Society in Melanesia.* Berkeley: University of California Press.

Strauss, A. (1988). The Articulation of Project Work: An Organizational Process. *Sociological Quarterly,* 29(2), 163–178.

Suber, P. (2012). *Open Access.* Cambridge, MA: MIT Press.

Suchman, L. (1995). Making Work Visible. *Communications of the ACM,* 39(9), 56–64.

Suchman, L. (2007). *Human-Computer Reconfigurations.* Cambridge: Cambridge University Press.

Sudnow, D. (1983). *Pilgrim in the Microworld: Eye, Mind, and the Essence of Video Skill.* New York: Warner Books.

Suits, B. (1978). *The Grasshopper: Games, Life, and Utopia.* Peterborough: Broadview Press.

Sundberg, M. (2011). The Dynamics of Coordinated Comparisons: How Simulationists in Astrophysics, Oceanography and Meteorology Create Standards for Results. *Social Studies of Science,* 41(1), 107–125.

Sverdlik, A., Hall, N. C., McAlpine, L., & Hubbard, K. (2018). The PhD Experience: A Review of the Factors Influencing Doctoral Students' Completion, Achievement, and Well-Being. *International Journal of Doctoral Studies,* 13, 361–388.

Szalay, A. S. (2018). From SkyServer to SciServer. *Annals of the American Academy of Political and Social Sciences,* 675 (January 2018), 202–220.

Szalay, A. S. & Gray, J. (2001). The World-Wide Telescope. *Science,* 293, 2037–2040.

Tenopir, C., Dalton, E., Allard, S., Frame, M., Pjesivac, I., Birch, B., Pollock, D., & Dorsett, K. (2015). Changes in Data Sharing and Data Reuse Practices and Perceptions among Scientists Worldwide. *PLoS One*, 10(8), e0134826 (24 pp).

Thompson, E. P. (1991). *Customs in Common*. New York: The New Press.

Thompson, S. M. (2019). The Carnegie Image Tube Committee and the Development of Electronic Imaging Devices in Astronomy, 1953–1976. PhD Thesis, Tempe, AZ: Arizona State University.

Ting, Y.-S. (2025). Statistical Machine Learning for Astronomy. *arXiv:2506.12230v1*.

Tousignant, N. (2013). Insects-as-Infrastructure: Indicating, Project Locustox and the Sahelization of Ecotoxicology. *Science as Culture*, 22(1), 108–131.

Traweek, S. (1988). *Beamtimes and Lifetimes: The World of High Energy Physicists*. Cambridge, MA: Harvard University Press.

Tsujimoto, M., Guainazzi, M., Plucinsky, P. P., et al. (2011). Cross-Calibration of the X-Ray Instruments Onboard the Chandra, INTEGRAL, RXTE, Suzaku, Swift, and XMM-Newton Observatories using G21.5-0.9. *Astronomy & Astrophysics*, 525, A25 (15pp).

Tufte, E. R. (1983). *The Visual Display of Quantitative Information*. Cheshire, CT: Graphics Press.

Tukey, J. W. (1959). Bias and Confidence in Not Quite Large Samples. *Annals of Mathematical Statistics*, 29(3), 614–623.

Tukey, J. W. (1962). The Future of Data Analysis. *Annals of Mathematical Statistics*, 33(1), 1–67.

Tukey, J. W. & Wilk, M. B. (1966). Data Analysis and Statistics: An Expository Overview. *Proceedings of the November 7–10, 1966, Fall Joint Computer Conference*. San Francisco, CA: AFIPS, 695–709.

Tuomela, R. (2007). *The Philosophy of Sociality: The Shared Point of View*. Oxford: Oxford University Press.

van de Sandt, S., Dallmeier-Tiessen, S., Lavasa, A., & Petras, V. (2019). The Definition of Reuse. *Data Science Journal*, 18(22), 1–19.

van der Wel, A., Noeske, K., Bezanson, R., et al. (2016). The VLT LEGA-C Survey: The Physics of Galaxies at a Lookback Time of 7 Gyr. *Astrophysical Journal Supplement Series*, 223(2), 29 (12 pp).

van der Wel, A., Straughn, A. N., Rix, H.-W., et al. (2011). Extreme Emission-Line Galaxies in CANDELS: Broadband-Selected, Starbursting Dwarf Galaxies at $z > 1$. *Astrophysical Journal*, 742, 111 (10pp).

Veigl, S. J. & Currie, A., eds. (2025). *Methods in the Philosophy of Science: A User's Guide*. Cambridge, MA: MIT Press.

Velden, T. (2013). Explaining Field Differences in Openness and Sharing in Scientific Communities. In C. Lampe & S. Counts, eds., *CSCW'13. Proceedings of the 2013 Conference on Computer Supported Cooperative Work, San Antonio, Texas, USA, 23–27 February 2013*. New York: Association for Computing Machinery, 445–458.

Vertesi, J. (2015). *Seeing Like a Rover: Visualization, Embodiment, and Interaction on the Mars Exploration Rover Mission*. Chicago, IL: University of Chicago Press.

Vertesi, J. (2020). *Shaping Science: Organizations, Decisions, and Culture on NASA's Teams*. Chicago, IL: University of Chicago Press.

vom Lehn, D. (2016). *Harold Garfinkel: The Creation and Development of Ethnomethodology*. Abingdon: Routledge.

Vygotsky, L. (1978). *Mind in Society: The Development of Higher Psychological Processes*, eds. M. Cole, V. John-Steiner, S. Scribner & E. Souberman. Cambridge, MA: Harvard University Press.

Wagenknecht, S. (2016). *A Social Epistemology of Research Groups: Collaboration in Scientific Practice*. London: Palgrave Macmillan.

Wallis, J. C., Rolando, E., & Borgman, C. L. (2013). If We Share Data, Will Anyone Use Them? Data Sharing and Reuse in the Long Tail of Science and Technology. *PLOS One*, 8(7), e67332 (17 pp).

Wang, H., Fu, T., Du, Y., et al. (2023). Scientific Discovery in the Age of Artificial Intelligence. *Nature*, 623(3 August 2023), 47–60.

Ward, A. & Webster, M. (2016). *Sociality: The Behaviour of Group-Living Animals*. Cham: Springer.

Warwick, A. (1995). The Laboratory of Theory, or, What's Exact about the Exact Sciences? In M. N. Wise, ed., *The Values of Precision*. Princeton, NJ: Princeton University Press, 311–351.

Weber, M. (1978). *Economy and Society*, vol. 1, eds., G. Roth & C. Wittich. Berkeley, CA: University of California Press.

Weick, K. (1979). *The Social Psychology of Organizing*, 2nd ed. New York: McGraw-Hill.

Weick, K. (1995). *Sensemaking in Organizations*. Thousand Oaks, CA: SAGE.

Wells, D. C. & Greisen, E. W. (1979). FITS: A Flexible Image Transport System. In G. Sedmak, M. Capaccioli & R. J. Allen, eds., *International Workshop on Image Processing in Astronomy*. Trieste: Osservatorio Astronomico di Trieste, 445–471.

White, H. (1973). *Metahistory: The Historical Imagination in Nineteenth-Century Europe*. Baltimore, MD: Johns Hopkins University Press.

White, S. D. M. (2007). Fundamentalist Physics: Why Dark Energy Is Bad for Astronomy. *Reports on Progress in Physics*, 70, 883–897.

White, S. D. M., Clowe, D. I., Simard, L. et al. (2005). EDisCS – The ESO Distant Cluster Survey: Sample Definition and Optical Photometry. *Astronomy and Astrophysics*, 444(2): 365–379.

White, T., Bok, E., & Calhoun, V. D. (2022). Data Sharing and Privacy Issues in Neuroimaging Research: Opportunities, Obstacles, Challenges, and Monsters under the Bed. *Human Brain Mapping*, 43, 278–291.

Wieder, L. (1974). *Language and Social Reality: The Case of Telling the Convict Code*. The Hague: Mouton.

Wilf, E. (2013). Toward an Anthropology of Computer-Mediated, Algorithmic Forms of Sociality. *Current Anthropology*, 54(6), 716–739.

Williams, B. (1985). *Ethics and the Limits of Philosophy*. London: Fontana Press.

Williams, B. (1986). Reply to Simon Blackburn. *Philosophical Books*, 27(4), 203–208.

Williams, R. (2018). *Hubble Deep Field and the Distant Universe*. Bristol: Institute of Physics Publishers.

Willis, A. J. (2013). The International Ultraviolet Explorer: Origins and Legacy. In A. Heck, ed., *Organizations, People and Strategies in Astronomy*, vol. 2. Dordrecht: Kluver, 395–416.

Wimsatt, W. C. (1990). Taming the Dimensions – Visualizations in Science. *Proceedings of the Biennial Meeting of the Philosophy of Science. Volume Two: Symposia and Invited Papers*, 111–135.

Wimsatt, W. C. (2007). *Re-Engineering Philosophy for Limited Beings: Piecewise Approximations to Reality*. Cambridge, MA: Harvard University Press.

Winch, P. (1958). *The Idea of a Social Science and Its Relation to Philosophy*. London: Routledge & Kegan Paul.

Wise, M. N., ed. (1995). *The Values of Precision*. Princeton, NJ: Princeton University Press.

Wittgenstein, L. (1960). *The Blue and Brown Books*. New York: Harper Perennial.

Wittgenstein, L. (1969). *On Certainty*, eds. G. E. M. Anscombe & G. H. von Wright, transl. D. Paul & G. E. M. Anscombe. Oxford: Blackwell.

Wittgenstein, L. (1978). *Remarks on the Foundations of Mathematics*, transl. G. E. M. Anscombe. Oxford: Blackwell.

Wittgenstein, L. (2009 [1953]). *Philosophical Investigations*, 4th ed., transl. G. E. M. Anscombe, P. M. S. Hacker, & J. Schulte. Oxford: Blackwell.

Wolf, C., Meisenheimer, K., Röser, H.-J., et al. (2001). Multi-Color Classification in the Calar Alto Deep Imaging Survey. *Astronomy and Astrophysics*, 365, 681–698.

Woolgar, S. (1991). Configuring the User: The Case of Usability Trials. In J. Law, ed., *A Sociology of Monsters: Essays on Power Technology and Domination*. London: Routledge, 58–100.

Worswick, S. P. (1976). Electronographic Photometry. In M. Duchesne & G. Lelievre, eds., *Astronomical Applications of Image Detectors with Linear Response*. Proceedings of the I. A. U. Colloquium n° 40, Paris: Observatoire Paris-Meudon, 38-1–38-14.

Wray, K. B. (2007). Who Has Scientific Knowledge? *Social Epistemology*, 21(3), 337–347.

Wray, K. B. (2017). The Impact of Collaboration on the Epistemic Cultures of Science. In T. Boyer-Kassem, C. Mayo-Wilson & M. Weisberg, eds., *Scientific Collaboration and Collective Knowledge: New Essays*. Oxford: Oxford University Press, 117–134.

Wu, L., Wang, D., & Evans, J. A. (2019). Large Teams Develop and Small Teams Disrupt Science and Technology. *Nature*, 566, 378–382.

Wuchty, S., Jones, B. F., & Uzzi, B. (2007). The Increasing Dominance of Teams in Production of Knowledge. *Science*, 316, 1036–1039.

Wyatt, S. (2008). Technological Determinism Is Dead; Long Live Technological Determinism. In E. J. Hackett, O. Amsterdamska, M. Lynch & J. Wajcman, eds., *The Handbook of Science and Technology Studies*, 3rd ed. Cambridge, MA: MIT Press, 165–180.

Wylie, C. D. (2019). Socialization through Stories of Disaster in Engineering Laboratories. *Social Studies of Science*, 49(6), 817–838.

Wynholds, L., Fearon Jr., D., Borgman, C. L., & Traweek, S. (2011). When Use Cases Are Not Useful: Data Practices, Astronomy, and Digital Libraries. *JCDL11: Joint Conference on Digital Libraries*. New York: Association for Computing Machinery, 383–386.

Yakel, E., Faniel, I. M., & Maiorana, Z. J. (2019). Virtuous and Vicious Circles in the Data Life-Cycle. *Information Research*, 24(2), paper 821.

Yoon, A. (2017). Data Reusers' Trust Development. *Journal of the Association for Information Science and Technology*, 68(4), 946–956.

York, D. G., Adelman, J., Anderson, J. E., et al. (2000). The Sloan Digital Sky Survey: Technical Summary. *Astronomical Journal*, 120, 1579–1587.

Zimmerman, A. S. (2008). New Knowledge from Old Data: The Role of Standards in the Sharing and Reuse of Ecological Data. *Science, Technology and Human Values*, 33(5), 631–652.

Zimmerman, D. H. & Pollner, M. (1971). The Everyday World as Phenomenon. In J. D. Douglas, ed., *Understanding Everyday Life: Toward the Reconstruction of Sociological Knowledge*. London: Routledge and Kegan Paul, 80–103.

Index

For EU product safety concerns, contact us at Calle de José Abascal, 56–1°, 28003 Madrid, Spain or eugpsr@cambridge.org.

www.ingramcontent.com/pod-product-compliance
Ingram Content Group UK Ltd.
Pitfield, Milton Keynes, MK11 3LW, UK
UKHW021902070626
471968UK00004B/14